Investing in Emerging Fixed Income Markets

The Frank J. Fabozzi Series

Fixed Income Securities, Second Edition by Frank J. Fabozzi

Focus on Value: A Corporate and Investor Guide to Wealth Creation by James L. Grant and James A. Abate

The Handbook of Global Fixed Income Calculations by Dragomir Krgin

Managing a Corporate Bond Portfolio by Leland E. Crabbe and Frank J. Fabozzi

Real Options and Option-Embedded Securities by William T. Moore

Capital Budgeting: Theory and Practice by Pamela P. Peterson and Frank J. Fabozzi

The Exchange-Traded Funds Manual by Gary L. Gastineau

Investing in Emerging Fixed Income Markets

Edited by

Frank J. Fabozzi, Ph.D., CFA

and

Efstathia Pilarinu, Ph.D.

JOHN WILEY & SONS

ISBN: 0-471-21836-7

Printed in the United States of America.

10 9 8 7 6 5 4 3 2 1

About the Editors

Frank J. Fabozzi is editor of the *Journal of Portfolio Management* and an adjunct professor of finance at Yale University's School of Management. He is a Chartered Financial Analyst and Certified Public Accountant. Dr. Fabozzi is on the board of directors of the Guardian Life family of funds and the BlackRock complex of funds. He is an Advisory Analyst for Global Asset Management (GAM) with responsibilities as Consulting Director for portfolio construction, risk control, and evaluation. He earned a doctorate in economics from the City University of New York in 1972 and in 1994 received an honorary doctorate of Humane Letters from Nova Southeastern University. Dr. Fabozzi is a Fellow of the International Center for Finance at Yale University.

Efstathia Pilarinu is a consultant specializing in the derivatives and emerging market fixed income areas. She has worked for several major Wall Street firms, including Salomon Brothers, Bankers Trust, and Société General. She has a doctoral degree and an MBA in finance from the University of Tennessee and an undergraduate degree in mathematics from the University of Patras, Greece.

Contents

Contributing Authors

Andrew M. Aran	Alliance Capital Management Corporation
Tsvetan N. Beloreshki	National Economic Research Associates, Inc.
Jane Sachar Brauer	Merrill Lynch
Frank J. Fabozzi	Yale University
Stephen Gilmore	Morgan Stanley
Laurie Goodman	UBS Warburg
Costas C. Hamakiotes	Lehman Brothers
James C. Kennan	BNP Paribas
Marcelo Fernandes de Lima Castro	BNP Paribas
Luis R. Luis	International Research & Strategy Associates LLC
Maria Mednikov Loucks	UBS Asset Management
Paul A. Pannkuk	Morgan Stanley
John A. Penicook, Jr.	UBS Asset Management
Efstathia Pilarinu	Consultant
Uwe Schillhorn	UBS Asset Management
David Sohnen	Merrill Lynch & Co.
Bruce Stanforth	BNP Paribas
Christopher Taylor	ING Barings
Allen Vine	Merrill Lynch & Co.

Chapter 1

Introduction

Frank J. Fabozzi, Ph.D., CFA
Adjunct Professor of Finance
School of Management
Yale University

Efstathia Pilarinu, Ph.D.
Consultant

It was not until after the implementation of the innovative Brady debt restructuring plan in the 1990s that emerging fixed income markets began to be treated as a separate asset class. The "clientele" for these assets were institutions of emerging countries and dedicated international emerging market funds. As these markets developed, there was also interest for these securities from high-yield international funds and institutions.

Emerging markets have become a rather well-known asset class even to the layman, especially in the aftermath of the crises that started in 1997 in Asia and continued for the subsequent three years. The globalization of the economies increased the interdependence of the fully developed economies to the emerging countries. The ease with which capital moves around the world changed the risks associated with both the G7 economies and the rest of the world. One of the idiosyncrasies of emerging markets is the need of these "lesser" developed countries to rely on international markets for access to capital. From a more positive perspective, emerging markets have benefited and speeded their economic and political progress on many fronts as they interact with the developed countries.

Even though there is no formal consensus on the definition of an emerging country, there is an understanding amongst institutional and retail investors. According to one definition, a country is classified in the category of emerging markets (EMG) if it has defaulted at least once on its international debt obligations. A second definition is based on certain macroeconomic criteria of the country, and a rather loose emerging market universe is one that includes all countries that are not considered industrialized or already "developed" and are thus named "lesser developed countries" (LDC).

This book brings forth 12 years (1989-2001) of history in emerging market fixed income securities that has seen extremely positive economic, political, and market changes happen to these countries, but has also witnessed crises that had, in many cases, worldwide effects. During this period market participants have acquired experience in trading, risk management, and credit analysis of emerging fixed income markets.

We consider that the Brady bond market has evolved over the past decade, with the retirement of large amounts of Bradys from the market (buybacks from countries) and with the unfortunate default of the Ecuador Brady bonds. We also consider the emergence of the Eurobond market as a very positive development that adds depth to the emerging markets fixed income asset class. Looking at the local side of emerging markets, the currency markets of these countries have also undergone substantial changes, from fixed and crawling peg currency regimes to some freely convertible spot markets. Finally, the local debt markets have evolved with the introduction of a variety of products[1] and with the general lengthening of yield curves.

Securities traded in emerging fixed income markets must be treated as a separate asset class even though many products are similar to the ones in developed markets. Valuation models, risk, and credit analysis need to be adjusted to take into account the particularities of these markets. Initially, the securities traded in these markets had been treated as assets whose prices traded according to stock market principles rather than based on the well-recognized principles of fixed-income securities. However, these markets have changed qualitatively and quantitatively. Sophisticated quantitative analysis has been applied to price and access relative value in these markets. Arbitrage-like opportunities that take advantage of mispricings among various instruments (e.g., Brady bonds versus eurobonds, local debt versus dollar instruments, financing discrepancies) became common types of trades in emerging markets. New standards for risk management and credit analysis have been developed over time to capture the structural changes in these markets and the features of their evolving economies.

As a result of the evolution of emerging debt markets (from non-tradable bank loans to a rich variety of tradable products), many investment houses have either merged their emerging market departments with their high-yield operations or at least allowed for significant overlap in these businesses.

OVERVIEW OF BOOK

This book covers a variety of topics that are important to those who wish to participate in emerging fixed income markets. The contributors to this book describe the characteristics of the fixed income instruments and address valuation, trading, and risk issues. They also discuss credit issues and present some case studies. The contributors are all investment professionals specializing in emerging markets and holding positions in various functions (research, credit, trading, and money management).

---

[1] There is a rich variety of local products in emerging markets, depending on the barriers to entry and legal restrictions in each country. Also there is an important offshore market with nondeliverable products for the nonconvertible currencies.

The book is organized into three sections. Section I contains six chapters covering market characteristics, including a description of the instruments and the nuances of this asset class. Chapter 2 by Jane Brauer describes the Brady bond market, its evolution, and valuation issues, and in Chapter 3 by James Kennan there is a thorough description of local Latin American markets. Chapter 4 by Steve Gilmore deals with the CE3 European local emerging markets and their developments as they adopt new policies in order to join the European Union and adopt the Euro. An investment management view of emerging fixed income markets and local currency markets is provided in Chapter 5 by Luis Luis. Chapter 6 by Maria Mednikov Loucks, John A. Penicook, Jr., and Uwe Schillhorn provides extensive coverage of issues pertaining to investing in emerging debt markets. As explained by the authors, this process entails benchmark selection, various valuations, then portfolio construction and risk management, and finally an attribution model. Chapter 7 by Laurie Goodman covers the collateralized debt obligation market (CDO) in emerging markets and compares it to the CDO high-yield market.

Valuations on fixed income securities and trading issues are covered in Section II. The section begins with an in-depth examination of the effect of swap spreads on the valuation of floating-rate bonds in emerging markets, in Chapter 8 by Costas Hamakiotes. In Chapter 9, Costas Hamakiotes discusses a methodology that quantifies the dollar differential between emerging bond markets in yield terms—an important methodology for accessing relative of bonds. Chapter 10 by Marcelo Castro is an account from a Brazilian local fixed income trader of the events that took place from the 1997 Asian crisis to the 1999 Brazilian devaluation. In Chapter 11 Marcelo Castro provides a description of the Brazilian local markets, with a detailed analytical account of some complex instruments. Using the Argentine peso as an example during the convertibility era, James Kennan in Chapter 12 addresses the issue of pricing options on pegged currencies.

In Section III, credit issues are addressed, along with some case studies. Chapter 13 by Christopher Taylor is an in-depth examination of the issues of emerging market corporate bond valuations, the factors to be considered, and the risks that need to be closely monitored. Allen Vine and David Sohnen in Chapter 14 discuss debt covenants, a standard high-yield mechanism that has been progressively adapted in emerging markets. In Chapter 15, Paul Pannkuk proposes new practices for credit analysis and risk management that have been motivated by the lessons learned from the 1997 Asian crisis. Chapter 16 by Tsvetan Beloreshki provides an analytical framework for default probabilities and recovery rates in emerging market bond valuation, along with a historical perspective and some economic analysis.

The last two chapters of the book provide case studies. Chapter 17 by Bruce Stanforth is a case study of a Brazilian company, Tevecap. The case pinpoints the potential pitfalls and risks in emerging market bond valuation. Chapter 18 by Andrew Aran takes a close look at an Asian bank, Dao Heng, during the crisis of 1997 and demonstrates the particularities of emerging market risks.

Section I

Emerging Market Characteristics

Chapter 2

Brady Bonds

Jane Sachar Brauer, Ph.D.
First Vice President
Merrill Lynch

T he term Brady bond refers to a series of sovereign foreign-currency denominated bonds issued by several developing countries in exchange for their rescheduled bank loans. The term comes from a U.S. government program, which combined U.S. government and official multilateral support in obtaining debt and debt-service relief from foreign commercial bank creditors for those countries that successfully implemented comprehensive structural reforms supported by the International Monetary Fund (IMF) and the World Bank. Typically, a country negotiating a Brady restructuring has significant external debt outstanding and cannot meet its debt repayment schedule when new financing becomes unavailable. By restructuring its debt, the country obtains some debt forgiveness while simultaneously deferring a portion of the principal and interest payments for a few years to allow time for reforms to ripple through the economy and improve its cash flow and balance of payments.

The first Brady agreement with Mexico in 1989-90 was the prototype for other ensuing Brady-type accords. A total of seventeen countries have since taken advantage of the program, with a cumulative face value of $170 billion of Brady bonds issued. The majority of Brady debt has been issued by Latin America, with Brazil, Mexico, Argentina, and Venezuela representing 74% of the current outstanding amounts in the Brady bond market (See Exhibit 1.). Almost all countries with defaulted commercial bank debt from the 1980's have exchanged that debt for Brady bonds or restructured loans. Since then, most countries have been able to improve their financing budget and have subsequently been able to raise more funds in the eurobond market.

The Brady market is unique in two respects. First, the yields are relatively high. Second, some issues are extremely large and liquid, especially compared to typical sovereign eurobonds. This chapter gives a general background of the evolution of the Brady market, the basic instruments, how they are viewed, and how to evaluate them.

Exhibit 1: Original Brady/Exchange Issue Amounts (US$ bn)

Country	Pars	Discounts	Other Brady Debt	Total Brady Debt Issued	Percent of All Bradys
Latin America					
Argentina	12.67	4.32	8.47	25.45	15.0%
Brazil	10.49	7.29	32.88	50.66	29.9%
Costa Rica	na	na	0.59	0.59	0.4%
Dominican Republic	na	0.33	0.19	0.52	0.3%
Ecuador	1.91	1.44	2.78	6.13	3.6%
Mexico	22.40	11.77	2.73	36.90	21.7%
Panama	0.26	0.045	2.92	3.22	1.9%
Peru	0.18	0.57	4.12	4.87	2.9%
Uruguay	0.53	na	0.54	1.07	0.6%
Venezuela	7.33	1.27	9.95	18.55	10.9%
Non-Latin					
Bulgaria	na	1.85	3.28	5.13	3.0%
Ivory Coast	na	0.07	1.26	1.33	0.8%
Jordan	0.49	0.16	0.09	0.74	0.4%
Nigeria	2.05	na	na	2.05	1.2%
Philippines	1.89	na	2.32	4.21	2.5%
Poland	0.90	2.99	4.02	7.90	4.7%
Vietnam	0.23	0.02	0.29	0.55	0.3%
Total	61.34	32.11	76.43	169.88	100%
Percent	36.1%	18.9%	45.0%	100.0%	

Source: Merrill Lynch

THE BRADY PLAN

The Brady Plan of 1989 grew out of the less developed countries (LDC) debt crisis of 1982-88. In the early 1980s, sluggish growth of industrial countries, rising global interest rates, and falling commodity prices triggered a significant economic contraction in developing countries. As a consequence, isolated from the international capital markets and lacking the level of domestic savings needed to service external obligations, most developing countries began to experience severe debt servicing problems. The first strategy adopted to address the crisis was a program of concerted new lending by commercial banks and multilateral organizations combined with structural adjustment efforts by the debtor countries. By 1988 it had become clear that this strategy was less than successful, the LDCs were not emerging out of the debt crisis, and a new strategy involving "debt relief" was necessary.

In 1989, the Brady Plan structure, named after former U.S. Treasury Secretary Nicholas Brady, was introduced. It provided debtor countries with debt relief through restructuring their commercial bank debt at lower interest rates or allowing them to write it down, enabling them to exchange that debt for tradable foreign-currency denominated fixed income securities. In return, the developing countries agreed to adopt macroeconomic reforms. Banks were given the choice of mainly debt (face) or debt-service (interest) reduction options. By the late 1980s many banks had written off as much as 25% of the face value of their commercial loans to LDCs. Since commercial banks at that time held these assets at face value, this enabled the banks to participate in a restructuring wherein the LDC obtained some formal debt relief.

The first collateralized restructuring issue, the predecessor to the Brady exchanges, was done in March 1988 by Mexico in the form of a $2.6 billion 20-year bond whose principal was fully collateralized with special purpose zero-coupon bonds issued by the United States Treasury. The bank creditors had accepted 30% forgiveness on the face amount of the existing loans in exchange for "Aztec" bonds. The exchange had been done in conjunction with public-sector financing from the IMF, the World Bank, and other official creditor agencies, together with the use of the country's foreign reserves for the purchase of the collateral enhancement. The Aztecs and all succeeding Brady bonds are callable at par; however, the Aztecs were the only bonds issued with a floating rate coupon as high as Libor +1.625%. Within the eight years following the issuance of the Aztecs, Mexico had recovered enough financially to allow the government to retire the outstanding Aztec bonds by calling them in February 1996.

The first country to reach a Brady agreement was Mexico, in September 1989. The deal covered approximately $48 billion face of the country's eligible foreign debt to commercial banks. In exchange for their illiquid defaulted loans, the banks were given three options, two of which included an exchange of defaulted loans for collateralized bonds. The first option was an exchange for Discount bonds, also known as principal reduction bonds. These bonds required a 35% reduction on the face value of the defaulted loans, providing Mexico with debt relief (in terms of the principal amount), but requiring what was then termed a "market" coupon rate of Libor + 13/16. The second option, Par bonds (also known as interest reduction bonds) had no reduction in the face value, though they included a below-market coupon of 6.25% at a time when Libor was over 10%. Both types of bonds included full principal collateral in the form of a special-purpose U.S. Treasury zero coupon bond, similar to the Aztec exchange. The two issues also included a rolling interest guarantee (RIG) covering 18 months worth of interest payments. The third option allowed the banks to carry the full principal amount of their Mexican loans on their books, while requiring the banks to provide additional new lending ("New Money") to Mexico of at least 25% of their existing exposure over a three-year period.

The Mexican Brady agreement, which included three basic options (Pars, Discounts, and New Money bonds), set the standard for subsequent Brady accords. Over time the Brady exchanges have become more complex, offering a wider array of possibilities for debt and debt service reduction that would be more advantageous to the debtor countries. These exchanges included increasing the level of debt forgiveness and applying creative ways to account for the past-due interest. An example is Peru, which had a history of approximately twelve years of non-payment on its outstanding debt. For the period of 1984–1996, Peru was allowed to accrue interest on the unpaid coupon payments of its outstanding debt at a rate of 2.5%, when Libor over that period averaged close to 7.0%. In several of the later Brady Exchange Agreements, the RIG gradually decreased, so much so that in some cases it included a RIG on only one coupon, or in the case of Poland, none.

TYPES OF BRADY BONDS

Countries typically issue several types of Brady bonds covering the outstanding principal amount of their bank loans and one or more bonds covering the past-due interest. The particular bond types are chosen by creditors to provide debt and debt service relief to the sovereign issuer. During the negotiations, creditors were presented with a choice of possible debt restructurings and were given several months in which to choose. At the time of the presentation, all options were equally attractive and produced roughly the same net present value. In their selection, some creditors were constrained by their own internal accounting requirements, while others were able to select the bond that provided the highest present value. Typically, these decisions were mainly influenced by the expectation of the sovereign's spread risk and the movements in the U.S. Treasury markets.

Collateralized Principal Bonds

Two principal bonds, Pars and Discounts, are 25–30 year registered bullet bonds and represent the largest, most common assets in the Brady bond market. Pars and Discounts represent 45% of the current Brady bond market. Issue size ranges from $90 million to $22.4 billion, and in some cases is larger than the most liquid U.S. Treasury securities. Par bonds were issued at "par" in exchange for the original face value of the rescheduled loans, but they carry a fixed, below-market interest rate. Discount bonds, on the other hand, carry a floating interest rate, typically Libor +13/16, but are exchanged for fewer bonds than the original loan amount or at a discounted face value of the previously rescheduled loans, often ranging between 50%–65% of the original face.

Principal and Interest Collateral
Pars and Discounts generally have principal secured by U.S. Treasury zero coupon bonds[1] that were originally funded by a combination of IMF, World Bank loans, and the country's own reserves. In addition, the interest portion of the Pars and Discounts is partially collateralized by securities rated at least AA in amounts sufficient to cover a specified number of months (usually 12 months) of interest

---

[1] Collateralized bonds denominated in a currency other than USD may have their principal collateral guaranteed by: Deutschemark Series – Federal Post Office (Bundespost) Zero Coupon Treasury Notes; French Franc Series – Republic of France Compound Interest Bonds; Japanese Yen Series—Japanese Government Bonds; Swiss Franc Series – 30-Year Global Bonds (issued by Swiss Bank Corporation).

on the outstanding principal at a notional rate. The interest guarantee is character-ized as a rolling interest guarantee (RIG) because the guarantee rolls forward to the subsequent interest period if not utilized. Both the interest and principal col-lateral are maintained by an assigned collateral agent and held in escrow at the Federal Reserve Bank of New York. In the event that the country misses an inter-est payment, the trustee will pay the investor out of the interest collateral until the number of coupon payments guaranteed has been exhausted.

Although the earlier exchanges involved a special-purpose issue of a zero coupon bond by the U.S. Treasury, subsequent issues allowed the sovereign to buy U.S. Treasury strips from the growing open market. Such market transactions required the maturity of the strips to be no longer than that of the Brady bond, issued with the restriction that the face value be equal to the principal amount of the Par and Discount bonds. From 1993 to 1994, pre-Brady countries (primarily Argen-tina and Brazil) accumulated the largest collateral blocks of U.S. Treasury strips. During that period, demand from these Latin American countries had impacted the overall shape and level of the then-developing U.S. Treasury strips market.

Recourse to Collateral

Bondholders do not have recourse to the principal collateral until maturity, at which time the proceeds will be available to pay the full principal amount due. Regarding the recourse to the interest collateral, if the issuer does not make an interest payment within the grace period stipulated in the Brady Exchange Agree-ment,[2] the Collateral agent, at the request of the Fiscal agent acting upon the instructions of holders of at least 25%[3] of the aggregate principal, will release interest collateral sufficient to cover the interest payable on the bonds.

In August 1999, the Republic of Ecuador failed to make the timely cou-pon payment on its Brady bond debt. Ecuador was facing its most difficult finan-cial condition in decades.[4] This marked the first time a Brady country had failed to pay on its contractual date. Defaulting on an interest payment does not mean that the sovereign debtor will cease to pay interest on the bond; instead, the coun-try could continue to make payments in arrears after the interest collateral has been depleted, or the country may attempt to renegotiate the terms of the bond. In the case of Ecuador, the government paid only its non-collateralized Brady debt and asked the collateralized bondholders to tap the interest collateral account for the collateralized coupon payment, in order to give the sovereign time to restruc-ture its external debt without defaulting. Instead, the bondholders requested the acceleration of payments, based on a provision stating that the unpaid balance become immediately due and payable if the debtor fails to meet payments or becomes insolvent, leaving Ecuador in technical default. Subsequently, Ecuador defaulted on its next Brady and eurobond coupon payments. A year after the first

---

[2] This period is typically 15 or 30 days.
[3] The percentage varies with each Brady Exchange Agreement.
[4] For 1999, Ecuador's total external debt accounted for over 115% of its GDP.

missed payment, Ecuador negotiated a restructuring of its defaulted Brady and eurobond debt into new 30-year eurobonds, forgiving 22% of the face value of the noncollateralized past-due interest Brady bonds.

Embedded Options

Aside from the par call feature of Bradys, certain Par and Discount bonds carry "value recovery" rights or warrants, which give bondholders the opportunity to "recapture" some of the debt and debt-service reduction provided in the exchange if the future economic performance and the debt-servicing capacity of the sovereign debtor improves. The rights are a mechanism by which the issuing country shares with its creditors a portion of the incremental revenue generated by, for example, a consistent increase in oil prices or the sovereign's GDP. Often, these warrants are linked to indices of oil export prices or the country's oil export receipts, as in the cases of Mexico, Venezuela, and Nigeria, or the level of a terms-of-trade index in the case of Uruguay.

Non-Collateralized Brady Bonds

The types of bonds included in a given plan are determined during the debt restructuring negotiations between a consortium of creditors and the debtor country. The bonds often have varying coupon schedules and amortizations, and sometimes include the capitalization of interest. Each plan may also include principal types other than Par and Discount bonds, such as *debt-conversion bonds* (DCBs), *capitalization bonds* (C-bonds), *front-loaded interest-reduction bonds* (FLIRBs), and the related *new-money bonds* (NMBs). The DCBs, NMBs, and FLIRBs are typically non-collateralized amortizing bearer instruments with a significantly shorter final maturity and average life than the Pars and Discounts. DCBs are exchanged at full face value and carry a floating interest rate, but creditors who choose the DCB option have to commit to extending new funds to the sovereign issuer by buying short-term, floating-rate NMBs. FLIRBs carry collateral-securing interest payments, generally for 12 months, and the guarantee is available for the first five to six years of the life of the bond. C-bonds, also known as *payment-in-kind* (PIK) bonds, are capitalizing bonds that first appeared in the 1994 Brazil Brady plan. In the C-bond exchange agreement, Brazil agreed to an 8% interest accrual rate that initially paid only 4%. The remaining 4% capitalized, for example, increasing the par amount outstanding at the end of the first year to 104% of the original amount.

Past-due interest on several Brady plans have also been consolidated into *past-due interest bonds* (PDIs), *interest due and unpaid bonds* (IDUs), *eligible interest bonds* (EIs), *interest arrears bonds* (IABs), and *floating-rate past-due interest bonds* (FRBs). These instruments generally consist of a non-collateralized, 10- or 20-year amortizing floating rate bond. Past-due interest on defaulted loans can be exchanged for PDI bonds, which typically capitalize during several of the earlier interest payments periods and then amortize, as is the case in the PDIs issued under the Ecuador, Panama, and Peru Brady exchanges.

Non-Brady Restructured Loans

Perhaps the most speculative segment of this high-risk, high-yielding market has been bank loans (generally non-performing and available only through assignment or participation agreements with extended 21-day settlement periods). Bank loans can be higher yielding than bonds for the same country, since the issuing countries are more cautious about offending bondholders than bank lenders. The principally traded types of bank loans were the "pre-Brady" claims of countries expected to obtain debt and debt service relief under the auspices of the Brady initiative in future negotiations. They were often off-limits to investors.

By the mid-1990s, almost all countries that were eligible to exchange defaulted loans into Brady bonds had done so, though a few countries, such as Algeria, Morocco and Russia, chose not to be a part of the Brady program and opted to exchange their bank loans for new, restructured loans.

In the case of the Russian Federation, it had accepted responsibility for all Soviet-era commercial bank loans taken by the former USSR, but it had no direct legal obligation to service the debt. The Vneshcomenbank loans of the former USSR were restructured into a $20 billion principal loan (Prins) and a $6 billion interest arrears note (IANs). In the aftermath of the Russian financial crisis and the ruble devaluation in August 1998, Russia defaulted on the Prins and subsequently on the IANs. Many investors who were unaware of the seniority class difference between Russian and Soviet-era debt incurred heavy losses. Since the obligor of the restructured loans legally was not the Russian Federation and no cross default clauses existed, Russia was able to cease payments on the Prins and IANs while it continued to pay on its sovereign eurobond debt without jeopardizing the non-default status of those eurobonds. Fourteen months after the first missed payment, Russia negotiated a restructuring of its defaulted Prins and IANs into new 30-year eurobonds, forgiving 37.5% of the face value of the Prins and 33% of the IANs.

RETIRING BRADY BONDS: BUYBACKS AND EXCHANGES

Since the issuance of Brady bonds, many countries have sufficiently implemented economic reforms to enable them to access the capital markets in the form of eurobonds. Simultaneously, many countries have been retiring their Brady debt through various forms of buybacks. In the past several years, sovereign issuers of Brady bonds have been able to retire Brady debt through five main approaches:

- The issuer may *exercise the call option* on the bond, as Mexico had done with its Aztec issue. All Brady bonds are callable at par, usually on coupon payment dates.
- The sovereign country may *discretely buy back their Brady bonds* in the open market, as did Argentina, Brazil, Mexico, Panama, and Poland.

- A sovereign issuer may *initiate a formal Brady exchange* program whereby a price or spread is preset and bids are solicited for an exchange into a new eurobond issue. In 1996, Mexico was the first sovereign country to participate in a large scale Brady-to-eurobond exchange. At that time, emerging markets were providing extremely high returns, spreads were consistently tightening, and investors were glad to have an opportunity to exchange their collateralized Mexican Par and Discount bonds for a non-collateralized global issue that would outperform if spreads continued to tighten. This set the tone for subsequent formal exchanges that included Argentina, Brazil, Mexico, Panama, Uruguay, Venezuela, and the Philippines.
- *Private exchange agreements* are arranged whereby two to four holders of a sizable block of Brady bonds would agree to an exchange for a sovereign eurobond.
- Brady bonds have also been *accepted as payment in several privatizations,* particularly in Brazil.

If a country retires collateralized debt, it may release the collateral associated with the principal amount retired. Since the issuer has a cost of funds which is higher than the return on its invested interest collateral in AA-rated securities, the issuer suffers from a "negative carry" for the life of the bond. In various buybacks and exchange programs, the issuer has been able to gain significant savings on financing costs through retiring its Brady debt. There are restrictions on the timing and size of retiring special purpose zero-coupon bonds used as collateral, but no restrictions exist on the retirement of open market U.S. Treasury strips. Many of these Brady bond buybacks are often associated with corresponding activity in the U.S. Treasury strips market. As a result, U.S. Treasury investors often have a keen interest in knowing what the Brady countries are doing vis-à-vis retiring collateralized debt.

Eurobonds are typically plain vanilla bullet structures and there is some sense by investors that Eurobonds are less subject to default risk. Therefore, investors typically do not require as wide a spread on eurobonds as on Bradys. With tighter eurobond spreads, sovereigns have been able to reduce their cost of funds by occasionally using the proceeds from eurobond issues to retire outstanding Brady debt.

CREDIT RATINGS

When Moody's Investors Service began rating Brady bonds in 1990, it rated Mexico's registered Par and Discount bonds Ba3, even though Mexico had previously been assigned a ceiling rating of Ba2. Moody's had distinguished other sovereign bond debt (eurobonds, global bonds) as being senior to Brady bonds. The one-notch distinction was rationalized because the Brady bonds were perceived as more vulnerable to rescheduling in a potential debt crisis, since Brady bonds had traditionally comprised a significant portion of a country's debt. Also, the owner-ship of Brady bonds was concentrated with the original lending banks. The past rationale was that this concentration, in theory, made Brady bonds easier to rene-gotiate. Furthermore, for the approximately 60% of outstanding Brady bonds that were issued in registered versus bearer form, the bondholders were also easier to "trace". Moody's also believed that large holders of Brady bonds could be tempted to submit to renegotiation of the bonds, rather than face a significant decline in the market value of their holdings in the event of a payment crisis.

Since the first Mexican rating, the emerging markets investor base has changed substantially, and many emerging markets countries have returned to the international capital markets through the issuance of eurobonds. When Moody's first rated Brady bonds, the majority of holders were initially the same banks that were owed the defaulted loan, a relatively small and concentrated investor group familiar with the restructuring. In many instances these banks had ongoing finan-cial relationships with the countries involved. Since then, the ownership has changed as trading volume on Brady bonds has soared and holdings by non-banks have become more widespread. Many of the same portfolios that hold eurobonds also include Brady bonds of the same country. In addition, a sizable number of small investors have also entered the Brady market.

In 1996, Moody's Investors Service revised its approach. Today, like Standard and Poor's, who originally began assigning equal credit ratings to all foreign debt obligations of sovereign countries, Moody's no longer makes a dis-tinction between the credit risk of Brady bonds and sovereign eurobonds of the same issuer. Legally, Brady bonds rank *pari passu* (equal ranking) with other senior sovereign foreign currency debt obligations of the debtor country. When investing in high-risk securities, investors should take note of the cross-default clauses stated in the provisions of the bond agreement.

ASSESSING VALUE IN COLLATERALIZED BRADY BONDS

A bond with collateral requires a somewhat different method of assessing value than merely calculating yield-to-maturity based on price. Investors can think of a Discount or Par bond as having three components: the U.S. Treasury fully collat-eralized principal, the collateralized rolling interest guarantee (RIG), and the credit risk remainder of the bond's cash flows. Often, dealers may vary in their measures of the bond's stripped yield (yield to maturity without the principal and interest collateral embedded in the bond). The main difference in valuing collater-alized Brady bonds has been in the various approaches to valuing the RIG compo-nent. In valuing these Brady bonds to assess relative value, we will review two of the most common methods that allow an investor to more easily compare yields of collateralized and non-collateralized sovereign bonds.

The Modified Cash Flow

The modified cash flow (MCF) method is a simple and efficient way to account for the rolling interest guarantee of a bond with interest collateral. Though the interest collateral does not currently cover the later coupons, these coupons still benefit from the RIG as each interest payment is made. The objective of the MCF approach is to simulate the rolling nature of the interest collateral as each successive coupon is paid. This is accomplished by discounting each subsequent coupon beyond the interest collateral at U.S. forward rates as it becomes guaranteed.

Through a continuous manner of discounting and moving forward each coupon by the specified number of periods secured, an investor can simulate the process of selling each coupon for its present value as soon as each successive interest payment becomes guaranteed. The set of proceeds generated from the sales represent the modified cash flows. The investor can now calculate an internal rate of return (IRR) on a collateralized Brady bond using the MCF and a stripped price. The stripped price is the price of the bond less the present value of its collateralized principal (discounted at the Treasury STRIP rate) and the present value of its interest guarantee (discounted using the swap curve to reflect the AA-rate collateral). The stripped yield and stripped spread (the spread off the U.S. Treasury zero coupon curve) is perceived as a representation of the market's view of that country's level of sovereign risk.

Using these calculated risk values, an investor is able to identify relative value between collateralized Brady bonds and non-collateralized bonds.

The Implied Probability of Default

The Implied Probability of Default (IPD) method computes the expected present value of each cash flow payment, assuming a constant probability of default on each coupon payment, given that default can occur at any time during the life of the bond. If we assign p to be the risk-neutral default probability, then the probability of defaulting on a future coupon date n can be represented as $p \times (1 - p)^{n-1}$, conditional on the issuer having paid all previous coupons. The following equation generalizes the IPD valuation of a collateralized Brady bond.

$$\text{Full Price} = \Sigma PV[(1 - p)^n \times \text{Coupon}_n + p(1 - p)^{n-1} \times [\text{Value of RIG}]_n]$$
$$+ [\text{PV of Principal Collateral}]$$

To compute the stripped yield using the IPD approach, an investor would need to solve for the p that equates the value of the bond's cash flows to its price (see above equation). The PV of the equation is calculated at a risk-free rate, which is usually chosen from a zero-coupon U.S. Treasury curve. Once the value of p has been determined, the investor can calculate the value of the RIG today, where

$$\text{Present Value of the RIG} = \Sigma PV[p(1 - p)^{n-1} \times [\text{Value of RIG}]_n]$$

The stripped yield is then the discount rate that equates the present value of the bond's cash flows to its stripped price (Full Price – [PV of Principal Collateral] – [PV of the RIG]).[5]

ASSESSING VALUE IN FLOATING-RATE BONDS

Unlike most corporate bonds, many Brady bonds amortize and may pay floating rate coupons for some or all of the coupon periods. A common way to compare fixed rate and floating rate coupons is to "swap" the floating rate to a fixed rate, or assume that the floating rate coupon resets based on forward LIBOR, on the LIBOR swap curve, or on the Eurodollar futures curve. The computed yield of the resulting cash flows, without the collateral, can then be compared to U.S. Treasuries to identify cheap bonds (wide stripped spreads) versus rich bonds (tight stripped spreads).[6]

CONCLUSION

Brady bonds have provided high yields (see Exhibit 2), considerable price appreciation, security of the collateral, and with sufficient size and liquidity to accommodate the increasing demand of institutional investors. However Eurobonds have surpassed Brady bonds as the liquid assets of choice as buybacks, retirements, and large Eurobond issues continue the trend begun in the last several years. In addition to cash bonds, active derivatives and repo markets in both Bradys and Eurobonds have given institutional investors leverage and enhanced opportunities to express a view or to take advantage of relative mispricings in the market. These attributes have encouraged successive waves of institutional investors to enter emerging markets, especially the Brady market, for the first time.

---

[5] See Chapter 16, "Default and Recovery Rates in Emerging Markets" by Tsvetan N. Beloreshki, for further details about this methodology.
[6] See Chapter 8, "How Swap Spreads Affect the Performance of Floating-Rate Emerging Market Bonds" by Costas C. Hamakiotes, for further details on floating-rate bond valuations.

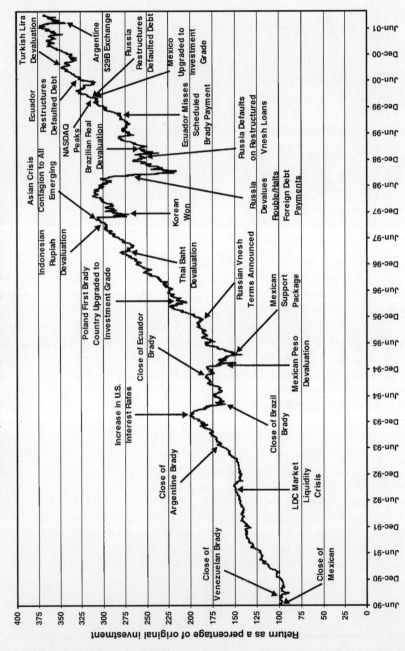

Exhibit 2: Emerging Market Returns since 1990
Total Return of Merrill Lynch Emerging Markets Index (IGOV)

Chapter 3

Latin American Local Markets

James C. Kennan
Vice President
BNP Paribas

T his chapter provides an overview of foreign exchange, interest rate, fixed income, and derivative products traded on the four major Latin markets: Mexico, Brazil, Argentina, and Chile.

BACKGROUND

Emerging markets remain an integral part of international commerce. Despite ups and downs, many of these markets are likely to converge with developed economies in the coming decades. A few broad themes provide background for this chapter.

Exchange Rates

All of the major Latin economies have employed FX regimes targeted to the US dollar, including both fixed and crawling pegs. Only Argentina continues to use a targeted FX rate, fixed at parity with the dollar. Mexico (1994), Brazil (1999), and Chile (1999) have abandoned FX targets, allowing the value of their currencies to be determined primarily by the markets.

Convertibility

Mexico has the only currency with both a liquid and freely convertible spot market. Most of the other Latin currencies have restrictions or barriers to trade of some type (legal, tax, or documentation requirements), and generally trade via non-deliverable contracts, such as NDFs.

Yield Curves

Local currency interest rates are generally higher than equivalent US dollar rates, a premium required to attract and retain funds or to counter high inflation rates.

Yield curves are generally lengthening, with liquidity beyond three years, though they generally remain shorter than their Central European or Asian counterparts.

Note: The information in this chapter was believed to be accurate as of September 2001; it is not to be relied upon for making investment or other decisions.

Derivatives

Derivatives are generally limited to FX options (with liquidity up to one year), with the same restrictions as the underlying currencies. Only Mexican peso options are traded with physical settlement at maturity, while the others are traded on a non-deliverable basis via NDOs.

STANDARD PRODUCTS

Standard products traded across several markets are described first, followed by those which are country-specific.

Non-Deliverable Forwards (NDFs)

NDFs are over-the-counter contracts which allow firms to hedge currency risks simply and efficiently. They are the primary tools used by offshore participants for managing currency and interest rate risk in restricted emerging markets.

Whether exposures are overseas assets or equity holdings, international subsidiaries or receivables in foreign currencies, investors can protect investments against currency and interest rate fluctuations.

Investors are often attracted to the high yields available in the developing world, but may find access limited due to currency restrictions. NDFs provide the means to invest in these economies without being locked into non-convertible or restricted currencies.

The advantages of NDFs are:

- Free of local regulations and restrictions
- Principal not subject to appropriation
- No convertibility or transferability risk
- Local bank accounts not required
- Eliminates spot unwind at maturity

NDFs thus serve the interests of both hedgers and investors.

In Latin America, NDFs are traded on the currencies of Brazil, Argentina, and Chile, as well as some of the smaller Latin markets such as Venezuela, Colombia, and Peru.

NDF Simplicity

A dollar-based investor taking a cash position in local markets must do the following:

- Borrow dollars at LIBOR
- Sell dollars spot and buy local currency
- Invest in local T-bills or deposits

- Receive principal and interest at maturity
- Sell local currency spot and buy dollars
- Repay LIBOR borrowing

These transactions must also be permissible under local law and the investor must maintain local bank accounts. Moreover, the client must be willing to risk an imposition of capital controls, as well as possible changes to local tax or other law. For many investors this is undesirable or impractical.

The convenient alternative is to sell dollars via an NDF, a far less complicated alternative than the underlying transactions but priced equivalently. This consolidates the six-step process into a single contract and eliminates the use of the balance sheet, as well as convertibility and transferability risks.

The same is true for buying NDFs, equivalent to shorting local bonds. Since deposit markets are frequently illiquid and repo markets often non-existent, borrowing local currency can be difficult. Buying NDFs (or buying dollars outright) is often a much more effective means of hedging local currency exposures.

How NDFs Work

Like standard forward contracts, NDFs are bought or sold depending on the desired currency or interest rate exposure. Unlike standard forward contracts, there is no physical delivery of the local currency at maturity. Instead, the difference between the agreed outright price and the prevailing spot rate at maturity is settled in the convertible currency of the contract (typically US dollars). The rate difference is multiplied by the notional amount to return a profit or loss amount (payout formula shown here for long dollar positions):

$$\left[1 - \frac{\text{forward rate}}{\text{settlement rate}} \right] \times \text{notional amount}$$

NDFs are generally short-term instruments (up to two years) and are usually quoted according to standard foreign exchange forward market conventions. In Latin America and Asia, they are quoted in forward points or as outright levels. For Central European currencies, they are typically expressed as interest rates.

NDFs employ a fixing mechanism, or reference rate, to determine profit and loss. These reference rates vary by currency and are shown in Exhibit 1.

Example: Capturing Yields with NDFs

Assume that Brazilian rates are falling and a New York fund manager wishes to lock in yields by investing in Brazilian T-bills for the next six months. Wishing to avoid the complex set of transactions noted above, he decides to sell a BRL NDF.

He calls a broker and asks for a 6-month BRL NDF on $10 million. He is quoted an outright exchange rate for an agreed fixing date and value date. The quote is "2.0270–2.0320," meaning the customer can sell USD in exchange for 2.0270 BRL in 6 months.

Exhibit 1: NDF Reference Rates

Currency	Fixing	Reference Rate	Fix Published
ARS Argentine Peso	T + 0	ARS Official Rate, or CME/EMTA ARS Industry Survey Rate	Between 3 and 5 pm Buenos Aires
BRL Brazilian Real	T + 2	PTAX 800 offer side, available on Reuters BRFR	Evening or next morning
CLP Chilean Peso	T + 2	Observado, available on Reuters CLPOB= or BCCHILG	Evening or next morning
COP Colombian Peso	T + 2	T.C.R.M., available on Reuters CO/COL03 or COT-CRM=RR	Next day
PEN Peruvian Sol	T + 2	Interbancario mid-rate, available on Reuters PDSC	11 am Lima
VEB Venezuelan Bolivar	T + 2	Tipo de Cambio Referencial mid-rate, available on Reuters page BCV28 or VEBFIX=	Evening

This forward rate implies a BRL interest rate, which can be calculated given a spot reference and a USD interest rate. With a prevailing spot rate of 1.9570 and a USD deposit rate of 6.30%, the implied BRL deposit rate is calculated as follows:

$$\text{outright} \ = \ \text{spot} \times \frac{1 + i_{BRL} \times \dfrac{\text{actual}}{360}}{1 + i_{USD} \times \dfrac{\text{actual}}{360}}$$

$$2.0270 \ = \ 1.9570 \times \frac{1 + i_{BRL} \times \dfrac{182}{360}}{1 + 6.30\% \times \dfrac{182}{360}}$$

This gives a BRL money market yield of 13.60%.

At maturity, the broker uses the official exchange rate (as published on the Central Bank of Brazil's Reuters page BRFR) to determine the settlement amount. If the Brazilian real depreciated to 1.9840 at maturity, the investor would receive a profit of:

$$\left[\frac{2.0270}{1.9840} - 1 \right] \times \$10\,\text{mio} \ = \ \$216,733.87$$

Note that this can also be calculated as the initial BRL amount of 20.27 million (\$10 mio × 2.0270) divided by the rate at maturity of 1.9840, giving the final amount of \$10,216,733.87.

Non-Deliverable Options (NDOs)

NDOs are the options equivalent of NDFs. They allow firms to hedge currency risks and investors to express views on currencies which are otherwise inaccessible.

Like standard FX options, NDOs are particularly attractive for firms which have contingent or nonlinear exposures, or who wish to assume risk within a defined range. For example, a firm submitting a competitive bid for a contract may buy an option to hedge the potential currency exposure, without assuming the greater risk of a forward contract.

As with standard options, NDOs can be combined to form multileg strategies, such as straddles, strangles, spreads, collars, and others.

The advantages of NDOs are:

- Free of local regulations and restrictions
- Local currency accounts not required
- Direct settlement of profit and loss
- Eliminates spot unwind
- Automatic exercise

In Latin America, NDOs are traded on the same restricted currencies as NDFs: Brazil, Argentina, and Chile, as well as the currencies of some of the smaller markets.

How NDOs Work

As with NDFs, NDOs are settled against an agreed reference rate, providing a net settlement in US dollars (or any other convertible and liquid currency). Unlike standard FX options, NDOs do not require the holder to notify his counterparty of an intention to exercise the option. They are automatically exercised if they are in the money at the time of expiration, even if by a single tick.

Since the reference rate for settlement is often not published until after expiry, the option holder (and writer) may not know if the option has been exercised until the following day. Because there is no physical delivery of the currency notional amounts, this generally does not pose a problem for the user.

Liquidity of NDOs reflects the corresponding liquidity of the underlying NDFs, and thus NDOs are typically short-term instruments (up to two years).

They are quoted using the same conventions as deliverable currency options, with two-way prices expressed either in terms of implied volatility (if the client exchanges the hedge with the bank) or in premium. Premiums cannot be quoted in terms of the local currency, since it is generally not convertible. The nondeliverable nature of NDO currencies may present difficulties in pricing barrier options, which rely on the liquidity of the underlying spot market. This typically results in larger exotic option bid/ask spreads than for deliverable currencies.

MEXICO

The local products covered for Mexico are:

- FX forwards
- FX futures

- FX options
- Exotic FX options
- TIIE swaps
- Cross-currency basis swaps
- Cross-currency inflation-indexed swaps
- Cetes
- Bondes
- Bonos
- BPAs
- BREMS
- Udibonos

FX Forwards: OTC Currency Forwards

Description

An FX forward contract is an obligatory agreement between two counterparties to physically exchange currencies at a fixed rate in the future, with the rate and time agreed at inception. It is traded over-the-counter (OTC), and since it is physically deliverable, among the Latin currencies it is traded only on the Mexican peso.

Valuation

The forward is the exchange rate that satisfies the relationship between the two currencies' interest rates, known as Covered Interest Parity (CIP). CIP basically states that an equal amount of money (calculated at the spot rate) invested in two countries must be worth the same at maturity. The rate that makes them equal is the forward rate. If they are not equal, one can profit by (1) borrowing one currency, (2) selling it, (3) lending in the other, and (4) trading the forward against it. The relationship between the spot and forward exchange rate is summarized by the following formula:[1]

$$F = S \times \frac{1 + i_{MXN} \times \dfrac{d}{360}}{1 + i_{USD} \times \dfrac{d}{360}}$$

F = Forward rate expressed in Mexican pesos per US dollar

S = Spot rate expressed in Mexican pesos per US dollar

i_{USD}, i_{MXN} = US and Mexican money market interest rates (actual/360 basis)

d = Number of days from spot date to value date

Example 1 Suppose the 1-year money market interest rate is 17.0% for the Mexican peso and 6.0% for the US dollar, and the spot rate is 10.00. If you invest $1

---

[1] For tenors longer than 360 days, the interest rate must be compounded.

in the US, it yields $1.0609 at maturity.[2] Likewise, if you invest 10 pesos in Mexico, it yields 11.7276 pesos in one year. If the forward rate does not equal 11.7236/1.0609 = 11.0546, an arbitrage opportunity exists. Say the forward rate is 11.50. Borrow 10.00 Mexican pesos at 17%, sell them spot for $1, and invest the $1 to receive $1.0609 at maturity. Meanwhile, sell $1.0609 forward at a rate of 11.50 pesos to receive $1.0609 × 11.50 = 12.2002 pesos in one year. The borrowing of 10.00 pesos at 17% is then repaid at maturity with 11.7276 pesos. The resulting profit is 12.2002 − 11.7276 = 0.4726 pesos per dollar traded.

The market convention for deliverable currency forwards is to trade the spot first, then the forward, expressed in two separate quotes: (1) the spot rate and (2) forward points. Forward points are usually expressed as the difference between the forward rate and the spot rate, with the decimal place moved five places to the right:

$$\text{Forward points} = (F - S) \times 10,000$$

Example 2 Suppose one wishes to sell 10.00 pesos 1-year forward. Spot and forwards are traded in two separate and specialized interbank markets, so there are typically three transactions comprising a standard-delivery forward. Using the rates in the preceding example, one first buys $1 and sells 10.0000 pesos in the spot market. In the forward market, one then simultaneously sells $1 spot at a rate of 10.0000 and buys $1 forward at a rate of 11.0546 (this price is expressed as "10,546"). Note that this largely insulates the forward market from moves in the spot rate. At maturity, one delivers 10.00 pesos and receives 10.0000/11.0546 = 0.9046 dollars. Since these are deliverable transactions, US dollar and Mexican peso bank accounts are required.

FX Futures: IMM Currency Futures

Description

FX futures contracts are standardized exchange-traded obligatory agreements, between a member and the clearinghouse, to physically exchange currencies at a fixed rate in the future, with the rate and time agreed at inception. Unlike forward contracts, they are traded on organized exchanges with standardized contract terms (such as amount and maturity), and are marked to market on a daily basis with corresponding margin accounts. The Mexican peso futures contract is traded in the International Monetary Market (IMM) division of the Chicago Mercantile Exchange (CME). Contract size is 500,000 pesos. The most actively traded contracts are the four quarterly maturities (March, June, September, December), though monthly contracts were recently listed. Contracts expire on the third Wednesday of the month and stop trading two business days before. Exchange

---

[2]
$$\left(1 + 0.06 \times \frac{360}{360}\right)\left(1 + 0.06 \times \frac{5}{360}\right) = 1.06088$$

trading hours are 7:20 am–2:00 pm Chicago time (the contract is also available on the IMM's Globex electronic trading system). A nondeliverable contract on the Brazilian real is also listed on the IMM, but has not been active since 1999.

Valuation

The valuation of futures is very similar to forward contracts. Some differences may arise from margining (forwards are usually traded on a credit or collateral basis). Provided there is no correlation between the futures rate and the margin interest rate, however, the relationship between the spot and futures exchange rates satisfies the same relationship between the two currencies' interest rates as for forwards, known as Covered Interest Parity (CIP). CIP states that an equal amount of money (calculated at the spot rate) invested in two countries must be worth the same at maturity; the rate that makes them equal is the futures rate. If they are not equal, one can profit *on average*[3] by (1) borrowing one currency, (2) selling it, (3) lending in the other, and (4) trading the futures against it. With no correlation between the futures rate and the margin interest rate, the relationship between the spot and futures exchange rates is summarized by the following:[4]

$$F = \frac{1}{S} \times \frac{1 + i_{USD} \times \frac{d}{360}}{1 + i_{MXN} \times \frac{d}{360}}$$

F = Futures rate expressed in US dollars per Mexican peso
S = Spot rate expressed in Mexican pesos per US dollar
i_{USD}, i_{MXN} = US and Mexican money market interest rates (actual/360 basis)
d = Number of days from spot date to value date

Unlike forwards, futures contracts are marked to market on a daily basis. The daily change in margin is:

$$\Delta \text{Margin} = (F_i - F_{i-1}) \times Q + \text{Margin Account} \times r \times \frac{1}{360}$$

F_i = Price of the contract on day i
Q = Number of contracts ($Q < 0$ means you are shorting contracts)
r = Relevant interest rate earned on margin

Example Suppose one wishes to sell 5 million Mexican pesos using the near-date quarterly futures contract, and the trade date is January 20. The next contract

---

[3] Unlike forwards, the arbitrage profit is not fixed due to the variable margin costs of futures contracts; instead, it is an expected value.
[4] For tenors longer than 360 days, the interest rate must be compounded.

maturity is March 21. One sells ten March contracts at a price of 0.9865 US dollars per Mexican peso, requiring the posting of a \$12,000 initial margin.[5] If the contract rallies the next day to 0.9910, the margin account will be credited:

$$(0.9910 - 0.9865) \times 500,000 \times 10 + 12,000 \times 6\% \times \frac{1}{360} = \$22,502$$

If the contract is not unwound prior to settlement, Mexican peso bank accounts are required for physical delivery.

FX Options: OTC Currency Options

Description

An option contract gives the holder the right to buy or sell an asset at a certain time and price. Since it is not an obligation, the buyer pays a premium to the seller. A call option gives the holder the right to buy the asset, while a put option confers the right to sell; in the case of currency options, the asset is a foreign currency. Given the symmetry of currency options (both assets are currencies), a call on the foreign currency is equal to a put on the local currency (and vice-versa).

Like other FX options, Mexican peso options are over-the-counter contracts which are physically deliverable at maturity. They are generally traded European-style (not exercisable prior to day of expiration), and expire at 12:30 pm New York time. They are usually traded against the US dollar, with occasional trades in cross-currency options (e.g., against the Canadian dollar). Options on Mexican peso futures are also listed on the IMM, but have been inactive in recent years.

Valuation

The standard model for quoting option prices is the Black-Scholes formula. While not an accurate description of observed market prices, the model is very convenient for quotation purposes: it allows options to be quoted in terms of implied volatility, which changes much less than the option price itself. For purposes of interbank trading, the model is used as a quotation yardstick rather than an estimation model. Interbank counterparties quote implied volatility to one another, with price subsequently agreed on using the Black-Scholes formula. Prices quoted in percent of the US dollar notional amount are equal to:

$$\text{US dollar call} = \frac{1}{S} \times e^{-rT}[F \times N(d_1) - X \times N(d_2)]$$

$$\text{US dollar put} = \frac{1}{S} \times e^{-rT}[X \times N(-d_2) - F \times N(-d_1)]$$

where

---

[5] Margin rates vary at the discretion of exchange management, depending largely on historical contract volatility.

$$d_1 = \frac{\ln\left(\frac{F}{X}\right) + \frac{1}{2}\sigma^2 T}{\sigma\sqrt{T}}$$

$$d_2 = d_1 - \sigma\sqrt{T}$$

e =   Constant equal to 2.71828182845904..., the base of the natural logarithm

$N(x)$ =   Cumulative normal distribution for x

S =   Spot rate, expressed in Mexican pesos per US dollar

F =   Forward rate, in MXN per USD

X =   Strike, in MXN per USD

s =   Implied volatility

T =   Time to maturity (in years)

i =   Mexican peso money market interest rate (implied by US D interest rate and forward)

r =   Mexican peso continuous interest rate = $\ln(1+i)$

Example A firm is bidding on a construction contract in Mexico. If it wins the contract, the firm will be paid in one year (365 days) in Mexican pesos, while its costs will be in US dollars. To protect against a potential weakening of the peso, management calls BNP Paribas for a quote on a 1-year at-the-money-forward option. The market level of implied volatility is 11.5%/12.0%, meaning the client may sell options at 11.5%, and buy options at 12.0% volatility. Using a spot rate of 10.00 and USD and MXN interest rates of 6.0% and 17.0% respectively, the strike is set at the forward rate of 11.0546. Based on the formula above, the corresponding premium is 4.51% of US dollars. MXN options are generally traded as a percentage of the USD notional, but can also be quoted in percent of MXN or in pesos per dollar.

Exotic FX Options: Barriers, Average Rates, and Baskets

Exotic options include custom-tailored properties to better suit investors' desired exposures, enabling almost any payoff profile to be structured. Following are examples of some popular types of exotic options. They are traded primarily on the Mexican peso, but may also be traded on other Latin currencies depending on market conditions.

Barrier Options

Barrier options are path-dependent. A barrier option's payoff depends on whether the underlying asset price (typically the spot rate) reaches a certain level during the option's life (or during a part of the option's life, called a "window option"). Examples include: (1) knock-out options, which expire if the underlying rate reaches (or "touches") the barrier; (2) knock-in options, which become active when the barrier is touched; and (3) double no-touch (or range) options, which pay out the notional if neither upper nor lower barrier is touched during the life of the option. Barrier options are often attractive to investors because (1) they can more closely match a particular view, and (2) they are less expensive than corresponding vanilla options.

Average Rate (Asian) Options

Average rate option payoffs depend on the average spot rate over the life of the option, rather than the spot rate at maturity. Spot is observed at specified intervals and averaged (with specified weights for each observation), which is then compared to the strike to determine the payoff. As a result, average rate options are always cash settled. They are particularly useful for companies with cash flows distributed over a given period of time, for which an average exchange rate has been budgeted. These options allow companies to ensure an average conversion rate for the series of cash flows. They are cheaper than standard options since the average of the underlying is less volatile than the underlying itself.

Basket Options

The payoff of a basket option is dependent on the value of a portfolio (or basket) of assets, rather than on a single asset. A standard basket option gives the holder the right to buy or sell a specified amount of different currencies in exchange for a specified amount of a local currency (usually US dollars). They are typically cash settled at maturity and are automatically exercised on behalf of the client if the option is in the money at expiry. The strike price is quoted in terms of a protected amount of local currency, based on a specific basket of assets. Their main appeal to investors is the often substantial premium savings relative to the sum of the corresponding vanilla options. This discount is a function of the assets' individual volatilities, correlations, and relative sizes.

Interest Rate Options: TIIE Caps and Floors

An interest rate cap is a sequence of calls on a reference interest rate, which can be used to hedge a floating-rate liability. Likewise, floors are a sequence of puts which can be used to hedge a floating-rate asset. Like swaps, they are determined in advance and paid in arrears. The interest rate option market in the Mexican peso is in the earliest stages of development. Most interest has been in short-dated TIIE caps.

Example

A firm funding itself at 28-day TIIE, which trades at 15.10% at the time of the firm's decision making process, believes rates are likely to remain at or below this level. However, management is concerned about a small probability that rates will move much higher during the next year, when they are particularly susceptible to cash flow constraints. They decide to purchase a one-year cap on 28-day TIIE struck at 17%, protecting the firm against the possibility of a large increase in funding costs. After 28 days, the prevailing TIIE rate is compared to the strike of 17%. If the TIIE has risen to 18.5%, the firm will receive the following payout (in 28 days):

$$\text{Notional} \times (18.5\% - 17\%) \times \frac{28}{360}$$

Every subsequent 28 days, the prevailing TIIE rate is compared to the strike, and a payment is made to the firm if the TIIE rate is above the strike.

TIIE Swaps: Tasa de Interés Interbancaria de Equilibrio Swaps (Interbank Equilibrium Interest Rate Swaps)

Description

- Type   OTC fixed-floating interest rate swap
- Payments   Netted in MXN, in arrears
- Maturity   Up to 3 years
- Floating Rate   28-day TIIE from *Diario Oficial de la Federacion*
- Rate Fixing   Determined via Central Bank auction of dealers with highest volumes of preceding week
- Rate Reset   One business day prior to payment date (Mexican business day convention)
- Tax Status   Onshore counterparties taxable, offshore counterparties tax-exempt
- Basis   Actual/360 on both legs

Valuation

Netted payments at the end of every 28-day reset period are equal to:

$$C_{\text{fix}} = \text{Notional} \times (\text{TIIE}_{28} - r_{\text{fix}}) \times \frac{d}{360}$$

$$C_{\text{TIIE}} = \text{Notional} \times (r_{\text{fix}} - \text{TIIE}_{28}) \times \frac{d}{360}$$

C_{fix} = Fixed rate payer receives from floating rate payer (if positive)
C_{TIEE} = Floating rate payer receives from fixed rate payer (if positive)
TIIE_{28} = 28-day TIIE rate observed at the beginning of reset period
r_{fix} = Fixed rate
d = Number of days in the initial period

Example A firm has funded itself with two-year fixed-rate Mexican pesos at 18%, but management believes rates will fall substantially over the near term. To offset the fixed-rate liability, they decide to enter into a 26×1 ("twenty-six by one") TIIE swap, comprising 26 periods of 28 days each ($26 \times 28 = 728$ days). The TIIE swap is quoted "18.40–18.80," meaning the company receives 2-year fixed at 18.40% and pays 28-day TIIE.

On the trade date, the current 28-day TIIE rate is 18.59%. This is used as the first reset and settled against the fixed rate at the end of the first period ("determined in advance and paid in arrears"). Since the TIIE rate is above the fixed rate, the company *pays* the following, on a notional of MXN 100 million, at the end of the first period:

$$\text{MXN 100 million} \times (18.59\% - 18.40\%) \times \frac{28}{360} = \text{MXN 14,777.78}$$

At the end of the first period, the TIIE rate has moved to 17.98%, which is used as the second reset. At the end of the second 28-day period, the company *receives*:

$$\text{MXN 100 million} \times (18.40\% - 17.98\%) \times \frac{28}{360} = \text{MXN 32,666.67}$$

On the same date, a new TIIE rate of 17.65% is then taken as the third reset, to be settled at the end of the third period. This process is followed until the maturity of the swap.

MEXIBOR Swaps
In July 2001, an association of 12 banks began quoting a reference interest rate designed to more closely mimic the popular LIBOR (London Interbank Offer Rate) mechanisms. MEXIBOR is quoted for a period of 91 days, to correspond with a 364-day year (91 × 4 = 364), maintaining the same day-count as the TIIE fixings (where 28 × 13 = 364). It is intended to provide an alternative reference of extended duration. Should it become popular, swap quotations will likely adopt the 91-day MEXIBOR as a standard reset reference, rather than the 28-day TIIE.

USD/MXN Cross-Currency Basis Swaps
Description

• Type	OTC cross-currency basis swap (floating-floating)
• Payments	Both legs physically exchanged (no netting)
• Maturity	Up to 3 years
• Resets	Every 3 years
• Principal	Exchanged at inception and maturity; using initial USD/MXN spot rate
• Floating Rates	USD: 1-month LIBOR MXN: 28-day TIIE
• Rate Resets	LIBOR set 2 business days prior to reset date TIIE published one business day prior to reset date
• Rate Sources	LIBOR as posted on Telerate page 3750 TIIE from *Diario Oficial de la Federacion*
• Tax Status	Tax-exempt
• Basis	Actual/360, both legs

Valuation

The following cash flows are exchanged on the reset dates:

$$C_{USD} = \text{Notional}_{USD} \times (\text{LIBOR}_{USD} + s) \times \frac{d}{360}$$

$$C_{MXN} = \text{Notional}_{MXN} \times \text{TIIE}_{28} \times \frac{d}{360}$$

C_{USD}, C_{MXN}	=	Coupon payments in USD and MXN
LIBOR_{USD}	=	1-month LIBOR rate
TIIE_{28}	=	28-day TIIE reference rate
s	=	Spread over LIBOR
d	=	Number of days in the past period

Example A multinational with a short-term project in Mexico wishes to fund its Mexican peso liabilities. Since US dollar funding is cheaper and easier for the firm to obtain, management decides to borrow $100 million US dollars at 1-month LIBOR flat, and subsequently swap it into Mexican pesos. The quote for a 1-year USD/MXN cross-currency basis swap is "5/10," meaning the firm can receive 1-month LIBOR + 5 bp and pay TIIE flat. When the swap is executed, the spot USD/MXN rate is set at 9.6500. With the value date two business days after the trade date, the firm pays $100 million and receives $100 million × 9.6500 = MXN 965 million. At maturity, the firm pays MXN 965 million and receives $100 million, in addition to the coupon payments over the life of the swap.

USD/UDI Cross-Currency Inflation-Indexed Swaps

Description

• Type	Cross-currency inflation-indexed swap
• Reference	UDI (*Unidad de Inversion*, or Unit of Investment), accumulated consumer price inflation index denominated in MXN (1 UDI = 1 Mexican peso as of 1 April 1995)
• Payments	Both USD and MXN legs physically exchanged (no netting)
• Maturity	Up to 5 years
• Resets	Semiannual
• Principal	Exchanged at inception and maturity; using initial USD/UDI spot rate
• Rates	USD: 6-month LIBOR UDI: fixed
• LIBOR Reset	Two business days prior to reset date
• LIBOR Source	As posted on Telerate 3750, calculated to the 5th decimal place

• Tax Status   Tax-exempt
• Basis   Actual/360, both legs

Valuation

The following cash flows are exchanged on the reset dates:

$$C_{USD} = Notional_{USD} \times LIBOR_{USD} \times \frac{d}{360}$$

$$C_{MXN} = UDI \times Notional_{UDI} \times i_{UDI} \times \frac{d}{360}$$

C_{USD}, C_{MXN} = USD- and MXN-denominated coupon payments
UDI = *Unidad de Inversion* rate for the payment date (in Mexican pesos per UDI)
$LIBOR_{USD}$ = 6-month LIBOR rate
i_{UDI} = UDI fixed rate
d = Number of days in the previous period

Example A multinational firm investing in a long-term project in Mexico must purchase raw land, which it expects to appreciate with Mexican inflation. Since US dollar funding is cheaper and easier to obtain, management decides to borrow $100 million US dollars at 6-month LIBOR flat for 5 years and swap it into inflation-indexed Mexican pesos, to match its assets. The quote for a 5-year USD/UDI cross-currency swap is "7.75/8.10," meaning the firm can receive 6-month LIBOR flat and pay 8.10 percent denominated in UDI. At inception, spot USD/MXN is 9.6500 and UDI/MXN is 2.9241, so the rate for exchange of principal at inception and maturity is set at 3.3002 UDIs per USD. With value two business days after trade date, the firm pays $100 million and receives 330.02 million UDI equivalent of MXN, or 330.02 million × 2.9241 = MXN 965 million. The first period LIBOR reference is also set at inception at the prevailing rate of 5.50%.

After 6 months, the UDI/MXN rate is 2.9963 (reflecting average annual inflation of 5%) and the firm pays:

$$8.10\% \times \left(\frac{182}{360}\right) \times 330.02 \text{ million} \times 2.9963 = MXN 40,492,954.02$$

On the dollar leg, the firm receives:

$$5.50\% \times \left(\frac{182}{360}\right) \times 100 \text{ million} = \$2,780,555.56$$

At maturity, the firm repays 330.02 million UDI worth of MXN at the prevailing UDI/MXN rate. If UDI/MXN is 3.7320, the firm then repays 330.02 million × 3.7320 = MXN 1.232 billion.

Cetes: Certificados de la Tesoreria de la Federation (Federal Treasury Certificates)

Description

- Type — MXN-denominated zero-coupon bond
- Issuer — SCHP (*Secretaria de Hacienda y Credito Publico*) via *Banco de Mexico*
- Amortization — Bullet
- Maturity — 28, 91, 182, and 364 days
- Coupon — None
- Rate — Quoted on a yield-to-maturity basis
- Face Value — 10 MXN
- Tax Status — Capital gains and interest tax-exempt for local and foreign investors
- Custodian — Local custodian required
- Basis — Actual/360
- Issuance — Weekly for 28- and 91-day, bi-weekly for 182-day, every 4 weeks for 365-day
- Bid Process — Modified discriminating (US Treasury style)
- Bid Format — Multiple bids allowed, specifying amount and discount offered

Valuation

Cetes are priced using the standard bond pricing formula:

$$\text{Price} = \frac{V}{1 + y \times \dfrac{d}{360}}$$

V = Face value
y = Annual yield-to-maturity
d = Number of calendar days

Example A company wishes to invest in a Mexican short-term security and decides to buy 50 Cetes maturing in 8 months. It contacts BNP Paribas and asks for a quote on recently issued Cetes with maturities around 8 months. BNP Paribas quotes a yield of 17.10% for bonds maturing in 255 days. The bond price is:

$$10{,}000 \times \frac{1}{1 + 17.1\% \times \dfrac{255}{360}} = \text{MXN } 8{,}919.61$$

The total price is:

$$50 \times 8{,}919.61 = \text{MXN } 445{,}980.60$$

Bondes: Bonos de Desarrollo del Gobierno Federal con Cupones Revisables (Federal Government Development Bonds with Floating Coupons)

Description

- Type   MXN-denominated floating-rate coupon-bearing bond
- Issuer   SCHP (*Secretaria de Hacienda y Credito Publico*) via *Banco de Mexico*
- Amortization   Bullet
- Maturities   2, 3, and 5 years
- Coupon

Maturity	Period	Reference rate
2 years	28 days	Cetes
3 years	91 days	Cetes adjusted rate
5 years	182 days	Cetes adjusted rate

- Rate Option   For 3- and 5-year bonds, greater of current Cetes rate or corresponding UDI inflation rate, determined at end of period
- Face Value   100 Mexican pesos
- Tax Status   Tax-exempt for local and foreign investors
- Custodian   Local custodian required
- Basis   Actual/360
- Issuance   Weekly; 2-year has not been issued since January 2000
- Bid Process   Dutch or Modified Discriminating (US Treasury style) auction at discretion of *Banco de Mexico*; US treasury style is currently used
- Bid Format   Multiple bids allowed, specifying amount and price to five decimal places

Valuation

Market convention is to quote the spread over the current Cetes rate for the specified maturity. A single, constant Cetes reference is used for the life of the bond, such that the values of all floating coupons are identical. This gives the following pricing formula:

$$\text{Price} = \frac{V}{(1+y)^{1-\frac{d}{T}}}\left[C + C \times \left(\frac{1}{y} - \frac{1}{(1+y)^{n-1}}\right) + \frac{1}{(1+y)^{n-1}}\right]$$

$$y = (\text{Cetes}_T + s) \times \frac{T}{360}$$

$$C = \text{Cetes}_T \times \frac{T}{360}$$

V = Face value

T = Coupon tenor in days (equal to 28, 91, or 182)

Cetes_T = Current Cetes reference rate

s = Spread over Cetes rate

y = Bond yield

C = Coupon

d = Number of days since last coupon payment

n = Number of coupon payments remaining

Bonos: Bonos de Desarrollo del Gobierno Federal (Federal Government Development Bonds)

Description

- Type   MXN-denominated fixed rate coupon-bearing bond
- Issuer   SCHP (*Secretaria de Hacienda y Credito Publico*) via *Banco de Mexico*
- Amortization   Bullet
- Maturity   3 and 5 years
- Coupon   Every 182 days for both maturities
- Face Value   100 Mexican pesos
- Tax Status   Tax-exempt for both local and foreign investors
- Custodian   Local custodian required
- Basis   Actual/360
- Issuance   Every 4 weeks for the 3-year bond and every 6 weeks for the 5-year bond
- Bid Process   Dutch or Modified Discriminating (US Treasury style), as determined by *Banco de Mexico*. The US Treasury type of auction is currently used.
- Bid Format   Multiple bids allowed, specifying amount and price to five decimal places

  For incremental auctions of previously issued bonds (re-openings), clean price is quoted. Accrued interest is calculated as:

$$\text{Accrued Interest} = V \times \left(\frac{d \times i}{360} \right)$$

V = Face value

d = Number of days since the last coupon payment of the bond

i = Annual interest rate

Valuation

Market convention is to quote the annualized yield-to-maturity, which is used in the standard bond pricing formula:

$$\text{Price} = \frac{V}{(1+y)^{1-\frac{d}{T}}}\left[C + C\times\left(\frac{1}{y} - \frac{1}{y\times(1+y)^{n-1}}\right) + \frac{1}{(1+y)^{n-1}}\right]$$

$$C = R_c\times\left(\frac{182}{360}\right)$$

$$y = \text{YTM}\times\left(\frac{182}{360}\right)$$

V	=	Face value
n	=	Number of coupon payments remaining
d	=	Number of days since last coupon payment or issue
T	=	Coupon tenor in days (equal to 182)
R_c	=	Annualized coupon rate
C	=	Coupon payment
YTM	=	Yield-to-maturity of the bond
y	=	Bond yield

BPAs: Bonos de Protection al Ahorro (Savings Protection Bonds)

Description

- **Type** — MXN-denominated, floating-rate coupon-bearing bond
- **Issuer** — IPAB (Institute for the Protection of Bank Savings) via *Banco de Mexico* (intermediary for issuance, interest payments, and redemption). In case of IPAB default, *Banco de Mexico* automatically debits the Federal Treasury's account to cover principal and interest.
- **Amortization** — Bullet
- **Maturity** — Determined by IPAB ad hoc. The first issue had a 3-year maturity.
- **Coupon** — Every 28 days
- **Rate** — The higher of the 28-day Cetes and the Central Bank's gross annual rate for one-month corporate notes. In practice, the Cetes28 rate is used.
- **Face Value** — 100 Mexican pesos
- **Tax Status** — Revenues derived from interest and redemption are tax-exempt for individuals. For corporations, the tax regime as defined in the Mexican Income Tax Law (*Ley de Impuestos sobre la Renta*) is applicable.
- **Custodian** — Local custodian required
- **Basis** — Actual/360
- **Frequency** — Weekly

- Bid Process   Dutch or Modified Discriminating (US Treasury style) auction at discretion of *Banco de Mexico*. Currently, auctions are Modified Discriminating style.
- Bid Format   Multiple bids allowed, specifying amount and price

Valuation

Market convention is to quote the spread over the Cetes$_{28}$ rate for the yield to maturity. For quotation purposes, a single, constant Cetes reference is used for the life of the bond, such that the values of all floating coupons are identical. This gives the following formula:

$$\text{Price} = V \times \frac{1}{(1+y)^{1-\frac{d}{28}}} \times \left[C + C \times \left(\frac{1}{y} - \frac{1}{y \times (1+y)^{n-1}} \right) + \frac{1}{(1+y)^{n-1}} \right]$$

$$y = (\text{Cetes}_{28} + s) \times \frac{28}{360}$$

$$C = \text{Cetes}_{28} \times \frac{28}{360}$$

V	=	Face value
Cetes$_{28}$	=	28-day Cetes reference rate
s	=	Spread over the Cetes rate
y	=	Bond yield
d	=	Number of days since last coupon payment
T	=	Coupon tenor in days (equal to 28, 91 or 182)
n	=	Number of coupon payments remaining
C	=	Coupon payment

BREMs: Bonos de Regulacion Monetaria (Monetary Regulation Bonds)

Description

- Type   MXN-denominated floating-rate coupon-bearing bond
- Issuer   *Banco de Mexico*
- Amortization   Bullet
- Maturity   3 years
- Coupon   Every 28 days
- Rate   Overnight interbank funding rate; published daily by the Central Bank
- Face Value   100 pesos
- Tax Status   Tax-exempt for local and foreign investors

- Custodian   Local custodian required
- Basis   Actual/360
- Issuance   Weekly [First auctioned 3 August 2000; used by Central Bank to conduct monetary policy]
- Bid Process   Modified Discriminating (US Treasury style)
- Bid Format   Multiple bids allowed, specifying amount and discount offered

Valuation

Market convention is to quote the spread over the average funding rate for the yield to maturity. This rate is published daily and is estimated based on previous observations. For quotation purposes, this reference rate is assumed constant for the life of the bond, such that all future coupon payments are known.

$$\text{Price} = \frac{V}{(1+y)^{1-\frac{d}{28}}} \times \left[C_1 + \frac{1}{(1+y)^{(n-1)}} + \sum_{i=1}^{n-1} \frac{C}{(1+y)^i} \right]$$

$$C_1 = \left(1 + R_d \frac{d}{360}\right) \times \left(1 + \frac{r}{360}\right)^{28-d} - 1$$

$$R_d = \left[\prod_{i=1}^{d} \left(1 + \frac{r_i}{360}\right) - 1 \right] \times \frac{360}{d}$$

$$C = \left(1 + \frac{r}{360}\right)^{28} - 1$$

$$y = \left(1 + \frac{r+s}{360}\right)^{28} - 1$$

V = Face value
y = Implied yield
d = Number of days since last coupon payment or bond issue
n = Number of coupon payments remaining
C_1 = Next coupon payment
C = Future coupon payments (excluding C_1)
R_d = Interest rate for period between last coupon payment (or issuance) and trade date
r_i = Historical interbank overnight interest rate reference published by Central Bank of Mexico
r = Central Bank of Mexico estimate of future interbank overnight interest rate
s = Market spread over r

Udibonos: Bonos de Desarrollo del Gobierno Federal Denominados en Unidades de Inversion (Federal Government Development Bonds Denominated in Units of Investment)

Description

- **Type**: UDI-denominated fixed-rate coupon; UDI (Unidad De Inversion) represents accumulated inflation since 1 April 1995, denominated in Mexican pesos. Udibonos provide a "real rate of return," akin to US Treasury Inflation-Protected Securities.
- **Issuer**: SCHP (*Secretaria de Hacienda y Credito Publico*) via *Banco de Mexico*
- **Amortization**: Bullet
- **Maturity**: 5 and 10 years (3-year Udibonos ceased issuance in August 1998)
- **Coupon**: 182 days
- **Rate**: Fixed yield expressed in UDI. Corresponding MXN price obtained using current MXN/UDI exchange rate. CPI figures announced by *Banco de Mexico* semimonthly. Extrapolated value of UDI published daily based on previous two CPI figures; step adjustment made upon official release of next CPI level.
- **Nominal Value**: 100 UDI
- **Tax Status**: Foreign investors exempt from ISR tax
- **Custodian**: Local custodian required
- **Basis**: Actual/360
- **Issuance**: Every 6 weeks for both maturities
- **Bid process**: Modified Discriminating (US Treasury style)
- **Bid format**: Multiple bids allowed, specifying amount and price

Valuation

Market convention is to quote the annualized yield-to-maturity, using the standard bond pricing formula:

$$\text{Price} = \text{UDI} \times \frac{V}{(1+y)^{1-\frac{d}{T}}} \left[C + C \times \left(\frac{1}{y} - \frac{1}{y \times (1+y)^{n-1}} \right) + \frac{1}{(1+y)^{n-1}} \right]$$

UDI = Current UDI/MXN exchange rate

V = Face value

y = Implied yield for period = annualized yield to maturity as quoted $\times\ 182/360$

C = Coupon payment in UDI = annualized coupon rate $\times\ 182/360$

d = Number of days since last coupon payment

T = Number of days in coupon period (182 days)

n = Number of coupon payments remaining

BRAZIL

The local products in Brazil that will be covered are:
- US dollar futures and options
- DI futures
- Adjusted DI futures
- DDI futures
- Pre-DI swaps
- USD/DI cross-currency swaps
- USD/BRL fixed-floating cross-currency swaps
- LFTs
- LTNs
- NTN-Cs
- NBC-Es
- TDAs

US Dollar Futures: BM&F Currency Futures

Description

• Type	Nondeliverable FX futures contract
• Payment	Cash-settled in BRL at maturity, using PTAX rate (offer side)
• Reference Rate	Daily weighted average of all spot trades as reported to Central Bank of Brazil
• Maturity	Up to 24 months, as determined by the BM&F
• Contract	Monthly
• Expiration	Last business day of the month preceding the contract month
• Settlement	First business day of the contract month
• Quotation	BRL per USD 1000, to three decimal places
• Contract Value	USD 50,000
• Exchange	Mercantile and Futures Exchange (BM&F) in São Paulo

Example

On February 1, a Brazilian exporter wishing to hedge its US dollar receivables of $500,000 for three weeks calls BNP Paribas to execute March futures, which expire on February 28. She plans to unwind the 10 futures contracts on February 21, when she receives her dollar payment and will convert them to reals in the spot market. The quote is "1.9535/1.9540," meaning she can sell US dollars for 1.9535 Brazilian reals for settlement on March 1. Were she to keep the contract until expiry, it would be settled against the PTAX fixing of February 28. All spot trades reported to the Central Bank by financial institutions in Brazil on that date would be averaged, based on size, and the average published by the Central Bank by the morning of March 1. If this rate is 1.9310, net payment to the exporter is $(1.9535 - 1.9310) \times \$500,000 = BRL\ 11,250$.

US Dollar Options: BM&F Currency Options

Description

• Type	Non-deliverable FX option
• Style	European
• Payment	Cash settled in BRL at maturity using PTAX rate (offer side)
• Strike Price	BRL per 1,000 USD, as established and published by the BM&F
• Maturity	Up to 24 months, as determined by the BM&F
• Contract	Monthly
• Expiration	Last business day of the month preceding the contract month
• Settlement	First business day of the contract month
• Quotation	BRL per 1,000 USD, expressed to three decimal places
• Contract Size	USD 50,000
• Exchange	Mercantile and Futures Exchange (BM&F) in São Paulo

Example

A Brazilian exporter may receive a $500,000 cash payment if she wins a contract, but will not know whether the contract is signed until April 30. Since there is a good chance of winning the contract and BRL appreciating significantly in the near term, and since she does not want to be locked into a forward contract, she decides to buy an option. On April 1, she calls BNP Paribas for a quote on ten of the May 1950 (1.9500 BRL per USD) put option on USD, which expires on April 30. With spot at 1.9700 and the outright forward at 1.9820, the quote is "27.75 28.75," implying a volatility level of 8.0/8.5.

DI Futures: BM&F Futures on Interbank Deposit Rates (Mercantile and Futures Exchange)

Description

• Type	Exchange-traded, daily-adjusted futures on overnight interbank deposit rates
• Payment	Marked to market daily in BRL

- Underlying   Accumulated DI (*Deposito Interbancario*)[6] rate from trade date (inclusive) to expiry (exclusive)
- Rate   Daily weighted-average overnight interbank deposit rate as calculated by CETIP [7]
- Maturity   Up to 24 months, as established by BM&F
- Contract   First four months, then first month of every subsequent calendar quarter (January, April, July, October)
- Expiration   Last business day of the month preceding the contract month (last trading day)
- Settlement   First business day of the contract month
- Contract Size   BRL 100,000
- Quotation   Zero coupon (face value discounted by implied DI interest rate)
- Exchange   Mercantile and Futures Exchange (BM&F) in São Paulo

Valuation

$$\text{Price} = \frac{\text{BRL 100,000}}{\prod_{j=0}^{n-1}(1 + \text{DI}_j)^{1/252}}$$

n = Number of business days
DI_i = Implied DI rate of day j

DI futures are marked to market daily. The daily variation in margin (i.e., daily profit or loss) is equal to:[8]

$$N \times [F_j - F_{j-1} \times (1 + \text{DI}_{j-1})^{1/252}]$$

N = Number of contracts ($N < 0$ if short)
F_j = Price for day j
DI_j = DI rate for day j

Example

A firm wishes to hedge its exposure to overnight interest rates. On January 15, it sells 10 of the July futures at a price of 93,425, implying an overall DI rate of

---

[6] Also referred to as CDI (*Certificado de Depósito Interbancário*), or DI-Over (*Overnight Depósito Interbancário*).

[7] *Central de Custódia e de Liquidação Financeira de Títulos,* or Central Custody and Settlement System for Private Certificates and Securities.

[8] Initial and maintenance margin are usually placed in the form of interest-bearing securities; excess cash in the margin account does not earn interest, but may be withdrawn on a daily basis at the discretion of the account holder.

$(100,000/93,425)^{252/116} -1 = 15.922\%.$[9] The contract closes the day unchanged. Prior to the open on January 16, the exchange reflects the actual DI rate for the preceding business day (on January 15) of 16.50%, giving a new futures rate of $93,425 \times (1 + 16.50\%)^{1/252} = 93,482$, giving a new implied DI rate of $(100,000/93,482)^{252/115} = 15.916\%.$

Adjusted DI Futures:
BM&F Adjusted Interbank Deposit Futures
(Mercantile and Futures Exchange)

Description

• Type	Exchange-traded futures on overnight interbank deposit rates
• Payment	Marked to market monthly (last business day of each month, for value first business day of following month) in BRL
• Underlying	Accumulated DI (*Depósito Interbancário*)[10] rate from trade date (inclusive) to expiry (exclusive)
• Rate	Daily weighted-average overnight interbank deposit rate as calculated by CETIP[11]
• Maturity	Up to 5 years, as established by BM&F
• Expiration	As established by BM&F (no standardized date schedules)
• Settlement	One business day following expiry
• Quotation	Effective interest rate, expressed in percentage per annum, to three decimal places
• Basis	Actual business days/252 (compounded daily)
• Contract Size	BRL 1,000,000
• Exchange	Mercantile and Futures Exchange (BM&F) in São Paulo

Valuation

$$\text{Price} = \frac{\text{BRL } 1,000,000}{\displaystyle\prod_{j=0}^{n-1}(1 + DI_j)^{1/252}}$$

n = Number of business days from trade date (inclusive) to expiry (exclusive)

DI_i = Implied DI rate of ith day

---

[9] This assumes that there are 115 business days between January 15 (inclusive) and June 30 (exclusive).

[10] Also referred to as CDI (*Certificado de Depósito Interbancário*), or DI-Over (*Overnight Depósito Interbancário*).

[11] *Central de Custódia e de Liquidação Financeira de Títulos,* or Central Custody and Settlement System for Private Certificates and Securities.

Example

A firm's management believes rates will fall in the near term. On January 15, it buys 100 futures maturing on the 10th of December when the DI rate is 16.50%. The contract is quoted "16.10 – 16.20," meaning the firm can lend BRL at an effective interest rate of 16.10%. The reference price at which the firm enters the contract is:

$$\text{Price} = \frac{1,000,000}{(1 + 16.10\%)^{227/252}} = \text{BRL } 874,177.35$$

Suppose further that on January 31 (12 business days later), the DI rate is still 16.50% and the current adjusted DI future quote is "15.88–15.92." The contract is marked at 15.90%, and the price of the contract is 881,709.74 BRL. The profit credited to their margin account is:

$$100 \times \left[881,709.74 - 874,177.35 \times (1 + 16.5\%)^{12/252} \right] = \text{BRL } 115,182.10$$

DDI Futures: BM&F Futures on Cupom Cambial
(Futures on Foreign Exchange Coupon)

Description

• Type	Futures on US dollar equivalent return of overnight BRL interest rates
• Payment	Marked to market daily in BRL
• Underlying	Accumulated DI (*Depósito Interbancário*)[12] rate from trade date (inclusive) to expiry (exclusive), adjusted by difference between PTAX exchange rate[13] from trade date to expiry
• Rate	DI, capitalized daily weighted-average overnight interbank deposit rate, calculated by CETIP[14]
• Maturity	Up to 60 months, as established by BM&F
• Contract	First four months, then first month of every subsequent calendar quarter (January, April, July, October)
• Expiration	Last business day of month preceding contract month (last trading day)
• Settlement	First business day of contract month
• Quotation	Interest rate representing spread between DI and variation of exchange rate (known locally as *cupom cambial*), expressed in percent per annum, to two decimal places
• Contract Size	USD 50,000

---

[12] Also referred to as CDI (*Certificado de Depósito Interbancário*), or DI-Over (Overnight *Depósito Interbancário*).

[13] USD/BRL daily weighted-average exchange rate offer side as calculated by the Central Bank of Brazil.

[14] *Central de Custódia e de Liquidação Financeira de Títulos,* or Central Custody and Settlement System for Private Certificates and Securities.

• Basis   Actual business days/252 (compounded daily)
• Exchange   BM&F (Brazilian Mercantile and Futures Exchange)

Valuation

The price of the *Cupom Cambial*, representing the US dollar return on domestic rates, is equal to:

$$\left[\frac{\displaystyle\prod_{j=0}^{n-1}(1 + DI_j)^{1/252}}{\dfrac{PTAX_{n-1}}{PTAX_{t-1}}} - 1 \right] \times \frac{360}{n}$$

$PTAX_j$ = Implied (expected) PTAX rate for day j
$PTAX_{t-1}$ = PTAX for day preceding trade date
DI_j = Implied (expected) DI for day j
n = Number of business days

DDI futures are marked to market daily, where the variation in margin is:

$$N \times [F_j \times PTAX_{j-1} - F_{j-1} \times PTAX_{j-2} \times (1 + DI_{j-1})^{1/252}]$$

N = Number of contracts ($N < 0$ if short)
F_j = DDI price of day j
DI_j = DI rate of day j

Pre-DI Swap: Fixed-Floating Interest Rate Swap

Description

• Type   Over-the-counter (OTC) BRL-denominated (pre)fixed-floating interest rate swap
• Payment   Cash-settled and netted in BRL at maturity
• Underlying   Accumulated DI (*Depósito Interbancário*)[15] rate from trade date (inclusive) to expiry (exclusive)
• Maturity   Up to 5 years
• Coupon   None (single payment exchanged at maturity)
• Rate   Capitalized daily weighted-average overnight interbank deposit rate as calculated by CETIP[16]
• Rate Reset   Daily (beginning on trade date)

---

[15] This rate is also referred to as CDI (*Certificado de Depósito Interbancário*), or DI-Over (Overnight *Depósito Interbancário*).
[16] *Central de Custódia e de Liquidação Financeira de Títulos,* or Central Custody and Settlement System for Private Certificates and Securities.

- Rate Source   Published daily by CETIP
- Tax Status   Tax-exempt
- Quotation   Effective interest rate, expressed in percentage per annum, to three decimal places
- Basis   Actual business day/252 (compounded daily), both legs

Valuation

$$C_{\text{fix}} = \text{Notional} \times \left[\prod_{j=0}^{n-1} (1 + \text{DI}_j)^{1/252} - (1 + r)^{n/252} \right]$$

$$C_{\text{float}} = \text{Notional} \times \left[(1 + r)^{n/252} - \prod_{j=0}^{n-1} (1 + \text{DI}_j)^{1/252} \right]$$

n = Number of business days
C_{fix} = Fixed rate payer receives from floating rate payer (if positive)
C_{float} = Floating rate payer receives from fixed rate payer (if positive)
r = Fixed rate
DI_j = DI rate of day j

Example A firm with operations in Brazil has funded itself with a 1-year, fixed rate Brazilian real at 21.50%, but management believes rates in Brazil will fall substantially over the next year, and they wish to reduce their fixed rate liabilities. On November 6, they enter into a one-year Pre-DI swap with a notional of 5,000,000 BRL. The firm pays floating and receives fixed, offsetting its existing fixed rate liability. The swap is quoted "21.61–21.65," which means the company receives 1-year fixed at 21.61% and pays compounded DI for the period. On the first day of the swap, the DI is 18.70%. At the end of the year, the geometric average of DI rates for the period (comprised of 250 business days) is 19.62%. At maturity, the firm receives a net payment of:

$$5,000,000 \times [(1 + 21.61\%)^{250/252} - (1 + 19.62\%)^{250/252}] = \text{BRL } 98,563.60$$

USD/DI Swaps: OTC Cross-Currency Swap

Description

- Type   Fixed USD vs. overnight BRL zero coupon, non-deliverable, cross-currency swap[17]

---

[17] The spot rates used at inception and maturity in USD/DI swaps are different, being the prevailing spot rates at the time of each principal exchange, unlike most G7 cross-currency swaps which set the spot rate used for both principal exchanges at inception. USD/DI swaps thus carry FX spot exposure, while most G7 swaps do not.

- Payments   Cash-settled and netted in BRL at maturity
- Maturity   Up to five years
- Coupon   None (net payment at maturity)
- Rates   USD: fixed
                BRL: floating DI (*Depósito Interbancário*), overnight interbank rate
                USD/BRL spot rate: PTAX (weighted average USD/BRL exchange rate)
- Rate Reset   Daily for DI (beginning on trade date); at inception and maturity for PTAX
- Rate Sources Central Bank (for PTAX) and CETIP (for DI); published daily
- Tax Status   Tax-exempt
- Basis   Actual/360 for USD; actual business days/252 (compounded daily) for BRL

Valuation

$$C_{\text{fix}} = \text{Notional} \times \left[\prod_{j=0}^{n-1} (1 + \text{DI}_j)^{1/252} - \left(1 + r_{\text{US}} \times \frac{d}{360}\right)\left(\frac{\text{PTAX}_{n-1}}{\text{PTAX}_{t-1}}\right) \right]$$

$$C_{\text{float}} = \text{Notional} \times \left[\left(1 + r_{\text{US}} \times \frac{d}{360}\right)\left(\frac{\text{PTAX}_{n-1}}{\text{PTAX}_{t-1}}\right) - \prod_{j=0}^{n-1} (1 + \text{DI}_j)^{1/252} \right]$$

C_{fix} = USD fixed rate payer receives from BRL floating rate payer at maturity (if positive)

C_{float} = BRL floating rate payer receives from USD fixed rate payer at maturity (if positive)

r_{US} = Fixed rate

DI_j = Daily DI rate for day j

n = Number of business days

d = Number of calendar days

PTAX_{t-1} = Initial USD/BRL reference exchange rate (determined one day prior to trade date)

PTAX_{n-1} = Final USD/BRL reference exchange rate (determined one day prior to maturity)

Example A firm has invested BRL 100 million cash in 1-year, zero-coupon bonds, yielding the daily DI rate. Management wishes to reduce its exposure to short-term BRL rates and to a potential weakening of the exchange rate by swapping into a fixed USD rate, and enters into a USD/DI swap. At the current USD/BRL spot rate of 1.9120, the initial USD value of the investment is

$$\frac{100 \text{ million}}{1.9120} = \$52,301255.23$$

The 1-year USD/DI is quoted "9.69–9.74," which means the company receives an unadjusted rate of 9.69% in US dollars[18] and pays compounded DI in Brazilian reals. PTAX on the day preceding the trade is 1.9010. At maturity the PTAX fixing is 2.1140, and the geometric average DI is 16.62% over the period. The US dollar-equivalent payoffs for the firm at maturity are:

$$C_{\text{float}} = \frac{100 \text{ million}}{2.1140}$$

$$\times \left[\left(1+9.69\% \times \frac{360}{360}\right)\left(1+9.69\% \times \frac{5}{360}\right)\left(\frac{2.1140}{1.9010}\right) - (1+16.62\%)^{\frac{252}{252}} \right]$$

$$= \$2,613,303.19$$

$$\text{Bond Return} = \frac{100 \text{ million}}{2.1140} \times (1+16.62\%)^{\frac{252}{252}} = \$55,165,562.91$$

The strategy's total return is

$$\frac{\$57,778,866.10}{\$52,301,255.23} - 1 = 10.47\% \text{ (before tax)}$$

Though both bond and swap are denominated in BRL, currency exposure for the strategy above is hedged, locking in a total return in USD.

USD/BRL Fixed-Floating Cross-Currency Swaps
Description

- Type   OTC non-deliverable, fixed-floating, cross-currency swap
- Payment   Cash-settled and netted in USD
- Maturity   Up to 4 years
- Coupon   Semiannual
- Principal   Computed using initial USD/BRL rate (no initial exchange; only at maturity)
- Rates   USD: 6-month LIBOR
                BRL: fixed
- LIBOR Reset   Set 2 business days prior to each reset date
- LIBOR Source As posted on Telerate 3750 calculated to the 5th decimal place

---

[18] Before adjusting for the difference between the preceding day's PTAX rate and the prevailing spot rate at the time of the trade.

- Tax Status   Tax-exempt
- Basis   Actual/360 for USD leg; 30/360 for BRL leg

Valuation

The initial spot FX reference for the swap is the PTAX fixing one business day prior to trade date, which is used to compute the notional amounts. Netted semi-annual coupon payments are:

$$C_{BRL} = \text{Notional}_{USD} \times \text{LIBOR}_{USD} \times \frac{d}{360} - \frac{\text{Notional}_{BRL}}{\text{PTAX}_{j-1}} \times r_{fix} \times \frac{180}{360}$$

$$C_{USD} = \frac{\text{Notional}_{BRL}}{\text{PTAX}_{j-1}} \times r_{fix} \times \frac{180}{360} - \text{Notional}_{USD} \times \text{LIBOR}_{USD} \times \frac{d}{360}$$

At maturity, principals and final coupons are notionally exchanged:

$$C_{BRL} = \text{Notional}_{USD} \times \left(1 + \text{LIBOR}_{USD} \times \frac{d}{360}\right) - \frac{\text{Notional}_{BRL}}{\text{PTAX}_{j-1}} \times \left(1 + r_{fix} \times \frac{180}{360}\right)$$

$$C_{USD} = \frac{\text{Notional}_{BRL}}{\text{PTAX}_{j-1}} \times \left(1 + r_{fix} \times \frac{180}{360}\right) - \text{Notional}_{USD} \times \left(1 + \text{LIBOR}_{USD} \times \frac{d}{360}\right)$$

C_{USD} = USD floating rate payer receives from BRL fixed rate payer (if positive)

C_{BRL} = BRL fixed rate payer receives from USD floating rate payer (if positive)

PTAX_{j-1} = Relevant USD/BRL reference exchange rate (determined one day prior to reset date)

LIBOR_{USD} = 6-month LIBOR rate paid by USD rate payer

r_{fix} = BRL fixed rate

d = Number of days in preceding period

LFTs: Letras Financeiras do Tesouro Nacional (National Treasury Finance Notes)

Description

- Type   BRL-denominated, floating rate, zero-coupon note
- Issuer   STN (Treasury) via the Central Bank of Brazil
- Amortization   Bullet (returns face value adjusted for accumulated SELIC rate over life of note)
- Maturity   Established by Ministry of Finance at time of auction; most common are currently 4-year
- Coupon   None (zero-coupon)

- Reference Rate   SELIC (*Serviço de Liquidação e Custódia* or Settlement and Custody System) rate, the overnight repo rate on government bonds
- Face Value   BRL 1000
- Tax Status   Nonfinancial local institutions: (1) buyer subject to CPMF tax, currently at 0.3%; (2) if investor buys and sells LTN within 28-day period, profits are subject to IOF tax, with specific rate depending on number of days between purchase and sale; (3) profits after IOF tax (if applicable) subject to flat 20% income tax at source
                    Financial local institutions: not subject to tax
                    Foreigners: (1) 0.3% CPMF tax on FX amount (both in and out); (2) 15% income tax on BRL profits
- Custodian   SELIC (Settlement and Custody System)
- Basis   Actual business days/252 (compounded daily)
- Frequency   Weekly (currently on Tuesdays)
- Bid Process   Competitive electronic auction; priority given to highest bidders
- Bid Format   Up to five competitive bids allowed per institution, specifying quotation rate (expressed as percentage of face value) and quantity (in multiples of 50 bills)

Valuation

Market convention is to quote the spread over the SELIC rate, to two decimal places. The price (locally referred to as *PU*, or unit price) is calculated using this spread:

$$\text{Price} = V \times \frac{1}{(1+s)^{d/252}} \times \prod_{j=k}^{t-1} (1 + \text{SELIC}_j)^{1/252}$$

V = Face value, expressed in BRL
SELIC_j = SELIC rate of day j
s = Spread over SELIC rate, in percent
d = Number of business days to maturity
k = Date of issue
t = Trade date

Example A company wishing to invest in a Brazilian short-term security buys 10,000 LFTs maturing in 3 years. BNP Paribas quotes a spread over the SELIC rate of 0.03% for 4-year bonds issued 1 year ago. The geometric average SELIC rate for the past year is 16.82%, with 249 business days in the year. The total price is:

$$10,000 \times 1,000 \times \frac{1}{(1 + 0.03\%)^{\frac{249}{252}}} \times (1 + 16.82\%)^{\frac{249}{252}} = \text{BRL } 11,656,943.94$$

LTNs: Letras do Tesouro Nacional
(National Treasury Notes)

Description

• Type	BRL-denominated, zero-coupon bill
• Issuer	STN (Treasury) via Central Bank of Brazil
• Amortization	Bullet
• Maturity	Minimum 35 days; currently, 180- and 360-day bills are most common; 2-year bills have been issued
• Coupon	None
• Rate	Yield-to-maturity, expressed as a spread over the SELIC rate
• Reference Rate	SELIC (*Serviço de Liquidação e Custódia* or Settlement and Custody System) rate, the overnight repo rate on government bonds
• Face Value	1000 BRL
• Tax Status	Nonfinancial local institutions: (1) buyer subject to CPMF tax, currently at 0.3%; (2) if investor buys and sells LTN within 28-day period, profits are subject to IOF tax, with specific rate depending on number of days between purchase and sale; (3) profits after IOF tax (if applicable) subject to flat 20% income tax at source
	Financial local institutions: not subject to tax
	Foreigners: (1) 0.3% CPMF tax on FX amount (both in and out); (2) 15% income tax on BRL profits
• Custodian	SELIC (Settlement and Custody System)
• Basis	Actual business days/252 (compounded daily)
• Issuance	Weekly (currently on Tuesdays)
• Bid Process	Competitive electronic auction; priority given to highest bidders
• Bid Format	Up to five competitive bids allowed per institution, specifying unit price (expressed in BRL, to the sixth decimal place) and quantity (in multiples of BRL 50,000)

Valuation

The price (locally referred to as PU, or unit price) is calculated as follows:

$$Price = \frac{V}{(1 + SELIC)^{d/252}}$$

V = Face value
SELIC = Implied geometric average SELIC rate for the period
d = Number of business days

NTN-Cs: Notas do Tesouro Nacional—Série C (National Treasury Notes—Series C)

Description

• Type	BRL-denominated, coupon-bearing note paying fixed spread over inflation; provides a "real rate of return," akin to US Treasury Inflation-Protected Securities (TIPS)
• Issuer	STN (Treasury) via the Central Bank of Brazil
• Amortization	Bullet (returns face value adjusted for accumulated inflation, as measured by FGV/IGP-M inflation index over life of note)
• Maturity	Established by Ministry of Finance at time of auction; most common are currently 4-year
• Coupon	Semiannual (recently issued NTN-Cs pay a coupon of 6%)
• Rate	Effective annual yield over inflation, measured using IGP-M index (computed monthly by *Fundação Getúlio Vargas*); bonds issued with reference date for computation of inflation
• Face Value	BRL 1000 (at issue date)
• Tax Status	Nonfinancial local institutions: (1) buyer subject to CPMF tax, currently at 0.3%; (2) if investor buys and sells LTN within 28-day period, profits are subject to IOF tax, with specific rate depending on number of days between purchase and sale; (3) profits after IOF tax (if applicable) subject to flat 20% income tax at source Financial local institutions: not subject to tax Foreigners: (1) 0.3% CPMF tax on FX amount (both in and out) (2) 15% income tax on BRL profits
• Custodian	SELIC (Settlement and Custody System)
• Basis	Actual business days/252 (compounded daily)
• Issuance	Generally monthly (at month-end, with settlement on first day of subsequent month); NTN-Cs with specific inflation reference issued by Treasury as reoffering

- Bid Process   Two-stage Dutch; (1) notes tendered for cash payment; cutoff rate adopted for second stage, (2) privatization monies (securitized Treasury liabilities) accepted as payment
- Bidding Format   First stage: up to five competitive bids allowed per institution, specifying rate (expressed as percentage of face value, to four decimal places) and quantity (in multiples of 50 notes)
Second stage: up to five competitive bids allowed for additional NTN-Cs for payment with privatization monies, specifying sale price (to six decimal places); priority given to lowest price bids for privatization monies (i.e., highest discount)

Valuation

$$Q = \sum_{j=1}^{n} \frac{C_j}{(1+y)^{\frac{d_j}{252}}}$$

$$V_{current} = V_{previous} \times (1 + IGPM)^{\frac{m}{d}}$$

Q	=	Quotation rate (or *cotação*), the BRL interest rate
C_j	=	Payment j
d_j	=	Number of business days for payment j
n	=	Number of coupon payments
y	=	Yield (incorporating IGPM inflation level, expected SELIC, and risk spread)
$V_{current}$	=	Current face value (adjusted for inflation)
$V_{previous}$	=	Previous face value, as published monthly by Treasury
IGPM	=	Expected IGPM level for the month
m	=	Number of business days month-to-date
d	=	Total number of business days in the month

Bonds are quoted in terms of the interest rate (Q); the price of the bond is equal to $Q \times V_{current}$. The Treasury retains the right to repurchase NTN-Cs, with price determined by a complex set of rules regarding interest accrual over full months and fractions of a month, as set out by MF/STN *Portaria* 442 of 5 September 2000.

NBC-Es: Nota do Banco Central—Série Especial (Central Bank Note—Special Series)

Description

• Type	BRL-denominated, US dollar-indexed, floating-rate coupon-bearing note
• Issuer	Central Bank of Brazil (also issued by Treasury, referred to as NTN-D)
• Amortization	Bullet (returns face value adjusted for total change in BRL/USD rate over life of note)
• Maturity	Established by Central Bank at time of auction; most common are currently 3- and 4-year
• Coupon	Semiannual (current issues pay coupon of 12%)
• Reference Rate	PTAX rate published daily by Central Bank of Brazil
• Face Value	BRL 1000, adjusted for variation of BRL/USD exchange rate over life of note
• Tax Status	Nonfinancial local institutions: (1) buyer subject to CPMF tax, currently at 0.3%; (2) if investor buys and sells LTN within 28-day period, profits are subject to IOF tax, with specific rate depending on number of days between purchase and sale; (3) profits after IOF tax (if applicable) subject to flat 20% income tax at source
	Financial local institutions: not subject to tax
	Foreigners: (1) 0.3% CPMF tax on FX amount (both in and out) (2) 15% income tax on BRL profits
• Custodian	SELIC (Settlement and Custody System)
• Basis	ISMA 30/360
• Issuance	No predetermined auction frequency; dollar-indexed notes commonly issued when outstanding dollar-indexed notes mature; Central Bank has established policy of gradually reducing outstanding stock of dollar-indexed debt, but in volatile markets has rolled over entire amount of dollar-indexed debt due for amortization; auctions announced two business days prior to auction date
• Bid Process	Competitive electronic auction; priority given to highest bidders
• Bid Format	Up to five competitive bids allowed per institution, specifying quotation rate (expressed in percent of face value) and quantity (in multiples of 50 bills).

Valuation

For secondary market trading, the rate of return is quoted on a semiannual bond basis to two decimal places, using a 30/360 day-count convention. For bidding at the primary auction, the quotation rate is used (based on this rate):

$$Q = \frac{1}{\left(1 + \frac{r}{2}\right)^{\frac{d_n}{180}}} + \sum_{j=1}^{n} \frac{C}{\left(1 + \frac{r}{2}\right)^{\frac{d_j}{180}}}$$

$$\text{Price} = Q \times V \times \frac{\text{PTAX}_{t-1}}{\text{PTAX}_{i-1}}$$

Q	=	Primary auction quotation rate
V	=	Face value
r	=	Nominal rate of return (quoted rate in secondary market)
n	=	Number of coupon payments
C	=	Coupon payment
d_j	=	Number of days between trade date and payment j
PTAX_{t-1}	=	PTAX on day preceding trade
PTAX_{i-1}	=	PTAX on day preceding issuance

TDAs: Título da Dívida Agrária
(Agricultural Debt Instruments)

Description

- Type   BRL-denominated, floating-rate, coupon-bearing note
- Issuer   Treasury (pre-June 1992, INCRA, or National Institute for Colonization and Agrarian Reform)
- Amortization   Bullet
- Maturity   Up to 20 years
- Coupon   Annual, with rates as follows:

Type	Issue	Coupon
TDA-E	5, 10, 15, & 20-year	6%
TDA-D	15-year	3%
TDA-D	18-year	2%
TDA-D	20-year	1%

- Rate   TR (*Taxa da Referência,* or Reference Rate), product of market CDB (Certificate of Deposit) rates and a "reduction factor," as established by Central Bank
- Face Value   Published monthly by Treasury on first business day; face value of TDAE and TDAD bonds for month t is adjusted by TR ("Reference Rate") of month $t-1$; as of December 2000, TDA face value was BRL 75.57

- Tax Status   Nonfinancial local institutions: buyer subject to CPMF tax, IOF tax if applicable, and withholding tax of 20% on profits

    Foreign investors and financial local institutions: not subject to tax
- Custodian   CETIP (*Central de Custódia e de Liquidação de Financeira de Títulos*), a custody and clearing system for private securities jointly administered by the Central Bank and ANDIMA
- Basis   Actual/365
- Issuance   No primary auctions; issued as payment for liabilities incurred by agrarian reform program as needed; issued on first business day of month, in separate series, classified by maturity; created to finance compensatory payments for land nationalized for agrarian reform purposes, as per Law 4504 (November 1964)
- Call Option   Treasury may repurchase TDA bonds 2 years after issue at its discretion

Valuation

$$Q = \sum_{j=1}^{n} \left(\frac{C}{1 + r_{TR}} \right)^{\frac{d_j}{365}}$$

$$\text{Price} = Q \times V \times (1 + TR)^{\frac{m}{d}}$$

Q = Quoted rate in percent of face value, adjusted for TR variation

TR = *Taxa da Referência,* or Reference Rate

C_j = Payment j expressed as percent of face value and adjusted for TR value

r_{TR} = Implied interest rate (a function of TR)

d_j = Number of calendar days between trade date and payment j

m = Number of business days from beginning of month

d = Total number of business days in month

n = Number of payments

V_j = Face value at beginning of month j, adjusted for TR monthly by Treasury

ARGENTINA

The following three local products in Argentina are described:

- USD/ARS fixed-floating cross-currency swaps
- Letes
- Bontes

USD/ARS Fixed-Floating Cross-Currency Swaps

Description

- **Type** — OTC non-deliverable, fixed-floating cross-currency swap
- **Payment** — Net settled in USD; ARS flows converted into USD at prevailing spot fixing reference
- **Maturity** — Up to 3 years
- **Coupon** — Semiannual
- **Principal** — Computed using initial USD/ARS spot rate; principal exchanged only at maturity
- **Rates** — USD: 6-month LIBOR
  ARS: fixed
- **LIBOR Resets** — Set two business days prior to each reset date
- **LIBOR Source** — As posted on Telerate 3750, calculated to the 5th decimal place
- **Tax Status** — Tax-exempt
- **Basis** — Actual/360 for USD leg; 30/360 for ARS leg

Valuation

The spot FX fixing reference is the ARS Official Rate or the CME/EMTA ARS Industry Survey Rate as defined by EMTA (Trade Association for the Emerging Markets).[19] Netted payments are:

$$C_{\text{ARS}}$$

$$= \text{Notional}_{\text{USD}} \times \text{LIBOR}_{\text{USD}} \times \frac{d}{360} - S_{\text{fixing}} \times \text{Notional}_{\text{ARS}} \times i_{\text{fix}} \times \frac{180}{360}$$

$$C_{\text{USD}}$$

$$= S_{\text{fixing}} \times \text{Notional}_{\text{ARS}} \times i_{\text{fix}} \times \frac{180}{360} - \text{Notional}_{\text{USD}} \times \text{LIBOR}_{\text{USD}} \times \frac{d}{360}$$

The principal and the last coupon payment are exchanged at maturity:

---

[19] EMTA's website (www.emta.org) provides more information.

C_{USD}

$$= S_{fixing} \times Notional_{ARS} \times (1 + i_{fix}) \times \frac{180}{360} - Notional_{USD} \times (1 + LIBOR_{USD}) \times \frac{d}{360}$$

C_{ARS}

$$= Notional_{USD} \times (1 + LIBOR_{USD}) \times \frac{d}{360} - S_{fixing} \times Notional_{ARS} \times (1 + i_{fix}) \times \frac{180}{360}$$

C_{ARS}	ARS fixed rate payer receives from USD floating rate payer (if positive)
C_{USD}	USD floating rate payer receives from ARS fixed rate payer (if positive)
$LIBOR_{USD}$	6-month LIBOR rate
S_{fixing}	USD/ARS reference spot rate
d	Number of days in preceding period

Letes: Letras del Tesoro (Treasury Notes)

Description

• Type	USD-denominated, zero-coupon bond
• Issuer	Republic of Argentina
• Amortization	Bullet
• Maturity	3, 6, and 12 months
• Coupon	None
• Rate	Yield to maturity
• Face Value	10 and 100 USD
• Tax Status	Tax-exempt on both interest and capital gains for both locals and foreigners
• Custodian	Local custodian not required
• Basis	Actual/360
• Issuance	Monthly (currently on the second Tuesday of the month)
• Bid Process	Dutch auction type on a discount-yield basis
• Bid Format	Amount and discount rate in percentage to two decimals

Valuation

Letes are quoted in terms of both percentage of face value and annualized yield-to-maturity. For yield quotations, the price is equal to:

$$Price = \frac{V}{1 + y \times \frac{d}{360}}$$

V = Face value
y = Annual yield to maturity
d = Number of calendar days

Bontes: Bonos Del Tesoro (Treasury Bonds)

Description

- Type — USD-denominated, fixed or floating rate, coupon-bearing bond
- Issuer — Republic of Argentina
- Amortization — Bullet
- Maturity — Generally 3 and 5 years (30 years also authorized)
- Rate — Fixed or floating (floating rate bonds have not been issued since 1998)
- Coupon — Semiannual for fixed rate; quarterly for floating rate
- Face Value — Minimum 100 USD
- Tax Status — Tax-exempt for local and foreign investors
- Custodian — Local custody not required
- Basis — 30/360 for fixed; actual/actual for floating
- Issuance — At discretion of Central Bank
- Bid Process — Dutch
- Bid Format — Amount and semiannual yield to two decimals (except reopenings, where price is used)

Valuation

Market convention is to quote the annualized yield to maturity (YTM), used in the standard bond pricing formula:

$$\text{Price} = \frac{V}{(1+y)^{1-\frac{d}{T}}}\left[C + C \times \left(\frac{1}{y} - \frac{1}{y \times (1+y)^{n-1}}\right) + \frac{1}{(1+y)^{n-1}}\right]$$

$$y = \text{YTM} \times \frac{180}{360}$$

$$C = R_c \times \frac{180}{360}$$

V = Face value
y = Yield to maturity for the period
YTM = annualized yield to maturity
C = Coupon payment = annualized coupon rate

R_c =   Annualized coupon rate
n =   Number of coupon payments remaining
d =   Number of days since last coupon payment

CHILE

For Chile the only local product covered is UF/USD forward.

UF/USD Forwards: Inflation-Indexed Currency Forwards (Unit of Increase Forwards)

Description
UF (*Unidad de Fomento*) forwards are USD/CLP forward contracts denominated in *Unidades de Fomento* instead of Chilean pesos. The UF is an inflation-indexed unit of account, denominated in Chilean pesos, similar to the UDI (*Unidad de Inversion*) used in Mexico.

Projections of the UF for each day of the forthcoming month are published by the Central Bank of Chile on the business day following the monthly CPI release (generally on the 9th of each month). The UF measure has a 30-day lag to the CPI and does not perfectly match current inflation. UF FX forwards are nondeliverable, being cash settled in US dollars at maturity using the *Dolar Observado* and the daily UF rates for settlement.

Valuation
The formula to price UF forwards is:

$$F_{USD/UF} = \frac{S_{USD/CLP}}{S_{UF/CLP}} \times \left(\frac{1 + r_{UF} \times \dfrac{d}{360}}{1 + r_{USD} \times \dfrac{d}{360}} \right)$$

Market convention for trading UF forwards, however, is to quote the interest rate differential between the *Dolar Observado* and the market exchange rate at inception. The *Dolar Observado* is published daily by the Central Bank and represents the previous day's fixing rate. The following is the relation between the quoted interest rate and the forward price:

$$r_{diff} = \left(F_{USD/UF} \times \frac{S_{UF/CLP}}{S_{Observado}} - 1 \right) \times \frac{360}{d}$$

$F_{USD/UF}$ =   Forward rate, in *Unidades de Fomento* per US dollar
$S_{USD/CLP}$ =   USD/CLP market rate at inception, in CLP per USD
$S_{UF/CLP}$ =   UF/CLP daily exchange rate, in CLP per UF

$S_{\text{Observado}}$ = *Dolar Observado* exchange rate at inception, in CLP per USD
r_{diff} = Quoted rate differential
$r_{\text{UF}}, r_{\text{USD}}$ = UF and USD interest rates
d = Number of days from trade date to settlement

The settlement amount at maturity is calculated using the *Dolar Observado* fixing rate:

$$\text{Notional} \times \left(F_{\text{USD/UF}} \times \frac{S_{\text{Observado Fix}}}{S_{\text{UF/CLP Mat}}} - 1 \right)$$

$S_{\text{Observado Fix}}$ = *Dolar Observado* fixing at maturity
$S_{\text{UF/CLP Mat}}$ = *Unidad de Fomento* rate at maturity

Chapter 4

The Convergence of the Central European EMGs to the European Union

Stephen Gilmore
Executive Director
Morgan Stanley

T his chapter takes a look at the Czech Republic, Hungary, and Poland (CE3)—the three major Central European "emerging markets."[1] The economic progress that these countries have made, their investment grade status, and their progress towards joining the European Union suggests they should perhaps be better described as "converging markets." The chapter reviews the European Union accession process and European Monetary Union and the impact that they have on the policy frameworks in the CE3 countries and the implications for the fixed income markets. The chapter discusses the importance of reducing inflation and the challenges to that process; the chapter concludes with a quick review of the debt management strategies and the market structure of the CE3 countries.

EUROPEAN UNION ENTRY

For the countries of Central Europe there is one overriding theme that dominates—the objective of joining the European Union (EU). That will be followed by entry into the European Monetary Union (EMU)—the adoption of the Euro. Judging by the results of the European Council Nice Summit in December 2000, the expansion of the EU to incorporate potentially up to ten new entrants looks likely to occur on January 1, 2004 or January 1, 2005. These ten countries include the so-called "Luxembourg Group"—Cyprus, Czech Republic, Estonia, Hungary, Slovenia, and Poland—and the second wave "Helsinki Group"— Latvia, Lithuania, Malta, and Slovakia. Bulgaria and Romania are likely to join

---

[1] CE3 is an abbreviation commonly used to refer to the three largest Central European "emerging markets."

I would like to thank Christian Schiweck and Letitia Rydjeski for their helpful comments.

at later dates. EMU entry could take place any time following a 2-year period after EU entry.[2]

Given that these objectives have provided a roadmap for the economic and legislative reform policies of the EU candidate countries and that the ultimate objective is adopting the Euro, it is appropriate to briefly look at what the EU and EMU entry processes entail. The implications for the exchange regime, capital account liberalization, monetary policy, and fiscal policy will then be apparent. Those implications are key when discussing and analyzing the bond markets in the candidate countries.

Candidate countries need to be able to satisfy the "Copenhagen criteria"—the criteria set out by the 1993 Copenhagen European Council. In broad terms, aside from meeting social goals such as democracy and the rule of law, the criteria require the existence of a functioning market economy. They also require that the member "has the ability to take on the obligations of membership, including adherence to the aims of political, economic and monetary union." More formally, all these obligations are embodied in a 31 chapter "acquis communautaire." The "aquis" must be adopted and implemented upon membership. Each year the European Commission assesses the progress that each of the candidate countries has made.

The monetary union obligations also require that the candidate countries eventually join EMU. They will not be able to "opt out" like the United Kingdom and Denmark. The candidate countries will have to ensure central bank independence, must not provide central bank financing for public sector deficits, must liberalize capital flows, and will have to adhere to the stability and growth pact. The specific criteria for EMU entry and the adoption of the Euro—the so-called "Maastricht criteria"—are set out in Article 121 of the Treaty on European Union.[3] Article 121 references Article 104 on avoiding excessive government deficits and further detail is provided in the Protocols to Articles 121 and 104.

The five "examination" criteria are as follows:

1. The achievement of a high degree of price stability. More specifically, a member state has to have a "price performance that is sustainable and an average rate of inflation, observed over a period of one year before the examination" that is not more than 1.5 percentage points more than the three best performing member states.

2. A general government deficit which does not exceed 3% of GDP.[4]

---

[2] That 2-year requirement is very likely to be maintained for the new EU member countries even if an existing EU member country but non-EMU member such as the United Kingdom were to enter EMU without having participated in ERM II for a 2-year period.

[3] Article 121 was formerly Article 109(j).

[4] Article 104 is not quite so strict, allowing some room if the deficit has declined substantially and continuously or if the excess is exceptional and temporary and close to 3%.

3. Gross general government debt to GDP of less than 60%—unless the deficit is declining and close to 60%.

4. The observance of the normal fluctuation margins provided for by the exchange rate mechanism of the European Monetary System without severe tensions for at least two years. (ERM II provides for bands of ±15% around a central parity.) More specifically, the member shall not have devalued its currency against the Euro.

5. The durability of convergence should be reflected in long-term interest rate levels. More specifically, over a 1-year period before the examination, average long-term (10-year) interest rates should not exceed by more than two percentage points those in the three best performing members.

While EU entry and the adoption of the Euro will not occur until 2004 and 2006 at the earliest, respectively, these future events have significantly shaped the policies of the candidate countries—with very important implications for the fixed income markets. The candidate countries are aiming to reduce inflation. That has implications for monetary conditions, the absolute level of yields, and the shape of the yield curve (with an expectation that yield curves will tend to be inverted while inflation rates remain high). The countries are also attempting to cap fiscal deficits and to keep general government debt levels down. In general, net debt issuance levels will tend to be modest—although the countries are typically aiming to reduce the foreign currency portion of debt and also trying to extend the length of domestic yield curves, the average duration of their debt and to improve the liquidity of benchmark issues. They have also been adapting their exchange regimes with the aim of eventually joining ERM II and then EMU. And with an eye to the interest rate test, several countries have also issued longer-dated bonds.

Of course, other countries have already been through the EU/EMU process. The classic examples are countries such as Greece, Italy, Portugal, and Spain which all had to successfully adapt to meet the Maastricht criteria. In the context of this chapter we focus on three candidate "emerging market" countries—the Czech Republic, Hungary, and Poland. Not only do the CE3 countries have the largest economies, but they also have the largest and most liquid local currency bond markets in the region (see Exhibit 1).[5]

While the CE3 countries all aim to join the European Union and EMU they have adopted slightly different approaches with a view to achieving these goals. That has had an implication for the development of the financial markets in each of the countries. We now take a brief look at the approaches to capital account liberalization, the currency regime, fiscal policy, government debt and inflation, before turning to the bond markets in each of the countries.

[5] This chapter uses the following exchange rates: EUR 1 = PLN 3.4 = HUF 2.45 = CZK 34 = USD 0.86.

Exhibit 1: Bond Market Size (in billions of EUR)

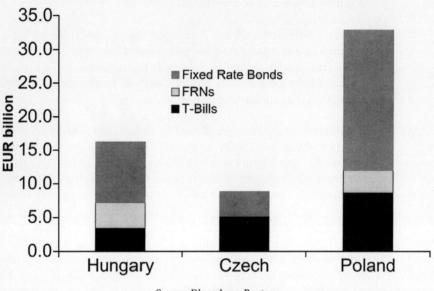

Source: Bloomberg, Reuters

Capital Controls

The countries have all given commitments to the European Union to liberalize capital flows. Hungary was the last of the CE3 countries to liberalize capital flows—moving in June 2001 following the earlier decision to widen the exchange rate trading bands for the currency.[6] This move has opened the way for the development of an active derivatives market. Prior to this move, non-residents were not able to purchase Hungarian government debt instruments with an original maturity of less than one year. Non-residents seeking to hedge currency exposure also had to use the offshore non-deliverable forward (NDF) market. The capital controls were strictly enforced and involved a considerable degree of extra administration. It was, for instance, necessary to specifically identify which securities were being sold in order for the forint proceeds to be convertible.

The Czech Republic had been the first to open up its markets. As a consequence it initially developed the most liquid foreign exchange market, although that is changing—with the Polish foreign exchange market now being more active than the Czech market. The Czech Republic was also the first market in the region to have an active, liquid, interest rate swaps market. The development of a swaps market in Poland has helped improve liquidity in the Polish bond market. An asset swaps market is gaining in stature.

---

[6] Although in Poland non-residents do not yet have access to the same borrowing rates (WIBOR – the Warsaw Interbank Offered Rate) as residents. Also, in Poland, pension funds still face very strict limits on their holdings of foreign assets.

Currency Regimes

EMU requires that member countries seeking to join have currencies that trade within "normal fluctuation margins" for at least two years, with ERM II defining those bands as ±15%. Here again the countries have taken different approaches with the Czech Republic and Poland floating their currencies, while Hungary has continued to set defined, if wide, bands for currency fluctuations.

The Czech Republic was the first to float its currency, the koruna (crown), when the currency came under pressure in 1997. Subsequently, the Czech National Bank has implemented a managed float arrangement. The koruna has tended to gradually strengthen against the Euro since 1999. That has in the past made the currency a favorite "carry trade" for Euro-based investors, even though the yield pick-up over Euro rates by 2001 was relatively low.[7]

Poland floated its currency, the zloty, in April 2000. Prior to that it had, like Hungary, followed a crawling peg arrangement for its currency. The Polish exchange rate bands had been gradually widened to ±15% by March 1999. Up until the float, the zloty traded against a basket that comprised 55% Euro and 45% USD.

Hungary has operated a crawling peg arrangement whereby the central parity of the forint has been allowed to depreciate by a pre-defined amount (0.2% per month as at mid-2001) against the Euro. The forint was allowed to fluctuate within bands of ±2.25% around that central parity up until May 4, 2001. The fluctuation bands were at that time widened to ±15% (shadowing an ERM II approach). The band widening has led to greater foreign exchange risk.

Fiscal Policy

Naturally, all of the countries aim to control their budget deficits. Poland set an objective of balancing its budget by 2003, although that goal seems unlikely given the economic slowdown in 2001. Hungary has typically focussed on running primary surpluses in an effort to keep debt to GDP ratios on a downward track. Hungary has also instituted a 2-year budget framework. The Czech Republic tends to be moving in the opposite direction. For much of the 1990s, it had very low budget deficits. However, it has had to foot the bill for significant bank restructuring costs. At the same time, it is set to benefit from significant privatization proceeds. Nevertheless, by 2001 it was running a structural deficit of the order of 5% of GDP.

Government Debt

History has shaped the approaches to government debt. In 1993, Hungary had a debt/GDP ratio approaching 90%. The reduction of this debt burden and the man-

---

[7] In a "carry trade" an investor buys the higher yielding currency (Czech koruna) funded in the lower yielding currency (Euro) in anticipation that the increased yield on the Czech instrument more than compensates for any currency depreciation of the koruna against the EUR.

agement of debt became a government priority. Hungary followed a two-pronged approach in this effort. It has used both privatization proceeds and primary budget surpluses to reduce the debt stock. Moreover, it continues to target small primary surpluses now that the debt/GDP ratio has fallen below 60% (see Exhibit 2).[8] Given the emphasis on reducing initially high debt levels, Hungary has developed the most sophisticated debt management policies of the CE3. Hungary was the first country in the region to issue a 10-year local currency bond.

Poland went through both an official and a commercial sector debt restructuring in the early 1990s. The 1997 Constitution places a limit on national public debt at 60% of GDP—the Maastricht criterion level. Like Hungary, Poland has also been developing a sophisticated debt management operation.

The Czech Republic continues to have the lowest debt/GDP ratio of the CE3 countries. However, bank restructuring costs and guarantees and a large structural budget deficit will see that debt burden grow. As a consequence of the relatively low debt outstanding and previously low budget deficits, the Czech Republic has tended to have the least developed domestic debt management policies.

Exhibit 2: Hungarian Government Debt (% of GDP)

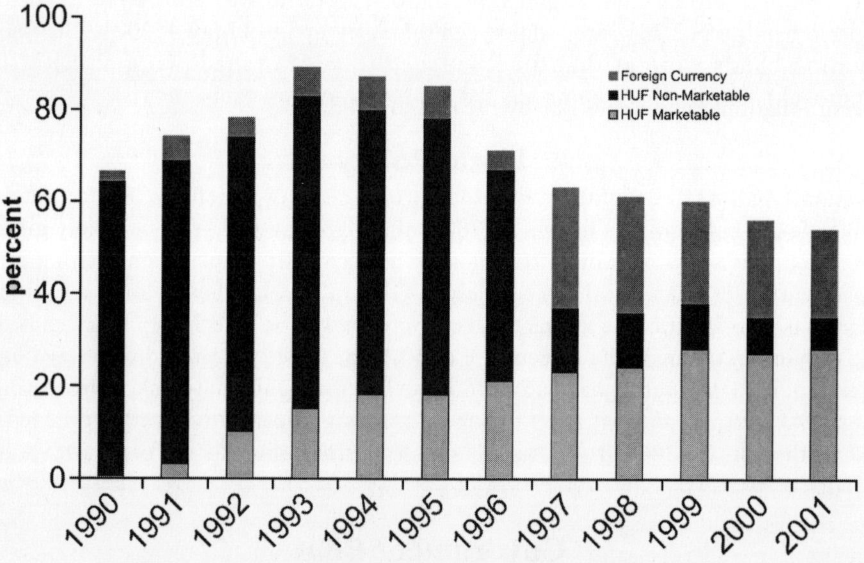

Source: Hungarian Debt Management Agency (AKK)

[8] Note that we have made a distinction between debt that is freely marketable and that which is not. The first marketable bond was issued in 1991. Prior to that the government had relied on central bank loans. Since 1997 the National Bank has not provided any financing to the government – with all government financing in the form of marketable government securities.

Exhibit 3: CE3 Inflation Targets

	Czech	Hungary	Poland
Actual – June 2001	5.5	10.5	6.2
2001		6 to 8	6 to 8
2002	3 to 5	3.5 to 5.5	
2003			Less than 4
2004		To meet the Maastricht	
2005	2 to 4	criterion on inflation	

Source: Czech National Bank, National Bank of Hungary, National Bank of Poland

Inflation

All of the CE3 now have formal inflation targets (see Exhibit 3). In the case of the Czech Republic, the Czech National Bank pursues an inflation target set "by agreement with the government." In April 2001 the target for annual headline consumer price inflation was expressed as a continuous range descending evenly from 3%–5% in January 2002 to 2%–4% in December 2005. The National Bank of Hungary (NBH) only formally set an inflation target—again in agreement with the government—for the first time in mid-2001 following the move to widen the exchange rate bands. The NBH aims to be able to bring inflation down to 3.5% from 5.5% by end-2002 and to meet the Maastricht inflation criterion by 2004/5. In Poland, the Monetary Policy Council of the National Bank sets the inflation target.[9] The target is 6%–8% for December 2001. The medium-term target is to bring inflation down below 4% by the end of 2003.

Interestingly, although the countries have similar inflation targets the curves are not pricing in similar interest rate paths.[10] Clearly if the market believed that there was a very high probability of a country entering EMU at a particular point in time, implied interest rates for that future period should be close to interest rates implied by the Euro curve. One way of assessing how much is "priced in" is to look at the forward forward, or implied forward interest rate. Exhibit 4 shows the Czech and Polish implied 5-year swap rates in 5 years' time as a spread to the Euro implied 5-year swap rate in 5 years' time. The Hungarian swap curve is not included given that the impetus for the development of the swap market only occurred with the capital account liberalization in June 2001.

There are a couple of points to note with curves. First, the spreads vary significantly throughout time. Partly that will reflect the relative bullishness or bearishness of the market or concerns about inflation or supply. But given the relatively young markets, the spreads will at times also reflect significant corporate hedging activity or position-taking. Second, the Czech implied forwards trade at a much narrower spread to Euro rates than do Polish rates—perhaps suggesting that

---

[9] There have been political noises about making the inflation target setting process more consensual. As of July 2001 it was not clear if the Monetary Policy Council would at some later date have to agree to an inflation target with the government.

[10] See Exhibit 11 for comparative yield curves.

the market anticipates that the Czech Republic will join EMU before Poland, or that inflation in the Czech Republic will likely remain lower than Polish inflation.

The Importance of Bringing Inflation Down

As we have noted, EU entry and EMU are likely to only take place in 2004 and 2006 respectively at the earliest for the CE3 countries. However, the experience of the existing EMU member countries provides an important lesson for the bond markets—bring inflation down and yields come down. The case of Italy (see Exhibit 5) is particularly instructive.[11]

The Czech Republic provides the same lessons. Headline inflation fell from 13% to 2.8% between May 1998 and February 1999. Exhibit 6 shows that in June 1998 the curve was inverted and rates were at high levels. Six months later the curve had shifted down and flattened as monetary policy was eased. By June 2001 yields at the short end had dropped by more than 1000 bps from their June 1998 level. The curve had also moved to a more traditional positive slope.

Exhibit 4: Czech and Polish 5-Year Swap in 5 Years' Time as a Spread over Euribor 5-Year Swap in 5 Years' Time (in basis points)

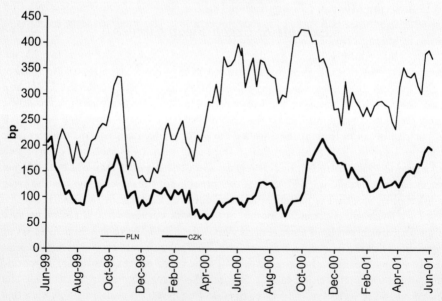

Source: Morgan Stanley Research

---

[11] The exhibit plots the spread between Italian Lire 5-year swap rates and German Deutschemark 5-year swaps against Italian inflation.

Exhibit 5: Italian Inflation and DEMITL 5-Year Swap Spread

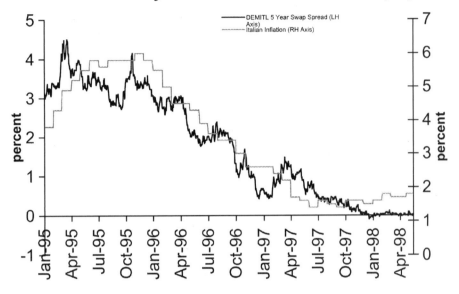

Source: Bloomberg

Exhibit 6: Czech Swap Curves

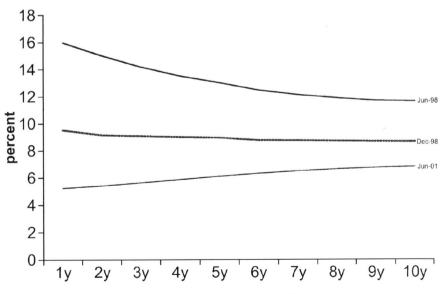

Source: Morgan Stanley Research

Exhibit 7: Hungarian Yield Curve

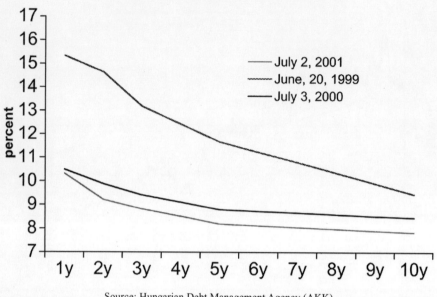

Source: Hungarian Debt Management Agency (AKK)

Hungary has not had the same success in bringing inflation down that the Czech Republic has had but yields there have also continued to move lower. Until June 2001, Hungary had been adopting an exchange rate target in an effort to bring inflation down. The narrow exchange rate band was highly credible (although there was always the possibility that the bands would be widened and the currency allowed to appreciate) and the yield pick-up and limited potential downside on the currency movements encouraged significant inflows of foreign money into the fixed income market. Yields fell as a consequence. With the move to wider exchange rate bands and the adoption of inflation targets, monetary conditions have been allowed to tighten through a strengthening currency. The Hungarian yield curve has remained inverted throughout (Exhibit 7).

The experience in Poland has been quite different (Exhibit 8). There, like in Hungary, the curve has remained inverted. However, yields backed up considerably between 1999 and 2000 as inflation moved higher and the Monetary Policy Council moved to raise its key interest rate—the 28-day National Bank bill rate—by 600 bp from 13% to 19% between January 1999 and August 2000. As inflation and official interest rates have declined, the curve has become less steeply inverted.[12]

---

[12] See Exhibit 13.

Exhibit 8: Polish Curves

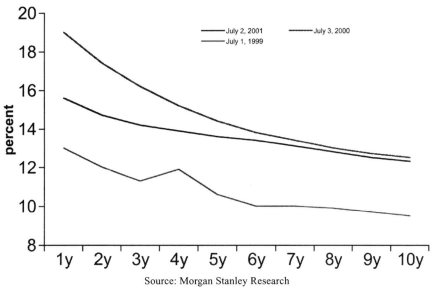

Source: Morgan Stanley Research

Key Challenges—Balassa-Samuelson and Initial Price Levels

The task of bringing inflation down imposes special challenges for the CE3. One of the important concepts here is expressed by the Balassa Samuelson hypothesis. In brief, the hypothesis uses the premise that the price of traded goods tends to converge across countries. However, prices of non-traded goods (such as some services) need not converge.

The prices of both traded and non-traded goods will have a wage component. Wages in turn will depend on productivity. But because workers can choose which sector they work in, wages in each sector should be linked.

In general, over time we can expect productivity gains in the traded goods sector to be higher than in the non-traded sector, as producers upgrade equipment or benefit from foreign investment. If productivity is higher in the traded goods sector but wages are the same in both the traded and non-traded goods sectors, we would expect the relative price of traded goods to rise less rapidly than for non-traded goods. In other words, price pressures in the non-traded sector will push inflation higher than it would otherwise have been. At the same time international competitiveness may be maintained even with an appreciating CPI-based real effective exchange rate. Exhibit 9 shows that CPI-based real effective exchange rates have indeed been strengthening throughout time. Nevertheless, that has not necessarily impacted competitiveness. NBH data show that in the case of Hungary, on a unit labor cost basis competitiveness improved significantly between 1995 and 2000.

Exhibit 9: REER Exchange Rates in CE3 (1996 = 100)

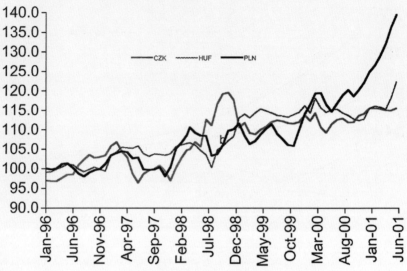

Source: IMF, Bloomberg, Morgan Stanley Research

Exhibit 10: Comparative Price Levels Germany = 100

Czech Republic	42
Greece	76
Hungary	43
Poland	58
Portugal	80
Slovakia	28
Spain	82

Source: OECD

The inflation challenge is also reflected in absolute price levels in the candidate countries. Over time price levels can be expected to converge toward those in the European Union. According to OECD data (Exhibit 10), price levels in the Czech Republic are just 42% of those in Germany, while those in Poland are 58% of German levels.[13]

These challenges to the disinflation process make it likely that the CE3 will have to maintain tighter monetary policies than the EMU countries. And as we noted earlier, yields will tend to be inverted (see Exhibit 11). CPI-based real effective exchange rates are also likely to continue generally strengthening—although the process is obviously unlikely to be a straight line one. We now take a look at each of the fixed income markets. Exhibit 11 shows yield curves as at June 2001.[14]

---

[13] Lower price levels in the Czech Republic and Hungary reflect in part a slower liberalization of regulated prices such as the prices of some utilities.

[14] Swap rates for Hungary in Exhibit 11 are estimated rates based off the bond curve.

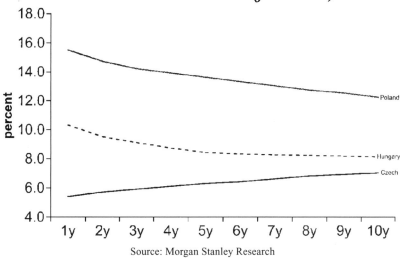

Exhibit 11: Yield Curves (June 2001)

Source: Morgan Stanley Research

Exhibit 12: Holdings of Polish Bonds as End-May 2001

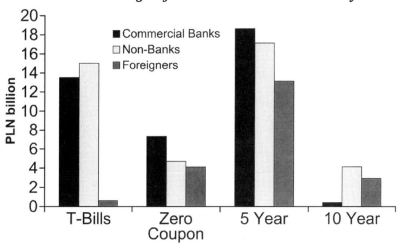

Source: Public Debt Department, Polish Ministry of Finance (preliminary data).

POLAND

Poland has the biggest and most liquid government bond market in the CE3, with USD 18 billion in total marketable fixed rate bonds outstanding (refer again to Exhibit 1). Foreign holdings of those bonds were approximately PLN 20 billion (USD 5 billion) at end-May 2001 (Exhibit 12).

In general, the expected total issuance for the year is defined in budget financing tables. In 2001, for instance, the original gross issuance of fixed-rate bonds was planned to be PLN 22 billion in cash terms. Given that bonds are issued at a discount, this is equivalent to approximately PLN 30 billion face value of bonds. In cash terms, the net issuance after redemptions was originally planned to be PLN 11.3 billion. The actual issuance depends on whether the other financing assumptions—such as privatization proceeds—are realized.

Bonds are issued via auctions. The auctions are discretionary price auctions with successful bidders getting bonds at the price at which they bid. Each month there is one issue of 2- and 5-year bonds. These bonds are auctioned together on the same day. Every second month there is also an issue of fixed rate 10-year bonds. The auctions take place on Wednesdays. The Public Debt Department of the Ministry of Finance announces in advance the auction schedule and usually announces the amounts to be auctioned each quarter. The longest dated bonds at mid-2001 were 10-year fixed-rate and floating-rate instruments. Fixed-rate bonds have an annual coupon and follow an actual/actual day count. Daily turnover in the bond market is estimated to be around USD 750–1500 million. As of June 2001, a buy and sell back market extended out to two months.

Treasury bills are auctioned each week on Mondays. These bills have tenors of 8, 13, 26, 39, and 52 weeks and follow an actual/360 day count. The interest rate swap market extended out to 20 years as of mid-2001, with swaps out to 5-years being more liquid than bonds.

Debt Management Debt Strategy

The Ministry of Finance has set out a strategy for 2001–2003. The main objectives of this strategy include:

- reducing the share of foreign currency debt in total debt;
- extending the average maturity of debt;
- smoothing out the debt repayment schedule;
- reducing the volatility of debt servicing costs and increasing their predictability;
- making the debt structure more flexible (or in other words, marketable);
- reducing debt servicing costs; and
- increasing the proportion of debt held by non-banks.

In sum, the implementation of these objectives should lead to a larger, more liquid, local currency fixed income market. At the same time, the average duration of that debt should increase.

The Ministry of Finance has been making progress in achieving these objectives. The foreign currency portion of government debt was 49% at end-1998. That had declined to 44% as at February 2001.

The average maturity of debt declined sharply in 1999, primarily because the government converted PLN 16.4 billion of debt held by the NBP and PLN 7.7

billion of debt to the health sector to fixed-rate marketable instruments. The Ministry of Finance also faced higher than anticipated borrowing costs in 1999 and decided to issue shorter-dated 2-year zero-coupon bonds. The average maturity of government debt declined from 4.6 years at the start of 1999 to 2.6 years at year-end. The plan is to increase the average maturity gradually to 3.3 years by end-2003.

As part of the effort to make debt servicing costs less volatile and more predictable, the Ministry plans to have the share of fixed-rate local currency debt to total debt grow from 39.5% at end-1999 to almost 70% by end-2003. That ratio was 47% at June 2000. The Ministry of Finance also aims to increase the share of marketable debt from 72.4% at end 1999 to just over 89% by end-2003. The Ministry has also embarked on creating larger, more liquid, benchmark bonds. In 2001, the Ministry moved from issuing three series of 5-year bonds during a year to just two series.

Market Structure

Exhibit 12 shows the breakdown in holdings of freely marketable domestic currency treasury bills and fixed-rate bonds. As at end-May 2001, preliminary data from the Ministry of Finance revealed that the total nominal value of marketable domestic securities outstanding was around PLN 135 billion (USD 34 billion). Of this total, PLN 29 billion were in the form of bills and PLN 106 billion in bonds. PLN 89 billion of the bonds outstanding were fixed-rate bonds—of which PLN 73 billion (USD 23 billion) were potentially available to be purchased by non-residents. By far the bulk of the bonds are 5-year instruments—comprising PLN 49 billion of the total.[15] PLN 16 billion of bonds were in the form of 2-year zero coupon bonds and PLN 7 billion were 10-year bonds. In addition to these fixed-rate bonds, there are approximately PLN 17 billion in floating-rate notes outstanding.

Exhibit 10 shows that the non-resident community is concentrated in the 5-year sector—the most liquid part of the curve. Benchmark 5-year issues typically have an issue size of between PLN 3 and 5 billion. Note that the bulk of 10-year fixed-rate bonds are held by domestic non-banks and that local banks typically hold very few 10-year fixed-rate bonds. Non-residents hold very few treasury bills. At the short end of the curve higher yields are available through foreign exchange forwards or euro-zloty issues. The total value of euro-zloty issues outstanding as of March 2001 was approximately PLN 22 billion.

Local pension funds are becoming a more and more significant participant in the market. In 2001, the government had originally planned to transfer around PLN 14 billion to the funds via the social security agency. Pension funds have typically invested around 60% of inflows in the bond market. The funds continue to be in a start-up phase. Through to the middle of 2001 they had tended to maintain a reasonably short duration (on average close to two years) given the higher yields available at the front end of the curve. Over the long run, they are likely to be natural buyers of the long end of the curve as they seek to match the duration of assets and liabilities.

---

[15] In Exhibit 12 the 5-year bond category represents those bonds that when issued had an original term to maturity of 5 years.

The Public Debt Department of the Ministry of Finance is not the only supplier of bonds. The NBP has also been selling government bonds that it holds on its books. The NBP initially held more than PLN 16 billion bonds with maturities out to 10 years. These bonds are sold via auction each Thursday but are only available to residents. The aim of the NBP is to reduce what it refers to as the "excess operational liquidity" in the system. That is, the NBP is using the sale of these bonds to reduce bank liquidity. The NBP's primary tool for withdrawing liquidity is the sale of 28-day NBP bills. But as excess operational liquidity is withdrawn, the lombard rate will become more important.

The asset swap market is developing quite rapidly. 10-year bonds tend to trade expensive to swaps. The benchmark 5-year bond also tends to trade reasonably expensive. However, as these bonds go off the run, they tend to cheapen up quite significantly.[16]

The Curve

Poland has pursued a very tight monetary policy in an effort to bring inflation down (refer to earlier Exhibit 8) and constrain domestic demand in an effort to limit the current account deficit. One consequence has been that yields are significantly higher than in the Czech Republic and Hungary—even though by mid-2001 the inflation outlooks for the three countries were not markedly different (see yields in Exhibit 11). This tight monetary policy has also meant that real interest rates have been high and the yield curve has been steeply inverted—although the extent of that inversion declined significantly during the first half of 2001 (see Exhibit 13).

That curve disinversion has provided high returns on shorter dated instruments. Morgan Stanley Capital International's (MSCI) index of 1–3 year Polish bonds gained 8.8% in PLN terms during the first 6 months of 2001. In EUR terms, the gain was more than 24%. For the 3-year period between June 1998 and June 2001, the 1–3 year bond index increased by 58% in local currency terms (and just under 78% in EUR terms). For the 3–5 year sector, the local currency return was just under 47%. Longer dated bonds have not performed so well, with local currency returns in the 7–10 year sector gaining only 7.5% between September 1999 and June 2001 (but a more respectable 38% in EUR terms). However, that performance masks what can at times be dramatic returns and significant sell-offs. For instance, between the end of October 2000 and the end of February 2001 the 7–10 year index increased by more than 20% in local currency terms. Likewise, those with longer memories will recall that 5-year bonds issued at 74.40 in late 1997 traded at above par in late 1998. And those bonds just happened to have a 12% coupon.

---

[16] In this example of an asset swap, one leg of the swap would involve a market participant paying or receiving flows linked to a Polish bond. A par bond trades "expensive" to swaps when a swap of similar maturity has a higher yield than the bond.

Exhibit 13: Polish 2-Year Swap – 5-Year Swap

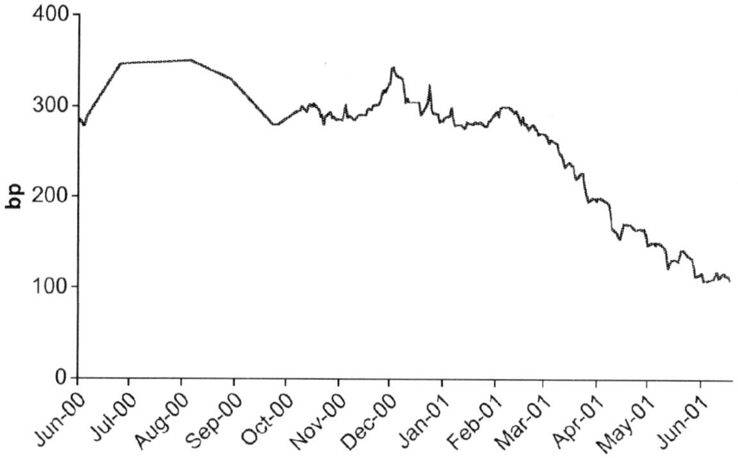

Source: Bloomberg

As at end-June 2001, 10-year swap yields were at 12.2%. Given the yield curve inversion, for a long position to break even, 9-year swap rates would need to be below 11.6% at end-June 2002. Clearly, with significant cost of carry considerations, the alternative of funding through a lower yielding currency (particularly EUR, or a basket of USD and EUR) has at times been attractive. Although the general weakness of the EUR since its launch, and a general perception that the zloty is too strong, has tended to make market participants cautious about this approach.

HUNGARY[17]

Hungary started with the highest debt to GDP levels of the CE3 and as a consequence has tended to have a relatively large and well-developed domestic debt market. As noted earlier in this chapter, Hungary was also the first of the CE3 to issue a 10-year bond. Hungary plans to issue longer-dated bonds at some point.

Debt Management Strategy

Hungary's debt management objectives have not been surprising. They have aimed to:

- increase the share of fixed rate publicly issued debt;
- extend the maturity profile and achieve a more even redemption schedule; and
- increase the share of retail securities

---

[17] Most of the information in this section can also be found on the excellent Hungarian Debt Management Agency website: http://www.akk.hu

Central government debt to GDP was at 55.4% as at end-2000. The Ministry of Finance expected that ratio to fall by 2 percentage points in 2001. Foreign currency debt to total debt was approximately 35%. The widening of the exchange rate bands in May 2001 and the subsequent strengthening of the forint will have helped decrease this ratio in 2001. Net debt sales of local currency denominated debt were expected to be HUF 552 billion in 2001. Gross issuance was expected to be around HUF 3,200 billion. Exhibit 1 shows that the bulk of Hungarian local currency debt is fixed-rate debt. At the end of September 2000, fixed-rate debt comprised 55% of the marketable government bonds. The average duration of that debt in September 2000 was just 1.28 years—with more than half of outstanding debt maturing in less than one year. That compares with an OECD average of 28% of debt maturing in one year. More tellingly, for OECD countries on average, 62.5% of debt outstanding has a maturity of more than two years. Not unsurprisingly, the Debt Management Agency was aiming to lengthen duration by selling bonds with an average maturity of 3.64 years during 2001.

Market Structure

One of the consistent characteristics of the Hungarian market is the steady increase in the participation of non-residents. Up until June 18, 2001, non-residents could only buy bonds with an original maturity of more than one year. That did not stop non-residents from increasing their holdings from just over HUF 140 billion following the Russian crisis in 1998 to around HUF 1000 billion at the end of May 2001—around 30% of marketable bonds outstanding.[18] The non-resident community was typically underweight duration in anticipation that the HUF trading bands would eventually be widened and that the currency would strengthen. That strategy proved to be the correct one, even though the timing of the band widening in May 2001 generally took the market by surprise. (See Exhibit 14.)

Bond auctions take place on Thursdays of every even numbered week of the year. Two bonds are auctioned at each auction. The auction will either be of 2- and 5-year bonds or a 3-year bond and a floater or a 10-year fixed-rate bond. The Debt Management Agency will announce the bonds to be auctioned and the amounts on the Friday preceding the auction. Auctions are on a discriminatory price basis—successful bidders get the bonds at the price that they bid. Three-month treasury bills are auctioned every Tuesday. Six-month bills are auctioned on odd numbered weeks and 12-month bills on Thursdays of odd numbered weeks.

Most Hungarian bonds are now issued with semiannual coupons. An actual/365 day count convention is followed for both bonds and bills. Daily turnover is estimated to be of the order of USD 700 million. The average trade size for bonds in the over-the-counter market is HUF 500 million.

The AKK also conducts reverse auctions. These auctions are used to smooth the redemption of larger issues.

---

[18] As at end-June 2001, the nominal value of bonds outstanding was HUF 3400 billion. The value of treasury bills outstanding was HUF 916 billion.

Exhibit 14: Holdings of Hungarian Government Bonds, NBH Bills, T-Bills, Q1 2001 (in HUF billions)

	Bonds	NBH Bills	T-Bills	Total
Non-financial corporations	102	104	160	366
Central bank	181	0	0	181
Credit institutions	1054	182	193	1428
Investment funds	149	271	86	505
Insurance companies, pension funds	707	45	138	890
Other financial corporations	65	14	41	120
Total financial corporations	2157	512	457	3125
Local government	59	21	60	140
Other general government	1	0	2	3
Total general government	59	21	62	143
Households	107	24	725	856
NPIs serving households	10	9	23	42
Rest of the world	853	0	0	853
Total	3288	670	1427	5384

Source: National Bank of Hungary

Hungary operates a primary dealer system. Primary dealers commit to purchase at least 3% of bonds and bills in the primary market over a 6-month period. They also agree to provide quotes on benchmark bonds in amounts of at least HUF 200 million and other bonds and bills of at least HUF 100 million.

The Curve

Even though nominal yields at the short end of the curve have fallen significantly since January 1999 (the issue date for Hungary's first 10-year bond), the curve remained inverted in mid-2001 (refer back to Exhibit 7). Unlike Poland during the first six months of 2001, the MSCI indexes for 1–3 years, 3–5 years, and 7–10 years all recorded very similar gains—up around 6%–7% in the first 6 months of 2001 in HUF terms and up around 16%–17% in EUR terms. If we extend the period back to November 1999, returns for the different curve segments continue to be close, ranging from 22%–25%.

CZECH REPUBLIC

As noted earlier, the Czech Republic has the lowest debt/GDP ratio of the CE3 countries. It is perhaps not surprising that the Czech bond market remains relatively small as of mid-2001. The absence of a pressing need to raise finance in the past has also meant that the Czech Republic has the least developed debt management policy of the CE3—in the past it simply did not need to have a sophisticated debt management framework. This looks likely to change significantly given the potential supply over the next few years as the general government deficit increases and as the government meets the costs associated with bank restructuring. As at end-2000, the total stock of outstanding bonds was approximately CZK 104 billion (EUR 3.1 billion), while the stock of bills was CZK 165 billion (EUR 4.86 billion). The main holders of government debt as of December 2000 were domestic financial institutions and insurance companies.[19] (See Exhibit 15.)

Government bonds go out to 15 years. The Ministry of Finance was the first in the CE3 countries to issue a bond of this tenor. Since 2001, bonds have typically been issued monthly. The Ministry of Finance publishes an auction schedule on its website.[20] Bonds are priced using a 30/360-day count. Bills are priced on an actual/360 day basis. In addition, there is an active Euro-CZK market, with more than EUR 2 billion outstanding as of mid-2001. From 2001, CZK eurobonds have been priced using an actual/actual day count convention. As noted above, there is an active swaps market that extends out to 15 years. As of mid-2001, swaps were liquid out to 10 years.

Exhibit 15: Czech Government Bonds and Bills as at End-2000 (CZK billion)

	Amount	Percentage
Total Bills and Bonds	270	100.0
Total Treasury Bills	165	61.3
13 Week Bill	68	25.2
26 Week Bill	39	14.6
39 Week Bill	35	13.0
52 Week Bill	23	8.0
Total Bonds	104	38.7
2 Year Bonds	12	4.5
3 Year Bonds	10	3.8
4 Year Bonds	5	1.9
5 Year Bonds	53	19.7
7 Year Bonds	12	4.5
10 Year Bonds	12	4.5

Source: Czech Ministry of Finance

Holdings of Czech Local Currency Government Bonds and Bills

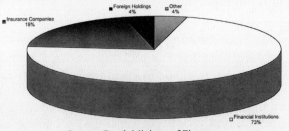

Source: Czech Ministry of Finance

---

[19] Of the CZK 195 billion held by financial institutions, CZK 44 billion was held by institutions that were foreign controlled.

[20] http://www.mfcr.cz

The Curve

As noted earlier, the Czech yield curve has both shifted down and moved from an inverted curve into a positively sloped curve during the three years from mid-1998 to mid-2001 (see Exhibit 6). A tight monetary policy and fiscal policy that were used to reduce the current account deficit and take pressure off the currency helped push the Czech economy into recession. That, in turn, helped bring inflation down and interest rates followed. Indeed, despite the significant cuts in interest rates, the Czech National Bank has outperformed on inflation. It was only in 2001 that the upper end of the Bank's inflation target looked like it was being threatened. That inflation increase, the growing economy, and the potential supply of debt, both from banking sector restructuring costs and an increasing structural budget deficit, have caused the yield curve to steepen. At some point in the future it is not inconceivable that the Czech monetary conditions would need to tighten sufficiently to again bring about an inverted curve.

CONCLUSION

The overriding aim of the CE3 countries is to join the European Union. They could potentially be new members in 2004 and possibly members of European Monetary Union two years after that. That goal of joining the European Union provides an anchor and has shaped policies in all countries. While all countries share the same objectives and hope to reach the same end point, they have started from slightly different positions and have taken slightly different approaches. The markets are dynamic and are developing rapidly. The convergence process makes the fixed-income markets interesting from an outright basis. And the different adjustment paths for the CE3 countries make them interesting from a relative value perspective.

Chapter 5

Emerging Fixed Income and Local Currency: An Investment Management View

Luis R. Luis, Ph.D.
Principal
International Research & Strategy Associates LLC

Investment managers had an early and important role in the development of emerging markets fixed income as an asset class following the developing-country debt crisis of the 1980s. Investment companies were created to take advantage of opportunities for excess return from investing in emerging bonds and defaulted bank loans to developing countries. Some of these initial investment vehicles were established as offshore entities, beginning in 1989, to facilitate access to the market by global retail investors who often resided in emerging countries themselves.[1] Thereafter, investment companies registered in the United States provided diversified emerging market portfolios for investors in developed countries. These dedicated funds generally aimed at providing high income with substantial potential for capital appreciation.

A second stage in the development of investment management involved the use of emerging market instruments as part of broader portfolios, often global and international bond portfolios. Emerging bonds also found their way to accounts and investment vehicles focused on U.S. bond markets. At the same time, dedicated accounts were established for institutional clients, mainly in the United States, and more recently in Europe, Japan, and other developed areas. As investors became better informed, emerging bonds were included in a variety of financial structures involving the use of leverage and derivative securities. These structures were available to institutional investors and to hedge funds and other specialized investment vehicles.

A third stage, evolving alongside deepening capital markets in emerging countries, is the management of local currency fixed income. The initial development of emerging fixed income was centered primarily in bonds and defaulted

---

[1] The first offshore vehicle to invest in emerging bonds is generally acknowledged to be the Sovereign High Yield Investment Company registered in Curacao, Netherlands Antilles, in 1989. This investment company was designed to invest primarily in bearer bonds issued by governments in emerging countries.

bank loans largely denominated in dollars and, to a lesser extent, other currencies of industrial countries. Although some use was made of instruments issued in the currencies of emerging markets, these were complementary rather than central to the asset class. They mostly comprised Treasury bills and other money market securities of a handful of countries, most prominently Mexico and other Latin American nations. The Asian currency crisis of 1997–1998 discouraged many investors from venturing into fixed income investments in local currency. However, by the year 2000, investors began to return prominently to local fixed income in such instruments as Polish government notes and Mexican T-Bills.

Investment managers face multiple challenges in seeking value while managing risk in the asset class. Value is derived from analysis of credit quality, market risk, and pricing relationships within the asset class and in relation to established bond markets. Information gaps played a major role in the early evolution of the asset class. Long lags in the availability of data, large voids in the data, and, most importantly, partial understanding of economic and political variables determining sovereign credit quality created opportunities to add value while presenting substantial risks. Value is enhanced and risk reduced in direct relation to analysis, information, and investment discipline.

As countries and other emerging issuers have strived to improve the flow and transparency of information following the 1994 Mexican peso crisis, the limiting factor is analysis of variables that determine credit quality and vulnerability to random events or shocks, not the lack of basic data and qualitative information.

As the marginal issuers in global capital markets, emerging countries are highly exposed, as may be expected, to shifting financial patterns and liquidity effects derived from core bond markets. As analysis improves and average credit quality rises, these effects are likely to diminish in size but will not be eliminated. Because relationships are not easily predictable, portfolio shifts within the asset class and in relation to other investments will characterize this market in the foreseeable future. This means that investment managers, possibly more than in other fixed income classes, are expected to design and manage portfolios in ways that take advantage of these shifts.

INVESTMENT OBJECTIVES

Investment managers view emerging markets as capable of satisfying a broad set of objectives. In general, portfolios and investment vehicles are classified into two main categories: those primarily seeking high income and those principally aiming at obtaining total return. Because price appreciation is most often a secondary objective and sometimes the primary goal, emerging markets fixed income is sometimes viewed as a "quasi-equity" asset class in contrast with traditional investment-grade fixed income investments. A third type of investor views emerging markets as primarily a means to diversify global or domestic fixed income portfolios.

Emerging market bonds are expected to provide high yield, certainly compared to investment-grade securities and even when placed against speculative grade corporate bonds. Most emerging countries are rated below investment grade. In mid-2001, emerging markets sovereign bonds had an average credit quality approximately equivalent to a BB/Ba as rated by the major agencies. Moreover, emerging bonds denominated in dollars have historically traded at wider spreads to benchmark U.S. Treasury bonds than other bonds of similar credit rating. For example, at the end of May 1997 emerging market bonds yielded approximately 890 basis points (bps) (net of collateral) and 800 bps (collateral included) over equivalent maturity U.S. Treasuries while similarly BB-rated U.S. high yield bonds yielded 620 bps.[2]

Spread curves for emerging market bonds in relation to U.S. Treasury bonds are upward sloping with the slope increasing in proportion to duration. This relationship holds for both normal Eurobonds and non-collateralized Brady bonds, as well as for Brady bonds which have collateralized principal and partial interest payments. In this case, market price reflects the view of the major rating agencies that collateral does not significantly improve the credit quality of the bond. This apparent paradox, captured by market pricing as well as rating agency views (even when the percentage of present value composed of high grade U.S. Treasury collateral increases as average maturity declines) provides a source of excess return for investors. Downward-sloping spread curves often appear when perceived default probabilities increase. In these cases the market is assuming that an upcoming default may be remedied promptly by an agreed restructuring which will not affect longer maturities.

Many investment vehicles seek to generate *steady* as well as high *current* income from a portfolio of emerging bonds. Portfolios can be designed to optimize current income at the expense of other objectives such as price appreciation or stability of net asset value. As emerging market bonds comprise a wide variety of fixed- and floating-rate securities, portfolio management strategies can be found that help optimize or stabilize current income throughout the interest rate cycle. Utilization of interest rate swaps or other derivatives can contribute substantially to achieving income objectives. As an illustration, during the period of low short-term interest rates from 1992–1993, swapping floating-rate Brady cash flows to fixed rates added over 200 bps in current yield.

Investment vehicles can also be designed to generate steady *dividends* composed of current income, realized capital gains, and, depending upon accounting conventions, accretion of discount. Exhibit 1 shows the historical cumulative dividends and total return in U.S. dollars per share of the Sovereign High Yield Investment Company. The main investment objective of this fund is to provide high income with a secondary objective of capital appreciation. A steady dollar dividend has been maintained for long periods since the inception of the fund.

---

[2] These are the approximate yields of the Emerging Markets Bond Index (EMBI) of J. P. Morgan (sovereign yield and blended yield) and of the Lehman Brothers BB index (long) of U.S. high yield bonds.

Exhibit 1: SHYIC Returns

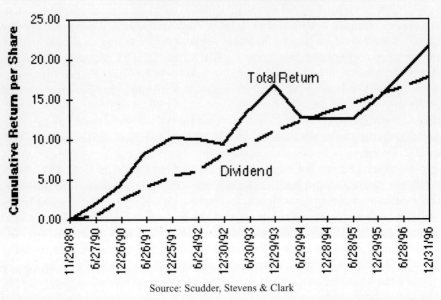

Source: Scudder, Stevens & Clark

Investment vehicles aiming at total return are managed differently from those that primarily seek high income. Among the many differences in management and orientation, vehicles seeking total return will often consider a wider set of potential investments, particularly highly discounted bonds and loans or high spread duration bonds. Collateralized Brady bonds are also favored for strategies involving higher interest duration as the U.S. Treasury zero-coupon bonds backing the principal value of the bonds supplies additional interest duration.

A wide range of risk profiles is consistent with a total return orientation. Although discounts from par value—and the potential for above average price appreciation—are larger for issuers of lower credit quality, there are ample opportunities to invest in highly discounted securities of issuers with improving credit. Success in recent years in rapidly and effectively turning around countries involved in acute financial instability—Argentina, Brazil, Korea, Mexico, Peru, and Poland, to name a few—provides evidence that even in cases of fragile credit quality framed in unstable macroeconomic conditions, successful turnaround can be produced within short periods of time. The record also shows that most of these major turnaround cases have led to sustained improvements in creditworthiness, breaking the cycle of stop-go progress that characterized major developing economies for most of the post-1945 years of the last century.

A number of portfolio management styles and techniques can be used to reach a total return objective. These range from long-term, research based portfolios which seek capital appreciation based on steady or improving fundamental conditions to trading-oriented vehicles which aim to take advantage of country- or issuer-specific events, U.S. bond market trends, or the global liquidity cycle. The deepening of emerging bond markets is providing increased liquidity for many benchmark issues, reducing the transaction costs of trading-oriented strategies. A trend towards lower return volatilities lowered the cost of hedging and entering into derivative strategies which can enhance total return. Growing demand for hedging products will tend to lower transaction costs for derivatives as the markets mature.

Aggressive total return portfolios, as can be anticipated, are highly susceptible to conditions outside of the emerging markets, both of a fundamental nature and liquidity related. Brady bonds and long duration emerging Eurobonds are often more sensitive to fluctuations in the U.S. Treasury yield curve than implied by interest duration, spread duration, and other parameters that measure price sensitivity to yield or spread changes. While this sensitivity will tend to decline as discounts to par recede, markets mature, and the quality of information and analysis improves, emerging dollar bonds are likely to be more exposed to shifts in Treasury bonds than other asset classes. Liquidity effects are another important consideration, particularly for portfolios that aim at boosting total return by employing a wide variety of trading strategies.

This pattern of sensitivity does not apply to local currency instruments, which have short duration and are segmented from global capital markets. Although the incipient development of local yield curves provides for only partial evidence, it appears that long duration bonds issued in local currencies have also reduced sensitivity to events in major global markets as compared to dollar pay issues. The segmentation of local fixed income markets from global markets results from the use of flexible exchange rates, restrictions or taxes on capital flows, and the lack of effective arbitrage between the local and international markets.

A third investment objective is asset diversification within a comprehensive investment program. It is not a distinct objective. Rather, it is achieved jointly with the other two objectives. Brady bonds and long-dated Eurobonds are sensitive to conditions in the U.S. bond market. Hence, these instruments are often not considered to provide much risk diversification for U.S. or dollar-based global bond investors. It is possible, however, to construct emerging bond portfolios which offer much greater potential for diversification by weighting more heavily emerging regions less associated with the U.S. bond market. Bonds of Asian, Central European, and Middle Eastern issuers historically have a lower correlation with the U.S. bond market than Latin American bonds. The latter account for about 65% of the mid-2001 capitalization of Brady and emerging Eurobonds.

Total return correlations of local currency markets with the U.S. and other developed country bond markets in recent years are generally not statistically different from zero at a high level of significance and as such can provide diversification advantages for U.S. and global bond investors. The substitution or addition of local currency instruments to U.S. or global portfolios can significantly reduce portfolio volatility and may potentially increase returns. These results apply to local currency portfolios of short duration. The diversification benefits of local currencies are also enhanced because of the low correlation among the local currency markets themselves which helps explain the low volatility of local currency portfolios.

Asset diversification can be managed tactically or strategically to enhance returns during perceived favorable conditions in U.S. or global bond markets. Alternatively, diversification can be a primary defensive tool, for example by increasing the allocation to local currency investments. It too can help achieve interest duration objectives in diversified global portfolios.

ANALYTICAL ISSUES

The central principle behind a fundamental approach to emerging bond investments is that value, consistency, and risk control can be enhanced by systematic analysis. In a largely speculative asset class such as emerging markets fixed income, return optimization requires particular emphasis on risk control as the basis for portfolio construction and management. Analysis is needed as the centerpiece in gauging risks, determining relative value, and establishing potential arbitrage opportunities.

Although there are a number of ways to integrate analysis into the investment process, tilting research attention and resources towards particular aspects of the asset class, a fundamental approach, at a minimum, involves the following: sovereign risk, corporate credit, security analysis, market sensitivity, and for local currencies, currency or exchange rate risk.

Sovereign Risk

Sovereign risk encompasses several dimensions of risk. In its more general form, it measures transfer risk, sometimes denoted as *convertibility risk*. This is the probability that a government will not make foreign exchange available to meet foreign currency obligations. As such, sovereign credit quality will depend on the ability of the government to obtain foreign exchange and its willingness to maintain unimpeded flows of international capital to public and private borrowers.

The probability of default is a parameter that can be estimated either explicitly or implicitly. Ordinarily, however, the evaluation of sovereign risk involves more subtle differentiation among sovereign credits than just estimating a probability of default. Such probability tends to approach zero for periods of one year or less for investment-grade credits, but increases non-linearly as credits decline in quality below the investment-grade frontier. Nonetheless, markets are very sensitive to gradations in the perception of sovereign risk trends. Experience also indicates that markets tend to discount swiftly perceived improving trends in creditworthiness.

A key element for investment managers is the anticipation of changes in sovereign credit quality. A method to determine such changes is very useful as a guide to potential value and pricing of specific sovereign issues. This can be approached in a number of ways. The most desirable method is a thorough evaluation of macro-, financial, and policy variables which will determine the government's ability and willingness to supply foreign exchange to entities operating within the country. Alternative approaches, which can be used as consistency checks, involve the use of quantitative models, indicators of creditworthiness, and check lists.

Among the key determinants of sovereign credit quality, to be assessed by thorough analysis, quantitative estimation, or other methods, are the following: the structure of the government's debt and debt service (external and internal), its international asset position, the fiscal position of the government, prospects for domestic output and demand, and a projection of dollar cash flows for the country derived from international trade and investment. The quality of economic policies in place, which can be quantified by indicators such as the status of International Monetary Fund programs, are also an important determinant. It is far more difficult to analyze and quantify institutional and political stability. Nonetheless, it is clear that both markets and rating agencies devote considerable importance to this element, which often helps to explain discrepancies in rating from that implied by more objective criteria.

Econometric analysis suggests that the structure of external debt is the central element involved in ratings of emerging markets by the major agencies. That this is the case should not be a surprise. After all, the probability of continuing to service external obligations will vary inversely with the burden of the debt. This is also the most readily quantifiable indicator of creditworthiness. It can be represented in simple form by the ratio of external debt to exports of goods and services. Other alternative ratios are also calculated, for example, the ratio of external debt to GDP. Likewise debt service ratios are often used to measure the current burden of servicing external debt.

Statistical analysis of sovereign debt ratings of the two major rating agencies, Moody's and Standard and Poor's, suggests that a small set of debt and economic indicators fits well the variation of ratings from a sample of 23 of the most important emerging countries. The results of two regressions, shown in Exhibit 2, indicate that the ratio of external debt to total exports, the ratio of total interest payments to exports, the trend growth of real GDP (average of the last three years) and the level of inflation for the last year account for 82% of the variance of Moody's ratings and 75% of the variance of ratings from Standard and Poor's. These results do not imply that the rating process used by the agencies is based solely or even primarily on these commonly used indicators. The standard errors, of 0.39 rating and 0.53 rating respectively, indicate that these equations are approximations of the process. Likewise, having 11 of 23 ratings split between the two agencies point out the important judgmental elements involved in the rating process. A statistical difference between the agencies appears to be that Standard and Poor's assigns somewhat greater weight to macroeconomic stability and growth than does Moody's, as can be seen in the larger coefficients for trend growth and inflation in the regressions.

Exhibit 2: Determinants of Sovereign Credit Ratings*

	Constant	Debt/Exports	Interest/Exports	Trend Growth	CPI Inflation	
Moody's	4.58	0.008	−0.027	−0.072	0.0084	$R^2 = 0.82$
(t ratio)	19.2	2.85	−0.58	−2.88	2.2	s.e.= 0.39
Standard & Poor's	4.51	0.009	−0.049	−0.077	0.016	$R^2 = 0.75$
(t ratio)	13.95	2.33	−0.79	−2.29	3.13	s.e. = 0.53

* Estimated from data in the Institute of International Finance, *Near Term Prospects for Emerging Market Economies* (Washington, D.C., April 1997). Ratings are those in effect as of June 1, 1997. For purposes of estimation, ratings were converted to a numerical equivalent where BBB/Baa is equal to 5.00 and BB/Ba equals 6.00 and so forth.

An evaluation of the mix of economic policies used by the government to attain financial and price stability and to help foster investment, growth, and financial deepening is essential in determining whether a country is on its way to achieving sustainable economic growth. Largely because of the diffusion of policy know-how and evidence that market-led policies instill confidence on investors and consumers, the quality of policies followed by developing countries has improved greatly in the 15 years since the debt crisis of 1982, the debacle which deeply set back development prospects for many middle-income countries. The lesson of the 1990s is that markets are rapid to acknowledge the benefits of stabilization based on a sound fiscal, monetary, and deregulatory policy mix. Likewise, selling state assets can rapidly provide signals to markets of a change in direction and an increase in the potential for solid fiscal policies.

A checklist can be a useful device to gauge the quality of the institutional and political environment in a country. The checklist may include factors such as the likelihood of a smooth transition of power, the stability of governing coalitions, and the chances for continuity of policies. Absent high political instability, which can lead to sharp reversal of policies, shifting coalition governments and other nonviolent signs of political change are not necessarily a huge negative in the evaluation of credit quality. It is when policies are affected negatively by either peaceful or violent political change that potential for a major reversal in credit trends exists.

Corporate Credit

Debt securities of emerging country corporations provide a means to enhance returns in emerging debt, high yield, or other fixed income portfolios. Credit research is essential in determining proper valuation and the identification of investment opportunities. Corporate credits can also be a source of diversification as a complement or an alternative to sovereign credits. On the other hand, corporate credits can be very sensitive to movements in sovereign credit quality in the country of corporate residence. It follows that corporate credits do not always provide much diversification to emerging debt portfolios.

Evaluation of corporate risk in emerging markets presents formidable challenges. Rapidly evolving operating environments, accounting and legal systems, and rapid shifts in financial variables compound uncertainty in assessing credit risk for corporations. Management quality is arguably even more of a determining variable in developing countries than in industrial ones. Because of these factors, financial outcomes for emerging country companies are often subject to greater estimation error than is the case in developed economies.

The operating environment for companies in developing countries is deeply affected, almost by definition, by rapid structural change arising out of institutional development, liberalization of markets, the creation and transformation of regulatory systems, and the opening to competition from foreign companies. It is also characterized by greater cyclical variation in demand and output than in developed countries.

Accounting standards are shifting rapidly in many emerging countries and are converging gradually to U.S. GAAP. Some countries, such as Chile and Argentina, now use accounting standards which are close to those of the United States and other developed countries. The issuance of American Depository Receipts and international bonds by many emerging country corporations also forces these companies to restate their financial statements in harmony with either U.S. or commonly accepted international standards. Privatization is another force pressing for updating accounting standards, as widening interest in state companies by potential strategic or portfolio investors requires a thorough restatement of financial data. The pace of change is strongest among many larger Latin American and East Asian companies which are now accessing the international capital market. Central European, South Asian, and African companies lag in these efforts.

There is a debate regarding the relative evaluation of corporate and sovereign credits. Traditionally, the sovereign ceiling, or the credit rating given to the government, has set a limit on the rating of corporations residing and largely operating in that country. In some cases, however, market prices signaled that investors viewed corporations as a better credit. For example, some Argentine corporate credits traded for substantial periods of time with spreads through sovereign bonds of comparable duration or maturity. Recently major credit agencies, among them Standard and Poor's, Fitch, and Moody's, have indicated conditions under which corporate credits could be subject to a higher hard currency credit rating than the sovereign.[3]

Historical price behavior gives some support to the view that corporate bonds may be more susceptible to systemic shocks than sovereign bonds. A shock is an unexpected shift in a financial or real variable that substantially alters the

---

[3] This refers mainly to "dollarized economies" where there is little or no difference between credit quality measured in local currency or in dollars. The limiting case of a dollarized economy is one where the dollar is legal and sole legal tender, such as Panama. Countries with a currency pegged to the dollar through a "currency board" system or other mechanism that maintains full backing of the monetary base by dollar reserves or equivalent assets can be considered dollarized. For a company operating in a fully dollarized economy, transfer risk approaches zero.

probabilities given by investors and consumers to normal economic outcomes. A sudden devaluation of the currency or a large drop in the price of a key commodity, such as copper for Chile or oil for Nigeria, can generate shocks. After the devaluation of the Mexican peso in December 1994, spreads of Eurobonds issued by Mexican and other Latin American companies widened significantly over comparable maturity sovereigns. In this case, the currency devaluation in one of the most prominent emerging debtors provided a systemic shock to the market, which deeply hit corporate credits. A systemic shock affects a set of international investors and markets as opposed to a country-specific shock which disrupts only investors in a given country and its securities.

Banks and other financial companies in emerging countries are especially sensitive to the stress generated by structural change and to the dislocations provided by shocks. The combination of rapid credit growth, often prevalent in emerging economies during price stabilization and deregulation of the financial sector, and inadequate risk management and other controls at lending institutions leads to a deterioration of loan portfolios. Shocks can exacerbate the situation by causing rapid downward shifts in economic activity or an increase in key prices and interest rates. Banking difficulties are common throughout the developing world and, paradoxically, in the more rapidly developing countries. Analyzing financial credits is one of the most challenging aspects of corporate credit evaluation in emerging markets.

Bonds issued by companies facing steady demand through the economic cycle and capable of reacting rapidly to shocks offer less risk and at times present opportunities for yield and yield-compression significantly over the sovereign. This is the case of some electric utilities and companies in the food processing sector. Transformation of energy pricing and regulation in emerging countries to systems based on fuel and capacity costs or, alternatively, on marginal cost pricing, such as in Argentina and Chile, are reducing uncertainty in evaluating company cash flows while increasing the likelihood that adequate interest coverage ratios can be maintained.

Investing in debt securities of all but the largest listed companies in emerging markets requires specialized credit work and wide access to local data and company management. Locally traded debt securities as well as private placements offer ample opportunities for excess return. However, this is a market segment which remains terra incognita for most investors located outside of the domestic market. The comments above regarding credit analysis, which pertain largely to the better capitalized corporations, are even more applicable to this much larger set of companies where the problems of risk evaluation are compounded by local operating environments, regulatory questions, and limitations of data and institutional understanding.

Security Analysis

Sovereign and corporate credit analysis provide essential inputs for security evaluation, country selection, and portfolio management. Additional evaluation is necessary to proceed with security selection in the investment process. Much like other debt securities, emerging bonds can be analyzed in terms of parameters determining yield and return, price sensitivity, and properties of the yield curve. The analytical issues are similar to those encountered in the evaluation of other debt securities. Analytical questions of special relevance for emerging market bonds concern collateral and unusual coupon structures in many Brady bonds, the abundance of floating-rate issues, and embedded options.

Collateral associated with Brady bonds requires calculation of stripped yields and spreads or, as alternatively called, sovereign yields and spreads, apart from the usual yield-to-maturity calculations. A stripped yield is derived from the cash flows net of collateral. This is straightforward when only the principal is collateralized, typically by a matching U.S. Treasury zero. It becomes more complex as two, or sometimes three, coupons are also collateralized. Such coupon collateralization can be evaluated by using alternative methodologies which incorporate the probability of default per coupon period.

Spread duration measures the sensitivity of price to changes in sovereign yield, as contrasted to ordinary yield-to-maturity (YTM) or "blended yield." This calculation is necessary for all Brady bonds except fixed-rate, non-collateralized bullets, where ordinary YTM calculations produce identical results. Spread duration is a central parameter in Brady bond evaluation and portfolio construction and management. It provides a measure of the sensitivity of total return of Brady bonds to changes in sovereign spreads over comparable U.S. Treasury bonds or other base yields.

Floating-rate bonds of intermediate and long-maturities were issued by the 15 countries that completed Brady debt restructurings in the 1989–1996 period.[4] Floating-rate syndicated loans of several countries, among them Russia and Morocco, trade actively in international markets. Several countries issued floating-rate Bradys and Eurobonds of varying maturities as part of their financing programs. These floaters have low or negative modified interest duration. Because of the discounts on most of these floating-rate bonds, interest duration provides a weak measure of the sensitivity of these bonds to shifts in the U.S. Treasury curve as well as to the sensitivity of the bonds to shifts in credit spreads. It is therefore essential to evaluate sovereign spread duration for these floaters as part of relative value, total return, and other portfolio summary statistics.

Call options to the issuer are embedded in most Brady bonds and in some sovereign Eurobonds. Corporate bonds are also issued in callable form. As long as call options on Brady bonds were deeply out-of-the-money, their value was safely ignored by investors. Brady bonds traded at deep discounts immediately after their issuance upon exchange of restructured loans. As Brady prices approach levels where the call options offer significant value, option-adjusted-spread (OAS) calculations become necessary as a means of establishing precise valuation, helping portfolio construction, and trading. OAS evaluation methodologies for Brady bonds are not yet standard and tend to produce substantial differences. This partly follows from Brady bonds' complex structures with one or two types of collateral and discrete

---

[4] These countries are Albania, Argentina, Brazil, Bulgaria, Costa Rica, Dominican Republic, Ecuador, Jordan, Mexico, Panama, Peru, The Philippines, Poland, Uruguay, and Venezuela.

coupon patterns. Furthermore, the probability distribution of Brady prices appears to differ appreciably from the lognormal distribution utilized widely to price options.

Market Sensitivity

Emerging market bond prices show, as a rule, high sensitivity to random events and to the impact of changes in international markets. For example, emerging bonds show more responsiveness to shifts in the U.S. yield curve than indicated by intrinsic measures of price sensitivity such as interest and spread duration. That this is so should not be a big surprise. Partly, it can be explained by the prevailing discount in most emerging bonds or other measures of risk premium.

Brady bonds are highly sensitive to conditions in U.S. markets. Sensitivity of the Emerging Markets Bond Index of J.P. Morgan, which is composed mostly of Brady bonds, to changes in the U.S. yield curve in the period December 1990 to March 1996 is −11.9. This means that a change in U.S. rates on average produces a percentage change about −12 times larger in the EMBI index. This was calculated by regression of the EMBI on a U.S. yield curve (3 months to 30 years) weighted to produce interest duration equal to that of the EMBI plus a variable for emerging market shocks (such as the Real Plan in Brazil and the Mexican peso shock of December 1994).

Fixed-rate Bradys show a sensitivity of −15 compared, for example, to interest duration of 10.7 years. The data also show clearly that Brady floating-rate bonds are also very sensitive to shifts in U.S. interest rates. While the interest duration of floating Bradys (April 1996) is only 0.4 years, they show a statistical sensitivity of −8.7. Markets overshoot when U.S. rates fall as credit risk is perceived to decrease. Conversely, markets react negatively to rising interest rates partly because credit risk is negatively impacted. Vanishing liquidity, in turn, compounds these effects. This applies to both fixed- and floating-rate Bradys. Consequently, in periods of weakness in U.S. markets, Brady bonds will tend to overreact. Market sensitivity of Brady bonds to the U.S. yield curve may be presumed to fall as discounts recede.

There is an additional explanation for the sensitivity to the U.S. market. Emerging countries are the marginal issuers in international debt markets and they—and the holders of their debt securities—will be among the first to be affected or benefited by changing patterns of international capital flows. As risk is perceived to decrease, either because of changes in fundamental trend or improved information and analysis, sensitivity may tend to decline.

Can market sensitivity be measured in any systematic and reliable way? Usual calculations, including those implied by the capital asset pricing model, such as betas, or other statistical relationships, similar to those in Exhibit 3, are typically not very stable. Likewise, there are reservations about usual measures of variability, such as the standard deviation, since total return of individual emerging debt securities may show deviations from normality. The U.S. Treasury rally of 1999–2001 was accompanied by mild sensitivity of emerging bonds to the decline in U.S. yields, even in credits with stable credit fundamentals.

Exhibit 3: Sensitivity to Changes in U.S. Yield Curve (December 1990 to April 1996)

	Sensitivity	Interest Duration (years)
EMBI	−11.9	5.4
Fixed Rate Bonds	−15.0	10.7
Floaters	−8.7	0.4

Source: Calculated from J.P. Morgan's Emerging Markets Bond Index.

The heightened volatility of emerging debt securities appears to be related to the size of the risk premium. It may also be argued that often this risk premium may be larger than is implied by the excess volatility of emerging debt securities. While this is debatable, the risk premium is a potential source of excess returns and arbitrage opportunities.

Options on emerging bonds suggest as well that there is a premium paid for excess volatility, apart from premia caused by other factors such as liquidity and shortcomings in option modeling. Implied volatilities usually exceeded actual volatilities for the main Brady bonds in the six years to mid-2001. This is probably derived from generally declining volatility in the market. Nonetheless, the additional risk premia has probably hindered the use of hedging strategies.

Currency or Exchange Rate Risk

Investment in emerging debt securities issued and payable in local currencies presents separate analytical issues in addition to the topics covered above. The central issue presented by these local currency investments is the evaluation of currency risk. This is the risk of devaluation of the currency in terms of dollars. In most instances, devaluation risk could be narrowed further as the risk of a real devaluation of the exchange rate, or a devaluation in excess of the inflation differential with the United States. Measuring the risk of real devaluation enables comparisons among currencies of exchange rate risk.

Investing in local currency securities can provide excess returns over those securities of similar duration in developed markets. Part of this return arises from prevailing local yields which in real terms are higher than required by underlying credit and currency risks. This could be the result of the need to maintain high positive real interest rates during financial stabilization and disinflation or derived from rigid expectations of policy or market behavior.

Evaluating the probability of a real devaluation enables the quantification and cross country comparison of currency risk. In most emerging countries, this requires the evaluation of the exchange rate regime and the policy rule followed. Some emerging currencies are managed according to preset rules, i.e., by pegging to the dollar or a basket of hard currencies, by keeping the currency within limits of a peg, or following a crawling peg. Quantification of the expected devaluation then involves evaluation of the policy rule and the ability of the central bank to follow it.

Following the Asian currency crisis, many emerging countries in Asia and Latin America switched to floating exchange rate regimes. While these make currencies more volatile, in most countries the exchange rate remains a key variable for policy. This means that monetary authorities will employ interest rate or open market operations as tools to influence the exchange rate. Such "dirty floats" and their accompanying intervention may encourage speculation rather than discourage it.

INVESTMENT PROCESS AND PORTFOLIO CONSTRUCTION

Portfolio construction and management are designed to reach the investment objectives within the risk tolerance indicated in the investment guidelines or prospectus. Alternative approaches to portfolio construction are determined by the investment process established to manage the portfolio. The investment process integrates all the elements needed to achieve investment objectives.

Investment Process

Emerging debt securities are generally in the lower segment of the credit quality spectrum. Investing in emerging debt consequently requires an especially rigorous process of country, security, and asset allocation as a means to control risk and provide for consistency of returns. It also requires comprehensive knowledge of trading conditions to provide for efficient timing of entry, exit, and hedging decisions.

While conceivably a variety of investment processes may produce superior and consistent performance, all of them require close integration of research and analysis on the one hand, and portfolio management and trading on the other. Likewise, a variety of investment styles will produce a number of investment processes, for example, very active, arbitrage-oriented portfolios or longer-term, value-oriented approaches.

Independent of the characteristics of the investment process, analytical support for the process involves a top-down component centered on fundamental sovereign, sector, and market analysis and a bottom-up component that incorporates security, corporate, or sub-national analysis. This is then integrated with the timing decision, which requires a sharp understanding of trading conditions for specific securities.

Some investment processes emphasize security selection and the bottom-up aspect of the process. A more technical approach based on pricing volatility as well as credit is also often utilized. Bottom-up investment may be akin to traditional corporate high yield investments. However, in emerging markets, companies operate within a wide variety of macroeconomic and institutional environments. So it is not easy to succeed with a pure bottom-up approach to the investment process, and a foundation of macro analysis is required to provide for differentiation across countries and interpretation of national and global events. Inasmuch as emerging markets become more integrated into the international economy through lifting of barriers to trade and capital, national operating conditions could become somewhat less important. The central premise in a bottom-up approach is security valuation.

A second type of process emphasizes the top-down component and the identification of potential gains from credit improvement or pricing divergence derived from analysis of fundamental country and macro trends. Just as the first approach requires integration with macro analysis, the top-down orientation must involve security analysis as an essential input in the determination of value. This said, since the majority of emerging countries are issuers of a few or even only one liquid security, country and security analysis often converge to the establishment of relative value in terms of individual securities.

In practice, disciplined investment processes involve both a top-down and a bottom-up component. The differentiation comes from the relative importance of each approach and the time dimension of investment decisions. Trading-oriented approaches may emphasize flow analysis, event appraisal, and global market effects, for instance, as the force driving investment decisions. These approaches can be viewed as complementary where they make most sense in managing global emerging market portfolios. For specialized portfolios, they can be considered stand-alone processes, for example, in managing country funds, where the investment process will largely be driven by security analysis.

Portfolio Construction

Construction of emerging market portfolios follows the same principles as other fixed income portfolios. Conceptually, this involves estimating, over the investment horizon, total return and its components for each security in the investable universe as well as estimation of risk characteristics. Research inputs are necessary in the estimation of total return. Risk characteristics could formally be projected from historical data on price and spread movements or from appropriate matrices of correlation coefficients. In practice, however, experience quickly teaches that such calculations have wide confidence intervals and are not stable enough to be interpreted without a great amount of care and sophistication. Quantitative analysis of risk and return and the use of optimization techniques can provide a rough and useful guide to the return and risk parameters for a portfolio.

One approach to portfolio construction involves having core and trading positions within the portfolio. Core positions will be driven by fundamental value to be realized within an intermediate investment horizon, say, three to six months, which in the dynamics of emerging countries can contain a sizable number of fundamental events. Core positions are adjusted as fundamental views change. They are changed in response to price action to realize price targets or implement a stop loss. Positions can also be altered as risk patterns change, for example, because of major deviations in volatility or security correlations. Nonetheless, the idea behind the core is that it should represent long-term views of credit direction, value, and relationship to the U.S. and other more developed bond markets.

Maintaining a core position requires much portfolio discipline and reliable inputs from analysis and research. By reason of the rapid change in emerging nations and the young stage of their financial institutions, governance, and markets, investors are continuously exposed to a substantial flow of information denoting the evidence of change and the resistance to and costs of change. Inevitably, this will be mixed news, often suggesting signals of some impending catastrophe. Exposed to this information flow and accompanying events, it helps to understand why turnover ratios in emerging debt portfolios are high.

A good example of the virtues of having core portfolios is provided by the massive correction and spectacular recovery that followed the devaluation of the Mexican peso in December 1994. The veritable collapse of the Brady bond market after the devaluation was followed with a sharp turnaround. Liquidity effects, including deleverage, rather than any sharp deterioration of fundamentals explained the market reaction, as well as the rapid recovery of prices. Sustaining core positions through this massive upheaval was no mean task, but it paid in terms of ultimately benefiting with the rapid recovery in prices. This would have required strong conviction derived from competent analysis. Instead, most investors tried timing the turning points in such rapid recovery, and a few succeeded.

Trading positions aim to take advantage of mispricing, event anticipation, and other elements which can give rise to temporary deviations from fundamental value. To be effective and to maintain overall control of risk, trading positions should be separate from the core. Of course, in a limiting case, the entire portfolio can be viewed as a collection of trades, subject to constant adjustment. This may work well, but strict accounting of trading and hedging costs must be made to ascertain the merits of the strategy.

Buy-and-hold portfolios are the other limiting case, when there is no adjustment of positions other than resulting from a change in core views. This could be derived from long-term fundamental views, or, in another limiting case, because the portfolio may be entirely passive, tracking a given benchmark. The latter are not used very widely, and it is not difficult to show that emerging market benchmarks are unlikely to be optimal from return or risk characteristics. Buy-and-hold portfolios may have limited room for flexibility when they are designed to match, directly or synthetically, certain desired characteristics such as maturity, duration, or current income. Specific purpose investment structures composed of emerging debt securities often fit well in the portfolios of insurance companies, banks, and other financial institutions.

Ordinarily, portfolio adjustments are made continuously as a result of changes in pricing or trading opportunities, and, less frequently, following the appreciation of shifts in fundamental value. Adjustments are also made when the portfolio profile no longer is within desired characteristics of spread and interest duration, currency exposure, or risk.

In a smoothly working investment process, initiative for portfolio changes may come from traders and portfolio managers, who are close to the price action, or from analysts who gauge credit or macro trends. In cases when fundamental variables drive adjustments, analysts can become involved in the process, even as origination may come from the portfolio management team. In practice, rapid events challenge the portfolio management process, as communication lags, for example, can lead to incomplete integration of the investment process and decisions which do not fully use the potential of the investment management team.

Failure to perform consistently up to expectations is usually the consequence of a failure in appraisal of fundamentals and not of errors in market timing. Of course, gauging the probability and impact of powerful positive or negative events adds value. It does and can provide for a large measure of success in managing emerging debt portfolios. Market and event related decisions, such as the timing of Brady buyback announcements, which have been made by several of the most prominent issuers of Brady bonds (Mexico, Argentina and Brazil), can be gauged by analysis of government finances and cash flows but equally require a keen understanding of capital market conditions.

One of the crucial aspects of managing emerging portfolios is the need to appraise the impact upon emerging borrowers of variables outside the investable universe, that is, financial and economic changes and expectations in advanced countries. This calls for an investment process integrated closely with fundamental and market analysis of U.S. and international bond markets. The flow of causality is almost exclusively from developed to emerging markets. Defensive or hedging strategies, as well as strategies to take advantage of patterns in benchmark markets, are a key part of the portfolio management process.

CONTROLLING RISK

Risk management is an essential ingredient in emerging markets fixed income. Risk management can be viewed in several ways, depending on the dimension of risk. In emerging markets, limiting credit risk, sovereign and corporate, is a central aim of the investment process and of portfolio management.

Risk control also involves mitigating market risk. This often involves reducing price or total return volatility. Investors will have widely differing levels of tolerance for volatility, depending on their ultimate aim. For an equity investor who views emerging debt as an equity alternative, maintaining low or moderate portfolio volatility may not be important. On the other hand, a fixed income investor who aims at seeking excess return over U.S. bonds but maintaining volatility within some upper bound of the U.S. bond market will want to have a different portfolio profile than an equity-oriented investor.

Risk could also be viewed asymmetrically, for example, reducing downside risk. This can also be approached in a number of ways. The selected strategy to reduce downside risk will vary with the prospectus or guideline restrictions. At one end, it may require capping downside price movement by purchasing put options. Or, it may involve selling call options, matching assets and liabilities, or simply lowering interest duration. The cost of reducing downside risk will be gauged in the context of overall investment objectives and may not always be by itself a determining variable.

Another potential area for risk control would be to reduce the risk of under-performance versus a established benchmark or appropriate index. This can be thought of as aiming to keep tracking error within bounds from a benchmark. Tracking error is the standard deviation of the difference in performance (usually total return) between a portfolio and the benchmark. A portfolio guideline or constraint may be to maintain tracking error within 2% for a given benchmark or reference index. Since emerging market portfolios can have high volatility, there could be a sizable cost in potential return for keeping tracking error low, for example, at less than 1%. Limiting tracking error is probably best viewed as an exercise in performance management rather than risk management as it merely focuses on a narrow aspect of the risk dimension.

Comprehensive risk management can also be viewed from a value-at-risk perspective. This would involve ascertaining the potential loss resulting at a given level of confidence from a change in some variable. It could measure, for instance, the impact of a change in the price of the 10-year U.S. Treasury note on emerging Eurobonds in the portfolio at a 95% level of confidence.

Managing Credit Risk

Management of credit risk requires making sound judgments on sovereign and corporate credits. Fiduciary responsibilities usually require that investment managers make independent evaluation of credit risk and do not rely on the judgment of credit rating agencies, brokers, or other intermediaries. Credit agency ratings are an important guide to credit quality and have great bearing on security pricing and price movements. In many cases, investment guidelines impose a constraint based on agency credit ratings. This means that agency ratings have to be taken as a central reference point for investment managers, who, nonetheless, will have to form their own opinions regarding the quality and direction of the credit.

Managing sovereign risk requires continuing assessment of factors that may imply or signal a deterioration of risk. Such monitoring can be done by research analysts or portfolio managers. Dependence on market information, made available by third parties such as banks, brokers, consultants, and the press does not relieve investment managers of their responsibilities versus clients.

The following steps are recommended as part of a continuing credit review process: (1) weekly, or at least monthly, review of all credits in a portfolio; (2) assessment of the impact on capacity to service debt of major changes in operating capability, government policies, external factors, or other exogenous changes; (3) analysis of interrelations among credits focusing on material impact that changes in one credit may have on other credits; (4) mitigation of elements that can lower the probability of serious impact upon the credit; and, (5) use of a value-at-risk or similar approach to quantify overall sensitivity to changes in key variables.

Exhibit 4: EMBI+ Volatility

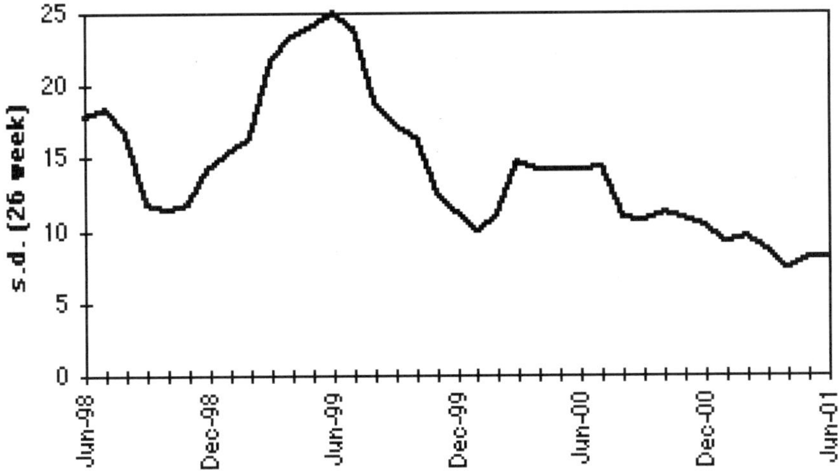

Source: Calculated from J.P. Morgan Emerging Markets Bond Index Plus.

While quantitative techniques and management systems will enhance capabilities, management of credit risk involves a continuing assessment of fundamental variables that affect valuation. A review of technical, flow, or statistical associations that may affect market prices is very useful but not the central aspect. That is, managing credit risk involves making fundamental judgments about intrinsic risk that can potentially be expressed in fundamental value.

Managing Market Risk

Investors in emerging debt usually concern themselves with two types of market risk—volatility and pricing risk. The first is associated with variation of total return or prices as measured by traditional statistical measures such as the standard deviation or the standard error of estimate. In this section we will direct our comments mainly to the management of volatility and not to pricing risk.

Pricing risk is often a consequence of the lack of liquidity in issues with thin secondary markets. While a concern in portfolios that seek value and diversification by investing in minor sovereign and, especially, corporate issues, pricing risk is generally low in all the major Brady bonds and large sovereign issues. One obvious way to reduce pricing risk is to confine investments to major liquid issues.

Emerging debt is usually viewed as one of the most volatile fixed income asset classes. This is generally the case for long duration emerging bonds, particularly Brady bonds and long Eurobonds. On the other hand, as discussed in the next section, portfolios of local currency investments exhibit low volatility when properly diversified.

In the two years since the Mexican peso crisis, the volatility of Bradys and liquid Eurobonds declined steadily as indicated in Exhibit 4. By June 1997, the volatility of the Emerging Brady Bond Index Plus produced by J.P. Morgan (EMBI+), the most widely used benchmark, reached a little over 8% (26 week annualized volatility) from levels of around 25% at the beginning of 1995. Lower volatility is reflected in pricing of options on Brady bonds. Volatility hovered largely around the 8% level in 1998-2001, except during periods of crisis in a key sovereign issuer. The Argentine financial crisis which raised expectations of sovereign default to a high level resulted in an increase in volatility to about 21% in August 2001.

Investors assign variable degrees of importance to volatility. For some investors it is of secondary importance in the context of attaining investment objectives and no restrictions are desired to limit volatility beneath a given threshold. For others high volatility may be undesirable or must be kept within bounds to match liabilities, complement other assets, or to keep within a range of the benchmark.

The following approaches to managing volatility can be used in emerging debt portfolios: portfolio diversification, asset allocation, and sell disciplines. Option strategies are a fourth alternative, which can be used tactically or as an integral part of core portfolios.

Portfolio Diversification

One of the virtues of portfolio diversification is that it can dampen market risk as well as provide a mechanism for managing other types of risk (sovereign, credit, currency, event) over a set of securities. The capability of diversification to dampen market risk is a function of the interaction of price and return among emerging debt securities and with securities in other asset classes.

Correlations and other statistical measures of association show that Brady bonds and Eurobonds are closely correlated. In addition, as mentioned before, volatility is not necessarily dampened in close proportion to the bonds' duration and other intrinsic properties. This means than when considering portfolios consisting mainly of Bradys and Eurobonds, there is only reduced scope for limiting low volatility by diversification within this asset class.

Other alternatives, such as strategies which imply use of options and other derivatives, can reduce volatility but their cost is generally high. This limits derivatives-based techniques to tactical and trading strategies, where they can add the most value. Ordinarily they do not provide an efficient approach to capping downside risk to the entire portfolio. As a comprehensive approach, extensive use of put options, covered calls, and other protective techniques is too costly for all but the most defensive strategies. Derivatives have an important role, when allowed by investment guidelines, in tactical positioning of portfolios or as a means of attaining implicit leverage. The growth of emerging debt derivatives trading in over-the-counter markets and in exchanges offers smooth execution and much more efficient pricing than was possible in the early stages of the evolution of the asset class.

Exhibit 5: Emerging Markets Correlation Matrix
(Monthly data—December 1993 to March 1997)

Index*	Annualized Volatility	EMBI+	EMBI	ELMI	ELMI-EW	S&P 500	Lehm G/C	G. Govt.	MS EAFE
EMBI+	17.81	1.00							
EMBI	17.75	0.98	1.00						
ELMI	7.62	0.54	0.50	1.00					
ELMI-EW	3.74	0.42	0.34	0.82	1.00				
S&P 500	10.22	0.48	0.52	0.13	0.07	1.00			
Lehm G/C	4.89	0.45	0.47	0.02	0.07	0.60	1.00		
G. Govt.	5.14	0.03	−0.01	0.04	0.32	0.27	0.52	1.00	
MS EAFE	10.85	0.20	0.20	0.15	0.05	0.45	0.12	0.36	1.00

Source: Calculated on the basis of index data from J.P.Morgan, Lehman Brothers, and Morgan Stanley Capital International.

*Indices are as follows:
   EMBI+: J.P. Morgan Emerging Market Bond Index Plus
   EMBI: J.P. Morgan Emerging Market Bond Index
   ELMI: J.P. Morgan Emerging Local Markets Index
   ELMI - EW: Adjusted Equal-Weighted ELMI
   S&P 500: Standard and Poor's 500 Stock Index
   Lehm G/C: Lehman Brothers Government/Corporate Index
   G. Govt: J.P. Morgan Global Government Index
   MS EAFE: Morgan Stanley Capital International, Europe, Australia and the Far East Index

One possible diversification strategy, blending Bradys and emerging Eurobonds on one side and local currency emerging debt on the other can often provide desirable risk-return characteristics and a substantial reduction in portfolio volatility.

Asset Allocation

Brady bonds and emerging market Eurobonds have lower correlation with other fixed income and equity securities than among themselves, providing for the possibility of constructing portfolios that will meet a wide range of desired objectives. The correlation matrix in Exhibit 5 illustrates correlations for 1993–1997 among the main emerging market debt indices—the EMBI and EMBI+ and other fixed income and equity indices. In particular, it shows that whereas the EMBI+ and EMBI have moderate correlation with the U.S. bond and equity markets (Lehman G/C and S&P 500), correlation with global bonds (G. Govt) is essentially not statistically different from zero. This suggests that emerging bonds can be a useful complement to global and international bond portfolios. It implies also that adding global bonds to emerging market portfolios could be an efficient strategy in terms of risk-return trade-off for many investors who do not wish to have full exposure to emerging market risk.

Sell Disciplines

Emerging markets debt management requires strict sell disciplines in portfolios and trading strategies. There are several reasons for this emphasis on sell disciplines. Emerging countries are in the process of solidifying policies, institutions, and regulations aiming at providing a constructive environment for long-term investments and market development. But, unfortunately, setbacks and failures occur frequently, sometimes in difficult-to-predict conditions. This calls for continuing evaluation of positions and the taking of swift action to reduce, alter, or eliminate positions from the portfolio.

The high sensitivity of emerging bonds to conditions in global fixed income markets also calls for strict sell disciplines as a defensive posture when faced with potential setbacks in the U.S. bond market or, for many Asian issuers, in Japanese money or bond markets. Alternative management techniques can be used to complement sell disciplines such as careful management of interest and spread duration. As explained above, however, duration strategies do not always work well in emerging debt securities.

Trading-oriented investment processes likewise need to be based firmly on precise sell disciplines. This is, of course, critical in leveraged portfolios or those which employ short positions. Even in portfolios where leverage or short positions are not allowed by prospectus or investment guidelines, tactical positions must be controlled and gains taken or losses curtailed as price action surpasses set limits.

Derivatives can substitute for sell actions and can frequently be a superior alternative. As pricing efficiency increases, options can be employed at lower cost to cushion portfolios from adverse price movements. The long-term fall in price volatility in Brady and Eurobonds supports arguments that volatility is priced reasonably low compared to the historical trend in the market. The contrary argument is that implied volatilities remain higher than historical volatilities for most Brady bonds.

LOCAL CURRENCY MARKETS

Local currency markets are a fast growing component of the emerging debt asset class, driven by the rapid development of capital markets in developing nations. Three factors argue for a swift development of liquid markets for local debt securities: (1) the deregulation of local capital markets; (2) the revolution in pension and savings systems in developing countries; and, (3) advances in price and financial stability by nearly all large emerging nations.

Local debt markets are now the largest part of the emerging debt asset class. Money markets instruments and local bonds in 75 emerging countries exceeded $950 billion by the end of 2000, according to estimates derived from International Monetary Fund, World Bank, and national data. By contrast, the market value of Eurobonds including Bradys issued in international markets by governments and corporations in the same countries is estimated at $310 billion. Some $420 billion of local markets securities are located in Asia, \$290 billion in Latin America, \$100 billion in Africa south of the Sahara, and the rest in Central and Eastern Europe and the Middle East. These numbers exclude many government and corporate bond issues and commercial paper.

The bulk of liquid local assets are money market instruments, mainly government securities. Commercial paper is usually placed privately. A handful of countries have developed liquid bond markets, most importantly Argentina, South Africa, and, to a lesser extent, Chile, the Czech Republic, and Poland. Government bills and notes are traded extensively in most countries, mainly in the interbank market but also in other active secondary markets. Clearing and custody are often sophisticated with book entry at the central bank or other central depository a common practice.

Local instruments are rarely traded offshore in direct form. However, liquid forward markets for local currencies are rapidly developing in major emerging countries and others that do not have strict capital controls. Offshore markets are also found in lesser currencies. By mid-2001, forwards and offshore notes were available in some 35 emerging currencies, most with reasonable liquidity. Banks are also active in designing offshore structures to capture the properties of local money market instruments when trading may be hindered by local operational practices such as lack of proper custody or certain types of exchange controls. These services are gradually becoming more competitive as international banks set up operations in new countries and local banks begin to enter the business through their offshore subsidiaries.

Exhibit 6 provides a sample of monthly money market returns in dollar terms comprising the ten emerging countries in J.P. Morgan's Emerging Local Markets Index (ELMI). The exhibit shows an average correlation of 0.11 from inception of the index in December 1993 to October 1996. Most coefficients in the exhibit are not statistically significant or negative among pairs of countries. Even among countries in some regions, the correlations are low. For example, the average correlation among the four Southeast Asian countries in the matrix is only 0.09.

Exhibit 6: Local Currency Correlation Matrix
(Monthly data—December 1993 to October 1996)

	Argen	Czech	Indon	Malay	Mexico	Philip	Poland	S.Afri	Thaild	Turkey
Argentina	1.000									
Czech Republic	−0.279	1.000								
Indonesia	0.200	−0.260	1.000							
Malaysia	0.239	0.240	−0.032	1.000						
Mexico	0.218	−0.219	0.384	0.145	1.000					
Philippines	0.218	−0.119	0.135	0.191	0.196	1.000				
Poland	0.098	0.564	0.030	0.183	−0.216	−0.086	1.000			
South Africa	−0.161	0.208	0.160	−0.204	−0.178	0.019	0.346	1.000		
Thailand	0.026	0.637	−0.046	0.375	0.106	−0.089	0.583	0.019	1.000	
Turkey	0.239	0.134	0.183	0.198	0.084	0.152	0.049	−0.023	0.154	1.000

* Based on portfolio of 90-day money market securities at market exchange rates.

Source: SS&C on the basis of data from J.P. Morgan.

Correlations increased as shocks hit one or several regional currencies as demonstrated by the Asian currency crisis. A successful speculative attack on one currency encourages speculators and investors to attack a neighboring currency or pull out massively from the currency. Evidence indicates that there are links between attacks on currencies in separate regions, such as pressure on the Philippine peso following the Mexican peso 1994 devaluation and spillover effects from the Thai baht to neighboring currencies and the Czech koruny. On the other hand, the Mexican peso devaluation of December 1994 had little impact on other Latin American currencies. Its impact was largely concentrated on bond and equity markets. Only Argentina experienced a sustained increase in money market rates resulting from the Mexico crisis. Long-term volatility of emerging currency instruments is well below that of emerging bonds, because of lower duration and lower correlation among currencies. For example, volatility of the ELMI+ index of local currency investments of J.P. Morgan has generally oscillated between 2% and 5% in the four years to mid-2001. During the Turkish lira crisis and devaluation of February-April 2001, volatility approached 14% augmented by the sharp movement in interest rates in many emerging economies.

As shown in Exhibit 5, the Emerging Markets Correlation Matrix in the previous section, ELMI had a correlation of 0.02 with the U.S. bond market as expressed by the Lehman Brothers Government/Corporate Index. The correlation with J.P. Morgan's Global Government Index was 0.04 and 0.15 with the EAFE index of Morgan Stanley Capital International. The correlation with the Emerging Markets Bond Index of J.P. Morgan was 0.50, reflecting the ELMI's nearly 25% average weight in Mexican pesos in most of the sample period of December 1993 to March 1997.

Greater diversification can reduce the volatility of local currency investments. This is shown by the use of an equally-weighted ELMI index or ELMI-EW, which could be considered as a potential alternative benchmark. This involves giving a 10% weight to each of the ten components of the standard J.P. Morgan index. Calculations were performed using a monthly sample for the period from the end of 1993 to March 31, 1997. As can be expected, this significantly improves the performance of the index in terms of portfolio volatility and lowers the correlation with the EMBI and EMBI+ index. Annualized monthly volatility of total return of the ELMI benchmark during the period was 7.62% as against 3.74% for the ELMI-EW. Correlation of the ELMI-EW with the EMBI was 0.34 compared with 0.50 for the ELMI. Comparisons with the EMBI+ are 0.54 and 0.42.

Aggressive investors may want to look at high yielding local currency investments such as those provided by countries in earlier stages of stabilization and reform than other emerging countries. In these cases also, diversification of local currency portfolios will help lower volatility as interest rates and currencies are determined principally by domestic factors and events.

The next stage in the development of local currency markets is the formation of full yield curves. In nearly all emerging countries, bonds with an average life longer than two years issued by governments and corporations are held to maturity by local banks, insurance companies, pension funds, and wealthy individuals. Thus there is no liquid secondary market. In some countries, there is limited liquidity of corporate and municipal bonds which can trade at the main security exchanges. Only in a few countries such as Argentina, Poland, and South Africa is there extensive secondary trading of sovereign and corporate bonds issued in Argentine pesos, rands, and zlotys with ample participation by local and foreign investors. With the improvement in credit quality and the growth of financial savings in many emerging countries, issuance in local currency is likely to be transformed in coming years. Corporate and municipal issuers look at the local securities markets as a largely untapped and natural source of financing which could provide an alternative to bank financing as a source of long-term funds.

Chapter 6

A Disciplined Approach to Emerging Markets Debt Investing

Maria Mednikov Loucks, CFA
Director, Emerging Markets Debt Portfolio Manager
UBS Asset Management

John A. Penicook, Jr., CFA, CPA
Managing Director, Emerging Markets and High Yield Debt
UBS Asset Management

Uwe Schillhorn, CFA
Director, Emerging Markets Debt Portfolio Manager
UBS Asset Management

Valuation, risk management, and attribution are familiar tools for professional money managers. An emerging markets debt (EMD) investor can use these tools to build a disciplined investment framework that captures the unique and constantly evolving nature of the EMD asset class. In this chapter, we will outline a complete process for EMD investing including:

- benchmark selection
- overall market, country and instrument valuation
- portfolio construction and risk management
- attribution

The historically high price volatility and low intra-country correlation of EMD creates opportunities for the disciplined investor to outperform his or her benchmark and the peer group. A fundamentally based valuation process provides

---

The authors gratefully acknowledge comments and inputs from their colleagues at UBS Asset Management—Sandra Bieri, Stefano Cavaglia, Norman Cumming, Christoph Kessler, YuChen Lin, Oleg Movchan, Joe Pratt, Günter Schwartz, Parvathy Sree, and Kevin Terhaar.

an anchor to investors when prices wildly fluctuate. Risk management allows the portfolio manager to examine alternative factors that influence a portfolio's return relative to its benchmark. Valuation and risk management come together during portfolio construction so that only well-compensated risks are taken. Finally, attribution provides investors with crucial feedback about the strengths and weaknesses of their investment decisions.

EMERGING MARKETS DEBT INDICES

Although we do not provide a detailed description of emerging market bonds in this chapter, it is worthwhile mentioning several basic characteristics of the asset class before reviewing the selection of an appropriate benchmark.

The EMD universe encompasses both sovereign and corporate issuers; emerging market bonds may be denominated in hard currencies (U.S. dollar, euro, yen) and local currencies. U.S. dollar-denominated, sovereign bonds are the easiest way for investors to gain exposure to EMD because of liquidity and ease of trading. Therefore, this chapter will be written for an investor that gains exposure to EMD mainly through investing in U.S. dollar-denominated, sovereign debt. The approach used here can be expanded to include multiple currencies and corporate issuers.

Due to poorly developed domestic capital markets, emerging market issuers must rely on international investors for capital. Although emerging market issuers differ greatly in terms of credit risk, dependence on foreign capital is the most basic common characteristic of the asset class. After the Asian crisis in 1997, investors realized that even investment grade sovereign issuers can run into problems when access to foreign capital is constrained.

The criteria used for issuer inclusion in EMD indices are either based on ratings, similar to other bond indices, or structural statistics. Non-ratings-based inclusion criteria are favored by investors that believe that emerging market sovereigns share similar risks, particularly the need for foreign capital, regardless of rating.

JPMorgan EMBI Global

The JPMorgan Emerging Markets Bond Index Global (EMBI Global) is currently the most widely used benchmark by EMD investors. The EMBI Global consists of only U.S. dollar-denominated, sovereign bonds and does not use ratings as an inclusion criterion for issuers. The EMBI Global contains countries with investment-grade long-term foreign-currency ratings, such as China, non-rated issuers such as Nigeria, and defaulted issuers, such as Côte d'Ivoire. There are currently 27 issuers in the EMBI Global.[1]

---

[1] All EMBI Global statistics are for 4/30/2001, unless stated otherwise.

Exhibit 1: Emerging Markets Debt Index Comparison
(April 1995 versus April 2001)

Date	April 30, 1995	April 30, 2001
Index	JPMorgan EMBI	JPMorgan EMBI Global
Market Capitalization	$59,519 million	$188,022 million
# of Countries	8	27
# of Securities	20	130
% Latin	88%	65%
Largest Issuer	Brazil (33.4%)	Brazil (19.7%)
Average Quality (Moody's)	Ba3	Ba2/Ba3

In order for a country to be included in the EMBI Global it must meet either an *income per capita criterion* or a *debt restructuring criterion*. Countries that meet the income per capita criterion are classified in the lower or medium income per capita tier by the World Bank.[2] Countries that meet the debt restructuring criterion have restructured their external or local debt within the last 10 years. Popular emerging markets equity indices also use income per capita to classify countries for inclusion.

Once a country meets the criteria to be included in an EMD index, a particular bond must meet certain liquidity requirements. The liquidity requirements used by EMD indices are stringent in comparison to those used by other bond indices. In order to be included in the EMBI Global, a bond must have at least $500 million face amount outstanding, at least 2.5 years to maturity, verifiable prices, and verifiable cash flows.[3] The liquid nature of the EMBI Global Index facilitates the trading of index swaps and allows investors to quickly implement top down strategy changes.

Issuer Diversification Concerns

Lack of diversification is the greatest complaint voiced by investors regarding the EMD asset class in general and about EMD indices in particular. EMD indices have historically had high exposure to a small number of large individual issuers, such as Argentina, Brazil, and Mexico and to the Latin American region overall.

Index providers have responded to investor concerns by switching from ratings-based to GDP/capita-based country inclusion criteria (thus including higher rated sovereigns) and by lowering liquidity requirements. Exhibit 1 compares the composition of JPMorgan Emerging Markets Debt indices as of April 1995 and April 2001. Over this period, the proportion of Latin American issuers in these EMD indices has fallen from 88% to 65%.

There is no argument that EMD indices continue to have extremely poor issuer diversification when compared to U.S. high yield and U.S. investment grade credit indices. While most U.S. high yield and U.S. investment grade credit indices have hundreds of issuers, the EMBI Global only contains 27 sovereign issuers.

[2] In 1999, a low or middle per capita income country would have an income per capita less than $9,635.

[3] As of 4/30/2001, the minimum face outstanding for the Lehman Investment Grade Corporate Index and the Merrill Lynch High Yield Index was $150 million and $100 million, respectively.

Four issuers in the EMBI Global have a market weight in the index that is over 10%: Argentina (19.1%), Brazil (19.7%), Mexico (15.5%), and Russia (10.8%).

The lack of issuer diversification contributes to the large spread volatility of EMD. Between April 1991 and April 2001, the annualized volatility of emerging market spreads was 8.7%, while the annualized volatility of U.S. high yield spreads was 4.7% over the same time period.[4] The impact of large issuers on spreads is magnified by regional and sometimes global contagion within the asset class.

In order to reduce issuer concentration, some investors have moved towards using EMD indices that are not market-capitalization-weighted. These indices shift a greater weight to countries outside of Latin America and increase the percentage of the index represented by less liquid sovereign issuers. The EMBI Global Constrained, for example, is a non-market-weighted index that limits the face amount of debt that is included in the index from a specific issuer. The EMBI Global Constrained has 53% of its market capitalization in Latin America compared to 65% in the EMBI Global.

Exhibit 2 compares the returns, volatilities, and Sharpe ratios of the EMBI Global Index with those of the EMBI Global Constrained. The exhibit shows that between December 1993 and April 2001, the EMBI Global Constrained had higher annualized returns and lower return standard deviation than the EMBI Global.

An investor should not assume that the higher measured Sharpe ratio of the EMBI Global Constrained is necessarily due to better diversification. Since the EMBI Global Constrained shifts more weight to less liquid and lesser known issuers, a higher return may be necessary to compensate investors for increased risk (similar to the small stock effect in equities). Less liquidity also helps to reduce measured volatility because bonds that trade infrequently appear less volatile even though it is difficult to sell these securities at quoted prices. Managers of funds with regular inflows and outflows may have difficulty managing their exposure relative to an index with high weights in less liquid issuers.

Exhibit 2: Comparison of Market-Weighted and Non-Market-Weighted Indices
(April 1994 through April 2001)

	EMBI Global*	EMBI Global Constrained
Type of Index	Market Weighted	Non-Market Weighted
Annualized Return	14.25%	14.53%
Standard Deviation**	17.28%	16.37%
Sharpe Ratio***	0.49	0.53

* The EMBI Global Index was introduced by JPMorgan in the summer of 1999. Exhibit 2 uses back history that was created by JPMorgan.
** Annualized standard deviation measured from monthly returns.
*** U.S. Eurodeposit rate used as cash in Sharpe ratio formula.

[4] Monthly EMD spreads from JPMorgan: EMBI (4/1991-2/1996), EMBI+ (3/1996-5/2000), EMBI Global (6/2000-4/2001) adjusted for defaulted issuers; monthly U.S. high yield spreads from Merrill Lynch (option-adjusted spreads used after 12/31/96).

Exhibit 3: Yield and Spread Change Correlation Matrix for Various U.S. Fixed Income Sectors*
(April 1991 through April 2001)

	EMD	Treasury/Agency	Inv Grade Corp	HY Corp
Emerging Markets Debt Spread	1.00			
U.S. Treasury/Agency Yield	(0.01)	1.00		
U.S. Investment Grade Corp Spread	0.33	(0.27)	1.00	
U.S. High Yield Spread	0.34	(0.24)	0.86	1.00

* Merrill Lynch monthly data used for Treasury/Agency yields, Investment Grade Corporate spreads and U.S. High Yield spreads (option adjusted spreads used after 12/31/96). EMD monthly spreads from JPMorgan are adjusted for defaulted securities.

For non-market-weighted indices, the increased complexity of the weighting rules make it difficult for managers to predict how market events, such as new issuance, will impact the index. Furthermore, the issuer weighting rules are vulnerable to change by the index provider as the market grows.

When investors decide on the appropriate index to use, they have to weigh the potentially improved diversification offered by a non-market-weighted index against the better liquidity and ease of use offered by a market-weighted index. Since an EMD portfolio is usually a small piece of an institutional investor's portfolio, issuer diversification should be less of a concern.

Despite the relatively high volatility of market-weighted EMD indices, their lower correlation with other fixed income markets improves the risk/return characteristics of U.S. bond portfolios. Exhibit 3 shows the correlations between EMD spread changes, U.S. Treasury/agency yield changes, U.S. investment grade corporate spread changes and U.S. high yield spread changes. Yield and spread correlations are measured instead of return correlations to separate the movement of spreads from the movement of Treasuries. Exhibit 3 shows that changes in U.S. investment grade corporate spreads and U.S. high yield spreads have a high correlation with each other, while changes in EMD spreads have a low correlation with changes in both U.S. investment grade corporate spreads and U.S. high yield spreads. Changes in EMD spreads are uncorrelated with changes in U.S. Treasury/agency yields, while changes in U.S investment grade corporate spreads and U.S. high yield spreads have a negative correlation with changes in U.S. Treasury/agency yields.

For the remainder of this chapter, we will discuss how to manage an EMD portfolio against the EMBI Global. EMBI Global is liquid, transparent and widely used. We think it is an appropriate benchmark for investors that incorporate EMD within a diversified portfolio.

VALUATION OF OVERALL MARKET

This is the first of three sections that describe fundamentally based valuation techniques that can be applied in the management of EMD portfolios. This section will discuss valuation techniques for the overall market; the following sections will discuss valuation techniques for countries and instruments.

From April 1991 to April 2001, EMD has returned 14.02% annually with an annualized volatility of 15.77%.[5] This high volatility was exacerbated by a series of crises beginning with Mexico in 1994.

In 1993, Mexico was rated BB+ by S&P. The increasing importance of NAFTA and the expectation that Mexico would soon be investment grade drove spreads to levels lower than warranted by fundamentals. When Mexico devalued the peso, spreads on Mexican debt widened substantially. This triggered similar spread widening in other emerging market countries, especially in Latin America, because investors feared wide range defaults in the region.

After a successful resolution of Mexico's liquidity crisis, optimism returned to the market. Private capital flows to emerging markets and EMD trading volumes reached unprecedented levels.[6] In 1998, in the aftermath of several Asian devaluations, Russia devalued and defaulted on its domestic debt and part of its external debt. The unwinding of leveraged positions following the Russian default caused an increase in risk aversion leading to a dramatic widening of EMD spreads that was not warranted by fundamentals.

These episodes illustrate that an investor must take into account both the potentially large returns and the considerable risks in the EMD asset class. In evaluating EMD, the following issues should be considered:

- relationship of EMD spreads to credit quality
- trends in EMD credit quality
- EMD spreads relative to other asset classes

Relationship between Bond Spreads and Credit Quality

Sovereign credit ratings, provided by the rating agencies, are an assessment of each government's capacity and willingness to repay debt according to its terms.[7] We compare ratings and spreads by assigning a numerical score to the rating of the overall market (calculated by combining historical country ratings according to their market weight).[8] We then standardize the two time series (ratings and market spreads) by calculating their z-scores[9] for each month. We inverted the z-

---

[5] Emerging debt daily return data from JP Morgan: EMBI (4/1991-2/1996), EMBI+ (3/1996-5/2000), EMBI Global (6/2000-4/2001)

[6] According to the Institute of International Finance, net private capital flows increased from US$ 229 billion in 1995 to US$ 330 billion in 1996. According to the Emerging Markets Traders Association, trading volume increased from US$2.738 trillion in 1995 to US$5.296 trillion in 1996.

[7] David T. Beers and Marie Cavanaugh, "Sovereign Credit Ratings: A Primer," Standard & Poor's Research (December 1998)

[8] We took Moody's sovereign ratings. Our rating score starts with 10 for A3 and then declines one point for each rating. All C-rated sovereigns have a score of 0; non-rated and B3-rated sovereigns have a score of 1. We tried different scaling methods but the essence of the results did not change.

[9] The z-score of a value (z) for a variable (v) is calculated as follows: z-score = $(z - \text{mean of } v)/\text{standard deviation of } v$.

score for the spread so that improving credit quality and a declining spread move in the same direction. Exhibit 4 plots the standardized rating against the standardized inverted spread of the market to see how closely the spreads move with the credit quality indicated by the rating score.

Spreads had an annualized volatility of 8.7% between April 1991 and April 2001.[10] Since ratings are long term and change infrequently, they do not provide a timely explanation for spread movements. Even the addition of rating outlooks would not greatly increase the movement of rating changes relative to spreads.

The underlying economic fundamentals of a country determine the capacity of a country to pay its debts. A complementary approach to using ratings is to use the macroeconomic fundamentals directly to assess the credit quality of the market. We measure the market-weighted macroeconomic fundamentals of the individual countries and then aggregate them to compute an indicator for the entire market.

The Market Fundamental Indicator (MFI) is calculated up from the country level. We use eight macroeconomic variables to calculate a Country Fundamental Indicator (CFI) for each country. The variables include short-term serviceability variables such as basic balance, medium-term solvency variables such as debt service ratio, and long-term structural variables such as inflation. Serviceability variables measure short-term debt service and liquidity risks. Solvency variables measure the medium-term financial health of a country. Structural variables are indicators for structural imbalances in the economy that can influence solvency and serviceability in the long run. The definitions of the variables used and an explanation of why these variables are important is provided in a later section describing relative valuations of countries.

Exhibit 4: Emerging Market Debt Spreads (Inverted) versus Market Rating

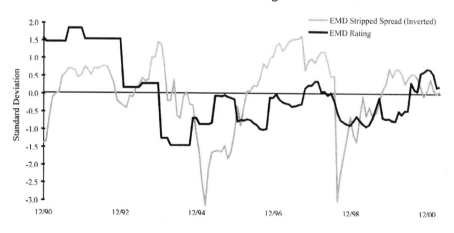

Exhibit 5: Emerging Markets Debt Spreads (Inverted) versus Market Fundamental Indicator

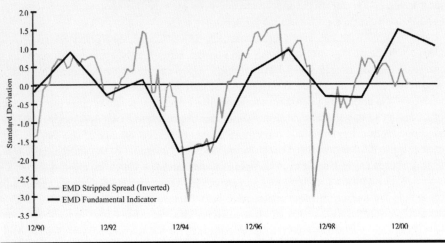

To construct a Country Fundamental Indicator, a country receives a score on each variable for every year.[11] The score is a z-score where the mean and standard deviation are calculated across countries and across time.[12] By calculating the mean and the standard deviation in this fashion, we compare a country's performance both relatively (across country) and historically (across time). A higher Country Fundamental Indicator signifies better macroeconomic fundamentals. Outliers, such as inflation over 1,000% distort the mean and standard deviation, so we place limits on variables. Essentially, this method assumes that once a variable reaches a particular threshold, further deterioration has limited negative impact on the economy.

Country Fundamental Indicators are combined according to their market weights to calculate the Market Fundamental Indicator. Political factors are captured in the Market Fundamental Indicator only in so far as they impact macroeconomic estimates. We can assume that specific political events in the different countries are uncorrelated and neutral for the market as a whole.

Exhibit 5 shows the Market Fundamental Indicator versus the inverted standardized spreads of the market. The historical values for the MFI are calculated from real (ex post) data; the 2001 value is calculated from Institute of International Finance (IIF)[13] macroeconomic forecasts.

---

[11] The annual data are updated on a quarterly basis.

[12] The z-score of country A at time t is equal to $(X_{A,t} - \overline{X})/\sigma_X$ where $X_{A,t}$ is the value of variable X in Country A for time t, $\overline{X}$ is the average of variable X across all countries and time periods, and σ_X is the standard deviation of variable X across all countries and time periods. The Country Fundamental Indicator for country A at time t is the average of the variable z-scores for country A at time t.

[13] The Institute of International Finance, Inc. (IIF) is a global association of financial institutions, created in 1983 in response to the international debt crisis.

Three observations can be drawn from Exhibit 5:

1. Emerging market spreads (inverted) and macroeconomic fundamentals tend to move in the same direction. Accurate macroeconomic forecasts can therefore serve as useful indicators for the direction of EMD spreads.

2. Spreads are more volatile over short periods than are measurable economic fundamentals. They are influenced by global financial conditions and the relative value of other asset classes. Euphoria and contagion seem to be able to explain at least part of the departure of the spreads from their underlying fundamentals.

3. Economic fundamentals have been on an improving trend since the mid-1990s. The deterioration after the Asian crisis in 1997 and the Russian default in 1998 was much less severe and of shorter duration than the decline of economic fundamentals at the beginning of the 1990s.

Long Term Credit Trends

We attribute the improvement in economic fundamentals of emerging market countries to structural reforms implemented in the 1990s and to the general acceptance of capitalism and democracy.

Economic crises in emerging markets have often been associated with high fiscal deficits, weak banking systems, or overvalued currencies.[14] Since the mid 1990s, many emerging market countries have improved important parts of their political and economic systems that address these three issues. In addition, many countries have moved away from isolation towards greater integration with the global economy.

After initial difficulties, functioning democracies and market economies with low fiscal deficits have been created in most of Eastern Europe. Large parts of the banking systems in many EM countries are now controlled by well capitalized foreign banks. Many large countries in the EMD universe liberalized their exchange rates. Mexico abandoned its pegged exchange rate in 1994; Russia, Turkey, Korea, Thailand, Brazil, and Colombia substituted their managed currency regimes with floating exchange rates between 1997 and 2001.

Trade barriers and ownership restrictions for foreigners have been reduced throughout the emerging world. Most Latin American governments have reduced their stakes in loss-making or inefficiently managed enterprises. According to the Institute of International Finance, net foreign direct investments in emerging markets increased from $81 billion in 1995 to $151 billion in 2000.

Democracy and capitalism are now accepted political and economic models in most emerging market countries. Previously, governments' heavy involvement in the allocation of production factors and the fixing of exchange rates

---

[14] For an overview of financial crises in Latin America see Sebastian Edwards, *Crisis and Reform in Latin America* (Washington, Publishing House, 1995).

masked the informational value of economic variables and lowered efficiency. Managed exchange rates, fixed domestic interest rates, and bank financing provided no price feedback for policy makers, increasing the risks of periodic crises. Fiscal accounts and financial statements of government-owned enterprises were not transparent and the ruling political class protected itself from being held responsible. Now, market economies give the necessary price feedback to expose bad economic management and the politicians at fault at an early stage. Better functioning democracies and increased political competition have led to the demise of many incompetent and corrupt politicians and have helped market-oriented reformers.

Emerging Markets Debt Relative to Other Asset Classes

In addition to economic fundamentals, investors should consider the attractiveness of other asset classes relative to emerging markets debt. EMD is a small, risky portion of investors' portfolios. Returns in other asset classes can influence the demand for EMD. According to a study by Goldman Sachs,[15] performance of the U.S. stock market and U.S. high yield spreads are important factors in explaining EMD spreads. In addition to dedicated EMD investors, cross-over investors from other asset classes actively invest in EMD. Because of its similar overall rating, investors view U.S. high yield and EMD as competing asset classes.

Exhibit 6 shows that EMD spreads have been higher and more volatile than U.S. high yield spreads. Market participants have attributed the higher risk premium of EMD relative to U.S. high yield to the following factors:

- EMD historical recovery rates are lower.
- EMD historical volatility is higher.
- EMD is a less diversified asset class.

The first factor (lower historical recovery rates) is based on data that do not reflect the current structure of EMD. The second factor (high volatility adjusted returns) is difficult to assess because of the composition changes and liquidity differences between U.S. high yield and EMD. The third factor (less diversification) is accurate, but it may not be significant to an investor who puts EMD in a diversified portfolio.

The median recovery rate for senior unsecured corporate debt from 1970-1998 was 48% according to Moody's survey of defaulted debt. This recovery rate is based on secondary market prices for corporate bonds one month after they default. Recent recovery rates on defaulted corporate debt have been lower than in the past. For EMD sovereign bonds, a recovery rate of only 20% is typically assumed. This is based on secondary market prices for the commercial bank debt restructurings in the 1980s and 1990s. Since EMD sovereigns have moved from bank to bond financing, low historical recovery rates for EMD might not be a good indicator for

---

[15] Alberto Ades, Rumi Masih and Daniel Tenengauzer, "EMD Valuemetrics," Goldman Sachs Emerging Markets Bond Views (October 23, 2000).

future recovery rates. According to a study conducted by Deutsche Bank, more recent sovereign defaults suggest that the recovery rates on publicly traded sovereign bonds have been at least as high as those on U.S. corporations.[16]

The restructuring of Russia's defaulted Soviet debt and Ecuador's Brady Bonds in 2000 suggest that EMD recovery rates may be higher than U.S. corporate recovery rates. Before restructuring, Russian and Ecuadorian bonds traded at 33 and 36, respectively. Prior to credit deterioration and subsequent default, these bonds traded around 50. The exact recovery amount for these bonds is difficult to calculate because, being themselves the result of a former debt restructuring, they were not issued at par and traded immediately at deep discounts. But investors that bought these bonds in the secondary market prior to credit deterioration/default realized recovery values even higher than the historical corporate bond recovery rate of 48%.

Exhibit 7 shows that historical spread volatility for U.S. high yield has been lower than that of EMD. Because the composition of both markets has changed considerably since the early 1990s, one has to be cautious when using these data to compare the two asset classes.

It is difficult to compare spread volatility in the U.S. high yield market with EMD volatility. In times of high market volatility, U.S. high yield bonds often trade "by appointment" in the secondary market; actual sales often take place two to three points below the quoted bid. EMD has tighter bid-offer spreads and quoted prices are generally executable.

Exhibit 6: Emerging Markets Debt Spreads versus U.S. High Yield Spreads*

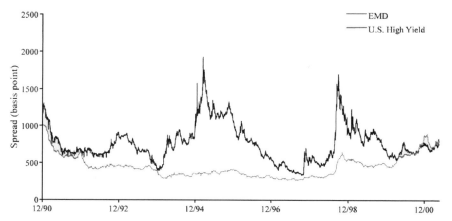

* Emerging debt monthly return data from JP Morgan: EMBI (4/1991-2/1996), EMBI+ (3/1996-5/2000), EMBI Global (6/2000-4/2001); U.S. High Yield monthly return data from Merrill Lynch.

[16] Peter Petas and Rashique Rahman, "Emerging Markets versus Corporate Bond Recovery Values," *Deutsche Bank Emerging Markets Weekly* (April 7, 2000), pp. 7-10.

Exhibit 7: Emerging Markets Debt and U.S. High Yield:
*Return and Volatility Statistics**
(April 1991 through April 2001)

	Annualized Returns		Sharpe Ratios	
	EMD	USHY	EMD	USHY
3-Year	6.12%	0.98%	0.09	−1.35
5-Year	12.64%	5.60%	0.52	0.39
10-Year	14.02%	9.63%	0.60	2.16

* Emerging debt daily return data from JP Morgan: EMBI (4/1991-2/1996), EMBI+ (3/1996-5/2000), EMBI Global (6/2000-4/2001); U.S. High Yield daily return data from Merrill Lynch.

Because EMD consists of a rather small number of different sovereign issuers, as an asset class it is much less diversified than U.S. high yield. The extra risk premium required for this lack of diversification depends on whether EMD is viewed as a stand-alone asset class or as part of a broader fixed income portfolio. As the previous section on EMD indices shows, compared to U.S. high yield, EMD offers less diversification when combined with U.S. Treasury bonds and more diversification when combined with investment grade U.S. corporate bonds.

RELATIVE VALUATION OF COUNTRIES

Despite the fact that emerging market debt is not a very diversified asset class, the performance of individual bonds often differs significantly. During the year 2000, 10-year bonds in Argentina, Brazil, Colombia, and Mexico returned 4.4%, 13.0%, 1.8%, and 12.7%, respectively. These large performance differences show that, even within the same geographical region, country selection can have a substantial impact on portfolio returns.

Relation between Bond Spreads and Credit Quality

Following the approach we used to investigate the price versus value relationship of the overall market, we start by investigating the hypothesis that the movement in country spreads is captured by rating changes. We use Colombia as an example.

On August 11, 1999, Moody's changed Colombia's long-term foreign-currency debt rating from Baa3 to Ba2. As of April 30, 2001, Colombia's Ba2 rating remains unchanged by Moody's. Exhibit 8 shows the spread movements of the Colombia Republic 9¾% due 2009 while the Ba2 rating was in place.

The high spread volatility in Exhibit 8 cannot be explained by the rating, which remained unchanged during the period. Looking at spread changes for bonds in other countries during a period of unchanged ratings leads to similar conclusions.

Since sovereign bond spreads change significantly without corresponding changes in the underlying country rating, we follow the approach used in the market valuation section and calculate a Country Fundamental Indicator (CFI).[17] Exhibit 9 shows spreads versus CFIs for various countries at one point in time. It shows that spreads for countries with similar CFIs vary significantly and that countries with better CFIs don't necessarily have lower spreads. If CFIs explained spreads perfectly, we would see spreads decline with better fundamentals along a line similar to the one drawn on the graph.

Exhibit 8: Spread of Colombia Republic 9¾% due 2009

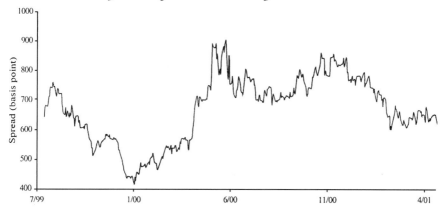

Exhibit 9: Country Fundamental Indicators versus Country Spreads[18]

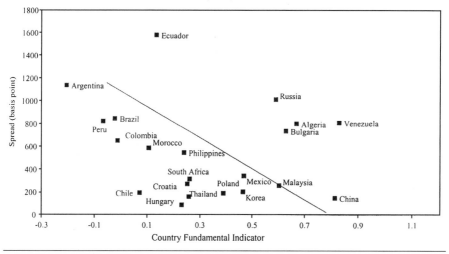

[17] See market valuation section for a detailed description of how Country Fundamental Indicators are cal-culated.

[18] Spreads of 10-year benchmark Eurobonds are used as country spreads. If a country has no Eurobonds, then the country spread is calculated from a liquid Brady substitute.

Sometimes, discrepancies between Country Fundamental Indicators and theoretical spread levels represent opportunities where the market is not properly pricing country risk. Other times, CFIs and theoretical spread levels do not converge because the Country Fundamental Indicator does not adequately measure a country's credit risk. Potential weaknesses of the CFI include the methodology by which different factors are combined to create the indicator, the lack of a time dimension, and the absence of qualitative variables.

Quantitative and Qualitative Considerations in Assessing Country Risk

A country's bond spreads are related to willingness and capacity to repay its debt. The latter depends directly on the amount of obligations coming due at any point in time and the foreign exchange resources and refinancing opportunities available at that time. Country Fundamental Indicators not only contain variables that measure a country's immediate risk (serviceability variables), but they also contain variables that measure the intermediate and long-term risks facing a country (solvency and structural variables). Intermediate and long-term variables, such as the budget deficit and level of inflation, do not directly measure a country's capacity to service the debt in any given period. They do, however, serve as indicators for the quality of economic policy and structural soundness and therefore indirectly determine serviceability by influencing the availability of external financing.

All risk variables (immediate, intermediate, and long-term) have the same weight in the CFI, however their relative importance differs by country. In explaining the spreads and credit worthiness of a country, we look at each variable in the CFI and provide a dynamic analysis of how the different variables might interact. For a given variable, we determine over what time frame it may become important and we analyze how quantitative variables interact (i.e., the transmission mechanisms between variables).

When we valued the overall market, we ignored qualitative variables, such as politics. We assumed that political factors in different countries are independent of each other and that positive developments in some countries would compensate for negative developments in other countries. On an individual country basis, qualitative factors, particularly political factors, become increasingly important, so we include them in our country analysis.

Exhibit 10 shows quantitative and qualitative variables that influence credit quality and spreads. The variables are shown along a timeline. Variables on the left side of the exhibit have an immediate impact on credit quality, variables in the middle of the exhibit have a medium-term impact on credit quality, and variables on the right side of the exhibit affect spreads over the long term.

Quantitative Variables

Most emerging market countries depend on continued access to external financial markets to refinance their debt, to stay current on their obligations, to continue to grow, and to reduce their debt ratios. The variables we consider in our analysis measure the external financing needs of a country and the riskiness of a country's financing position. We calculate our quantitative variables from macroeconomic forecasts provided by the IIF.

Serviceability Variables (Immediate Risk) Serviceability variables measure short-term debt service and liquidity risks. *Refinancing Risk* is an indicator of the size of the debt service that has to be refinanced from external financing sources and is measured as follows:[19]

Refinancing Risk

$$= \left(\frac{\text{short-term}}{\text{debt stock}} + \frac{\text{interest}}{\text{payments}} + \frac{\text{amortization on medium}}{\text{and long-term debt}}\right) \Big/ \text{reserves}$$

A low value indicates less risk.

Different financing sources do not have the same degree of uncertainty. Financing from official sources (multilaterals and bilaterals)[20] does not depend on capital market conditions but is affected by longer term agreements between the borrower and the creditor. Such flows are not subject to market sentiment. Availability of financing from capital markets is more uncertain. It depends on the ongoing credit assessment of the country by the potential investors and on capital market cycles. A high degree of dependence on financing from capital markets puts a country in a much riskier position than a country that depends on official financing sources.

Exhibit 10: Country Variables along a Timeline

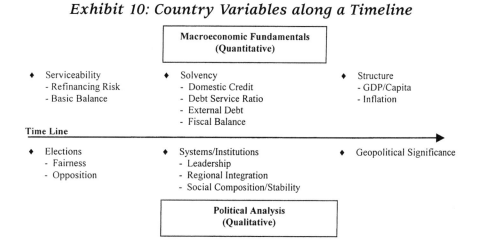

---

[19] The measure includes only interest payments and debt amortizations for external debt, which is total disbursed debt in foreign currencies owed to nonresidents. Short-term debt has a maturity of one year or less.

[20] This includes financial aid from multilateral institutions such as the International Monetary Fund and the World Bank and bilateral aid and loans from individual countries.

Basic balance measures the amount of foreign currency (excluding portfolio flows) that enters the country in any given year. A high value indicates less risk.

Basic Balance = [current account balance + foreign direct investment]/[GDP]

In order to pay foreign currency debt service, a country must attract foreign currency inflows through trade (current account) or through capital inflows. Capital flows can be divided between foreign direct investment and portfolio flows. Foreign direct investments are usually based on long-term planning that is less dependent on business cycles and capital market cycles than portfolio investments, while portfolio flows are a riskier source of financing. A negative basic balance would indicate a potential need for riskier sources of financing.

Some countries have exports that are highly dependent on commodity prices. Since commodity prices tend to be much more volatile than prices for other goods and services, the basic balance for these countries is much more volatile.

Solvency Variables (Intermediate Risk) Strong solvency ratios support a country's access to the external financial market in order to refinance its immediate obligations. The *Domestic Credit Ratio* estimates the ratio of domestic credit to GDP in three years and is computed as follows:

$$\text{Domestic Credit Ratio} = \frac{\left(1 + \dfrac{\text{expected 3-year}}{\text{domestic credit growth}}\right) \times \text{domestic credit}}{\left(1 + \dfrac{\text{expected 3-year}}{\text{GDP growth}}\right) \times \text{GDP}}$$

A low value indicates less risk.[21]

An efficient allocation of credit to productive investment projects should result in higher GDP growth than credit growth over time. If credit is not allocated efficiently, the investment will not produce the desired GDP growth and the domestic credit ratio will increase, indicating over-investment or credit allocation that is not based on profit maximization.

Inefficient allocation of domestic credit was one of the reasons for the Asian crisis. In 1997 and 1998, South Korea and Malaysia had domestic credit ratios of over 150% and Thailand's domestic credit ratio was above 130%. After having addressed some of the problems in their banking systems, domestic credit ratios in all three countries are declining but remain over 100%, well above the 65% benchmark average.

In countries with low credit intermediation, credit growth rates can be significantly higher than GDP growth rates over an extended time period without being a sign of inefficient credit allocation. This phenomenon is well captured in the domestic credit ratio because it is a ratio of absolute levels of domestic credit

---

[21] This is generally the case for emerging market countries but a very low level can also indicate a lack of domestic investment opportunities in the real economy.

to GDP, projected forward. Only countries with high credit intermediation and inefficient allocation will have a high ratio.

The *External Debt Ratio* and *Debt Service Ratio* are indicators for the size of the debt and debt burden in a given period. The calculation of both ratios follows:[22]

External Debt Ratio = [external debt]/[GDP]

Debt Service Ratio

$$= \frac{\text{(interest payments + amortization on medium and long-term debt)}}{\text{(exports of goods and services + income receipts)}}$$

A low value in these variables indicates less risk.

For example, Argentina's debt service ratio exceeds the emerging market country average and has grown from 47% in 1997 to a forecasted 80% in 2001. The debt service ratio is high not only because of Argentina's large interest and amortization payments but also because of Argentina's low exports. Argentina's export to GDP ratio is only 6%. A low export ratio makes it more difficult for Argentina to earn foreign exchange to repay foreign currency denominated debt. In contrast, Chile has a higher debt to GDP ratio but a much lower debt service ratio because of its high level of exports.

Our variables for refinancing risk, debt service ratio, and external debt ratio include corporate and bank obligations because, taken as a whole, corporate and bank debt is a contingent liability for the sovereign. The Republic of Korea provides a recent example of this contingent liability when it assumed a large part of the corporate and bank debt in the 1997 Asian crises.

Primary fiscal balance and interest payments compose the Public Sector Borrowing Requirement, which is measured as follows:[23]

Public Sector Borrowing Requirement
= [primary fiscal balance + interest payments]/[GDP]

Fiscal deficits add to the re-financing burden because they have to be financed, so a low public sector borrowing requirement indicates less risk.

The composition of the public sector borrowing requirement is important. Primary fiscal deficits are an indicator of current fiscal problems and countries with primary fiscal deficits will have increasing debt service in the future. Large public sector borrowing requirements resulting from high interest payments can be an indicator of past fiscal problems. For example, due to high interest rates on past borrowing, Brazil had a 4.6% public sector borrowing requirement in 2000 despite a significant primary fiscal surplus.

---

[22] The debt service ratio includes only interest payments and debt amortizations for external debt, which is total disbursed debt in foreign currencies owed to nonresidents.

[23] Includes central, provincial, and local governments, as well as public sector enterprises.

Structural Variables (Long-Term Risk) Structural variables show potential imbalances that could weaken solvency ratios and debt service ability. Structural imbalances, such as low growth or high inflation might not be alarming if they are transitory. The challenge of examining structural variables lies in predicting when the market will focus on them and when they will lead to a deterioration in serviceability and solvency variables and therefore to a rapid increase in bond spreads.

1. *5-Year Average GDP Per Capita Growth*
Low GDP per capita growth over a sustained period of time make it difficult for a country to reduce poverty, form a stable society, and reduce debt ratios. Higher GDP per capita growth rates indicate less risk.

     Argentina in 2001 illustrates how sustained structural imbalances can lead to deteriorating debt ratios and make an otherwise manageable re-financing program very hard to achieve. Between 1998 and 2001, Argentina was in a recession with below average GDP per capita growth. Despite a large IMF package that reduced refinancing needs, capital markets closed to Argentina at the beginning of 2001 and Argentine spreads widened dramatically. The market doubted whether the economic and monetary model in Argentina could produce sufficiently high growth to avoid a debt trap where debt ratios increase past an unsustainable level.

2. *Inflation (Average Change Year-Over-Year)*
High inflation numbers, especially when combined with high fiscal deficits, can reflect structural imbalances that require drastic adjustment programs entailing fiscal as well as monetary measures.

     In the past, countries have tried to lower inflation by management of the exchange rate. When the government implements a managed exchange rate system, nominal interest rates do not immediately adjust downward, so real interest rates on short term debt instruments (T-bills) become very high. The government creates quasi-arbitrage conditions with no exchange rate risk and high real rates, encouraging speculation as investors borrow money at low rates off-shore and invest in the domestic T-bill market.

     If the government would quickly proceed with the other structural reforms required to put the economy on a sustainable path, interest rates and inflation would decline, the government could free the exchange rate and leveraged positions in the local T-bill market would decline. Unfortunately, an abundance of short-term financing, due to the high real interest rates in T-bills, allows governments to run a fiscal deficit and proceed slowly with structural reforms. High real interest rates increase the country's debt stock quickly. Eventually, the currency peg breaks (Russia 1998, Turkey 2001) with disastrous results for the local banking system and for investors.

Caveats to Using Publicly Available Statistics
According to IMF methodology, external debt is not only issued in a foreign currency but also debt held by foreign investors. This distinction is important in coun-

tries, such as Argentina, where local investors held approximately 60% of foreign currency-denominated debt at the end of 2000. Not including debt held by locals in external debt statistics may understate debt ratios. Statistics regarding the proportion of locally held, foreign currency-denominated bonds vary from country to country.

Publicly available statistics do not take the concessional character of bilateral financing (i.e., financing from one country to another) into account. Bilateral debt service has a political element and may be restructured or rescheduled rather than refinanced. In Ukraine, for example, the official data show that external debt service is $8.2 billion in 2001. As a result, the refinancing risk variable for Ukraine is over 800% (versus an average refinancing risk of 176% for all emerging market countries in 2001). Roughly $6.9 billion of Ukraine's obligations is owed to Russia for gas supplies. This debt is political and is likely to be renegotiated rather than paid in cash. Therefore, Ukraine's refinancing risk is effectively lower than it seems from looking at the size of its official debt service.

Domestic debt is excluded from external debt data. Some countries have very large amounts of short-term domestic debt, and reliable statistics are often unavailable. It is estimated that Brazil had over $130 billion of short-term domestic debt at the end of 2000 compared to an external debt service of $60.3 billion.

Fiscal accounts in different countries often don't follow the same standard methodology. Differences result from the treatment of provincial balances and balances of government agencies. In Mexico, for example, the official deficit in 2000 was 1.1% of GDP versus 4.7% when government agencies and provinces were included.

Qualitative Factors

Anecdotal evidence suggests that certain qualitative variables have in the past often been associated with a change in a country's risk premium. Qualitative factors, even if they are not pressing, need to be constantly monitored because credit events erupt very quickly. By the time an event reaches the headlines of international newspapers, bond spreads have already widened out. Although qualitative weaknesses are often known beforehand, they are not the focus of the market unless they develop into a major problem. Focusing research efforts on pertinent qualitative factors is better than watching events unfold and spreads widen.

Many emerging market countries have defaulted in the past and have gone through periods of sharp economic adjustments and political instability in the last 20 years. Because of the need for many emerging market countries to constantly access international capital markets, the importance of investor confidence in a country's politics and institutions is more important in emerging markets than in developed countries.

Qualitative Factors of Immediate Importance Issues regarding *fairness of elections* and the political program of *opposition parties* can influence a country's risk premium during the election period. The Peruvian spring 2000 presidential election was colored by allegations that the incumbent president Alberto Fujimori orchestrated election fraud. During the election period, bond spreads in Peru widened out over 200 basis points compared to the JPMorgan EMBI Global. Because of the political pressure resulting from these allegations and the discovery of a widespread corruption scandal within the government, new elections were held in June 2001. One of the main contenders in the new election was ex-president Alan Garcia, who had pushed the country into a debt crisis in 1987 because of his populist politics. Political uncertainty that resulted from the candidacy of Alan Garcia lead to another relative spread widening in Peruvian bonds compared to the EMBI Global of 200 basis points before the elections.

Qualitative Factors of Intermediate and Long-Term Risk High economic volatility often requires governments in emerging market countries to implement harsh fiscal adjustment programs. *Political leadership* is required to overcome initial resistance of legislators that often respond to particular interest groups instead of following the government's agenda. It is difficult for a government to function effectively when it does not have a majority in congress, when the government coalition is based on a desire for power-sharing rather than ideology, or when the President is a weak leader.

Potential *integration* into trading blocks or membership in international organizations that are dominated by industrial countries can be powerful anchors of stability and can greatly accelerate a country's reform process. The European Union, for example, requires prospective new members to pass certain economic and political reforms. Because EU membership is strongly backed by the population of the prospective new member state, there is much less resistance to reforms than in countries that don't have that external anchor. In contrast, Mercosur, the Latin American trading block of Argentina, Brazil, Paraguay, and Uruguay, does not have a strong industrialized country as a member. Although Mercosur led to an improvement in trade among its members, it did not lead to milestone political and economic reforms.

Political crises or violent up-risings occasionally occur in countries that have disenfranchised minority groups. An extreme example is Colombia, where guerilla and paramilitary terrorist activities constantly provide negative headlines and keep risk premiums high. A less dramatic example is the uprising in Chiapas, Mexico in 1994, which contributed to a loss of investor confidence that led to the Mexican crisis in December 1994. Countries that don't have these kinds of *social issues*, like Argentina, are likely to avoid this kind of crisis.

The *geopolitical significance* of a country might only become relevant if a country has a major credit crisis. Industrialized countries have in the past, either directly or via multilateral institutions like the IMF, devoted significant resources to prevent economic collapse and political instability in countries if they perceived larger global repercussions. Mexico's common border with the United States and NAFTA membership was a contributing factor in the $48 billion official package for Mexico in 1995. Multilaterals devoted significant financial resources to Russia in 1998 to prevent a devaluation and default; however, the political and economic situation was so chaotic that the problem escalated. Geopolitically less important Ecuador and Ukraine did not enjoy the same kind of support in their latest financial crisis; multilaterals actually actively encouraged both countries to default on private creditors.

Valuation Process Example

To make relative value decisions across countries, one must compare the credit quality and pricing of the different countries to each other. The challenge is to have the resources to acquire in depth credit knowledge of every country and to put their credit quality on the same scale, independent from possible biases of individual analysts. A solid starting point is an analysis of the quantitative variables of a country that can be objectively compared to the values of all other countries in the investment universe. This puts countries on a level playing field and focuses research on the relevant variables. As an example for our general valuation process, the following Russia case study starts with a relative valuation of the quantitative variables and then adds qualitative factors to complete the analysis.

Exhibit 11 shows a comparison of Russia's quantitative variables in 1995 and 1997 in a radar chart. The serviceability ratios start at the 12 o'clock position of the chart, solvency and structural variables follow clockwise. The mean for each variable is calculated by averaging across countries in the investment universe and is represented by the dotted line in the middle of the graph. The gray line represents Russia's relative position in 1995 and the black line represents its relative position in 1997. Variables are measured in standard deviations from the benchmark average. Variables inside the dotted line are better than average, while variables outside the dotted line are worse than average. The external debt variable for Russia in 1997, for example, was one standard deviation better than the benchmark average. The radar chart provides a quick overview of the relative weakness and strengths of a country compared to the average country in the benchmark. The radar chart, combined with a country's spread relative to the market, provides the starting point of our country analysis process.

In 1995, Russia was in the middle of its IMF-led, post-communist macroeconomic stabilization program and was attempting to create a market economy. Inflation was running at over 100%, GDP was declining, and fiscal deficits were high. These weaknesses are clearly shown by the 1995 radar chart. However, external debt write-offs of old Soviet debt left the country with little external debt. Serviceability ratios and solvency ratios (with the exception of public sector borrowing requirement) looked very healthy. To control inflation, Russia's currency was managed in a crawling peg to a basket of Deutschmarks and U.S. dollars. The inflation reduction strategy via a pegging of the exchange rate showed positive results. Inflation declined from 280% in 1992 to 40% in 1996. As described in the section on structural variables, the crawling peg and rapidly declining inflation led to high real interest rates and a sharp inflow of capital into the local currency-denominated T-bill market. Private and government-owned Russian banks provided foreign investors with currency hedges that guaranteed dollar returns far superior to the return on the longer-dated, dollar-denominated Russian Eurobonds.

By 1997, Russia's refinancing position had dramatically worsened and fiscal deficits were still very high. The inflation problem had been reduced but a short-term serviceability problem had been created.

Qualitative variables were worrisome. The country was at war in Chechnya. Red tape, white-collar crime, and corruption were obstacles to foreign investment. Institutions did not work properly, the federal government had little control over the regions, and president Yeltsin had lost his ability to actively lead and govern the country. Exhibit 12 shows that Russia's Eurobond spreads, trading only 30 basis points wider than market spreads in the spring 1998, did not reflect the looming quantitative and qualitative risks. Comparing relative spreads with quantitative and qualitative factors in early 1998 supported underweighting Russian bonds in early 1998.

International investors speculated that, because of its geopolitical significance, Russia was "too big to fail" and that the international community would come to rescue if needed. In fact, the IMF approved an $11.2 billion financial support program in July 1998 and immediately disbursed $4.6 billion. A month later, Russia devalued and contemporaneously defaulted on its local currency-denominated T-bills and Soviet era external debt. Russia did not, however, default on its Eurobonds.

Exhibit 11: Russian Quantitative Variables in 1995 and 1997 (Radar Chart Comparison)

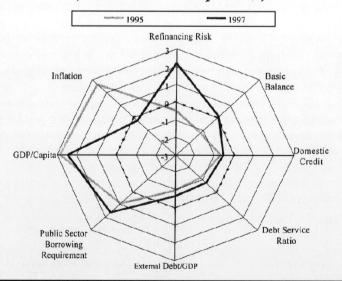

Exhibit 12: Spread of Russia Republic 10% due 2007 less Market Spread

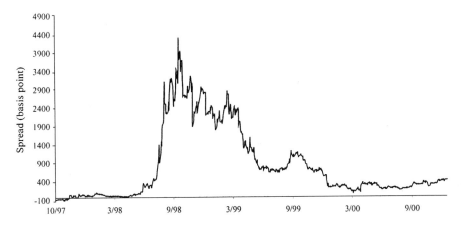

Exhibit 13: Russian Quantitative Variables in 1997 and 2000 (Radar Chart Comparison)

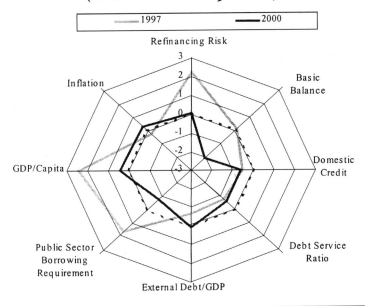

Exhibit 13 is a radar chart comparing Russian macroeconomic variables in 1997 and 2000. Default on its Soviet-era external debt greatly improved Russia's refinancing picture. Currency depreciation and high oil prices led to an 18% current account surplus and a positive 18.8% basic balance in 2000. Accurate forecasts for Russia's serviceability position in 2000 were available in fall 1999 when Russia's Eurobond spreads were still trading 1,400 basis points above the market as indicated in Exhibit 12. Comparing relative spreads with quantitative and qualitative factors in late 1999 supported overweighting Russian bonds.

In spring 2000, the government under President Putin had secured a working coalition in the Duma for the first time since communism and was able to actively approve market friendly and institution building reforms. Although Russia's Eurobond spreads had declined substantially relative to market spreads, improved political conditions supported a continued overweight of Russian bonds in the Spring of 2000.

Overall Market Valuation Implications for Country Selection

Overall market spread expectations should be taken into account in country allocation. EMD country spreads tend to move in the same direction if there are no overriding country issues. When market spreads decline, countries with relatively high spreads (high risk) tend to outperform countries with lower spreads (low risk). If the valuation of the overall market indicates that EMD is undervalued, a portfolio's cash position should be small and the portfolio should have more weight in riskier countries. If the valuation of the overall market indicates that EMD is overvalued, a portfolio's cash position should be increased and the portfolio should have more weight in defensive, low risk countries. The risk management and portfolio construction section elaborates further on the relative riskiness of countries.

RELATIVE VALUATION OF INSTRUMENTS

Overall market exposure and country weights are the most important return contributors in emerging markets. Therefore, most research and investor interest is concentrated at the market or country level. However, performance of bonds within the same country can differ substantially and contribute significantly to performance. This section describes features of emerging market bonds that can cause differences in instrument performance and discusses some techniques to value different bonds within the same country.

Analysis of the Eurobond Spread Curve

The purest form of a country's credit risk is represented by internationally-issued, bullet-maturity, fixed-coupon Eurobonds; all other instruments usually carry an extra premium to basic Eurobonds. Exhibit 14 shows the spreads of Mexican and Argentine dollar-denominated Eurobonds versus their spread duration. Most of the spreads of Eurobonds within the same country can be explained by spread duration, spread convexity, and the implied probability of default.

Exhibit 14: Eurobond Curves in Mexico and Argentina
(4/30/2001)

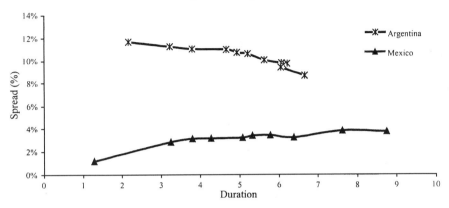

Spread Duration

Spread duration measures the price sensitivity of a bond due to changes in spread (risk premium). The shapes of the two spread curves in Exhibit 14 are quite different from each other. Mexico's spreads are much lower and the curve is relatively smooth and upward sloping. Argentina's spreads are much higher, the individual bonds are more scattered, and the curve is inverted.

Mexico's spread curve is a typical upward sloping spread curve. An upward sloping spread curve is consistent with risk aversion if we assume parallel shifts in the spread curve because higher-duration bonds will have greater price volatility than lower duration bonds.

Spread Convexity

Spread convexity measures the rate of change of duration as spreads change and is used (along with duration) to approximate the change in a bond's price when spreads change.[24] A high convexity adds value to a bond. Due to the long duration and high spread volatility of many sovereign bonds, spread convexity plays a more important role in the management of emerging market bond portfolios than interest rate convexity plays in the management of U.S. corporate bond portfolios. Spread convexity explains the slight downward slope at the very end of the Mexican Eurobond curve because longer maturity bonds have more convexity. The longest instruments on the Mexican Eurobond curve are due in 2016 and 2026. The difference in spread convexity between the Eurobond due in 2026 and the Eurobond due in 2016 is 46.52. If we estimate the potential Mexican Eurobond spread change by their 90-day historic standard deviation (15.5%), then the con-

---

[24] The percentage change in dollar price due to spread movements can be approximated by the following formula: price change = (spread duration) × (spread change) + ½ (spread convexity) × (spread change)^2

vexity value of the Eurobond due 2026 is 54 cents (½ × 46.52 × 0.1552) higher than that of Eurobond due 2016. A 54 cent convexity value equates to 5 basis points of value in the Eurobond due 2026 relative to the Eurobond due 2016 and may explain why the long end of the Mexican curve is downward sloping.

Implied Probability of Default

Bonds with a very high probability of default trade on a percentage-of-par (i.e., price) basis instead of a spread basis because past debt restructurings have been done on a percentage-of-par basis. In a percentage-of-par restructuring, the potential loss for high dollar priced bonds is higher than for low dollar priced bonds; this leads to an inverted spread curve because shorter bonds typically have higher prices. The precedent of percentage-of-par restructurings is changing. During Ecuador's debt restructuring in the summer of 2000, debt write-offs were calculated on a net present value (NPV) basis. If investors expect a NPV-based debt restructuring, an issuer's spread curve should be flat, not inverted.

The inverted spread curve in Argentina in Exhibit 14 indicates high default risk and investor expectation of a percentage-of-par debt write-off. Investor expectations regarding the probability of default can be calculated from bond prices. The *implied probability of default* (IPD) is the default probability that sets the expected return on the bond equal to the risk free rate. Therefore, it is also called *risk neutral default probability*. The implied probability of a bond with three years to maturity and annual coupon payments can be calculated by solving the probability tree shown in Exhibit 15 for q.

Exhibit 15: Solving for Implied Probability of Default (IPD) using a Probability Tree

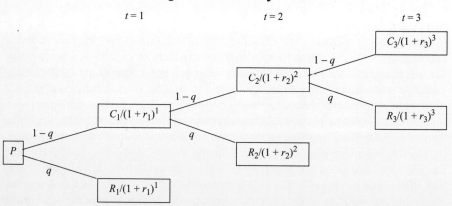

Where P denotes the price of the bond, q is the IPD, C are cash flows (coupons and principal, discounted at the risk free rate, r), and R is the present value of the recovery rate (discounted at the risk-free rate).

Exhibit 16: Implied Probability of Default Term Structure in Argentina (4/30/2001)

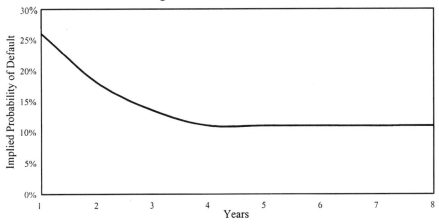

When bonds trade on price and the spread curve is inverted, the IPD of short duration bonds is higher than the IPD of long duration bonds. A higher IPD in the short term makes economic sense because high IPD levels are unsustainable for a long period of time (either the country defaults or it overcomes the crisis and default probability starts to decline). Since investors cannot accurately assess a country's default risk in the long run, a country in crisis will have a IPD term structure that is declining for the first few years and then constant after a certain period of time.

Applying the probability tree approach to bonds independent of one another will lead to different IPDs for overlapping cash flows; this is inconsistent. To generate a consistent term structure of default, one can calculate the IPD for short-term bonds and then apply the short-term IPD for the cash flows of longer-term bonds to find the longer term IPD (bootstrapping method). Applying this method to the spread curve in Argentina and assuming that the probability of default remains constant after four years generates the term structure of default probability in Exhibit 16.[25]

An investor can use this term structure of default probabilities to calculate consistent prices for long duration bonds. These prices can then be compared to market prices to make relative value decisions.[26]

There are more elaborate ways to calculate IPD such as taking the volatility of a country's credit risk into account. Elaborate methods often suffer from too much complexity and judgmental input. In the end, a model that is able to describe bond price behavior will serve the investor best.

---

[25] Because Argentina does not have a Eurobond with maturity in 2002, we calculated the IPD for the first year from default swap rates.
[26] This approach ignores the influence of different repo rates and differences in default swap rates.

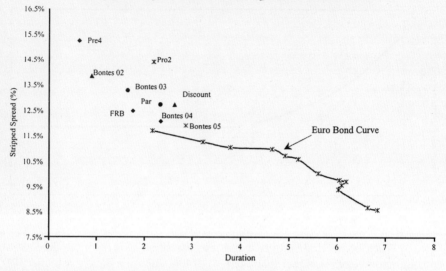

Exhibit 17: Argentine Instruments:
Stripped Spread versus Spread Duration

Emerging Market Bonds that Do Not Trade on the Eurobond Spread Curve

So far, we have concentrated our analysis only on Eurobonds. Exhibit 17 shows spreads and durations for a variety of U.S. dollar-denominated bonds in Argentina including Eurobonds, Brady bonds, and domestically issued bonds. Exhibit 17 illustrates that Argentine U.S. dollar-denominated bonds can have radically different spreads despite similar durations.

Spread differences between bonds with similar durations can be attributed to differences in credit ranking, collateralization, liquidity and repo rates, and instrument type. Below the characteristics of different EMD instruments relative to basic Eurobonds are outlined.

Credit Ranking

Credit ranking of an emerging market bond depends on the bond's original issuance, the legal status of the bond, payment guarantees and the identity of the issuer.

Original Issuance Some bonds are issued as a result of a debt restructuring or forced debt exchange. If a country has insufficient financial resources to service all its debt, it may choose to selectively default on previously restructured debt and continue to service its regularly issued Eurobonds. Eurobonds represent a country's future access to the capital markets, so there is an incentive to service Eurobonds above other types of debt. Sometimes restructured debt has the same legal protection as new Eurobond debt, and sometimes it clearly does not; in many cases it is unclear. Legal recourse for bondholders against sovereigns that selectively default is limited and has only rarely been tested in courts.

Brady bonds resulted from a comprehensive sovereign loan restructuring. Because they had been restructured before, Brady bonds were initially rated lower than Eurobonds and traded at significantly higher spreads than Eurobonds. The rating agencies eventually increased the rating of Brady bonds to that of Eurobonds. Many countries have been buying back their Brady bonds or exchanging Brady bonds for Eurobonds. This has led to a reduction in the spread difference between Brady bonds and Eurobonds. Although Brady bonds are legally *pari passu* to sovereign Eurobonds and carry the same rating, in many cases the spread difference between Brady bonds and Eurobonds has not completely gone away.

Russia successfully selectively defaulted on previously restructured Former Soviet Union (FSU) bank debt.[27] The FSU bank debt was issued by Vneshekonombank, a fully government-owned export bank in Russia. The market generally viewed the FSU bank debt as obligations of the Russian Republic. When Russia issued its first Eurobond in 1997, it made the Eurobond senior to the FSU debt in order to secure lower funding costs; the prospectus of the new Eurobond did not include cross-default language to the FSU debt.

In 1998, Russia defaulted on its restructured FSU debt, but continued to service its Eurobonds. The subsequent restructuring of the FSU debt resulted in the issuance of more Eurobonds. To make the restructuring acceptable to the holders of the FSU debt, the Russians had to include prospectus language that would prevent the new Eurobonds from being subordinated again to regularly issued Eurobonds. Even so, it is unclear if such language will effectively protect bondholders from a selective default. As of April 2001, Russian Eurobonds that were issued in the FSU debt restructuring still trade at higher spreads than regularly issued Russian Eurobonds.

Due to weak legal protection of sovereign bondholders, the issuer's incentives to selectively default should not be underestimated. History shows that doubts concerning effective subordination will lead to a relative spread widening of bonds issued as the result of a debt restructuring, particularly if default risk is high.

Legal Status Usually a sovereign issues domestic currency bonds and notes under domestic law and foreign currency bonds and notes under either New York or United Kingdom law. In some cases, however, sovereigns issue dollar-denominated instruments under domestic law. The enforcement of claims under domestic law is more difficult because the investor has to go through domestic rather than international courts, so bonds issued under domestic law usually trade at higher spreads than bonds issued under international law.

Exhibit 17 illustrates this point by comparing the spreads of the similar duration, dollar-denominated bonds in Argentina. The "Pro2 Bocones" and the "Bonte" due 2004 are domestically issued and the Eurobond due in 2003 is issued

---

[27] In contrast, Ecuador unsuccessfully tried to selectively default on part of its Brady bonds in 1999.

under New York law. The spread differential between domestic and internationally issued bonds is directional: it becomes larger when spreads increase and vice versa.

Partial Payment Guarantees Some countries have issued bonds that are partially guaranteed by the World Bank. For example, the cash flows of the Colombia World Bank-backed bond are structured as an annuity payable every six months with the World Bank (rated AAA) guaranteeing the first two consecutive payments. As long as Colombia is current on its interest and amortization payments, the World Bank guarantee will continue to roll forward to the next semiannual payment. If Colombia defaults on its payments to bondholders, the World Bank will make the next payment. This will trigger a default of the Republic of Colombia to the World Bank, which has preferred creditor status. The rating agencies posit that the likelihood of default to the World Bank is much lower than the likelihood of default on regular bonded sovereign debt.[28] Colombian World Bank-backed bonds are rated BBB/Baa1, whereas the Republic of Colombia has a rating of Ba2/BBB.[29]

Partially guaranteed sovereign bonds are relatively new to the market. They are not very well understood, and the relative credit quality of guaranteed bonds has not been fully tested. World Bank-backed bonds in Argentina actually widened out relative to the Argentine Eurobonds when Argentina's credit quality deteriorated in the spring of 2000.[30]

Issuer The central government, government agencies, provincial governments, and corporations issue external dollar-denominated bonds. These different issuers within a country have different credit quality. Sovereign bonds issued by the central government generally have lower credit risk than other bonds. There are, however, some cases where corporations have better credit quality than the central government either because of their unique credit features or because they have better access to capital markets. Both Moody's and S&P rate some corporations higher than their sovereign ceiling.

Bonds of government agencies that do not have explicit guarantees from the central government like *Banco Nacional de Desenvolvimento Economico e Social* (BNDES) in Brazil or Korean Development Bank (KDB) in Korea usually also have more credit risk and carry an extra spread over sovereign Eurobonds.

The spread difference between riskier bonds and the sovereign Eurobond curve declines when Eurobond spread levels decline and widens when sovereign spreads widens.

---

[28] Standard & Poor's, "How Preferred Creditor Support Enhances Ratings," *Standard & Poor's CreditWeek* (June 1999).

[29] The standard method of comparing spreads of partially guaranteed bonds to spreads of non-guaranteed bonds is to calculate their stripped spreads. The calculation of stripped spreads for collateralized Brady bonds is explained in the section on collateralization. However, applying a similar methodology to partially guaranteed bonds does not take into account the World Bank's preferred creditor status.

[30] Argentine World Bank-backed bonds were issued with an investment grade rating from S&P. Due to subsequent declines in Argentina's long-term debt rating, the World Bank-backed bonds were downgraded to BB.

Collateralization

The principal payments of some Brady bonds are collateralized by U.S. Treasury zero-coupon bonds. These bonds are effectively a combination of a risk-free Treasury bond and a risky emerging market bond. To compare the risk premium for collateralized bonds to the risk premium of non-collateralized bonds, one should calculate spreads after stripping out the collateral. The so-called "stripped spread" is found by discounting the collateral at the appropriate spot interest rate and subtracting this collateral value from the bond's market price. The remainder is the price of the risky sovereign cash flows for which the standard procedure of finding the credit spread can be applied.

Many investors cannot effectively hedge the Treasury component of collateralized Brady bonds and therefore receive a low blended yield, which is a combination of the stripped yield and the yield of U.S. Treasuries. To compensate for the lower blended yield, investors require an extra premium for holding collateralized bonds. Therefore, collateralized bonds trade at higher stripped spreads than non-collateralized bonds.

Liquidity and Repo Market Considerations

Different issuers within a country have different liquidity. Eurobond and Brady bonds issued by the central government can be traded in institutional scale and have better liquidity than other bonds. Liquidity in corporate bonds can be especially poor if the corporation has just one issue outstanding and is not covered by multiple dealers.

In the past, massive short sales of the more liquid bonds have led to very low or even negative repo rates. Investors that hold the shorted bond can generate extra returns in the repo market.

Instrument Type

Not all fixed income instruments are issued as bonds. Some are issued in other legal forms such as trust certificates and loan participations. Because settlement of these alternative issue types is sometimes more complex and some investors cannot invest in these issues for regulatory reasons, these instruments often carry an additional spread over standard bonds.

Country Relative Valuation Implications for Instrument Selection

Country spread expectations should be taken into account during instrument selection. If a country is undervalued and spreads are expected to decline, a portfolio should be overweight long duration bonds if the spread curve is upward sloping; if the spread curve is inverted, a portfolio should be overweight bonds with high implied probability of default (usually shorter duration bonds). Under a declining spread scenario, the following type of bonds would outperform: subordinated bonds, uncollateralized bonds, illiquid bonds, and bonds with a non-standard structure.

Conversely, if a country is overvalued and spreads are expected to increase, a portfolio should be overweight shorter duration bonds if the spread curve is upward sloping; if the spread curve is inverted, a portfolio should be overweight bonds with a lower dollar price. Under an increasing spread scenario, the following type of bonds would outperform: senior bonds, collateralized bonds, liquid bonds, and bonds with a standard structure. The risk management and portfolio construction section elaborates further on the relative riskiness of countries.

RISK MANAGEMENT AND PORTFOLIO CONSTRUCTION

How does an EMD investor incorporate his views regarding the overall market, relative country attractiveness, and instrument choices into a portfolio? How can an investor incorporate macroeconomic views into an EMD portfolio?

The valuation system described in the previous sections only provides part of the answer to the questions above. A valuation system compares value and price and determines the attractiveness of the overall market and the relative attractiveness of countries and instruments. A detailed risk management system allows the EMD portfolio manager to incorporate his valuation views in the construction of a portfolio.

An active investor establishes country and instrument over/underweights relative to his chosen benchmark. The exposure measurement techniques described in this section are calculated relative to a benchmark unless explicitly stated otherwise. Portfolio exposure can vary from simple percentage over/underweights to elaborate tracking error decomposition. We will discuss the pros and cons of various risk management techniques as they apply to an EMD portfolio.

Basic Exposure Measurement

Percentage market weight is the simplest way to measure risk exposure. It is the exposure of a portfolio to the return of a particular instrument or country. Instrument weights are summed together to calculate the weight for a particular country.

During periods of extreme market distress securities start to trade on a price basis rather than a spread basis.[31] When securities trade on a price basis, percentage exposure correctly measures a portfolio's exposure to a distressed issuer.

In a normal market environment the return of an EMD instrument is influenced by U.S. interest rate risk, instrument spread risk, country spread risk, and overall market spread risk. Percentage market weight does not specifically address these different risks.

An instrument's sensitivity to U.S. interest rate changes and issuer spread changes is measured by an instrument's interest rate duration and spread duration,

---

[31] When there is a high probability that an issuer will default, securities trade on a price basis rather than a yield or spread basis. This behavior is driven by the market perception that all bonds of a defaulted issuer will be restructured on a percentage-of-par basis as described in the instrument valuation section.

respectively. Spread duration is higher than interest rate duration for floating rate bonds; interest rate duration is higher than spread duration for collateralized bonds.

U.S. interest rate risk can be measured on an overall portfolio basis by calculating the interest rate duration of the portfolio relative to the benchmark. Investors may choose to hedge U.S. interest rate risk by using U.S. note and bond futures to separate their U.S. interest rate views from their EMD credit views.

While U.S. interest rate exposure is aggregated for the entire portfolio, contribution to spread duration (CTD) relative to a benchmark should be shown by country and by instrument so the portfolio manager can determine exactly where credit risk is taken. The calculations for instrument relative CTD are as follows:

$P(z)$ = weight of instrument z in portfolio
$B(z)$ = weight of instrument z in benchmark
$D(z)$ = spread duration of instrument z

Instrument relative CTD = $D(z) \times [P(z) - B(z)]$

Country relative CTD is the sum of instrument relative CTDs for all of the instruments in the country. The spread duration exposure for the overall portfolio is the sum of the CTDs.

Exhibit 18 is a risk report for an EMD portfolio relative to the EMBI Global benchmark. U.S. interest rate duration and spread duration are shown for the aggregate portfolio; percentage market weight exposure and relative CTD are broken out by country. Relative U.S. interest rate duration is hedged with U.S. Treasury futures.

The U.S. interest rate duration of the portfolio is similar to that of the benchmark. Despite a cash exposure of 3.4%, the portfolio has more spread duration relative to the benchmark because it has an overweight in higher spread duration instruments.

Country exposures vary depending on the risk measurement methodology used. For example, the portfolio has more percentage market weight exposure in Bulgaria than in Qatar, but Qatar contributes more to the portfolio's spread duration than Bulgaria. These results indicate that the portfolio has more exposure to spread movements in Qatar than in Bulgaria because the portfolio has longer duration Qatar securities. However, the portfolio has more exposure to a massive credit event in Bulgaria than in Qatar because the percentage market weight exposure to Bulgaria is higher.

Beta-Adjusting Spread Durations

Since EMD securities are risky assets, a decrease in investor risk tolerance can lead to an increase in spreads for EMD issuers. However, an increase in spreads for the overall market does not uniformly affect spreads of individual EMD issuers. Spreads of risky credits such as Russia and Brazil tend to increase more during a market selloff than spreads of less risky credits such as Mexico and Poland; risky credits tend to outperform when market spreads decrease. Exhibit 19 shows the spread change for the market and for various countries during a market rally and a market selloff using weekly data.[32] We define a spread decline of 50 or more basis points during a week as a market rally (18 instances) and a spread increase of 50 or more basis points during a week as a market selloff (21 instances).

Exhibit 18: Basic Risk Report (4/30/2001)

	Portfolio	Benchmark	Relative
Cash	3.4%	0.0%	
Interest Rate Duration	4.92	4.92	1.00
Spread Duration	4.96	4.66	1.06

	Percentage Market Weight (%)			Contribution to Spread Duration		
Country	Portfolio	Benchmark	Difference	Portfolio	Benchmark	Difference
Algeria	—	0.5	(0.5)	—	0.01	(0.01)
Argentina	19.0	19.1	(0.1)	0.65	0.73	(0.08)
Brazil	23.7	19.7	4.0	1.27	0.92	0.35
Bulgaria	5.8	1.9	3.9	0.26	0.08	0.18
Chile	—	0.3	(0.3)	—	0.02	(0.02)
China	—	1.1	(1.1)	—	0.05	(0.05)
Colombia	1.7	1.9	(0.2)	0.08	0.09	(0.01)
Côte d'Ivoire	—	0.1	(0.1)	—	0.00	(0.00)
Croatia	—	0.4	(0.4)	—	0.01	(0.01)
Ecuador	—	1.0	(1.0)	—	0.05	(0.05)
Hungary	—	0.4	(0.4)	—	0.01	(0.01)
Korea	1.7	5.6	(3.9)	0.09	0.21	(0.12)
Lebanon	—	0.3	(0.3)	—	0.00	(0.00)
Malaysia	—	2.5	(2.5)	—	0.13	(0.13)
Mexico	14.3	15.5	(1.2)	0.81	0.83	(0.02)
Morocco	1.1	0.9	0.2	0.03	0.03	0.01
Nigeria	—	1.6	(1.6)	—	0.04	(0.04)
Panama	1.9	2.1	(0.2)	0.15	0.14	0.01
Peru	0.1	1.1	(1.0)	0.01	0.07	(0.06)
Philippines	1.2	2.2	(1.0)	0.09	0.15	(0.06)
Poland	—	1.9	(1.9)	—	0.12	(0.12)
Qatar	3.3	—	3.3	0.31	—	0.31
Russia	19.2	10.8	8.4	1.06	0.56	0.50
SouthAfrica	—	1.0	(1.0)	—	0.06	(0.06)
Thailand	—	0.3	(0.3)	—	0.02	(0.02)
Turkey	—	2.8	(2.8)	—	0.13	(0.13)
Ukraine	0.8	0.4	0.4	0.02	0.01	0.01
Venezuela	2.7	4.8	(2.1)	0.13	0.20	(0.07)
Cash	3.4	—	3.4	—	—	—
Total	100.0	100.0	—	4.96	4.66	0.29

[32] Stripped spread data are from JPMorgan from 12/31/97 to 4/30/01. (Data series start at 12/31/97 because EMBI Global Country Sub-Indices are not available before that date.) EMD market spreads are adjusted for defaulted issuers.

Exhibit 19: Country Spread Changes During Market Rallies and Selloffs (December 1997 through April 2001)

Country	Average Weekly Spread Δ (bps)	
	Market Rally	Market Selloff
Market	−92	110
Argentina	−75	122
Brazil	−106	123
Bulgaria	−64	81
Colombia	−46	40
Ecuador	−140	158
Korea	−37	29
Mexico	−60	71
Morocco	−58	103
Nigeria	−63	108
Panama	−22	33
Peru	−49	55
Philippines	−41	41
Poland	−17	26
Russia*	−310	371
Turkey	−22	44
Venezuela	−132	137

* The spread change numbers are very high because the time period examined includes the Russian crisis, which had a significant impact on spreads of other emerging debt countries. To the extent that Russian spread changes influenced market spread changes, the large spread changes in Russia during rallies and selloffs exaggerate the true market risk in Russia.

Exhibit 19 shows that spreads in Brazil, Ecuador, and Russia typically change more than the market spread during rallies and selloffs, while spreads in Panama, Poland, and Korea change less than the market spread during rallies and selloffs. Spread changes that are smaller than market spread changes during a rally/selloff indicate that a country has less market risk but not necessarily less credit risk. For example, Turkey's spreads have increased and decreased dramatically over the time period examined in Exhibit 19. However, large spread changes in Turkey have not occurred at the same time as large market spread changes.

Instrument spread sensitivities to country spread movements also vary. The spreads of shorter maturity instruments and instruments with unique structures may increase by more than other bonds within a given country following a negative credit event; similarly, the spreads of these securities decrease by more than other securities following a positive credit event.[33] Exhibit 20 compares the spread change for the Brazilian EMBI Global Sub-Index and for various instruments in Brazil during a market rally and a market selloff using weekly data.[34] We define a spread decline for the Brazilian Sub-Index of 50 or more basis points during a week as a rally (22 instances) and a spread increase of 50 or more basis points during a week as a selloff (28 instances).

---

[33] For more details, refer to the section on relative valuation of instruments.

[34] Spread data are from JPMorgan from 12/31/97 to 4/30/01; EMBI Global Brazil Sub-Index is used for Brazil country spread.

Exhibit 20: Brazilian Instrument Spread Changes During Market Rallies and Selloffs
(December 1997 through April 2001)

Bond	Type	Coupon	Principal	Spread Duration	Average Weekly Spread Δ (bps)	
					Market Rally	Market Selloff
Brazil	Index			4.69	−115	118
Republic 11⅝% due 2004*	Eurobond	Fixed	Bullet	2.44	−120	160
Republic 9⅜% due 2008	Eurobond	Fixed	Bullet	4.81	−92	92
Republic 10⅛% due 2027	Eurobond	Fixed	Bullet	6.65	−81	86
EI	Brady	Floating	Amortizing	2.17	−147	161
FLIRB	Brady	Floating	Amortizing	3.67	−114	120
DCB	Brady	Floating	Amortizing	4.69	−115	116
C	Brady	Step-Up	Amortizing	4.80	−79	92
Par	Brady	Step-Up	Collateralized	2.95	−163	152
Discount	Brady	Floating	Collateralized	3.33	−191	166

* Due to short data history, the spread changes for the Brazilian Eurobond due 2004 were calculated by taking the ratio of the spread changes for the Eurobond due 2004 and the Eurobond due 2008 (for the period when spread information for the Eurobond due 2004 was available) and multiplying by the spread changes for the Eurobond due 2008 for the entire timeperiod.

Exhibit 20 shows that spreads of collateralized Brady bonds[35] (Pars and Discounts) and short duration Brady bonds (EI) typically change more than the Brazilian Sub-Index spread during rallies and selloffs, while spreads of Eurobonds and very liquid Bradys (C bond) change less than the Brazilian Sub-Index spread during rallies and selloffs. The spreads of short duration Brazilian Eurobonds change more relative to other Eurobonds during market rallies and selloffs.

A portfolio's overall spread duration is an accurate measure of market risk if one assumes that all of the spreads of the countries in the portfolio will increase/decrease by the same amount in response to a negative/positive market credit event. Similarly, a country's contribution to spread duration is an accurate measure of country risk if we assume that the spreads of the instruments within a country will increase/decrease by the same amount in response to a negative/positive country credit event. Exhibits 19 and 20 indicate that it is not realistic to assume that country and instrument spreads react identically.

Beta-adjusting spread durations can provide portfolio managers with an enhanced tool to measure the sensitivity of their portfolio to changes in overall market spreads and changes in the spreads of a particular country. Each instrument has two betas: a market beta and a country beta. A *market beta* measures an instrument's sensitivity to overall market spread changes; a *country beta* measures a bond's sensitivity to country spread changes. Betas are measured as the coefficient of a regression of the spread change of an instrument against the spread change of the overall market (market beta) or the spread change of a coun-

---

[35] Spreads for collateralized bonds are shown as stripped spreads (for the calculation of stripped spreads refer to the section on instrument valuation).

try (country beta). Exhibit 21 shows market and country betas for various instruments in Brazil and Panama.[36]

In Exhibit 21, the market betas for Brazilian instruments are higher than the market betas for Panamanian instruments indicating that Brazilian bonds are more sensitive to EMD spread movements. Within Brazil and Panama, sensitivity to country spread movements varies with Brady bonds having more sensitivity to spread movements than Eurobonds.

Since an instrument's market and country beta measure different sensitivities, the two risks should be shown separately or valuable information is lost. A portfolio's overall spread duration and a country's relative CTD can be adjusted by using market and country betas as follows:

$$
\begin{aligned}
P(z) &= \text{weight of instrument } z \text{ in portfolio} \\
B(z) &= \text{weight of instrument } z \text{ in benchmark} \\
D(z) &= \text{spread duration of instrument } z \\
BC(z) &= \text{spread beta of instrument } z \text{ relative to country} \\
BM(z) &= \text{spread beta of instrument } z \text{ relative to overall market}
\end{aligned}
$$

Country beta-adjusted instrument relative CTD $= BC(z) \times D(z) \times [P(z) - B(z)]$

Market beta-adjusted instrument relative CTD $= BM(z) \times D(z) \times [P(z) - B(z)]$

Country beta-adjusted instrument relative CTDs can be combined for all of the instruments within a country to more accurately show a portfolio's sensitivity to changes in spread for the particular country. Country beta-adjusted instrument relative CTDs are only applicable at the country level and should not be summed up to the overall portfolio.

Market beta-adjusted instrument relative CTDs can be combined for all of the instruments within a country to show how a particular country contributes to the overall market risk of the portfolio. Market beta-adjusted instrument relative CTDs can be summed up to measure the market risk of the overall portfolio.

Exhibit 21: Market and Country Betas (Brazil and Panama)
(April 2001)

Bond	Type	Coupon	Principal	Spread Duration	Beta Market	Beta Country
Brazil Republic 9⅜% due 2008	Eurobond	Fixed	Bullet	4.81	0.84	0.77
Brazil Republic 10⅛% due 2027	Eurobond	Fixed	Bullet	6.65	0.94	0.83
Brazil DCB	Brady	Floating	Amortizing	4.69	1.22	1.11
Panama 8¼% due 2008	Eurobond	Fixed	Bullet	5.19	0.50	0.87
Panama 8⅞% due 2027	Eurobond	Fixed	Bullet	9.02	0.53	0.94
Panama PDI	Brady	Floating	Amortizing	7.37	0.55	1.06

---

[36] Market and country betas are calculated from 18 months of weekly spread data. For instruments with limited history, a substitute instrument with similar characteristics may be used. Post-restructuring data were used for Russia and Ecuador.

Exhibit 22: Risk Report Containing Beta-Adjustments
(4/30/2001)

	Portfolio	Benchmark	Relative
Market Beta Adjusted Spread Duration	5.90	4.60	1.28

	Market Beta Adjusted CTD			Country Beta Adjusted CTD		
	Portfolio	Benchmark	Difference	Portfolio	Benchmark	Difference
Algeria	—	0.00	(0.00)	—	0.01	(0.01)
Argentina	1.14	1.12	0.02	0.75	0.71	0.04
Brazil	1.41	1.05	0.36	1.21	0.89	0.32
Bulgaria	0.24	0.08	0.17	0.25	0.08	0.17
Chile	—	0.00	(0.00)	—	0.02	(0.02)
China	—	0.01	(0.01)	—	0.05	(0.05)
Colombia	0.06	0.06	(0.00)	0.07	0.09	(0.02)
Côte d'Ivoire	—	0.00	(0.00)	—	0.00	(0.00)
Croatia	—	0.01	(0.01)	—	0.01	(0.01)
Ecuador	—	0.06	(0.06)	—	0.05	(0.05)
Hungary	—	0.00	(0.00)	—	0.01	(0.01)
Korea	0.05	0.05	(0.00)	0.22	0.19	0.03
Lebanon	—	0.00	(0.00)	—	0.00	(0.00)
Malaysia	—	0.03	(0.03)	—	0.13	(0.13)
Mexico	0.55	0.53	0.02	0.77	0.75	0.02
Morocco	0.02	0.02	0.00	0.03	0.03	0.01
Nigeria	—	0.03	(0.03)	—	0.04	(0.04)
Panama	0.09	0.08	0.01	0.16	0.14	0.01
Peru	0.00	0.05	(0.05)	0.00	0.07	(0.06)
Philippines	0.09	0.12	(0.03)	0.10	0.16	(0.05)
Poland	—	0.03	(0.03)	—	0.12	(0.12)
Qatar	0.10	—	0.10	0.31	—	0.31
Russia	2.00	0.97	1.04	1.21	0.59	0.62
South Africa	—	0.03	(0.03)	—	0.06	(0.06)
Thailand	—	0.00	(0.00)	—	0.02	(0.02)
Turkey	—	0.07	(0.07)	—	0.13	(0.13)
Ukraine	0.03	0.01	0.01	0.02	0.01	0.01
Venezuela	0.11	0.19	(0.08)	0.11	0.19	(0.07)

Exhibit 22 shows a risk report for an EMD portfolio versus the EMBI Global benchmark. Overall portfolio spread duration is adjusted by the market beta. Country relative CTDs are shown adjusted by market betas and adjusted by country betas.

The risk report in Exhibit 22 shows that the relative risk of the portfolio is considerably larger when spread durations are adjusted by a market beta because the portfolio has more exposure to countries that are particularly sensitive to market spread movements. In Exhibit 18, the spread duration of the portfolio was 1.06 times the spread duration of the benchmark, while the portfolio's market beta-adjusted spread duration is 1.28 times the benchmark's. Due to the high market sensitivity of Russia, Russia's contribution to the portfolio's risk has increased from 21% of the portfolio's spread duration to 34% of the portfolio's market beta-adjusted spread duration.[37]

Exhibit 18 showed a CTD underweight in Argentina, while Exhibit 22 shows a market beta-adjusted CTD overweight in Argentina. The increase in sensitivity to Argentina is due to the portfolio's higher exposure to instruments that are more sensitive to spread movements in Argentina (the portfolio's country beta-adjusted CTD for Argentina is higher than the benchmark's).

Tracking Error Decomposition

Does increasing an overweight to a country with a high market beta necessarily increase the overall risk of a portfolio? Can a risk model capture a portfolio's exposure to an external factor, such as oil prices?

The risk measurement techniques described in the previous sections do not provide a complete picture of a portfolio's risk because they calculate each country's/instrument's risk separately, without taking into account how a particular country's instrument's spread moves relative to other holdings in a portfolio. Increasing an overweight in a country with a large market beta can decrease the overall risk of a portfolio if the particular country has a low correlation with other holdings in a portfolio. Percentage market weights and CTDs (regular and beta-adjusted) do not take into account co-movement between countries, so they cannot tell a portfolio manager what trades will lower the overall risk of an EMD portfolio relative to a benchmark.

Tracking error measurement and decomposition is becoming the industry norm for measuring the risk of a portfolio versus a benchmark. Tracking error decomposition gives EMD managers a more complete picture of how their exposures are contributing to overall portfolio risk. Tracking error measurement incorporates not only the spread volatility of every holding in a portfolio, but also incorporates the correlation between the different countries and instruments within a portfolio and relative to benchmark holdings. Below we describe how a bond risk management system decomposes the tracking error risk of an EMD portfolio.

Tracking error measures (in terms of standard deviations) the risk of a performance difference between a portfolio and its benchmark.[38] To simplify the tracking error discussion, we analyze an EMD portfolio that is hedged against movements in U.S. interest rates and focus on risk from credit spread movements. The tracking error measurement will take into account the volatilities and correlations of spread changes for all of the countries held in the benchmark and the port-

---

[37] Exhibit 18 shows that Russia's contribution to the portfolio's spread duration is 1.06 (21% of the portfolio's total spread duration of 4.96). Exhibit 22 shows that Russia's contribution to the portfolio's market beta-adjusted spread duration is 2.00 (34% of the portfolio's total market beta-adjusted spread duration of 5.90).

[38] Assuming a normal distribution and zero value added from the active strategy, a tracking error of 2% for a given period implies that the portfolio will underperform or outperform its benchmark by less than 2% in that period approximately 68% of the time.

folio. The tracking error measurement will also take into account the specific risk (i.e. the difference in spread change between bonds in the same country).

The matrix formulas used to calculate the tracking error of a portfolio are shown as follows:

$$\text{Tracking Error} = (\text{Systematic Risk}^2 + \text{Instrument Specific Risk}^2)^{1/2}$$

$$\text{Systematic Risk}^2 = (\text{Country Active Exposure Vector})^T$$
$$\times (\text{Country Spread Variance/Covariance Matrix})$$
$$\times (\text{Country Active Exposure Vector})$$

$$\text{Instrument Specific Risk}^2 = [(\text{Instrument Active Exposure Vector})^2]^T$$
$$\times [\text{Instrument Residual Risk Vector}^2]$$

Systematic risks influence all of the bonds within a specific category. In this tracking error model, countries are treated as systematic risks. The systematic risk calculation contains a vector with active exposures across countries and a matrix that contains spread variances and covariances across countries in the portfolio and the benchmark. An active exposure is the difference in risk factor sensitivity between the portfolio and the benchmark. Since the risk in this tracking error model is spread movement, relative CTD is the appropriate risk factor sensitivity. Therefore, the country active exposure vector contains differences in country CTD between the portfolio and the benchmark.

Instrument specific risk captures performance differences between securities within a specific country. Instrument relative CTDs are placed in the instrument active exposure matrix. The active exposure vector is multiplied by a vector that contains residual risk information for every instrument in the portfolio and benchmark. Residual risk for a particular instrument measures the standard deviation of the spread difference between the instrument and the corresponding country spread. Factors such as instrument type (Brady, Eurobond, and local issue) and instrument duration influence residual risk.

In calculating overall tracking error, systematic risk and instrument specific risk are assumed to be independent (zero correlation).

Exposure vectors contain relative CTDs for a country or an instrument. Instrument residual risk vectors are estimated by calculating the historic spread change differences between bonds in the same country. Country spread variance/covariance matrices require more advanced calculations based on historical spread data analysis.

The country spread variance/covariance matrix is calculated through a process that takes into account the historical correlation of common factors that drive country spreads. For example, the positive correlation between spread movements in Russia and Venezuela is partly due to the fact that both countries are major exporters of energy products (oil and gas). Therefore, oil price is an underlying factor that helps explain the correlation between Russia and Venezuela. This risk model uses the following common factors: regional spread factors (Latin America, Asia, Eastern Europe), quality spread factors (investment grade, non-investment grade), U.S. equity, oil, U.S. high yield spreads, and foreign exchange rates (Euro/$ and Yen/$).

A variance/covariance matrix is calculated for the underlying factors using historical data. Then, analysis is performed to measure the sensitivity of a country's spread movement to the underlying factors. For example, Venezuela is sensitive to Latin American spread movements and oil prices. The underlying factor variance/covariance matrix is combined with the sensitivity analysis to create a country spread variance/covariance matrix that contains all of the countries in the portfolio and in the benchmark.[39]

Exhibit 23 shows a risk summary for an EMD portfolio that uses the EMBI Global as its benchmark. The risk summary shows the total tracking error and beta of the portfolio versus its benchmark as well as total volatility for the portfolio and the benchmark. Tracking error, beta, and volatility numbers are further separated into a systematic and an instrument specific component.

This exhibit shows that the portfolio is a lot riskier than the benchmark. The expected volatility of the portfolio is 11.1% versus 9.3% for the benchmark and the portfolio has an expected tracking error of 2.9%. The bulk of the risk comes from systematic (i.e., market) rather than instrument-specific risk.

The tracking error model estimates the portfolio beta at 1.16, which is above the relative spread duration of the portfolio measured in Exhibit 18 (1.06), but below the relative market beta-adjusted spread duration of the portfolio measured in Exhibit 22 (1.28). This makes intuitive sense. The tracking error model and the market beta-adjusted spread duration calculate higher relative risk for the portfolio because they account for both spread duration and the portfolio's overweight in certain high beta countries. The relative risk calculated by the tracking error model is lower than the relative risk of market beta-adjusted spread duration because imperfect correlation between country spread movements decreases the risk of the high beta portfolio.

Exhibit 23: Tracking Error Risk Summary
(April 2001)

	Risk		
	Total	Systematic	Instrument Specific
Benchmark Volatility	9.3%	9.2%	1.1%
Portfolio Volatility	11.1%	10.9%	1.6%
Expected Tracking Error	2.9%	2.5%	1.4%
Portfolio Beta	1.16	1.15	0.01

[39] Using underlying factors to build a variance/covariance matrix facilitates the modeling of countries with limited spread data history and is intuitively more consistent than calculating relationships from historical data.

Exhibit 24: Tracking Error Breakout by Country (April 2001)

	Total Contribution	Systematic Contribution	Instrument Specific Contribution
Total	2.85%	2.47%	1.43%
Algeria	−0.01%	−0.01%	0.00%
Argentina	0.18%	−0.13%	0.60%
Brazil	0.78%	0.69%	0.37%
Bulgaria	0.26%	0.29%	0.01%
Chile	0.03%	0.00%	0.05%
China	0.00%	0.00%	0.00%
Colombia	0.00%	−0.01%	0.01%
Côte d'Ivoire	0.00%	0.00%	0.00%
Croatia	−0.01%	−0.01%	0.00%
Ecuador	−0.08%	−0.10%	0.00%
Hungary	0.00%	0.00%	0.00%
Korea	−0.01%	−0.01%	0.01%
Lebanon	0.00%	0.00%	0.00%
Malaysia	0.00%	0.00%	0.00%
Mexico	0.00%	−0.01%	0.02%
Morocco	0.01%	0.01%	0.00%
Nigeria	−0.01%	−0.01%	0.00%
Panama	0.01%	0.01%	0.00%
Peru	−0.04%	−0.04%	0.00%
Philippines	−0.04%	−0.05%	0.01%
Poland	−0.01%	−0.01%	0.00%
Qatar	0.07%	0.08%	0.01%
Russia	1.72%	1.81%	0.30%
South Africa	0.01%	0.01%	0.00%
Thailand	0.00%	0.00%	0.00%
Turkey	−0.03%	−0.05%	0.02%
Ukraine	0.01%	0.01%	0.00%
Uruguay	0.00%	0.00%	0.00%
Venezuela	0.00%	0.00%	0.01%

Exhibit 24 shows a detailed breakout of an EMD portfolio's tracking error across countries. This exhibit shows that the bulk of the portfolio's tracking error risk is explained by overweights in Russia and Brazil, with the overweight in Russia explaining more than half of the portfolio's tracking error. The portfolio's underweight in high volatility Ecuador actually lowers the portfolio's tracking error. Instrument specific risk is important in countries that have a variety of bonds (Bradys's, domestic bonds, etc.) such as Argentina and Brazil. Argentina's contribution to the portfolio's tracking error comes mainly from instrument selection within Argentina.

Exhibit 25 provides a summary of the strengths and weaknesses of different portfolio risk management techniques just described.

Exhibit 25: Portfolio Risk Management Techniques for EMD Portfolios

Technique	Strengths	Weaknesses
Percentage Weight	- Simple. - Useful during periods of distress when securities trade on price.	- Does not separate spread risk from US interest rate risk. - Volatility and co-movement of spreads between countries not evaluated. - Cannot calculate overall portfolio risk relative to benchmark.
Contribution to Spread Duration (CTD)	- Simple - Captures sensitivity to spread movement. - Relative risk for overall portfolio can be calculated.	- Not as useful during periods of distress. - Volatility and co-movement of spreads between countries not evaluated.
Beta-Adjusted CTD	- Captures a volatility adjusted sensitivity to spread movement. - Relative risk for overall portfolio can be calculated.	- Co-movement of spreads between countries not evaluated.
Tracking Error Decomposition	- Decomposes sensitivity to spread movement adjusted for volatility and co-movement of countries. - Divides portfolio risk between systematic and security specific risk factors. - Allows flexibility to divide portfolio risk along various non-country dimensions.	- Relatively complex. Model is sensitive to assumptions made during construction. - Model correlation/volatility assumptions have to be re-calibrated if there is a market regime shift.

ATTRIBUTION

A detailed attribution model provides feedback to portfolio managers about the strengths and weaknesses of their decision-making processes. A portfolio manager's valuation process dictates not only an approach to risk management but also the structure of an attribution model. The valuation section described how to evaluate the attractiveness of the market, the relative attractiveness of countries, and the relative attractiveness of instruments within countries. The attribution model provides feedback on each of these decisions.

The return of an emerging market bond can be divided into four components: (1) Underlying Treasury Yield, (2) U.S. Yield Curve Change, (3) Spread Yield, and (4) Spread Change. The U.S. Yield Curve Change component measures the portion of a bond's return that is explained by movements in the underlying Treasury yield curve. Underlying Treasury Yield and Spread Yield are calculated by dividing up the Income and Accretion component of a bond's return. The Spread Change component represents the part of a security's return due to spread tightening/widening. Underlying Treasury Yield can be combined with U.S. Yield Curve Change to create a U.S. Yield Curve Factor that represents the total return of the

U.S. Treasury instrument equivalent to the EMD instrument. Similarly, Spread Yield and Spread Change can be combined to create a Spread Factor.

The components of an emerging market bond's return are then calculated as follows:[40]

$$\begin{array}{c}\text{Return of Emerging} \\ \text{Debt Instrument}\end{array} = \begin{array}{c}\text{Underlying} \\ \text{Treasury Yield}\end{array} + \begin{array}{c}\text{U.S. Yield} \\ \text{Curve Change}\end{array} + \begin{array}{c}\text{Spread} \\ \text{Yield}\end{array} + \begin{array}{c}\text{Spread} \\ \text{Change}\end{array}$$

Underlying Treasury Yield + Spread Yield
   = Income and Accretion of Instrument

U.S. Yield Curve Factor
   = Underlying Treasury Yield + U.S. Yield Curve Change

Spread Factor = Spread Yield + Spread Change

Return of Emerging Market Debt Instrument
   = U.S. Yield Curve Factor + Spread Factor

The components of an instrument's return are weighted by portfolio and benchmark percentage market weights and differences between the portfolio and benchmark are analyzed within the attribution process. Since U.S. yield curve exposure is measured at the overall portfolio level, it is not necessary to break out the difference between the portfolio's and the benchmark's U.S. Yield Curve Factor by country.

Since valuation and risk management for EMD portfolios is done on the basis of spread movements, an EMD attribution model decomposes the spread factor difference between the portfolio and the benchmark. The spread factor difference between the portfolio and the benchmark is divided into three factors: (1) market effect, (2) country selection, and (3) instrument selection. *Market effect* measures the contribution of the overall portfolio spread duration to the portfolio's relative performance. A portfolio with a spread duration that is greater than the benchmark's will have a positive market effect if the benchmark has a positive spread factor. *Country selection* measures how country relative CTDs contribute to the spread factor difference between the portfolio and the benchmark. Lastly, *instrument selection* measures how instrument relative CTDs contribute to the spread factor difference.[41]

Exhibit 26 shows an attribution report for a single month (April 2001) for an EMD portfolio. The return difference between the portfolio and the benchmark is divided between U.S. Yield Curve Factor and Spread Factor. Then, Spread Factor is divided into Market Effect, Country Selection, and Instrument Selection. Country Selection and Instrument Selection are shown by country. Instrument

---

[40] The equations show components of the underlying returns, not returns themselves.

[41] For a more detailed discussion on performance attribution for EMD portfolios see Brian Fischer and Fernando Cunha, "Performance Attribution for an Emerging Market External-Debt Portfolio," *JPMorgan Portfolio Strategies* (September 9, 1998).

Selection contribution can be displayed down to the individual instrument level, but are summarized at the country level in this exhibit.

Exhibit 26 shows the portfolio's exposure relative to the benchmark at the beginning of the month both in percentage weight and CTD. Also shown is the spread factor for each country; this is the country's return excluding the effect of U.S. Yield Curve Change and Underlying Treasury Yield. Turkey, Côte d'Ivoire, and Russia had the largest spread factors, while Peru, Ecuador, and Argentina had the lowest spread factors.

Exhibit 26: Detailed Attribution by Country (4/30/2001)

Portfolio less Benchmark		Contribution to Spread Factor	
US Yield Curve	0.07%	Market Effect	0.01%
Spread Factor	0.38%	Country Slct	0.27%
Total	0.45%	Instrument Slct	0.10%
		Total	0.38%

	Portfolio less Benchmark		Spread	Contrib to Spread Factor	
Country	Weight	CTD	Factor	Country Slct	Instrument Slct
Total	0.00%	0.12	0.69%	0.27%	0.10%
Cash	8.46%	0.00	0.00%	0.00%	0.00%
Algeria	−0.48%	−0.01	1.28%	−0.01%	0.00%
Argentina	−1.01%	−0.10	−2.42%	0.10%	−0.14%
Brazil	1.22%	0.25	−0.23%	−0.04%	0.05%
Bulgaria	3.96%	0.19	−0.48%	−0.03%	0.00%
Chile	−0.27%	−0.02	0.73%	0.00%	0.00%
China	−1.09%	−0.04	0.30%	0.00%	0.00%
Colombia	0.33%	0.01	1.78%	0.00%	0.02%
Côte d'Ivoire	−0.06%	0.00	4.99%	0.00%	0.00%
Croatia	−0.37%	−0.01	0.11%	0.00%	0.00%
Ecuador	−1.04%	−0.05	−5.06%	0.06%	0.00%
Hungary	−0.37%	−0.01	−0.19%	0.00%	0.00%
Korea	−4.52%	−0.15	0.73%	−0.08%	0.10%
Lebanon	−0.28%	−0.01	0.58%	0.00%	0.00%
Malaysia	−2.85%	−0.14	−1.45%	0.05%	0.00%
Mexico	−0.77%	0.01	2.57%	0.00%	0.07%
Morocco	0.19%	0.01	0.70%	0.00%	0.00%
Nigeria	−1.52%	−0.04	4.35%	−0.06%	0.00%
Panama	−0.03%	0.02	3.67%	0.01%	0.00%
Peru	−1.13%	−0.07	−10.60%	0.12%	0.00%
Philippines	−1.01%	−0.06	−0.32%	0.01%	−0.02%
Poland	−2.22%	−0.14	2.13%	−0.04%	0.00%
Qatar	3.23%	0.31	4.14%	0.12%	0.00%
Russia	6.92%	0.43	4.49%	0.35%	0.03%
South Africa	−0.95%	−0.06	1.51%	−0.01%	0.00%
Thailand	−0.34%	−0.02	1.78%	−0.01%	0.00%
Turkey	−2.52%	−0.12	9.34%	−0.23%	0.00%
Ukraine	0.43%	0.01	−0.95%	0.00%	0.00%
Venezuela	−1.91%	−0.06	2.13%	−0.03%	0.00%

The portfolio in Exhibit 26 outperformed the benchmark by 45 basis points. U.S. Yield Curve and Spread Factor contributed 7 and 38 basis points, respectively, to the portfolio's relative performance. The portfolio's overall duration overweight is captured by the market effect and explains only 1 basis point of the spread factor. Country selection explains 27 basis points of the spread factor, while instrument selection contributed 10 basis points to the spread factor. Positive contributors to country selection include CTD overweights in Russia and Qatar and CTD underweight in Peru and Argentina. A CTD underweight in Turkey negatively impacted country selection. Issue selection in Korea contributed to performance, while issue selection in Argentina detracted from performance.

CONCLUSION

The volatility of emerging markets debt requires using a fundamental valuation approach as an anchor. The analysis shows that while EMD spreads and macroeconomic fundamentals move in the same direction, spreads are more volatile than fundamentals, and EMD fundamentals have been on an improving trend since the mid-1990s.

A distinguishing feature of the EMD asset class is the need of emerging countries to rely on international investors for capital. A systematic framework for evaluating EMD sovereign issuers considers the interaction of quantitative and qualitative factors to determine the probability that a country receives the foreign capital that it needs.

Because of the variety of investment alternatives and their widely differing performance characteristics, there are many opportunities for relative value trades across countries and within the same country. High spread volatility and low legal protection make technical, as well as legal, considerations indispensable when evaluating individual bonds.

Due to the high volatility of EMD spreads, a portfolio manager benefits from using a variety of risk management techniques. Adjusting spread duration measurements by a volatility-based beta provides a more complete picture of the portfolio's sensitivity to movements in market spreads. Tracking error decomposition takes into account inter-country correlations and exposures to common risk factors such as oil prices.

All of the stages of a disciplined investment process are connected. After deciding on a benchmark that properly captures the investment universe, the investor considers overall market, country, and instrument valuation when making investment decisions. The different portions of the valuation process are reflected in risk and attribution models in order to assist the investor in portfolio construction and to provide performance feedback on prior decisions.

Chapter 7

Emerging Market CBOs: Considerations for Portfolio Managers

Laurie Goodman, Ph.D.
Managing Director
Head of the Mortgage Strategy Group
UBS Warburg

One of the faster growing sectors of the fixed income markets is the CDO (collateralized debt obligation) market, a subset of which is the CBO (collateralized bond obligation) market. A significant number of these CBO transactions have been backed by emerging market debt, and an even greater number have been backed by high-yield bonds. Many portfolio managers have invested a substantial amount of time and energy in understanding CBO structures. Most have become comfortable with CBO deals backed by both high-yield bonds and bank loans. However, these same portfolio managers are still quite uneasy about any CBO backed primarily by sovereign emerging market bonds, as they believe that all emerging market debt is tainted by high default experience.

In this chapter, we shed some light on the differences (that matter) between emerging market and high-yield CBO tranches. The picture that "emerges" (pun intended) may surprise you—positively, that is.

We first provide a brief introduction to the CBO market. We then turn our attention to contrasting the difference between CBOs backed by emerging market bonds and those backed by high-yield bonds. Key points include:

- There have actually been few defaults on U.S. dollar denominated sovereign emerging market (EM) bonds. The negative bias of many investors against EM CBOs is because they do not fully appreciate the differences between EM sovereign bank loans and EM sovereign bonds.

- Rating agencies are far more conservative in their assumptions when rating emerging market deals than in rating high-yield deals, as performance data on EM bonds are far more limited. So there is an extra credit cushion already built into comparable credit levels.

Exhibit 1: Global CDO Issuance Volume
(Rated by Moody's)

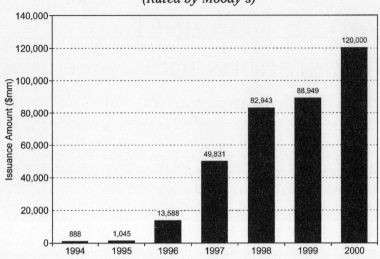

- EM CBOs generally provide much greater structural protection, as the average portfolio credit quality is higher, resulting in a lower probability of default on the underlying portfolio. Subordination for EM deals is also much higher, hence the equity itself is much less leveraged.

We discuss each of these points in turn. Indeed, we believe that EM CBOs are no more risky than high-yield CBOs, and the rated debt often yields much more.

A QUICK REVIEW OF CBOs

A CDO is a special purpose vehicle which invests in a pool of assets, the timing, amount, and value of which are dependent upon a set of identifiable risks. The assets are funded through the issuance of several classes of liabilities. The assets serve as collateral for the CDO liabilities, and the repayment of the liabilities is linked to the performance of the underlying assets. Thus, a CDO simply reallocates the risk of the underlying assets to different market participants, depending on their individual risk appetites.

This is one of the fastest growing fixed income sectors. Exhibit 1 shows indications of market growth based on the quantity of CDOs rated by Moody's Investor Services. Note that volume has grown from $1 billion in 1995 to $120 billion in 2000. When the underlying assets are bonds, the CDO is often referred to as a CBO (collateralized bond obligation). When the underlying assets are loans, the special purpose vehicle may be called a CLO (collateralized loan obligation). CDOs consist of both CBOs and CLOs. CBOs will be the focus of this chapter.

The securities issued by the CBO are tranched into rated and unrated classes. The rating of each class is primarily determined through the priority of the interest in the cash flows generated by the collateral. The senior notes are typically rated AAA, AA, and A, may pay a fixed or floating coupon (floating is more common), and have the highest priority on the cash flows. The mezzanine tranches are typically rated BBB to B, may pay either a fixed-rate or floating-rate coupon, and have a claim on cash flows that is subordinate to the senior notes. The rating is based on the ability of the collateral to generate sufficient cash to pay interest and principal on the rated liabilities.

The equity in the CBO (often referred to as *subordinated notes*) is the residual. These securities represent the first loss position; the coupon may be deferred or eliminated based on available cash flow. That is, investors in this tranche receive a coupon if cash is available after payment of expenses, the debt service on the securities that rank senior to the equity, and after satisfying tests that require a cushion be in place to safeguard the higher rated tranches in future years. The equity in the deal represents a leveraged investment in the underlying collateral.

High-yield bonds and emerging market debt are both used extensively as collateral for CBOs. Both asset classes have a relatively large yield spread, allowing the CBO to comfortably service the liabilities issued against them, as well as providing for a substantial cushion. We now look at emerging market CBOs, comparing them to high-yield CBO deals.

EM SOVEREIGN BOND DEFAULTS

EM debt has developed a bad rap. This tainted reputation stems from the fact that many potential investors do not distinguish between EM sovereign foreign currency bank loans and sovereign foreign currency bonds. In fact, the historical record on EM sovereign foreign currency bonds is very favorable. Sovereigns are far more likely to default on foreign currency bank loans than on foreign currency bond debt.

Let's look at the asset record, recently compiled in a Standard and Poor's study which covers both public and private debt. For example, Exhibit 2 shows that out of a universe of 201 sovereign issuers, 13.9% of the issuers were in default in 1999. This includes defaults on foreign currency debt (both bank loans and bonds), as well as in local currency debt. Note that 11.9% of the issuers are in default within the category of total foreign currency debt (which includes both bank loans and bonds). But a separate breakout of just the sovereign foreign currency bonds indicates that most of these issuers were in default only on their bank loans. In fact, the sixth column of Exhibit 2 shows that at the end of 1999 only 2.5% of the issuers were in default on their foreign currency bonds! Note that the 2.5% default on foreign currency bonds is lower than the 3.5% default on local currency debt.

Exhibit 2: Sovereign Default Rates

	Number of issuers	All issuers in default (%)	New Issuers in default (%)	All foreign currency debt* (%)	Foreign currency bonds (%)	Local currency (%)
1975	164	2.4	N.A.	1.2	0.6	1.2
1976	165	2.4	0.6	2.4	0.6	0.6
1977	166	2.4	0.0	1.8	0.6	0.6
1978	169	4.7	2.3	4.1	0.6	0.6
1979	173	6.4	2.3	5.8	0.6	1.2
1980	174	6.3	1.7	5.7	0.6	0.6
1981	176	10.2	6.3	9.1	0.0	1.1
1982	176	15.9	5.7	15.3	0.0	1.7
1983	177	24.9	10.2	23.7	0.0	1.1
1984	178	25.3	1.1	23.6	0.6	1.7
1985	178	24.7	2.8	24.2	0.6	1.1
1986	179	28.5	5.6	27.9	0.6	1.7
1987	179	30.7	3.3	29.1	1.1	2.2
1988	179	30.2	1.7	29.6	1.1	1.1
1989	179	30.2	1.7	29.1	2.2	1.7
1990	178	30.9	4.2	29.8	1.1	2.8
1991	198	27.3	3.0	26.8	1.0	1.5
1992	198	29.3	3.5	28.8	2.0	1.5
1993	200	27.0	0.5	26.5	1.5	2.0
1994	201	24.4	0.0	23.9	1.5	2.0
1995	201	22.9	1.5	21.9	1.5	3.0
1996	201	21.4	0.5	19.9	1.5	3.5
1997	201	15.9	0.0	14.9	1.5	2.0
1998	201	15.9	2.5	13.9	2.5	3.5
1999	201	13.9	0.5	11.9	2.5	3.5

N.A. = Not available
* Bonds and bank debt.

Source: David T. Beers and Ashok Bhatia, "Sovereign Defaults: Hiatus in 2000?" *Standard and Poor's Credit Week* (December 22, 1999).

This 2.5% default rate amounts to only five issuers out of 201 issuers (sovereign borrowers). They include Ecuador, Ukraine, the former Yugoslavia, Pakistan, and Russia. Ecuador was the only new issuer to default in 1999. That country first blew the whistle that it might not meet payments on its Brady debt during the summer, and then proceeded to default on the bonds. This shook the markets, since it was the first time that Brady debt had defaulted. However, realize that there was no contagion—other Latin American countries continued to make timely payments on their Brady bonds. Investors should realize that a sovereign can default on some bonds, while remaining timely on others. This would be reflected in Exhibit 2 as a default. For example, while Russia has defaulted on some if its bonds, it has continued to service on a timely basis its large public issues, including the Russian Federation's CCC rated Eurobonds. It is also keeping current four other Ministry of Finance foreign currency bonds.

Cumulatively, Standard and Poor's has identified a total of 78 issuers (38.8% of all sovereigns) that defaulted on their foreign currency bond and bank loans since 1975. (This constitutes a much smaller percent of all foreign currency debt in default.) Defaults usually took the form of late payments of principal and/or interest on bank loans. In fact, there were 75 bank debt defaults since 1975, and some sovereigns defaulted more than once. By contrast, only 14 issuers defaulted on foreign currency bonds in that same period. In most of these cases, the defaulted bonds had been issued by smaller countries which had little total debt outstanding. The bonds that the countries defaulted on tended to be held by banks, rather than being public issues held by a broad cross sector of investors.

This has been independently confirmed in a previous study by Moody's rating service. The Moody's study noted that "a review of worldwide sovereign default experience since World War II shows that when sovereign nations have defaulted on any of their foreign currency obligations...they have been more likely to default on bank loans than on sovereign bonds or notes."[1]

A BETTER DEFAULT TRACK RECORD OF EM SOVEREIGN BONDS

There are four reasons that EM sovereign bonds have a better track record than sovereign bank loans. First, there is a strong disincentive for a sovereign to default on foreign currency bonds; it will restrict capital market access going forward. The consequences of defaulting on (or rescheduling) bank loans has been more predictable, and far less detrimental to a nation's interest, than defaulting on its bonds. Defaulting on bonds could essentially bar a country from the international capital markets for a considerable period of time, and will result in much higher borrowing costs when the country is finally able to enter. Most of the developing nations depend on external financing for their growth, and hampering access to capital markets could sacrifice medium term growth.

Second, more sovereigns have access to cross-border bank financing than have access to bond issuance in the international capital markets. Yes, international bond markets have been receptive to issuance by speculative grade rated sovereign credits since the early 1990s. But relative credit sanity has prevailed, as there have been barriers to entry by sovereigns of less credit quality, notably those from sub-Saharan Africa.

Third, it is far easier to renegotiate debt held by a few banking institutions rather than a bond issuance held by large numbers of international investors. For one, identification of creditors in advance is not always easy. By definition, there are a large number of creditors, some of which may have relatively small holdings. All of which makes restructuring more complex. Also, any one of even the smallest

---

[1] See Vincent Truglia, David Levey, and Christopher Mahoney, "Sovereign Risk: Bank Deposits Versus Bonds," Moody's Investor Services, Global Credit Research (October 1995).

creditors can potentially bring legal proceedings against an issuer in a number of jurisdictions, depending on the security's documentation. The possibility of asset attachments is greater, simply because of the number of potential court cases.

The fourth and final major difference between bank loans and bond debt is that banks have multi-faceted relationships with borrowers, and usually receive sizeable fees for a variety of services. Banks often keep their long-term relationship with the borrower in perspective when agreeing to reschedule. Bondholders are not relationship-driven, and there are no business consequences for the bondholders in trying to extract the last possible dollar. The net result: sovereign default rates on bonds are much lower than on bank loans. Unfortunately, many investors do not distinguish between the two, and keep looking at sovereign debt as a homogeneous category, which clearly, it is not.

CBO RATING DIFFERENCES: EM VERSUS HIGH YIELD

The rating methodology for cash flow CBOs involves looking at the expected loss on the various tranches under various default scenarios, and probability weighting the results. This, in turn, requires making assumptions on how diversified the collateral is, how likely it is to default, and how much will be recovered if any default occurs. It is much harder for the rating agencies to feel comfortable with the parameters that they are using for EM bonds than U.S. high-yield bonds. Let's look at reasons for this.

First, consider EM sovereign debt. Default rate statistics on EM sovereign bonds are very limited. Moreover, EM economies are subject to greater economic instability than those of more developed countries. Corporate debt in EM countries is even more problematic for the rating agencies. Clearly, there is generally less publicly available information about companies in EM countries than about issuers in developed countries. Moreover, financial reporting in many foreign countries is often not subject to uniform reporting and disclosure requirements. Finally, and most importantly, the actions of local governments are far more likely to affect the ability or willingness of EM corporates to service their debt.

Given the issues that were mentioned above, the rating agencies react by rating EM assets in a more conservative manner than other collateral. As a result, additional levels of credit protection are built into EM CBOs beyond that which is structured into high-yield CBOs. We now review some major differences in those assumptions.

RECOVERY RATES

The rating agencies typically assume 30% recovery rates for high-yield debt and 50% on bank loans. For sovereign debt, Moody's assumes that base case recovery rates are 30% of the market value, or 25% of par, whichever is lower. For EM corporate debt, Moody's assumes that recovery rates are 20% of market value (15% of par value) if the issuer is domiciled in an investment-grade country, and 15% of market value (10% of par value) if the issuer is domiciled in a non-investment grade country. Bonds of countries that face unusually adverse political or economic conditions are treated as having a lower recovery rate, which in some cases, can be as low as zero.

In point of fact, historical recovery rates on sovereign bonds have proved far more favorable. A September 1998 Standard and Poor's study showed that since 1975, the recovery rate on foreign currency bonds has been around 75%.[2] It was higher in the majority of cases in which the defaults were cured quickly through the issuance of new debt. It was lower on bonds that remained in default for longer periods of time. Even for bonds that remained in default for longer periods, most of the recovery rates were just under 50%—far higher than the recovery assumptions made by the rating agencies. And the 75% overall recovery rate on sovereign foreign currency bonds is well above the 60% recovery rate on foreign currency bank loans.

Moreover, even though the rating agencies are more generous in the recovery rates they assume for U.S. high-yield borrowers than for sovereign borrowers, actual recovery rates for sovereign borrowers have been higher. A Moody's study showed that the recovery rates on senior unsecured U.S. corporate debt in the 1977-1988 period averaged 51.31%.[3] Compare this with the 75% recovery rate on sovereign bonds.

DIVERSITY SCORES

Each rating agency has its own set of tools for measuring the diversity of underlying collateral. Moody's methodology has become the industry standard. This treatment reduces the pool of assets to a set of homogenous, uncorrelated assets. For CBOs backed by high-yield or bank loans, a diversity score is calculated by dividing the bonds into one of 33 industry groupings, and each industry group is assumed to be uncorrelated. (See Exhibit 3.)

Exhibit 3: Moody's Diversity Score Table for CBOs

Number of Companies (Countries)	Diversity Score	Diversity Score for Latin America*
1	1.00	1.00
2	1.50	1.25
3	2.00	1.50
4	2.30	1.65
5	2.70	1.85
6	3.00	2.00

* Diversity = $1 + (\text{Standard Diversity Score} - 1) \times 0.5$
Source: UBS Warburg calculations

---

[2] See David T. Beers, "Sovereign Defaults Continue to Decline," Standard and Poor's (September 1998).
[3] See Sean C. Keenan, Igor Shtogrin, and Jorge Sobehart, "Historical Default Rates of Corporate Bond Issuers, 1920-1998," Moody's Investor Services (January 1999).

Assumptions are more conservative for EM bonds, reflecting rating agency fears of "contagion." Countries that carry an investment-grade sovereign rating from Moody's are each treated as a separate industry. Bonds from non-investment grade EM issuers are grouped into six geographic regions. These are Latin America, the Caribbean, Eastern Europe, Africa, East Asia, and West Asia. The latter includes the Middle East. Each region constitutes a single "industry." All bonds from a region, regardless of the industry they represent, are taken as part of the same group. Thus, the value of including corporate EM borrowers, which would customarily be seen as providing greater diversity and reduced risk from that diversification, is discounted entirely. In point of fact, many EM deals include up to 20% of the portfolio in corporate form.

For all regions except Latin America, the diversity score is the standard table used by Moody's, which relies on the assumption that defaults on bonds in the same region or industry have a correlation coefficient of approximately 30%. This is shown in the first two columns of Exhibit 3. For example, if there were equal amounts of debt from each of four Caribbean countries, the diversity score is 2.3. That is, the deal would be credited as if there were 2.3 uncorrelated assets. For Latin American it is assumed the correlation is about 60%, and the diversity score is shown in the third column of Exhibit 3. If there were four Latin American issuers, the diversity score would be 1.65. Thus, combining four Caribbean issuers and four Latin American issuers in equal amounts would "count" as 3.95 uncorrelated issuers.

To be even more conservative, all bonds from a particular EM country are taken as constituting one issue. Essentially, 100% correlation is assumed within each country. In effect, EM collateral does not receive diversity score "credit" for having multiple corporate issuers or industries. Thus, if one compares the diversity score on a pool of 100% emerging markets collateral with a pool of U.S. high-yield assets with similar industry diversification, the EM collateral would have a substantially lower diversity score.

STRUCTURAL PROTECTIONS

We have thus far focused on how Moody's deals with limited historical experience (by making more conservative assumptions). In practice, these more conservative assumptions mean several forms of additional built-in protection for the CBO buyer. First, the average credit quality is higher on an EM CBO than on a high-yield CBO. Second, subordination levels are also generally higher on an EM CBO than on a high-yield CBO.

HIGHER AVERAGE CREDIT QUALITY

The conservative approach used by Moody's means that average credit quality of an EM CBO deal is much higher than on a high-yield CBO. That is, CBO managers will generally choose to include higher credit quality bonds to compensate for the lower diversity scores and the more stringent recovery assumptions. Most EM deals have average credit qualities of Ba2 or Ba3. By contrast, most high-yield deals have an average credit quality of B1 or B2.

This difference is highly significant, as shown in Exhibit 4. The exhibit shows Moody's data for the average cumulative default rates by letter rating after 10 years. This groups corporate bonds with a given initial rating, and tracks those bonds through time. Data for the period 1970-1998 are included. We use Exhibit 4 to highlight cumulative default rates after 10 years, as that roughly corresponds to the average lives of CBO deals. The findings show that default rates tend to rise exponentially as credit letter ratings fall. Of the bonds that started out life with a Baa rating, 4.39% had defaulted by the end of 10 years. Bonds with an initial rating of Ba had a cumulative default rate of 20.63%, while bonds initially rated B had cumulative default of 43.91%. While numbers on sovereign debt are unavailable, the results are indicative that higher-rated bonds actually default much less than do their lower-rated brethren. Bottom line: the higher initial portfolio quality on sovereign EM CBOs is highly significant.

Moreover, actual EM portfolio quality may be slightly higher than even that indicated by the overall rating. EM corporate bonds (usually 5%–20% of the deal) can generally receive a rating no higher than the country in which it is based.[4] This is called the "sovereign ceiling." Thus, if a company is rated Aa2 based on "stand-alone" fundamentals, but is based in a country rated Ba2, the company itself can generally only receive that same Ba2 rating. This same methodology and rating effect is reflected throughout the overall portfolio.

Exhibit 4: Cumulative Default Rates After 10 Years as a Function of Credit Quality

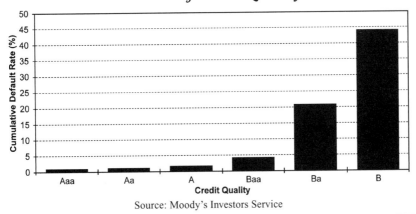

Source: Moody's Investors Service

[4] There have been a few CBOs backed primarily by Asian corporate bonds. These CBO "story bonds" driven by local investors, and have taken advantage of brief "windows of opportunity." This chapter focuses on CBOs backed by diversified sovereign EM bonds. In practice, the rating agencies criteria is such that it has never been economic to include more than 20% EM corporate bonds in a sovereign EM deal.

Exhibit 5: Comparison of Emerging Market and High-Yield Deal Structure

Class	Ratings Moody's/S&P/D&P	Amount ($M)	% of Deal	% Sub	Current Pricing Info
Representative Emerging Market Deal					
A1	Aaa/AAA/NR	163.00	68.6%	31.4%	+68 DM
A2	A2/A/NR	22.00	9.3%	22.2%	+250/10yr Tsy
Mezz	Ba1/NR/NR	10.00	4.2%	18.0%	+800/10yr Tsy
Equity	NR	42.74	18.0%	—	—
Total		237.74			
Representative High Yield Deal					
A1	Aaa/AAA/AAA	344.50	68.2%	31.8%	+57 DM
A2	NR/A–/A–	79.00	15.6%	16.2%	+225/10yr Tsy
Mezz 1	NR/NR/BBB–	22.00	4.4%	11.8%	+360/10yr Tsy
Mezz 2	NR/NR/BB–	20.00	4.0%	7.9%	+700/10yr Tsy
Equity	NR	39.79	7.9%	—	—
Total		505.29			

MORE SUBORDINATION

The more conservative rating methodology also means that the rating agencies require higher subordination levels. In particular, equity tranches are usually much larger on emerging market deals than in high-yield deals. Exhibit 5 shows a representative high-yield deal versus a representative sovereign EM deal, both brought to market at approximately the same time. Note that the equity tranche is 7.9% on the high-yield deal versus 18% on the EM deal. More generally, the tranches in the CDO deals which are rated investment grade receive much more protection on the EM deal than they do on the high-yield deal. One measure of this is the amount of the deal that is rated less than investment grade, and is available to support the investment-grade tranches. In the EM CDO, 22.2% of the deal is rated less than investment grade (18% equity tranche plus 4.2% Mezz tranche). By contrast, in the high-yield CDO, only 11.9% of the deal (7.9% equity tranche plus 4.0% Mezz 2 tranche) is rated less than investment grade.

The yields for each tranche are higher on the EM CBO than for the corresponding tranche on the high-yield CBO, in spite of the fact that the rating is as high or higher on the EM debt. The AAA rated bond on the EM deal is priced at 68 discount margin (DM), versus 57 DM on the high-yield deal. The A rated EM tranche is priced at +250/10-year Treasury, versus +225/10-year Treasury for a lower rated (A–) tranche of the high-yield deal. This translates into roughly a 50 b.p. differential, as the credit quality differential is worth 25 b.p.. The Ba1 mezzanine bond in the EM deal is priced at +800/10-year, versus +700/10-year for the BB– tranche of the high-yield deal. Here the EM investor is receiving a 100 b.p. higher spread, as well as higher credit quality. The equity on the EM deal is the only exception to this. It may yield slightly less than on high-yield deals, as the equity is far less leveraged. The difference in the leverage can be seen by the fact that the EM equity is 18% of the deal versus 7.9% of the high-yield deal.

CONCLUSION

It's unfortunate that many investors have been reluctant to look at CBOs backed by EM collateral, because of general misimpressions about the collateral. In this chapter, we have shown that there have been few actual defaults on sovereign EM bonds, which is the collateral used to back many EM CBOs. Many investors do not realize this, as they tend to clump together the experience of both sovereign bank loans and sovereign bonds. The former, sovereign bank loans, has clearly experienced more significant level of defaults. Moreover, when there is a default, the recovery rates are higher on the sovereign bonds than on the bank loans.

Moreover, because of the limited history of sovereign bonds, the rating agencies are far more conservative in their ratings. They are particularly harsh in the assumptions they make about recoveries, and on diversity characteristics. This more conservative rating methodology means that the average credit quality of bonds is higher in the EM deal.

Finally, EM CBOs have more subordination. This extra structural protection is clearly not priced in. EM CBOs trade wider than high-yield CBOs for every rated tranche.

Section II

Valuation and Trading Issues

Chapter 8

How Swap Spreads Affect the Performance of Floating Rate Emerging Market Bonds

Costas C. Hamakiotes, Ph.D.
Senior Vice President
Emerging Markets Fixed Income Strategy
Lehman Brothers

F loating-rate coupon bonds constitute 25.6% of the $218 billion market capitalization Lehman Brothers Emerging Markets Index. Out of the 211 securities in the index, 40 are floating and the remaining 171 are fixed. The former issues typically float over LIBOR at a non-zero spread—$^{13}/_{16}$, for example. This spread is known as "reset margin." For price/yield calculations, it is common practice among market participants to "swap" the asset. This means that implicit in the calculations is either a swap to maturity of the flows, or a series of successive swaps whereby the future stream of flows is determined by the Eurodollar futures (i.e., the forward LIBOR rates as implied by the swap curve). Consequently, swap spreads have an effect on the valuation of the bond, and the entire swap spread curve constitutes an independent input variable, much like the entire Treasury curve. Yet the effect of swap spreads is hardly ever discussed.

This chapter discusses the relationship between swap spreads and the performance of emerging markets floating-rate bonds. In particular, it demonstrates how long-term money managers and hedge, or "arbitrage," accounts are affected through their positions in such bonds by employing and analyzing real trades and return performances. Further, it discusses the link between swap and credit spreads, and the implications of swaps potentially replacing Treasuries as the benchmark someday. With their volatility at unprecedented levels (as of March 16, 2001), we demonstrate that their effect can be at least as important as that of the credit spread and Treasury components. Further, we prove that unless the asset is swapped into fixed, investors are far from assured of earning the yield of the bond (if held to maturity and all bond obligations of the issuer are honored). In fact, depending on the magnitude of Treasury, credit spread, and swap spread changes, it is conceivable that both the yield and the price of a floating-rate bond could decrease. Lastly, it shows that it is the whole of the Treasury and swap curves that affect bond valuations, rather than just any single point on these curves.

Exhibit 1: History of 2-, 3-, and 5-Year Swap Spreads

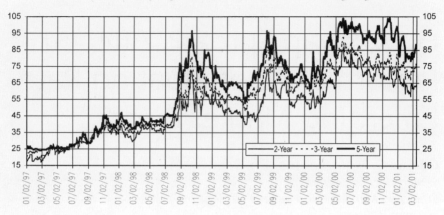

Exhibit 2: History of 10- and 30-Year Swap Spreads

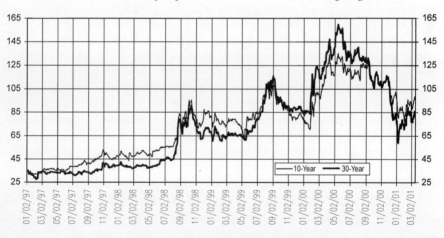

SWAP SPREAD HISTORY

Exhibits 1 and 2 show 2-, 3-, 5-, 10-, and 30-year swap spreads historically to January 1997. Given that many of the floaters in emerging markets have long average lives, we expect the wild swings of swap spreads to have a huge impact on the floaters' valuations. And we show that they do. To put the average life of the floaters in perspective, the floating portion of our Lehman Brothers Emerging Markets Index has an average life of 10.3 years and a stripped spread duration of 3.8. In contrast, the fixed portion of the index has an average life of 11.3 years and a stripped spread duration of 4.7.

Swap spreads first spiked significantly during the last calendar quarter of 1997, due to the Asia crisis. That spike was dwarfed by the widening almost exactly one year later at the advent of the Russia meltdown and the Long Term Capital Management blowup. Then, almost exactly one year after that, credit and swap spreads widened because of inflation fears, repeated Fed hikes, and concerns about Y2K. Finally, the wide spreads during most of 2000 were characterized by credit concerns (U.S. investment-grade and high-yield widened dramatically), and technical factors surrounding the U.S. government's buyback program's squeezing the Treasury market, causing it to invert in significant ways.

ANALYSIS

The price of a bond P with a set of cash flows F_i, at a yield R, is calculated as follows:

$$P = \sum_i \frac{F_i}{(1 + R)^i}$$

In the case of a floating-rate bond, each of the cash flows is a function of swap rates or, alternatively, Treasuries, T, and swap spreads, SS. Further, we rewrite the yield, R, as the sum of Treasuries, T, and some credit spread, CS. The above equation can then be written as:

$$P = \sum_i \frac{f_i(T_i, SS_i)}{g_i(T_i, CS_i)} \tag{1}$$

Equation (1) shows that the price of a floating-rate bond depends on three variables: Treasuries, credit spreads, and swap spreads. As a result, then, such a bond has three durations: Treasury duration, D_T, credit spread duration, D_{CS}, and swap spread duration, D_{SS}. These are defined as follows:

$$D_T \equiv \frac{-1}{P} \times \left.\frac{\partial P}{\partial T}\right|_{CS_i, SS_i}, \quad D_{CS} \equiv \frac{-1}{P} \times \left.\frac{\partial P}{\partial CS}\right|_{T_i, SS_i}, \quad D_{SS} \equiv \frac{-1}{P} \times \left.\frac{\partial P}{\partial SS}\right|_{T_i, CS_i} \tag{2}$$

Consequently, the percent change in price, $\%\Delta P$, caused by a change in Treasuries, ΔT, a change in credit spreads, ΔCS, and a change in swap spreads, ΔSS, is approximated to the first degree of accuracy by:

$$\%\Delta P = -D_T \times \Delta T - D_{CS} \times \Delta CS - D_{SS} \times \Delta SS \tag{3}$$

A NOTE ON THE SHAPE OF THE TREASURY AND SWAP SPREAD CURVES

As can be seen in equation (1), it is the shape of the entire Treasury and swap curves that affects valuation of floating-rate bonds, rather than just any one, single point along the curve. In this chapter, for the sake of simplicity and clarity, we do our analysis assuming all parallel shifts. As we will witness in later sections, this can be a gross simplification, especially when one considers the shifts that have taken place in both curves during the year 2000. For example, the Treasury curve as defined by 2s-to-30s was at pick 24 bp on January 1, 2000, give 65 bp on June 1, 2000, pick 48 bp on January 1, 2001, and pick 103 bp on March 16, 2001.[1] These are huge fluctuations, with huge implications for the performance of long-term asset holders. Further, it is also important to notice that parallel shifts of par curves (such as the Treasury and swap curves) do not translate to parallel shifts in the spot and forward curves.

LINKING SWAP SPREADS AND CREDIT SPREADS

By definition, any spread over Treasuries represents risk over Treasuries. As a result, we would expect swap spreads and credit spreads to be correlated. Exhibit 3 shows the history of the 10-year swap spread and the stripped spread of our Lehman Brothers Emerging Markets Index dating back to January 1, 1997. It could be possible, then, to link swap and credit spreads through the correlation of their behavior, thus reducing the dependency of price in equation (1) to just two variables: Treasuries and spreads in general. It should, however, be noted that in this case, the correlation would enter the equation, and it could be viewed as an independent parameter because it changes with time and over different time horizons.

Exhibit 3: History of 10-Year Swap Spreads and Stripped Spread of the Lehman Brothers Emerging Markets Index

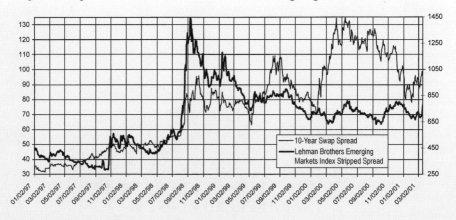

---

[1] "Pick" and "give" are used here to indicate the yield pick-up or give-up to extend from 2-year Treasury notes to 30-year Treasury bonds.

TREASURIES OR SWAP SPREADS AS A BENCHMARK?

During most of 2000, in the midst of the U.S. Treasury Department's ongoing buy-back program and diminishing Treasury bond and note supply, there was a lot of speculation about the long-term existence of Treasuries. Many market participants were and still are considering whether spread products should trade off swaps rather than Treasuries. Even if the market agrees to such a change, the mathematics of our analysis would change only slightly; its foundation would remain intact. In the scenario in which Treasuries disappear or no longer serve as the benchmark and are replaced by swaps, the independent parameters in the price equation would be reduced to two: swap rates, SR, (rather than swap spreads) and credit spreads, CS', which would now be a spread over swap rates. Equation (1) would then be written as:

$$P = \sum_i \frac{F_i(SR_i)}{g_i(SR_i, CS_i')}$$

In this case, the functional dependency of P on the two new independent variables, SR and CS', would lead to two new types of duration: one quantifying the exposure to swap *rates,* and one to the credit spread over swap rates.

RESULTS

To demonstrate the effect of swap spreads, we have constructed four sample bonds. All of them bullet bonds paying LIBOR + $^{13}/_{16}$. The 3-year bond is meant to simulate the 2- to 3.5-year average life sector Brady bonds, such as Argentina FRBs, Brazil EIs, and Venezuela DCBs. The 7-year bond is meant to simulate the 7- to 10-year average life sector Brady bonds, such as Brazil DCBs, Bulgaria FLIRBs, and IAB. The 20-year bond is meant to simulate the 20-year average life sector Brady bonds, such as all the Discount bonds, but looked upon in blended or cash flow fashion. The last type of bond we set up is a 20-year bond whose principal is collateralized (but without rolling interest guarantee), thus closely simulating all Discount bonds looked upon in stripped fashion.

Exhibits 4, 5, and 6 show the results of equation (2)—that is, the credit spread, Treasury, and swap spread durations for each of our four sample bonds parametrically as a function of the credit spread of the bond. Each of the durations gives the percent change in price caused by a 100 bp change in the underlying parameter, given that the other two variables remain unchanged.

Two points are evident. The first is that the effect of swap spreads is significant as manifested by the magnitude of the swap spread duration compared with the magnitude of the other two durations. The second is that the swap spread duration is negative. This means that, Treasuries and credit spreads unchanged, the price of the bond increases as swap spreads widen and vice versa. This makes sense because an increase (widening) in swap spreads implies a higher stream of flows forward. On the other hand, and counteracting this effect of swap spreads, widening of swap spreads is a manifestation of credit deterioration, which, in all likelihood, is accompanied by widening in credit spreads. As a result, the end effect depends on the relative changes of swap spreads, credit spreads, and Treasuries, and is quantified by equation (3).

To put the results of the matrices in Exhibits 4–6 in the context of emerging markets, we list select assets, their average lives, and spreads in Exhibit 7.

TRADING AND PERFORMANCE IMPLICATIONS AND STRATEGIES

These results have significant ramifications for most market participants, especially since many of them do not actually swap the floating-rate instruments into fixed. In this last section of the chapter, we demonstrate some of these ramifications with three examples.

Exhibit 4: Credit Spread Duration— All Bonds are Floating-Rate Paying LIBOR + 13/16

Spread	3-Year	7-Year	20-Year Uncollateralized	20-Year Collateralized
150	2.70	5.56	10.87	5.47
250	2.69	5.49	10.35	5.12
350	2.67	5.43	9.85	4.79
450	2.66	5.36	9.36	4.49
550	2.64	5.29	8.88	4.20
650	2.62	5.22	8.42	3.93
750	2.61	5.15	7.98	3.68
850	2.59	5.09	7.56	3.45
950	2.58	5.02	7.17	3.23
1,050	2.56	4.95	6.79	3.03
1,150	2.55	4.88	6.44	2.84

Exhibit 5: Treasury Spread Duration— All Bonds are Floating-Rate Paying LIBOR + 13/16

Spread	3-Year	7-Year	20-Year Uncollateralized	20-Year Collateralized
150	0.00	0.04	0.25	1.42
250	−0.04	−0.15	−0.57	1.63
350	−0.09	−0.34	−1.38	1.86
450	−0.13	−0.53	−2.15	2.09
550	−0.18	−0.72	−2.90	2.34
650	−0.22	−0.92	−3.61	2.59
750	−0.27	−1.12	−4.29	2.84
850	−0.31	−1.31	−4.92	3.10
950	−0.36	−1.52	−5.52	3.36
1,050	−0.41	−1.72	−6.08	3.62
1,150	−0.45	−1.92	−6.60	3.87

Exhibit 6: Swap Spread Duration—
All Bonds are Floating-Rate Paying LIBOR + 13/16

Spread	3-Year	7-Year	20-Year Uncollateralized	20-Year Collateralized
150	−2.70	−5.52	−10.61	−9.99
250	−2.73	−5.64	−10.93	−9.75
350	−2.76	−5.76	−11.23	−9.51
450	−2.79	−5.89	−11.51	−9.28
550	−2.82	−6.01	−11.78	−9.06
650	−2.85	−6.14	−12.03	8.84
750	−2.88	−6.27	−12.27	−8.62
850	−2.91	−6.40	−12.49	−8.41
950	−2.94	−6.53	−12.69	−8.21
1,050	−2.97	−6.67	−12.87	−8.02
1,150	−3.00	−6.80	−13.04	−7.83

Exhibit 7: Select Emerging Markets Floating-Rate Assets,
Their Average Lives, and Spreads

Asset	Average Life	Spread
Argentina FRB	2.0	1,035
Argentina Discount	22.0	1,161
Brazil EI	2.6	540
Brazil DCB	7.1	804
Brazil Discount	23.1	954
Bulgaria FLIRB	6.3	743
Bulgaria IAB	7.4	704
Bulgaria Discount	23.3	981
Mexico Discount	18.8	479
Panama PDI	11.8	461
Venezuela DCB	3.5	815

For Discount bonds, we list their stripped spreads. Data as of close March 20, 2001.

What Needs to Happen to Overcome Effect of
Swap Spread Changes

The matrices in Exhibits 8 and 9 show the change of credit spreads, in an environment of unchanged Treasuries, that is required to offset a change of −20 bp and −40 bp in swap spreads, respectively. For example, Exhibit 9 shows that if swap spreads *tighten* by 40 bp and Treasuries remain unchanged, the credit spread of a 7-year bond trading at a spread of 850 bp needs to tighten by 50 bp to offset the negative effect of the swap spread's tightening (i.e., just to break even). This is the case if the floating-rate bond is not swapped. If the bond were swapped, then the 40 bp swap spread contraction would actually be realized, and this alone would translate to a +2.56% return (the product of the swap spread duration from Exhibit 6 times the change in swap spreads, i.e., [−6.40] × [−0.40%]).

Referring to Exhibit 7, for example, we can see that the Brazil DCB, a 7-year average-life bond, trades at a spread of about 800 bp. Exhibit 9 shows that if the bond is not swapped, its spread needs to tighten by 50 bp just to offset the negative effect of a 40 bp tightening in swap spreads. Similarly, the Brazil Discount, a 23-year collateralized bond trading at about 950 bp stripped spread, needs to see its spread contract by 102 bp to offset the negative effect of a 40 bp contraction in swap spreads if it is not swapped.

Put a different way, take, for example, the Argentina Discount bond, a 22-year bond that trades at a stripped spread of 1,161 bp (Exhibit 7). On March 20, 2001, this bond traded about even stripped spread with the Argentina Par bond. In this case, we favor going long Pars and short Discounts. If we do not swap the Discount bond, then, in effect, we are long the fixed leg of the swap. In this case, even if the two bonds stay at even spread, as long as swap spreads tighten, we would generate positive P&L, and, conversely, if swap spreads widen, we would lose money. If swap spreads were to widen 40 bp, Discounts (not swapped) would need to widen by an additional 110 bp (Exhibit 9) to Pars just to break even on the trade.

Exhibit 8: Change in Credit Spreads Required to Offset −20bp Change in Swap Spreads for Break Even Return While Treasuries Remain Unchanged (in bp)

Spread	3-Year	7-Year	20-Year Uncollateralized	20-Year Collateralized
150	−20	−20	−20	−37
250	−20	−21	−21	−38
350	−21	−21	−23	−40
450	−21	−22	−25	−41
550	−21	−23	−27	−43
650	−22	−24	−29	−45
750	−22	−24	−31	−47
850	−22	−25	−33	−49
950	−23	−26	−35	−51
1,050	−23	−27	−38	−53
1,150	−24	−28	−40	−55

Exhibit 9: Change in Credit Spreads Required to Offset −40bp Change in Swap Spreads for Break Even Return While Treasuries Remain Unchanged (in bp)

Spread	3-Year	7-Year	20-Year Uncollateralized	20-Year Collateralized
150	−40	−40	−39	−73
250	−41	−41	−42	−76
350	−41	−42	−46	−79
450	−42	−44	−49	−83
550	−43	−45	−53	−86
650	−43	−47	−57	−90
750	−44	−49	−61	−94
850	−45	−50	−66	−98
950	−46	−52	−71	−102
1,050	−46	−54	−76	−106
1,150	−47	−56	−81	−110

Exhibit 10: Performance of Brazil DCB and C, May 31, 2000 - March 16, 2001

DCB	Price	Yield	Spread	Duration Spread	Duration Treasury	TROR
05/31/00	71.250	14.96	846	4.80	−0.82	10.14%
03/16/01	72.500	12.57	778	4.76	−1.07	
Change	1.250	−2.39	−68			

C	Price	Yield	Spread	Duration Spread	Duration Treasury	TROR
05/31/00	69.875	14.34	786	5.15	5.15	21.28%
03/16/01	78.625	12.46	758	4.91	4.91	
Change	8.750	−1.89	−28			

The bottom line is that investors may choose to swap a floating-rate asset, or not. Each action gives a different P&L and risk/reward profile that the investor needs to be cognizant of. Whether an investor decides to swap the asset or not is almost irrelevant as long as one is fully aware of the risks involved with each of the actions.

Performance from the "Real Money" Manager's Perspective

For the purpose of this example, we chose two bonds that are similar from every perspective except for the fixed- or floating-rate nature of their coupons: Brazil DCBs and Cs. DCBs pay a coupon of LIBOR + 7/8, amortize in 17 equal payments commencing April 2004 with an April 2012 final, and have a 7.1-year average life. Cs pay an 8% fixed coupon, amortize in 21 equal payments commencing April 2004 with an April 2014 final, and have an 8.1-year average life.

We calculated the total rates of return for each of these bonds from May 31, 2000, to March 16, 2001. Exhibit 10 shows the trading levels of the two bonds at the two points in time and their calculated total rates of return. The discrepancy in the performance of the bonds is evident and impressive. The yield of DCBs compressed by 239 bp, whereas that of Cs compressed by 189 bp. Yet DCBs returned 10.14%, almost half what Cs did, 21.28%.

Exhibit 11 shows the changes in the Treasury and swap spread curves for the same period of time. Not only is the magnitude of the changes evident, but also the change in the shape of both curves. This brings us to the point that we made at the beginning of this chapter regarding the shape of the entire curve influencing the valuation of floating-rate bonds.

Our last exercise is an approximate return attribution that tries to see where the returns came from or were taken away from. Exhibit 12 shows our results. On May 31, 2000, DCBs were trading at a spread of 846 bp (see Exhibit 10). We approximate their swap spread duration as −6.40 (see Exhibit 6). For the purpose of this approximate decomposition of returns, we consider the changes in the 10-year Treasury and the 10-year swap spread. It is clear that the answers would be different if we considered another point on the curves. The correct approach should account for the contribution of each part of those curves to the price of the bonds.

The final point is about the return of the floating-rate bond (i.e., the DCB). As noted earlier, the holder of a floating-rate bond is far from being assured to earn the calculated yield of that bond unless the bond has been swapped. If the DCB had been swapped, instead of losing 1.26% due to Treasuries and 2.37% due to swap spreads (i.e., a total cost of 3.63%), the bond would have earned it, thus bringing its estimated total rate of return to 18.92% (= 12.01 + 3.28 + 1.26 + 2.37). This is much closer to the return of its fixed-coupon counterpart, the C bond.

A Relative Value Trade from the Hedge Fund Manager's Perspective

Our final example is a relative value trade that calls for long and short positions. Once again and for the same reasons, we refer to the same pair of bonds: Brazil DCBs and Cs. On September 15, 2000, DCBs were trading at a yield pick-up of 12 bp over Cs (Exhibit 13). Suppose that at the time, one believed that DCBs would tighten even more to Cs, eventually trading through Treasuries. To capture that move, one would need to buy $1 million DCBs, sell $770,000 Cs, and buy $600,000 10-year U.S. Treasury notes (the amounts listed under the "Hedge Ratio" column in Exhibit 13). The trade would be a virtually neutral carry trade (marginally negative to the tune of 0.3 bp per month). Since managers typically do not swap the floating-rate bonds, we do the analysis here under the same terms and conditions.

Exhibit 11: Treasury and Swap Spread Curves, May 31, 2000 - March 16, 2001

	Treasuries				
	2-Year	3-Year	5-Year	10-Year	30-Year
05/31/00	6.693	6.641	6.537	6.292	6.021
03/16/01	4.236	4.319	4.487	4.761	5.269
Change (bp)	**−246**	**−232**	**−205**	**−153**	**−75**

	Swap Spreads				
	2-Year	3-Year	5-Year	10-Year	30-Year
05/31/00	85.70	92.50	104.00	132.50	156.50
03/16/01	63.00	76.00	87.50	95.50	80.75
Change (bp)	**−22.70**	**−16.50**	**−16.50**	**−37.00**	**−75.75**

Exhibit 12: Approximate Return Attribution, May 31, 2000 - March 16, 2001

	Contribution to Total Rate of Return					
		Changes			Total	Total
	Yield	Spread	Treasury	Swap	Estimated	Actual
DCB	12.01%	3.28%	−1.26%	−2.37%	11.66%	10.14%
C	11.40%	1.43%	7.88%	0.00%	20.71%	21.28%

Exhibit 13: Brazil DCBs and Cs on September 15, 2000 and March 16, 2001

	Price	Yield	Spread	DV01 Spread	DV01 Treasury	Hedge Ratio	Market Value
09/15/00							
DCB	76.125	13.04	701	380.29	−72.21	1.00	$761,250
C	75.875	12.92	686	494.07	494.07	−0.77	−$719,436
UST 5.75 8/15/2010	99.328	5.84			741.60	0.61	$595,969
		0.12					$637,783
03/16/01							
DCB	72.500	12.57	778	360.54	−80.97		$725,000
C	78.625	12.46	758	495.91	495.91		−$745,511
UST 5.75 8/15/2010	106.465	4.88			776.30		$638,789
		0.11					$618,278
Difference		0.00					**−$19,505**

Exhibit 14: Treasury and Swap Spread Curves, September 15, 2000 - March 16, 2001

	Treasuries 2-Year	3-Year	5-Year	10-Year	30-Year
09/15/00	6.062	6.013	5.916	5.839	5.900
03/16/01	4.236	4.319	4.487	4.761	5.269
Change (bp)	**−183**	**−169**	**−143**	**−108**	**−63**

	Swap Spreads 2-Year	3-Year	5-Year	10-Year	30-Year
09/15/00	69.50	75.50	92.70	117.20	117.20
03/16/01	63.00	76.00	87.50	95.50	80.75
Change (bp)	**−6.50**	**0.50**	**−5.20**	**−21.70**	**−36.45**

Exhibit 13 lists the trading levels on the initiation date of September 15, 2000, and on March 16, 2001. What should be noted is that although the relative level between the two bonds did not change, the trade actually *lost* $19,505 on just $1 million position. That is a loss of 1.95 points.

Exhibit 14 shows the changes in the Treasury and swap spread curves during the same period.

The way the trade was set up, both credit spreads and Treasuries were hedged. Almost. They were hedged to the extent that the curves moved in parallel fashion. The only risk left unhedged was the swap spread risk. In fact, the position as described above is effectively short the fixed leg of the swap. In the meantime, the 10-year swap spreads tightened by almost 22 bp, which the trade not only did not realize but incurred as a loss. On September 15, 2000, DCBs were trading at a spread of about 700 bp (see Exhibit 13). According to Exhibit 6, DCBs had a swap spread duration of about −6.2. The P&L effect of 22 bp on such a duration bond is 1.4%, which, given the full price of DCBs at the time, translates to 1.1 points. This still leaves us with $0.85 unaccounted for. Again, the difference is attributed to the effect of the whole curve that we discussed earlier.

Having hedged with the 10-year Treasury, we have implicitly accepted and assumed that the whole curve moves pretty much in a parallel fashion. But the Treasury curve during this particular period of time had dramatically different behavior. It steepened in an impressive fashion, with the 2-year going down in yield by 183 bp, while the 10-year did so by only 108 bp. Swap spreads changed by various amounts as well. A better approach would be to quantify the Treasury and swap spread exposures through buckets of durations, thus better capturing the effects of the moves of the various parts of the perspective curves. In that case, instead of hedging with just one Treasury bond almost arbitrarily chosen from a point on the Treasury curve, we would use a series of them.

Chapter 9

Quantifying Dollar Differentials Between Emerging Market Bonds in Yield Terms

Costas C. Hamakiotes, Ph.D.
Senior Vice President
Emerging Markets Fixed Income Strategy
Lehman Brothers

INTRODUCTION

This chapter presents a methodology to quantify, in yield terms, the dollar differentials between emerging market bonds of similar credit and maturity. Although our focus is emerging markets, the proposed methodology is applicable to all asset classes across fixed income. The approach is then extended to bonds of the same credit but different maturities. The methodology involves default swaps that exist in investment-grade, high-yield, and emerging markets. This chapter demonstrates how a position in one bond, typically a lower-priced bond, can be duplicated with a position in another bond and a default swap on a certain notional amount. Implicit is the assumption that the bonds are *pari passu* in seniority structure. The methodology is especially important for any fixed-income portfolio manager (whether dedicated emerging markets, investment-grade, high-yield, or crossover) who cannot take advantage of any special effects in the repo market and, secondarily, for any such manager who can repo securities out and hedge funds or arbitrage accounts. The thinking process described here is applicable to and useful for security selection and the pricing of new issues in the capital markets. In the latter case, it is especially relevant when a new issue is priced off a high- or low-dollar benchmark and is expected to come out at a different dollar price from the benchmark. When choosing between two similar bonds, the analysis can help investors choose the one that has the most upside, with the same downside risk as the other (at the limit of default).

THE METHODOLOGY

For purposes of illustration, suppose we have two 10-year bonds with the same issuer and seniority: one with a 14½% coupon, yielding 13.30% at a price of $106.533

(Bond 1), and one with a 9⅜% coupon, yielding 11.90% at a price of $85.460 (Bond 2). Given the equal creditworthiness of the two bonds, there should be a yield differential at which an investor should be indifferent between choosing either bond while assuming the same risk. The question is, given the yield of one of the bonds, what is the "fair" yield of the other? To answer this, we start by assuming a recovery value[1] for each of the bonds in case of default. We then calculate the percent drop in the price of each bond in case of default, given these recovery values. An investor should be indifferent in choosing between the two bonds if both yielded the same, and both were subject to the same percent drop in price in case of default. If one of the bonds had a greater downside than the other but no greater upside, in percentage terms, then the investor should demand a discount in price or a premium in yield.

Our approach consists of the following steps:

Step 1—Assume a recovery value in case of default. In this case, we assume this value to be $20 for each bond.

Step 2—Calculate the percent drop in price for each of the bonds in this default outcome. Bond 1 would lose 81.23% of its value, while Bond 2 would lose 76.60%.

Step 3—Calculate the amount of default protection we need to buy. We compute the amount of money we need to protect in order to be indifferent in case of default per dollar invested. To do this, we assume that we have only enough money to buy $100 face amount of the lower dollar price bond. In this case, the choice is between buying $100 face of the $85.460 bond (Bond 2), or $80.22 face of the $106.533 bond (Bond 1). In either case, we invest $85.460. In case of default, the investment in Bond 1 would lose 81.23%; the investment in Bond 2 would lose 76.60%. This means that if we opt for Bond 1, we need to protect an amount equal to the difference, i.e., 81.23% − 76.60%, or 4.63% of its value. This results in a dollar amount of $3.96 (4.63% of $85.460). A default swap[2] would allow us to capture 80% of the notional value in case of default (because we have assumed recovery value to be $20). So we would need to enter into a default swap of $4.945 notional ($3.96 divided by 0.80).

Steps 1–3 are shown in Exhibit 1.

Step 4—Calculate the tenor of the swap and its amortizing structure.[3] We amortize the swap downward by the coupon differential. For example, an investment in

---

[1] Recovery value is the value recovered by the bondholder in case of default by the issuer.

[2] Default swap is an agreement between two counterparties struck on a single asset or a group of assets. It works as follows: the buyer of the swap pays the seller a rate for the life of the swap. If default occurs at any point in time during the life, these payments cease and the buyer delivers the underlying bond to the seller in exchange for a cash payment equal to the face amount of the bond.

[3] Amortization refers to sequential retirement of principal. A bullet bond pays all principal at maturity, i.e., at one point in time. A bond that amortizes, on the other hand, pays the principal in sequential installments that may or may not be equal amounts but usually in equal time intervals, i.e., semiannually, for example.

Bond 1 entails buying $80.22 face of the 14½% coupon bond and a default swap of $4.945 notional, while an investment in Bond 2 entails buying $100 face of the 9⅜% coupon bond. The semiannual coupon cash flow of the Bond 1 position is $5.816 (= 0.8022 × 14.50/2), while that of the Bond 2 position is $4.6875 (= 9.375/2). We apply the coupon differential of $1.1285 to amortize the swap downward because the excess coupon cash flows provide a cushion toward the downside. Once we have constructed the amortizing swap, we can calculate its average life. In this case, it turns out to be 1.08 years.

Step 5—Price the swap. Suppose a one-year default protection swap is offered at 225 bp over LIBOR. We set up the flows on an amortizing swap such as the one we set up in the previous step, i.e., the flows obtained by the coupon flows only of a 2.25% coupon annuity (no principal) on an amortizing bond in the fashion of Step 4. We then discount these flows at a yield equal to the swap rate of equal average life (one year, in this case) plus the swap spread. With one-year swap rates at 6.65%, for example, and a swap spread of 225 bp, we get a discount rate of 8.90%. Discounting these flows at this rate, we get a price (present value) for the swap of $0.14. This amounts to 2 bp of Bond 1 equivalent yield.

Exhibit 1: Determining the Notional Amount of Default Protection that Needs to be Purchased Along with the Higher-Dollar Asset in Order to Provide the Same Downside for Both Assets in Case of Default

	Bond 1	Bond 2
Price	$106.53	$85.46
Default Recovery Value	$20.00	$20.00
Drop in Points	$86.53	$65.46
Drop in Percent Terms	81.23%	76.60%

Investor has $85.46 to spend ==> Can buy $100 face of Bond 2 or $80.22 face of Bond 1.

In order to be indifferent to default, investor needs to protect differential in percent price drop
==> Needs to protect (81.23% − 76.60% = 4.63%) of $85.46 ==> (4.63% of $85.46 =) 3.96 points.

How Default Swaps Work:
Investor buys default on $100 notional for certain term.
If default occurs in that term, investor delivers cheapest to deliver bond in terms of price and receives $100 in return. That means, investor pays, say, $20.00 to buy the cheapest to deliver bond and receives $100 in return, thus making $80.00.

Q: To make $3.96 in case of default, where an asset goes to the default recovery value, investor needs to buy default protection on what notional amount?

A: Investor needs to buy default on notional of ($3.96/80.00% =) $4.95.

Exhibit 2: Cheapness of Bond 1 Compared to its Trading Yield as a Function of Default Recovery Value Scenarios for Bond 1 and Bond 2

For default swap pricing at 225bp. one-year swap rates at 6.65%.
Analysis assumes bonds are pari passu
Hypothetical trading levels and bonds:
  Bond 1: 14 1/2% coupon, 10-year, trading at 13.30% yield, 106.533 price
  Bond 2: 9 3/8% coupon, 10-year, trading at 11.90% yield, 85.460 price

Default Recovery	Default Recovery Value of Bond 2					
Value of Bond 1	30	25	20	15	10	5
30	134	140	141	142	143	144
25	126	136	140	141	142	143
20	117	130	138	140	141	142
15	109	122	132	139	140	141
10	100	114	126	135	139	141
5	92	106	119	129	136	140

Step 6—Calculate the "fair" yield of Bond 1. If Bond 2, i.e., the lower dollar price bond, trades at a yield of 11.90%, what should the yield of Bond 1 be so that we have the same downside (as defined by percent loss in value) in case of default and the same upside (as defined by earned yield) if held to maturity? The answer is that Bond 1, since it has the greater downside, should trade at a yield higher than that of Bond 2 by the amount that it would cost to buy default protection. In other words, in our example, we have determined the cost of default protection to be worth 2 bp. "Fair" yield, then, for Bond 1 relative to Bond 2, is 11.92%. But Bond 1 is trading at 13.30%. Consequently, we term Bond 1 to be 138 bp cheap (13.30% − 11.92%) compared with the level it should be trading at relative to Bond 2. This relative richness/cheapness may be due to various other factors that we discuss later (e.g., repo, liquidity, size of issue, etc.).

Step 7—Adjust for different maturities. In most real cases, the bonds we compare are of different maturities. We resolve this maturity mismatch by assuming that the longer bond is shorter and of equal maturity to the shorter bond. Once we infer value between these two, we adjust for the curve extension. In other words, we determine how much we want to be compensated to extend X number of years between two bonds of the same price and issuer, since we have already adjusted for and quantified the dollar differential. To do so, because the framework of the model set up here is in terms of yield, we must account for yield pickup due to the Treasury yield curve steepness, as well as to the credit spread curve extension. Exhibit 2 shows the amount by which Bond 1 is "cheap" to its trading level when compared with Bond 2 and its trading level based on this methodology. We show the results parametrically, assuming various default recovery values for the two bonds. In this exhibit, we analyze the yield curves of certain emerging market countries that have a number of issues outstanding across a wide maturity spectrum.

A FEW NOTES ON THE METHODOLOGY

The determination of a bond to be cheap or rich, by a certain model or thinking process, should be valued only to the extent that its value can be captured. Here we discuss the realistic aspects of our methodology and its limitations.

The Repo Market

Some of the apparent "mispricings" in the market may be due to special effects in the repo market. Our methodology assumes that both bonds trade at about the same level in the repo market. Differences in the repo market would have to be taken into consideration, and used to adjust the level by which the model assesses that one bond is rich or cheap relative to the other. Even when this is done, however, arbitraging the relationship is difficult because such a step would entail going long the cheap bond, short the expensive bond, long or short a certain amount of default protection, and locking in the repo on both bonds for extended periods of time. Such long lock-up periods in the repo market are not feasible, making it impossible to express the trade in a truly arbitrage-type way. One can approximate, but not exactly capture, the apparent "mispricing" in a risk-free way. This whole issue of the repo market, however, is irrelevant to the investor who cannot repo securities out and take advantage of special situations. If this is the case, it would be misleading to build this argument in the valuation since it would not be able to be captured by that particular investor.

The Default Swap Liquidity

The investor who does the trade, and wants to unwind at some point, may have to deal with non-trivial bid-offer spreads on the default swap side, in addition to the bond side. This is one of the reasons that we don't make much of this or any model that points to marginal cheapness or richness. But we do pay attention when our models suggest rather significant mispricings. That being said, the proposed approach is one that can be truly duplicated in the marketplace.

"Tail Risk"

We refer to "tail risk" as the risk involved when applying this methodology to bonds of non-equal maturities. In most real cases, we have to assess value between bonds that rarely have identical maturities. In fact, typically, bonds are spread out across the credit curve of a certain issuer, and we have to evaluate them relative to each other. Take, for example, an issuer such as the United Mexican States (UMS), which has bonds spaced almost a year apart from maturities of 2005 to 2012, and then, bonds maturing in 2016, 2019, and 2026. The way we approach this problem is to assume that the longer bond is actually of equal maturity with the shorter bond. First, we assess the relative value, or a "fair" yield, of this hypothetical bond, given the trading level of the shorter bond. Then we assign a certain spread differential to the curve extension. Because we solve for yield, we must be careful to account for the excess yield pickup required due to both the credit spread curve and the U.S. Treasury yield curve. We first assign value to the price differential, largely due to the coupon, and then adjust for the curve. The first is a deterministic problem, as set out in our methodology above, and has a quantifiable answer, subject to our assumptions on default recovery values. The second is a less well-defined problem, and is assessed by market trading levels.

On Default Recovery Value

Unlike corporate bonds, it is difficult to assign a recovery or salvage value to sovereign bonds. For corporate bonds, recovery value can usually be derived from the seniority of the bonds in the capital structure and the assets of the issuer, a process not well defined for sovereign issuers. History is about the only source of experience we can draw on to assign some kind of value to default. Exhibit 3 shows the historical prices of the Russian Eurobonds around the time of Russia's default. Although Russia never defaulted on these particular bonds, it did on others, and uncertainty made all its instruments trade indiscriminately at default values. At the top of the crisis, all these bonds converged to a price of around $15, plus or minus a couple of points, according to the asset. The difference was driven by coupon, maturity, supply, and demand. It is impossible to quantify the effect for each; although, at such an extreme, psychology plays a big role. Prins (Principle Notes) and IANs (Interest Arrear Notes) (which the Russians did default on), on the other hand, traded as low as the single digits. In conclusion, assigning a value to default, especially in the case of a sovereign, is a less-than-exact science, and all we can do is make educated guesses to estimate the possible outcome.

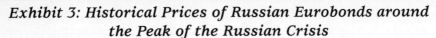

Exhibit 3: Historical Prices of Russian Eurobonds around the Peak of the Russian Crisis

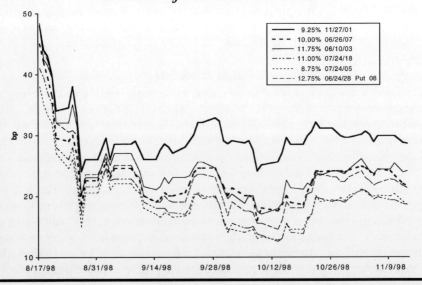

A NOTE FOR DEDICATED ACCOUNTS

The model we developed and described here is applicable to dedicated, investment-grade, high-yield, crossover, or any other fixed income accounts, most notably the ones with long-term approach and commitment to the market. It is even more applicable to accounts that cannot repo their securities out, thus taking advantage of any tightness in the repo market. We approached this problem from the perspective of these investors. Given the choice, an investor can spend a certain amount of money to buy one security with a certain yield and tenor, or another one of the same issuer with about similar maturity at a different yield and a certain amount of default protection. Our approach helps the investor choose the cheaper bond, in a way that can really be expressed in the marketplace, thus enhancing yield (should there be a mispricing according to our model) while maintaining the same risk per dollar invested.

THE APPLICATION

Exhibit 4 shows the results of applying this methodology to the curves of Argentina, Brazil, Mexico, Russia, and Turkey as of the close of March 22, 2001. Not surprisingly, we find notable mispricings as we move down the credit spectrum.

In Exhibit 4, we have listed all bonds in terms of increasing maturity (or average life). Every bond is compared with its previous one. For example, take the Brazil 14.50% of 10/15/09 and the 12.75% of 1/15/20. If Brazil 09 trades at a price of 107⅜, or a yield of 13.04%, we determine that to make it comparable with the Brazil 20 (assuming both bonds mature in 2009) we would need to enter into a 4.47-year average life default swap. Such a swap on Brazil would be offered at 650 bp. The present value of this swap would be worth $1.33, or, equivalently, 25 bp. What this means is that if Brazil 20s were the same maturity as 09s and 09s were trading at a yield of 13.04%, then 20s should be trading at a yield of 12.79%, i.e., 25 bp lower than the yield of 09s, because the swap would have to be bought alongside the 09 position (the higher dollar price bond). But 20s actually trade at a yield of 13.67%, which makes them 88 bp cheap to where they should be if they had an 09 maturity. The truth of the matter is that 20s do not have an 09 maturity. They are longer by 10.25 years. To adjust for that, we proceed as follows: 10s-to-30s along the Treasury curve are at about 50 bp. That is 2.5 bp per year. A 10.25-year extension, then, is worth about 25 bp. We assign an additional pickup of 25 bp in spread for the extension.

We conclude that in yield terms, the extension should be worth about 50 bp in yield. This tells us that "fair" yield of the 20s should be adjusted upward by 50 bp, from 12.79% to 13.29%. This makes their actual trading level about 38 bp cheap to where they should be, when compared with 09s based on this methodology. Although every step of this proposed model is quantifiable, the last step, the adjustment for the extension, is subject to market conditions and other less-than-well-quantifiable actions. In our opinion, the value of this platform far outweighs the shortcomings of the subjective nature of this last point.

Exhibit 4: Relative Value between Bonds in the Argentine, Brazilian, Mexican, Russian, and Turkish Yield Curves, as of Close March 22, 2001, Based on Flat Price

As of Close of 03/22/01 Based on Flat Price — Asset	Price	Average Life	Trading Yield	Default Swap — Average Life	Default Swap — Offer Price	Default Swap — PV Points	Default Swap — BP	"Fair" Yield Relative to Previous	Rich/Cheap Relative to Previous (bp)	Curve Extension Worth (bp)	Rich/Cheap Rel to Previous Adjusting for Curve (bp)
Argentina 8.375%, 12/20/03	85.002	2.73	15.281								
Argentina 11.000%, 12/04/05	86.000	4.69	15.277	0.23	2000	0.028	1	15.291	−1	10	−11
Argentina 11.000%, 10/09/06	85.002	5.54	15.090	2.89	2000	0.314	11	15.171	−8	5	−13
Argentina 11.750%, 04/07/09	84.499	8.03	15.149	3.80	1800	1.200	36	14.726	42	20	22
Argentina 11.375%, 03/15/10	82.504	8.97	14.983	1.88	2000	0.273	7	15.082	−10	5	−15
Argentina 12.375%, 02/21/12	84.999	10.90	15.231	0.71	2000	0.108	2	15.006	22	5	17
Argentina 11.750%, 06/15/15	83.000	14.22	14.612	0.71	2000	0.108	2	15.006	−39	5	−44
Argentina 11.375%, 01/30/17	82.505	15.85	14.168	0.22	2000	0.015	0	14.609	−44	5	−49
Argentina 12.125%, 02/25/19	85.995	17.92	14.307	1.49	2000	0.332	6	14.227	8	5	3
Argentina 12.000%, 02/01/20	85.001	18.85	14.311	5.17	2000	0.228	4	14.267	4	0	4
Argentina 9.750%, 09/19/27	73.252	26.48	13.470	2.13	1750	1.431	25	14.057	−59	0	−59
Argentina 10.250%, 07/21/30	75.252	29.32	13.708	1.29	2000	0.174	3	13.502	21	0	21
Brazil 11.625%, 04/15/04	102.501	3.05	10.638								
Brazil 10.250%, 01/11/06	96.499	4.79	11.205	0.60	300	0.057	2	10.616	59	5	54
Brazil 11.250%, 07/26/07	100.501	6.33	11.130	0.74	300	0.034	1	11.213	−8	5	−13
Brazil 9.375%, 04/07/08	91.000	7.03	11.261	1.14	440	0.164	4	11.093	17	5	12
Brazil 14.500%, 10/15/09	107.374	8.55	13.040	0.32	300	0.110	2	11.282	176	5	171
Brazil 12.750%, 01/15/20	93.748	18.80	13.675	4.47	650	1.331	25	12.790	88	50	38
Brazil 8.875%, 04/15/24	67.786	23.05	13.431	8.30	800	2.999	47	13.203	23	0	23
Brazil 10.125%, 05/15/27	76.003	26.13	13.462	13.82	850	1.547	28	13.707	−25	0	−25
Brazil 12.250%, 03/06/30	88.502	28.94	13.876	2.83	500	0.641	10	13.564	31	0	31
Brazil 11.000%, 08/17/40	77.874	39.39	14.138	16.64	850	2.524	40	13.475	66	0	66

Exhibit 4 (Continued)

As of Close of 03/22/01 Based on Flat Price — Asset	Price	Average Life	Trading Yield	Default Swap — Average Life	Default Swap — Offer Price	Default Swap — PV Points	Default Swap — PV BP	"Fair" Yield Relative to Previous	Rich/Cheap Relative to Previous (bp)	Curve Extension Worth (bp)	Rich/Cheap Rel to Previous Adjusting for Curve (bp)
UMS 9.750%, 04/06/05	107.126	4.03	7.658	0.37	100	0.013	0	7.654	34	10	24
UMS 8.500%, 02/01/06	101.998	4.85	7.990	0.63	100	0.011	0	7.992	33	10	23
UMS 9.875%, 01/15/07	107.003	5.80	8.324	0.87	100	0.019	0	8.320	16	10	6
UMS 8.625%, 03/12/08	100.744	6.96	8.479	1.09	140	0.040	1	8.486	14	10	4
UMS 10.375%, 02/17/09	109.878	7.90	8.621	1.10	140	0.013	0	8.619	8	10	-2
UMS 9.875%, 02/01/10	107.130	8.85	8.700	1.49	165	0.078	1	8.688	11	10	1
UMS 8.375%, 01/14/11	97.259	9.80	8.796	1.37	150	0.122	1	8.809	53	10	43
UMS 11.375%, 09/15/16	116.506	15.47	9.337	3.28	250	0.546	6	9.277	1	10	-9
UMS 8.125%, 12/30/19	89.800	18.75	9.286	6.92	340	1.225	11	9.395	-1	10	-11
UMS 11.500%, 05/15/26	120.251	25.13	9.386								
Russia 11.750%, 06/10/03	97.850	2.20	12.878	1.01	650	0.432	23	12.643	180	5	175
Russia 8.750%, 07/24/05	82.124	4.33	14.439	2.94	925	1.287	46	13.975	158	5	153
Russia 10.000%, 06/26/07	78.250	6.25	15.555	2.86	925	1.161	35	15.206	126	5	121
Russia 8.250%, 03/31/10	66.899	7.37	16.463	1.24	700	0.867	22	16.685	-113	5	-118
Russia 12.750%, 06/24/08	87.998	7.24	15.556	1.35	700	1.795	46	15.096	195	5	190
Russia 2.250%, 03/31/30	40.248	16.62	17.047	0.88	650	1.233	26	17.309	-205	20	-225
Russia 11.000%, 07/24/18	74.251	17.33	15.254								
Turkey 10.000%, 05/23/02	97.000	1.16	12.844	0.41	850	0.064	6	12.781	-35	5	-40
Turkey 8.875%, 05/12/03	93.503	2.12	12.435	0.13	800	0.021	1	12.443	104	5	99
Turkey 11.875%, 11/05/04	95.503	3.61	13.480	0.20	800	0.048	2	13.462	-86	5	-91
Turkey 9.875%, 02/23/05	91.753	3.91	12.607	2.52	975	0.483	17	12.438	21	5	16
Turkey 10.000%, 09/19/07	88.501	6.48	12.652	0.94	900	0.187	4	12.692	13	5	8
Turkey 12.000%, 12/15/08	96.000	7.72	12.822	4.98	1000	2.970	63	12.188	276	5	271
Turkey 12.375%, 06/15/09	88.007	8.22	14.947	3.95	1000	0.515	12	14.826	20	5	15
Turkey 11.750%, 06/15/10	83.877	9.22	15.027	6.00	1050	1.119	26	14.769	-19	30	-49
Turkey 11.875%, 01/15/30	81.754	28.80	14.575								

Exhibit 4 (Continued)

Note: The analysis has been done in following fashion:

1. Sort the bonds in increasing order of their average life.

2. Value every bond relative to the immediately prior (shorter) bond.

3. List resulting "fair" yield in the "'Fair' Yield Relative to Previous" column.

4. Next to that column list the number of BP by which this bond is cheap/rich relative to the previous one.

5. Steps 2–4 assume the two bonds we compare are of same maturity (average life).

6. Assign a value to the curve for the extension all else being equal in the second column from last.

7. Adjust the result of step 4 (column 10) by the curve value for the extension.

8. To compare bonds not directly adjacent in terms of average life, proceed in sequence and add the results.

9. For Russia, we have assumed the new 10- and 30-year to be of same seniority with the other Eurobonds.

Chapter 10

From the Asian Crisis to the Brazilian Devaluation: The View from a Trading Desk

Marcelo Fernandes de Lima Castro
Director
BNP Paribas

T his chapter covers the events that took place in emerging markets between the beginning of the Asian crisis in September 1997 until the Brazilian devaluation of the Real (BRL), in January 1999.

Although the story involves plenty of economic and financial concepts, it is not intended to be a rigorous economic essay. The objective is to show how events in distant parts of the world interconnect and cause abrupt changes on prices and expectations. It also attempts to show that "contagion" does not merely reflect an irrational herd behavior of international investors. Rather, contagion may have rational causes, based on liquidity considerations, relative value among assets, and the fact that when financial institutions lose money in a specific country, investors become overall more risk averse.

This chapter also tries to depict how the information flows, and how decisions are taken on a trading desk. As a trader of Brazilian local fixed income since 1993, I have based this recollection on my personal notes during the crisis. As often as possible, I have tried to provide independent sources to substantiate the events described.

OPTIMISM

In September 1997, Latin American markets enjoyed sheer optimism. The Asian financial crisis was touched off by the Thailand's Baht 20% devaluation, in July 1997. It was quickly followed by the capitulation of the Indonesian Rupiah, Malaysian Ringgit and Philippine Peso, but so far was not able to contaminate the bullish sentiment in Latin America. After a few days of market volatility, Latin countries resumed external borrowing at record high volumes and at the lowest credit spreads since the 1970s. On September 11, Venezuela placed USD 4 billion 30-year global bonds at 325 bp over U.S. Treasuries, and on the following day, Argentina announced the issue of USD 2.25 billion 30-year global bonds at 305 bp spread.

During the two years following the Mexican crisis there was no major crisis in Latin America. Any brave Brady bonds trader who aggressively bought at jittery moments—and there were quite a few hectic weeks—was the frank winner. Still, the absolute resilience of Latin America vis-à-vis the worrisome reports that came from Asia puzzled many trading desks. At risk meetings, traders, economists, and market strategists exhaustively discussed whether or not the events on the other side of the globe would ultimately hit Latin America.

Evidence against contagion was compelling: clients kept buying bonds, there was firm demand for new issues, a full-fledged privatization was taking place in Brazil, strong growth observed in Argentina, and Mexico fully recovered from the Tequila crisis. As the market climbed higher despite the unsettling news coming from the east, market participants wondered if Latin America was really different. After all, it hardly shared the faults that apparently caused the Asian debacle: lax credit and monetary policies, an excessively leveraged banking sector, crony capitalism, over-regulated capital markets, and inadequate bankruptcy laws. It seemed that the Tequila crisis had forced Latin American countries to do their homework in 1995. Adding to this positive view, the U.S. economy remained healthy and the buoyant Dow Jones had long shrugged off U.S. Fed Chairman Greenspan's "irrational exuberance" speech of December 1996. This contrasted with the bad dynamics that the ailing Japanese economy exerted upon southeast Asia.

MARKET TECHNICALS

Very few strategists had realized how much leverage there was in the system, until the Korean debacle and the speculation against the Hong Kong peg in late 1997 forced them to take a hard look into the numbers. To use the proper Wall Street jargon, "market technicals" were unusually bad in September 1997.

From the second half of 1995 to 1997, Latin American bonds yielded excellent returns with relatively low volatility; foreign banks, local dealers, wealthy individuals, and asset-management firms had built increasingly high profit expectations. As credit spreads compressed, they had to resort to leverage to keep the previous bond returns. For example in January 1996, a position of USD 100 million cash invested on Brazilian Eligible Interest (EI) bonds at the price of 74.50 yielded USD 7 million of revenues over one year, assuming that the credit spread would not change. This theoretical revenue, assuming the credit spread constant, is what market players call "carry." In September 1997, the same USD 100 million position in EI bonds at 93.50 price would have an annual carry of only USD 2.85 million; therefore, 59.3% lower. To make the carry the same as it was in January 1996, one had to resort to leverage or derivatives. During that time, two forms of boosting yield were very popular: repos and selling covered call options.

Repurchase Agreements

Repurchase agreements are essentially a form of secured lending. If an investor[1] has USD 100 million cash and wants to buy as many EI bonds as possible, he or she could spend USD 100 million to buy EI bonds[2] in the market, sell them to a dealer, and enter into a repurchase agreement (repo). To prevent changes in the bond price from creating an undesirable credit exposure with the client, the dealer usually retains part of the bonds as collateral. This cushion to cover eventual price fluctuations is called "haircut." Haircuts vary according to the volatility and liquidity of each bond. For the sake of the example, assume that the dealer retains 20% of the EI bonds as haircut, and does a repo on the remaining USD 80 million. The investor ends up with USD 80 million in cash and has USD 20 million of EI bonds in an escrow account as guarantee of a repurchase agreement of USD 80 million EIs. With USD 80 million the investor can repeat the transaction, and buy another USD 64 million EIs in repo and deposit an additional USD 16 million EIs as collateral. After the second repo, the investor would then have USD 64 million cash, USD 36 million EIs deposited as guarantee, and USD 144 million EIs in repos. This transaction could be repeated, until all the USD 100 million initial cash is deposited as collateral in the form of EI bonds, and the investor ends up with USD 400 million EI bonds in repos. In practice, the dealer processes all these steps simultaneously: the client delivers USD 100 million in bonds and enters into a USD 400 million repo. Notice that the USD 400 million repo is essentially a loan backed by USD 500 million EI bonds (cash value).

Back in 1997, the competition for clients was so fierce, that the average client would incur haircuts on Brazilian assets as low as 5%; that contrasts with a 12% haircut the same client would pay in April 2001. This repo mechanism multiplies the amount of bonds that cash can buy. It is essentially a geometric progression with ratio $(1 - h)$, where h is the haircut. In essence, the amount of bonds and the total return of a one-year repo transaction are given in the following equations:

$$\text{Bond amount at risk} = \text{Initial Cash}/h \tag{1}$$

$$\text{Repo total return} = \text{Initial Cash} \times \left[\left(\frac{R - r}{h} \right) + r \right] \tag{2}$$

---

[1] In this chapter, the term "investor" is used quite indiscriminately. If we were to follow Benjamin Graham's rigorous definitions of investment and speculation (in *The Intelligent Investor*), a great deal of the activities described in this chapter would fall into the latter category.

[2] EI bonds trade at a discount to face value, therefore the face value amount would be more than USD 100 million. In this chapter, whenever we mention a cash position in bonds we refer to their actual market value (i.e., it includes discount and accrued interests). One should not confuse market value (also denominated cash value) with the face value amount.

r = repo rate accrued in the period
h = haircut (notice that $1/h$ equals the leverage)
R = total return of the bond, therefore price change plus accrued interests.

Mathematically, the total return of a bond during a given period starting on date 0 and ending on date n is defined as:

$$R = \{[\text{Bond Price}_n + \text{Accrued Interest}_n + \text{CF}_{(0,n)}] \div [\text{Bond Price}_0 + \text{Accrued Interest}_0]\} - 1 \tag{3}$$

where

Bond Price$_n$ = Bond Price on date n
Accrued Interest $_n$ = Accrued Interest on date n
$\text{CF}_{(0,n)}$ = Cash flows paid to the bondholder (amortization and interests) between dates 0 and n, plus interests from the payment date until date n^3.

Notice on equation (2) that if the dealer asks for 100% haircut, then there is no leverage, and the repo total return equals R. For $h = 8\%$, which was the average haircut available in September 1997, the bond amount at risk would be multiplied by 12.5 times, and, assuming a repo rate of 7%, the repo would multiply the total return of an EI bonds position.

Writing Covered Call Options

The second popular way to enhance bond returns was to write covered call options. In this strategy, the investor sells the right to buy a bond at a certain strike price. If the investor owns a bond and writes a call option on it, this implies that he or she receives a premium, but gives away potential upside on the bond. This strategy makes sense if the investor has a positive long-term view on a bond, but does not believe that it will appreciate substantially in the short run. Thus writing a call on a bond and collecting the premium enhances the total return of the position if there is no significant increase on the bond price until the option maturity.

Analytically, a covered call position has the following total return R_{call}:

$$R_{\text{call}} = \frac{\text{Min}(R, R_k)}{(1 - \text{call})} \tag{4}$$

R follows definition of equation (3), R_k is the total return of the bond, if it is sold at the strike price k, and call is the call premium stated as a percentage of the initial bond "dirty price" (i.e., price plus accrued interests).

---

[3] To simplify notation, the Bond Price, Accrued Interests, and Cash flows are stated in U.S. dollars not as a percentage of the face value. This avoids complications of a changing face value, due to amortizations and capitalizations, both not unusual peculiarities of emerging market debt.

Exhibit 1: Total Return (%) of EI bonds position

EI Price after one month	Bond without leverage	Covered call without leverage	Bond 3 × leverage	Covered call 3 × leverage	Bond 15 × leverage	Covered call 15 × leverage
96.0	3.21	2.71	8.43	6.91	39.73	32.15
	45.08	*36.94*	*159.28*	*119.68*	*5,036.14*	*2,563.78*
93.5	0.61	1.14	0.64	2.21	0.78	8.66
	7.48	*14.28*	*7.79*	*29.42*	*9.63*	*165.93*
80.0	−13.41	−12.95	−41.42	−40.07	−209.52	−202.74
	−81.63	*−80.47*	*−99.82*	*−99.76*	n.a.	n.a.
70.0	−23.79	−23.39	−72.58	−71.39	−365.30	−359.34
	−95.92	*−95.66*	*−100.00*	*−100.00*	n.a.	n.a.
50.0	−44.56	−44.27	−134.89	−134.02	−676.87	−672.53
	−99.90	*−99.90*	n.a.	n.a.	n.a.	n.a.
Margin call price	n.a.	n.a.	61.20	60.86	87.03	86.56

Notes: Initial price = 93.50; Repo rate = 7% p.a.; Call price = 0.50 (10% vol); Theoretical purchase date = Sep/08/97; Repo tenor/Option maturity = Oct/09/97. (n.a. = not applicable)
Annualized return is compounded, base 365. For example:
$-81.63\% = \{[1+ (-13.406/100)]^{(365/31)} - 1\} \times 100$
(Bottom numbers in italics represent annualized return.)

A relevant point is the strike price of the call option. Notice that the more in-the-money the call (i.e., the lower the strike k), the higher is the call premium and the lower R_k. Combining the two effects, as the call strike gets lower, the less upside the investor has, since the bonds are more likely to be sold at the strike k. Generally, the investor prefers to write calls slightly out-the-money-forward, thus keeping some upside if the bonds appreciate during the option period.

Equation (4) describes a covered call position without leverage. In those days, investors would actually combine covered call positions (equation (4)) with repo positions (equation (2)), thus further increasing risk and expected returns.

Exhibit 1 simulates the one-month total return on an EI bonds position with different strategies and degrees of leverage. Taking market conditions as of September 1997, the repo rate was 7%, the initial EI price 93.50, and the call price 0.50 for a 95.00 strike, implying 10% volatility.[4] The bottom numbers in italics in Exhibit 1 show the annualized return.

Notice how the leverage substantially increases the potential upside and downside, and how the covered call strategy provides the best returns if the bond price remains unchanged. The bottom row is of particular interest: it shows the price under which the collateral posted as guarantee for the repo no longer covers the mark-to-market losses.

For example, a 15-times leveraged bond position with initial cash USD 1 million would have to pay at the end of the repo USD 14,084,389,[5] whereas the

---

[4] Based on a one factor model, bond price, no mean reversion, bond price is lognormal, and constant volatility.
[5] USD 14 million of loan, plus 7% interest in 31 days.

value of the collateral would only cover USD 8,315,693.[6] The USD 5,768,696 million difference must be covered with additional cash from the client. Therefore, if the price drops below a certain level (the "margin call price"), the uncovered difference between the loan value and the collateral value is a credit exposure and the dealer usually calls for more collateral.

As the bond price falls below the margin call price, the relationship between dealer and client becomes increasingly tense. The bank wants to cover the undesired credit exposure as quickly as possible, especially because under these stress situations the bank does not know the client's true financial situation, especially whether the client faces similar margin calls with other dealers. On the other hand, the client undergoes material losses and if the leverage is too high, may have difficulties in delivering additional collateral in a timely manner so as to keep the outstanding leveraged positions. At these stressful situations, the last thing the investor wants is to close the position at what may be perceived as the market bottom. However, as the market drops further, the repo dealer incurs further undesired credit exposure against the investor, and at some point is obliged to liquidate the client's collaterals, and compulsorily close the leveraged position. Depending on the degree of tension between client and dealer, who covers the difference between the value of the collaterals and the previously agreed bond repurchase price is often a matter to be decided in court.

Covered-call positions are particularly treacherous when volatility increases because the price of the bond and the price of the option do not move together. Using the technical terminology, the investor who sold covered calls is "short convexity." The real danger is that, if the underlying bond falls too much, the investor may be obliged to liquidate the bond without being able to buy back the option. In fact, during times of crisis, it is virtually impossible to find a dealer willing to write an out-of-the-money option. When this happens, the investor ends up short an out-of-the-money call option without any underlying bond to cover it. At that time, if the market suddenly rallies, the investor who already incurred severe losses on the downside will lose again on the upside.

During times of asset liquidation such as the one described above, market prices often lose touch with rational valuations and creditworthiness. Market participants cease to look at countries' creditworthiness, spread over Treasuries, implied probability of default, and other economic fundamentals to assess value. In fact, most market participants do not assess value at all. For some time, liquidity is all that matters. A long-term investor would then conclude that this is the perfect moment to buy—a strategy called "bottom-fishing."

While catching inversion points in the market are usually the most profitable moments of a trader's life, bottom-fishing is indeed much more difficult than it seems, and it may end up being a very painful experience. There are three major pitfalls.

First, since prices during asset liquidation lose their rationality, it is practically impossible to know when the market has reached a bottom. Prices can fall

---

[6] A face value of USD 15,735,589 × 0.50 (= price) × 0.99 (= principal factor) plus USD 526,576 (= accrued interests). This equals USD 8,315,693.

much more than anyone can expect, from an already very attractive entry level. For this reason, bottom-fishing must be done with plenty of liquidity and willingness to incur severe mark-to-market losses for an indeterminate period of time, otherwise one may fall into the same leverage trap as the previous players did. That is why a savvy trader used to say that "prices can behave irrationally for a longer period than one's capacity to remain liquid."

Second, very few market participants have the fortitude to stick to their initial views after a dramatic and adverse price change. There is perhaps no greater danger for a speculator when one misleadingly regards oneself as an investor. Long-term strong convictions mysteriously fade after a few days of big losses, contradictory rumors, and pressure from senior management.

Third, market prices do alter economic fundamentals. For example, a Latin American country that borrows at certain credit spread may enjoy a robust economy, but if the borrowing cost trebles due to some irrational market action, the country may face problems with the exchange rate and inflation which, if persistent, could trigger a political crisis that might ultimately lead to a sharp deterioration of the economic conditions. When bottom-fishing, the market players risk neglecting this key interaction between prices and fundamentals.[7]

These concepts of leverage and bottom-fishing help understand what happened to Latin America a few months after the Asian crisis. Exhibit 1 presented a numerical example with EI bonds, but up to September 1997, similar structures had been accumulated with other bonds as underlying assets, such as Brazil Global 2027, Brazil C bond, Argentina FRB, Russia MinFin, and specially Russian local bonds "GKO." In the Brazilian local market too, local banks had placed huge positions on interest rate swaps, expecting that the local interbank rate "DI-overnight" would fall further. The most aggressive Brazilian players—a few local but the majority foreign-owned banks—have conspicuously built positions well over USD 1 billion, mainly allocated between external debt, interest rate swaps, and currency derivatives. The optimism had spread to equity markets too. Brazil's state-owned telecommunications holding company Telebras, on the verge of being privatized, was the underlying asset of many creative equity derivative products.

Thus were the market technicals in September 1997. The leverage had multiplied the demand for emerging market bonds and stocks, because one dollar of cash could buy 10, even 20 dollars worth of assets. This explains the record high volumes observed in new issues during 1997.

THE DETERIORATION

On October 20, 1997, the Taiwan stock market fell 9.50% and the pressure on the Hong Kong dollar increased, the Hang Seng index was already down 14% for the

---

[7] George Soros has systematically profited from this interaction between prices and fundamentals. He calls it the "Theory of Reflexivity," and explained it in his book *The Alchemy of Finance*.

month. In the West, the Asian shock was offset by strong U.S. stocks and the full-flagged Brazilian privatization program. On October 21, the Dow Jones climbed 140 points, Brazil privatized CEEE—the electric utility—for USD 1.6 billion, almost USD 1 billion above the base price, and the JP Morgan Emerging Market Bond Index (EMBI) closed at the record tight spread of 334 bp.

On October 23, as New York traders arrived at work and looked at the market screens, they realized the mood was deteriorating fast. Hong Kong stocks were down overnight another 10%, rates implied in HK dollar forwards climbed to 40% p.a. for one-month maturity. The EMBI index widened 20 bp. So far the Latin American currencies had not been affected, at the London time zone, the South African Rand depreciated a meagre 1.8% in the month.

In Brazil, one year swaps opened at 21.90%, 23 bp higher than the day before and closed at 22.50%. In London, the C Bond opened October 23 trading at 86.5, or 400 bp spread over Treasuries. At 11:00 am New York time the spread was 435 bp, and at 12:30 pm the spread had already widened to 458 bp.

I remember trading BRL forwards that Thursday, October 23. I was looking to buy USD, sell BRL one year. In the morning, an American bank offered to sell USD 20 million and buy BRL for one-year maturity at 1.2265 BRL/USD rate. After a few seconds of hesitation, I told the broker to lift that offer, but somebody else had just done it before me. The market bid immediately climbed to 1.2265, and the offer retraced to 1.2330. On Friday, the one-year BRL/USD forward traded at 1.24, and on Monday, October 27, the same contract was 1.29 bid with 1.32 offer—that is 7.6% higher than the 1.2265 initial offer. This is an example of how fast expectations changed during those days.

On Monday, October 27, the damage to the market was already substantial. The EMBI index had widened 250 bp in a week, the Bovespa fell 15%, and C bonds traded at 78, or 540 bp spread. Short-term bonds were the worst hit, because of the increasing fear of default. Brazil IDU bonds fell 4 points to 95 cents, trading at 400 bp over Treasuries.

In the Brazilian local market, the pressure on the BRL and massive dollar outflows led one year rates to trade at 24.75% on Monday, 32% on Tuesday, October 28. The Central Bank sold more than USD 4 billion those two days.

In Asia, bonds that once were considered investment-grade and therefore were not part of the high-yield emerging market realm, had suddenly widened to very high spreads. For example, Thailand USD-denominated bonds, at 400 bp and Indonesian bonds offered at 450 bp over U.S. Treasuries introduced a new, unexpected aspect of global contagion. As countries were downgraded, their debt increased the global supply of high-yield bonds to several billion, thus posing severe competition to the mainstream Latin American bonds. There was an increasing fear that Korea would finally capitulate to the Asian crisis, causing more risk aversion to all emerging markets.

The most stressed market professionals were the derivatives and repo dealers. When the asset liquidation hit, rumors of margin calls hitting over-leveraged local banks were everywhere. Credit departments in every bank became adamant about the repo lines, and instructed repo dealers to sell collaterals and liquidate positions if margin calls were not met on time. On the other side, with trading volumes above USD 10 billion per day, the emerging markets payment system was also under tremendous stress. Clients, facing multiple margin calls and selling massive amounts of bonds, underwent operational difficulties in delivering bonds on time, even if their financial situation remained sound. During those days, traders that handled repos and structured products usually arrived at work when London opened, 4:00 am NY time, and stayed until late at night to figure out the situation of their books.

In Brazil, there were strong rumors that the Central Bank was buying Brady bonds in the international market, and also selling USD futures at the Brazilian Futures Exchange (BM&F). Local traders quickly confirmed the latter through an ingenious way. The BM&F issues a daily report on contracts held by different types of institutions, such as banks, non-financial companies, individuals, etc. In the last days of October, one of the categories had a very unusual USD 10 billion increase of BRL futures contracts. This category comprised local security companies ("Distribuidoras" or "DTVM"), usually small institutions that by no means have the balance sheet to buy or sell USD 10 billion futures. There was only one with such punch: Banco do Brasil DTVM, therefore the government.

On Tuesday, October 28, the Brazilian local market opened in panic, as USD 5 billion left the country in the morning, afraid of a currency devaluation and capital controls. On Wednesday, October 29, the markets underwent a relief rally as IBM announced a USD 3.5 billion stock buyback. Mr.Greenspan gave a speech playing down the impact of South East Asian crisis on the U.S. economy, implying that the deflationary impact coming from Asia could actually reduce the need for tightening monetary policy. Nonetheless, USD outflows from Brazil remained strong.

Given the low inflation level, the USD 55 billion international reserves, and the cost of keeping the BRL peg (unemployment, high interest rate), many players debated why the Central Bank had not simply let the currency depreciate. Whether due to fear of an inflation outbreak, confidence in the prevailing foreign exchange policy, or due to political reasons (presidential elections were less than a year away, and President Cardoso would run for a second term), the fact was that that the Central Bank had made the choice of defending the peg at any cost. To confirm that, on October 30, the monetary authority raised the repo rate to 43.40% p.a. from 20.70% p.a.. Additionally, the Central Bank bought back one-year local bonds at 28% p.a., signaling an inverted yield curve.

After this drastic measure, something very important happened: Brazilian Brady bonds fell. The C Bond, for example, traded as low as 59.50. A vicious connection had been established between local rates and external debt: high local rates had raised concerns over the country's creditworthiness. During that time, local experts in fiscal policy calculated that, given the high proportion of floating-rate bonds on the domestic public debt, for every 1% p.a. real rate increase there would be an additional impact of BRL 1.6 billion on the Public Sector Borrowing Requirement (PSBR). The interest rate shock announced on October 30 would then increase the PSBR by more than BRL 30 billion (around 3% of GDP), if rates remained that high for one year. With an already fragile fiscal situation, Brazilian external bonds dropped because investors understood the adverse impact of very high rates on the country's creditworthiness.

This connection between local rates and foreign bonds is important because it sets an upper boundary for monetary policy. At some very high level of local rates, monetary policy can no longer attract USD to the country because investors start raising issues about the country's solvency. Standard macroeconomic models for open economies assume that there is a stable relationship between the currency and domestic interest rates. This is also a key assumption for various models, ranging from currency boards to inflation targeting. And yet, for highly indebted emerging economies facing a fragile fiscal situation, this assumption may be unrealistic. In other words, under critical conditions, high domestic rates, without sound fiscal policy, cannot curb currency attacks. Too high interest rates might actually foster currency attacks, like throwing gasoline at the fire.

In the first week of November, the need for a more austere fiscal policy was under discussion inside the Brazilian government. The economic team prepared something to be announced in a week.

Meanwhile Korea was under attack. International reserves were below USD 30 billion and the country had USD 110 billion external debt, 70% of which matured in less than a year. If foreign banks did not roll over their short-term loans, default was inevitable. Korea is a much bigger economy than the other South East Asian ones; it is one of strategic importance for the United States, because of its border with communist North Korea. Though an IMF-led financial package was expected, with presidential elections to be held December 15, the country was in a political deadlock and could not implement financial reforms in the short term.

On November 10, the Brazilian government announced fiscal measures, with around BRL 20 billion fiscal adjustment. This surprised the market positively, which traded at a better tone. Externally, asset liquidation continued, making November 1997 a very volatile month, but with no clear trend.

FRAGILE RECOVERY

November was the peak of pessimism in Brazilian markets, when the one-year swap rate reached 40% p.a.. The Asian collapse would continue for a few more months with a substantial amount of bad loans reducing foreign banks' risk appetite. But the resilience of the U.S. stock market in the beginning of 1998 coupled with the confidence on the new Brazilian fiscal measures, and very high local rates, finally reduced USD outflows.

On December 4, the IMF announces a USD 55 billion financial aid package to Korea. The IMF would provide a USD 21 billion three-year stand-by credit, the World Bank would lend USD 10 billion, the Asian development bank USD 4 billion, Japan USD 10 billion, the United States USD 5 billion, the United Kingdom USD 1.5 billion, and Australia, Germany, France, and Canada USD 3.5 billion. This was the largest financial aid ever coordinated by the IMF. In exchange for that, Korea committed to several Western-style, market-friendly reforms, such as reforming its financial system and opening it up to foreigners, restructuring the "Chaebols,"[8] revamping the labor law, and reducing protectionism.

Yet the market remained worried about how the Korean banks would handle their short term liabilities. There was additional apprehension: (1) the Korean government might assume the local banks' liabilities and end up with a much worse public debt situation,[9] or (2) the Korean government might not assume these liabilities and the Korean banks would have no alternative but to default, causing more losses to the international financial system. Reflecting these concerns, Standard & Poor's revised the Korean sovereign credit rating from A– on November 25, to B+ on December 22, 1997. An astonishing seven-notch downgrade in less than a month. Korean Development Bank (KDB) bonds, in November 1997, traded as high as 800 bp over Treasuries, and on December 11, one week after the USD 55 billion package announcement, still traded at 550 bp.

1998 started with more weakness in Asia. Another round of currency depreciation took place at the end of December/first week of January 1998. The pressure on the HK dollar grew. There were mounting concerns that China would be forced to devalue the Renminbi to catch up with its neighbors' weaker currencies and keep its exports competitive. Moreover, the situation in Indonesia deteriorated sharply; the Indonesian Rupee lost 50% of its value against the USD throughout January 1998. A vast amount of information hit the Latin American market everyday, causing unprecedented volatility.

Indonesia declared a renegotiation of its IMF agreement on January 6. On January 7, the Hang Seng fell 6% on rumors that Peregrine Investment Holdings was going under. One of the most aggressive Hong Kong investment banks, Peregrine was rumored to have a USD 3 billion bond portfolio, with substantial exposure to China and Indonesia. The market feared that if Peregrine went under, more asset liquidation would take place. The one-year HK dollar rate reached 13.50%.

---

[8] These are Korean industrial and banking conglomerates. They had intricate balance sheets, with cross holdings and loans between companies of the same group. This increased leverage and reduced transparency.

[9] This alternative is a recurrent outcome of banking crises. Mexico's Fobaproa was a by-product of the Tequila crisis (1995). Similarly, in April 2001, many economists feared that the break of the Turkish Lira peg – January 2001 – might lead to a significantly higher public debt.

On Friday, January 9, Peregrine Investments Holdings collapsed, and on the following Monday, one-year HK rate reached 18% while the one-year Brazil rate jumped to 39.25%, 400 bp higher than the preceding week. The Brazilian market would not see a day like Monday, January 12 for the next nine months when the Russian default on GKO bonds led to an even more severe crisis.

During the balance of January, the pressures on the HK dollar eased and Latin American markets gradually decoupled from the Asian woes. The fact that Indonesia suspended payments to private debt on January 27 had a minor impact on Brady bonds. On January 28, Korea was on the verge of an agreement to roll its short-term bank loans and KDB bonds traded below 400 bp over U.S. Treasury. Finally, the agreement was announced on January 29: USD 24 billion loans would be rolled at Libor plus 225 bp, 250 bp, and 275 bp for one, two, and three years, respectively. On the same day, the Brazilian Central Bank cut the repo rate to 34.50% p.a..

With the bank debt agreement, Korea overcame both fears of debt default and debt assumption, leading a sharp rally in emerging markets. The improving sentiment created a temporary virtue circle, where liquidity in global capital markets allowed emerging countries to resume external borrowing which then reinforced the improving sentiment. On February 9, Brazil issued a 4-year Euro-denominated EUR 500 million bond at 390 bp over European governments. Nevertheless, the milestone would be Korea that on April 12, placed USD 1 billion 5-year Republic of Korea bonds at 390 bp and USD 3 billion 10-year at 405 bp over U.S. Treasuries. The total demand for these bonds reached the incredible amount of USD 12 billion.

RUSSIA

At the end of the first quarter of 1998, emerging markets were in a fragile balance. The massive IMF packages had managed to stem the Asian crisis, but the Asian countries still had plenty to do to resume sustained economic growth, especially in restructuring their battered financial and corporate sectors, as well coping with a massive amount of bad loans. Moreover, after the turmoil, governments were politically weak and had to tackle the economic problems facing increasing social unrest.

Perhaps the fundamental change that resulted from the Asian crisis and the global decrease on leverage was the drastic reduction of capital flows to emerging markets. Some market strategists were already alerted to the problem during the Asian crisis. They argued that, with banks and investors more risk-averse, there would not be enough funding for countries with high borrowing requirements. In other words, countries running big current account deficits, high budget deficits, or facing heavy amortization schedules might face liquidity problems going forward. By that time, there was no evidence of how drastic the decrease on funding could be, let alone its implications.

In Latin America, Brazil overcame the currency attack, but local interest rates remained very high, still implying an explosive path for the domestic debt.

To make matters worse, as the pressure on the currency eased, the government urgency to implement the BRL 20 billion fiscal austerity package also eased. In fact, only a small fraction of the measures announced in November 1997 was delivered. These problems were latent in April 1998; however, the market was actually focusing on the privatization of the telecommunications sector and the presidential election, to take place in July 1998 and October 1998, respectively.

Completing this bird's eye view of emerging markets in April 1998, there was Russia, the most profitable emerging market of 1997. The IFC Russian stock index closed that year up 53% in USD after having peaked in October, up 115%. Short-term ruble government bonds (GKO) were the ultimate carry-trade. Throughout 1997, the local interest rate dropped from the 30%–32% range to below 20% p.a.. If an investor bought GKO bonds and hedged the currency exposure with local ruble forwards, the USD yield would be around 15% p.a.. Contrary to the Brazilian market in 1995, there were no taxes, no intricate hedging required. There were some capital controls in Russia: foreigners had to open a special account to buy GKOs, and there was a set of regulations to convert rubles into dollars and remit the proceeds. Still, to earn 15% p.a. with very little volatility and holding securities with average maturity three-months was irresistible.

Since 1995, the foreign exchange rate policy was essentially a crawling peg. This had helped stabilize inflation from 130% in 1995, to 21.80% in 1996, and 11% in 1997. In 1997, the Russian ruble (RUR) devalued 7.3% to 5.958. This policy apparently reduced the risk of holding GKO bonds and stimulated local banks to borrow abroad. In July 1998, the eve of the Russian debacle, the RUR was trading around 6.21, having devalued 4.22% year-to-date.

Additionally, Russia did not seem to share the Asian problems. The foreign debt was below 30% of GDP, a virtually flat current account (deficit below USD 1 billion), and a trade surplus of USD 13.5 billion depicted an apparently robust balance of payments situation. The Achilles's heel of the balance of payments was the low level of international reserves, estimated at around USD 14 billion. There were no published figures on the Central Bank forwards that could bring net international reserves to dangerously lower levels.

The fiscal accounts did not look so good. The federal budget deficit closed 1997 at 6% of GDP, with more than 4% of GDP accounting for debt service. The state found difficulties in collecting taxes, and this had led to payment arrears to pensioners, soldiers, teachers, and public employees. According to trade unions, at the end of 1997, wage arrears amounted to 2% of GDP. To buy time and implement fiscal reforms, the Russian government resorted to loans from the IMF, domestic bond issuance, and eurobond placements. Investors looked at this picture and estimated that Russia had plenty of time. In fact, the government domestic debt was only 12.50% of GDP in the middle of 1997. The Russian situation looked indeed very similar to how Brazil was at the beginning of the 1990s. This resemblance attracted plenty of Brazilian investors, either Brazilian banks that invested their cash in GKOs, or Brazilians traders working for foreign banks who built sizeable positions in Russia. Foreign banks also marketed structured products on GKOs, providing leverage in a manner similar to the repo mechanisms described above.

Finally, Russia was the quintessential moral-hazard trade. If Korea had a USD 55 billion bailout package, in the worst case scenario, Russia at least deserved a similar amount. The risk of Russia breaking apart into smaller republics, causing military disarray, and eventually the trafficking of nuclear or biochemical weapons to Western-hostile nations seemed well worth a sizeable financial support to Mr. Yeltsin's administration.

Yet investors neglected a crucial point that would become clearer at the end of 1998—Russia lacked governance. If the Russian government could not show commitment to structural reforms, neither the IMF nor the Western governments could keep lending money. During 1998, allegations that corrupt Russian officials embezzled or misused IMF loans harmed Moscow's credibility, clouding the feasibility of a sizeable financial aid package.

By the end of 1997, the heavy borrowing schedule of the Russian government, coupled with the increasing risk aversion, led foreigners to redeem GKO bonds. This provoked a hemorrhage of international reserves. On December 3, the Russian Central Bank raised local rates to 36% p.a.. With inflation around 11% p.a., the real interest rate of 22.50%, as in Brazil, casted doubts over the domestic debt dynamics. The difference was that the Russian domestic debt was roughly a third the Brazilian domestic debt. Upon the Central Bank rate hike, 98-day GKO yields jumped 400 bp to 41% p.a..

Throughout the first half of 1998, the Russian situation deteriorated, with some sporadic, sharp rallies as the Russian government committed to budget improvements or on announcements of IMF new loans and eurobond placements.

On May 18, 1998, the Russian Central Bank increased the overnight rate to 50%. The Moscow stock market fell 12%. On May 27, with GKOs at 60% p.a. there were rumors of an IMF emergency credit facility plus additional loans from international banks. On June 1 the IMF package was not announced, causing GKO yields to widen to 71%. Meanwhile, Brazil started to suffer contagion, one month before the privatization of Telebras, and four months prior to presidential elections. One-year swap rates traded at 31% on June 1, compared to 26% p.a. at the beginning of May.

On June 3, with the market once again bullish on an IMF/G7 financial package, GKO yields backed down to 54% p.a.. The Russian Federation placed a 5-year EUR 1.25 billion bond with 11.75% coupon (650 bp spread over governments). On the following day, GKO yields dropped to 45% p.a..

In Brazil, the Central Bank tried to reverse worsening expectations with all its forces. The sale of USD futures through the BM&F had become a routine. On June 4, the monetary authority tried a further step, and intervened in the interest rate market. It announced a local bond buyback for 45 days at 22% p.a., while the market was forecasting a 25% rate for that maturity. The Central Bank not only wanted to control the currency, but now it also intended to control the interest rate. This certainly reduced the margin of maneuver to fight capital outflows.

The events in Russia took a hectic pace. On June 18, the Russian Federation issued another bond, USD 2.5 billion, 30-year maturity, and putable after 10 years. The Russia 2028 bond was issued at 12.75% coupon (753 bp over Treasuries). Three months later, this bond, issued at 98.4370, would be trading below 30.

In that same week, the IMF made its seventh quarterly review of the Russian program and postponed a USD 670 million loan tranche, alleging insufficient fulfillment of the targets. This decision caught the market by surprise. The new attitude of the IMF led to speculation that there was increasing opposition to a financial aid package that fostered moral hazard. The following comments from Mr. Alan Greenspan and excerpts from IMF publications support this new attitude:

> (...) private capital flows may temporarily turn adverse. In these circumstances companies should be allowed to default, private investors take their losses[10]

> With respect to bank's foreign creditors, it may be difficult to avoid moral hazard altogether, although there may well be scope for arrangements in which foreign banks agree to roll over short term loans at reasonable risk premia at times when they would not normally choose to do so. The issue of whether and how private creditors should assume a greater share of the burden of dealing with financial crises—the so-called bail in—will need to be considered carefully during the period ahead (...)[11]

July 1998 began on a very nervous tone. The delay of the long-awaited IMF package to Russia shrunk the demand for GKO bonds. On July 1, a GKO auction only raised half the redemption at the rate of 78%. In the following week GKO yields climbed to above 100%, with increasing speculation that the IMF package would contemplate a restructuring of the local bonds.

THE BEAR TRAP

On July 13, 1998, the IMF finally announced the Russian financial assistance—a USD 22.6 billion total package. Of the USD 22.6 billion, USD 17.1 billion was new money, 73.6% of which was available in 1998. GKO yields dropped 4,000 bp, to 60% p.a. on this news. To increase its lending to Russia, the IMF drew on its General Arrangements to Borrow (GAB) lines, which had been unused for 20 years. The actual release of the loans was tied to fiscal targets that required a tough negotiation between Mr. Yeltsin and the Duma (the Russian congress). The

---

[10] Alan Greenspan, Speech October 29, 1997.
[11] *World Economic Outlook* (May 1998).

market became more constructive, but remained apprehensive with a rumored exchange of GKO bonds and the votes on the Duma. The fears were indeed well founded. On July 22, the IMF withheld the first installment of the financial package, USD 800 million, expressing concern at the Duma's failure to pass the necessary austerity measures. Facing this political deadlock, the Russian situation remained unpredictable and caused more weakness to Latin American bonds.

Brazil had so far held up well due to the conspicuous action of the Central Bank in the currency, interest rate, and Brady bonds markets.[12] The privatization program reached a peak, and kept bringing much needed dollars to the country. On July 16, Enron, a U.S. group, purchased Elektro, an electric utility company, for BRL 1.48 billion (USD 1.25 billion i.e., 98.94% above the auction minimum price). That was a good test for the Telebras auction, scheduled for two weeks ahead. The foreign demand for Brazilian companies stemmed from the strong equity markets in Europe and in the United States and the wave of mergers and acquisitions in those markets. These multinational companies saw in the Brazilian privatization a once-in-a-lifetime opportunity to establish a strong presence in the domestic market, and their strategic approach hardly took into account the stress levels where bonds and interest rates were trading.

On July 29, the Brazilian government privatized its telecommunication sector for BRL 22 billion (USD 18.85 billion), 63.74% over the minimum price. The auction result exceeded all expectations; the most optimistic analysts had forecasted a 30% premium over the minimum price. Was that a clear sign that Brazil would be able to avoid contagion? To corroborate this view, on the last three days of July a net USD 6 billion entered the country and the C bond credit spread tightened 20 bp. That was the biggest bear trap of the year.

A common trading practice is to evaluate actions based on alternative scenarios that would imply different portfolio allocations. To choose among the scenarios, the trader follows several economic and financial data, and as the stream of data corroborates one of them, the trader allocates his portfolio accordingly. If new data start to contradict the chosen scenario, the trader cuts the position; in contrast, if the data confirm it, the scenario is more likely to be the right one, and the position is increased.

In July 1998 two elements played a major role in decisions. First, whether or not Russia would default, second, investors' perception on Brazil. From these two elements four scenarios were possible:

	Russia defaults	Russia does not default
Investors' perception on Brazil improves.	(A) Brazil suffers turbulence but may be able to avoid contagion.	(C) Brazil enjoys a sharp rally.
Investors' perception on Brazil worsens.	(B) Brazil devalues, with high risk of inflation outburst and/or local debt restructuring.	(D) Brazil remains under pressure, all depends on the economic policy after presidential elections.

---

[12] On December 31, 1998, the Brazilian Central Bank held USD 6.7 billion of Brazilian USD denominated bonds as part of the international reserves. Source: Central Bank of Brazil (www.bcb.gov.br).

Notice that scenarios A and D imply a continuing volatile market with no clear trend, scenario B is chaos, and scenario C calls for a strong bull market.

During the month of July, IMF financial assistance to Russia drastically reduced default fears. Additionally, the amazing success of the Brazilian privatization was perceived as a strong sign of investor confidence in the country. Given that, scenario C had a non-negligible probability of being the right one, and offered big upside, scenarios A and D were also likely, but the downside, if any, was small. Finally, scenario B would cause huge losses, but it became increasingly remote, given recent developments.

With this rationale, investors and speculators bought heavily, either to cut short positions or to establish bullish ones, causing a sharp rally on Brazilian assets. The follow-up on the events would show that there were serious flaws on the analysis above, and scenario B was more likely than previously assessed. First, the IMF attitude towards Russia was much more rigorous than previously thought, and the IMF was willing to show that the new "bail in" approach was not a mere academic concept. Second, the Brazilian debt dynamics had an overwhelming impact on investors' expectations that would wipe out the short-term optimism on the Telebras auction.

Sometimes the information available seems to confirm a scenario that, in fact, is the wrong one. In that sense, July 1998 brought a terrible lesson to both the novice and the seasoned trader. This trap is a clear danger to any professional who makes decisions with incomplete information, and it is tellingly illustrated in the excerpt below:

> By "intelligence" we mean every sort of information about the enemy and his country—the basis, in short of our own plans and operations. If we consider the actual basis of this information, how unreliable and transient it is, we soon realize that war is a flimsy structure that can easily collapse and bury us in its ruins. The textbooks agree, of course, that we should only believe reliable intelligence, and should never cease to be suspicious, but what is the use of such feeble maxims? They belong to the wisdom which for want of anything better scribblers of systems and compendia resort to when they run out of ideas.
>
> Many intelligence reports in war are contradictory; even more are false, and most are uncertain. What one can reasonably ask of an officer that he should possess a standard of judgement, which he can gain only from knowledge of men and affairs and from common sense. He should be guided by the laws of probability. These are difficult enough to apply when plans are drafted in an office, far from the sphere of action; the task becomes infinitely harder in the thick of fighting itself, with reports streaming in. At such times one is lucky if their contradictions cancel

each other out, and leave a kind of balance to be critically assessed. It is much worse for the novice if chance does not help him in that way, and on the contrary one report tallies with another, confirms it, magnifies it, lends it color, till he has to make a quick decision – which is soon recognized to be mistaken, just as the reports turn out to be lies, exaggerations, errors, and so on.[13]

The trading bear trap of July 1998 resembles in many ways the difficulty of assessment in a war situation, described above. In some market situations, information dangerously "tallies with another, confirms [a scenario], magnifies it, lends it color, till [the trader] has to make a quick decision—which is soon recognized to be mistaken." Similarly in July 1998, optimistic expectations from Russia and the unquestionable success of the Brazilian privatization led investors to overcome fears, and heavily buy Brazilian assets. Investors would soon realize their mistake.

In Brazil, Fernando Henrique Cardoso headed the polls for a second term. With the vote two months ahead, his re-election was virtually certain, the question being whether he would achieve more than 50% of the valid ballots in the first round so as to avoid a second vote. The market was extremely nervous and as political immobility delayed action, the risk of a collapse increased. The market expected very tough fiscal measures if Mr. Cardoso was re-elected, and possibly an agreement with the IMF, though the government denied the latter. Mr. Cardoso's prospects of re-election kept the hope that, once the elections were over, the reforms would be resumed, and the country would improve. Meanwhile, the central bank resorted to all sorts of tactics to defend the currency peg until the election.

On August 5, a series of events caused growing risk aversion in emerging markets: more speculation with the weak yen, at 143 and the Hong Kong dollar was once more under pressure with local rates above 10% p.a.. On August 7, GKO yields climbed to 91% p.a.. The deterioration in sentiment took a hectic pace. The speculation against the Hang Seng stock index and the Hong Kong dollar led the Hong Kong Monetary Authority to intervene, crushing the speculators in a very unorthodox way:

"As you know, over the past two weeks, with my approval the HKMA has been operating in the stock and futures markets with the aim of hitting those currency speculators engaged in a double play of dumping the Hong Kong dollar and shorting the local stocks and Hang Seng Index futures. The game plan of these speculators is to create extreme conditions in the money market by attacking the HK$ in order to cause panic and a sharp fall in the stock and futures markets. We have frustrated their plan.[14]

---

[13] Carl von Clausewitz's classic book on strategy: *Of War*, Chapter 6 (1832).

[14] Financial Secretary, Donald Tsang, at a press stand-up session, August 28, 1998.

Presenter: Making an educated guess, how much do you think these speculators have lost in this round of attack? *Mr. Tsang:* Well, as I said, the whole purpose is not to make people lose money. But we moved in the market two weeks ago, (and since then) the HSI has moved up 1,200 points. Say, for instance, (someone is) holding 20,000 contracts, short contracts. That movement would mean (someone) has to settle back about $1.2 billion."[15]

With $96 billion in international reserves—eight times what is needed to redeem all Hong Kong dollars in circulation—the HKMA could definitely be tough on speculators. That was not the case of Brazil, Russia, and other countries who depended on foreign money to finance their borrowing requirements.

On August 17, Russia abandoned the ruble crawling peg, and set a band at 6.30-9.20. Russia also announces a 90-day moratorium. Local government bonds such as GKO bonds were to be restructured. Three days later, market analysts estimated that the Central Bank spent USD 4.8 billion defending the band. Emerging markets saw a meltdown. On August 21, the Brazilian Central Bank (BCB) gave up intervening on interest rate futures, causing a 200 bp increase on 3-month rates to 22.50%. On August 24, the BCB announced more measures to attract short-term capital flows. The measures were valid until December 1998, in a clear attempt to muddle through until the presidential election. On August 25, the Russian government finally announced the terms for the GKO restructuring. The restructuring conditions shocked the market: it became clear that the losses incurred by GKO holders exceeded the most pessimistic expectations. A first analysis estimated the GKO's recovery value on 10 cents (i.e., causing a 90% loss to GKO holders). The first emerging market sovereign default after the Brady era caused another wave of asset liquidation.

A week after the Russian announcement, the ruble band was already gone, and the Russian currency closed the month at 12. Russian inflation closed 1998 at 86%, and the RUR at 20. In Brazil, C bonds reached a low of 50 (1,400 bp over Treasuries) on August 27. In the same week, a 2-year Bradesco eurobond, Brazil's largest privately-owned commercial bank, was offered at 40% p.a. yield. On September 1, Malaysia imposed capital controls. There was growing fear that Brazil could follow suit.

Five weeks prior to elections, the BCB had not resorted to the unpopular decision of raising interest rates. On August 31, President Cardoso, the frontrunner candidate for election, affirmed this. He stated: "do not even think of raising interest rates to fight the problem (of the USD outflows), we are not considering that." On September 3, the BCB in fact lowered the interest rate floor (TBC) 75 bp, to 19% but raised the interest rate ceiling (TBAN) 400 bp to 29.75%. The TBC was

---

[15] Remarks by the Financial Secretary, Donald Tsang, in an interview with Radio-3's program "HK Today," Saturday, August 29, 1998.

abolished on September 8, and the TBAN ceiling became the new target. On the evening of September 10, the BCB raised the TBAN 2,000 bp, to 49.75%.

On September 14, U.S. President Clinton and Treasury Secretary Robert Rubin talked about concerted action in the world economy and called for a global meeting in 30 days. Mr. Clinton called it the "worst financial crisis in half a century." Brazilian authorities were in secret talks with the IMF and U.S. undersecretary Lawrence Summers. It was then clear that there would be an IMF package after the election. The question was whether the IMF would require the flotation of the BRL.

September was also the month when Long Term Capital Management (LTCM) went under. On September 23, in an action coordinated by the Fed's New York branch, a pool of banks injected USD 3.5 billion in the ailing hedge fund, preparing for the liquidation of its super-leveraged positions. On September 29 the Fed cut the fed funds target 25 bp, citing "increasing weakness in foreign economies" and "less accommodative financial conditions domestically."

THE IMF RESCUE

President Cardoso was re-elected for another 4-year mandate on October 4. In the global economy, the risk aversion escalates. The liquidation of LTCM prompted an unheard-of widening of spreads on the investment-grade market: on U.S. Treasuries, off-the-run bonds widening against on-the-run bonds, illiquid AAA bonds, mortgage bonds. On October 7, the yen appreciated 9% in less than 48 hours, to 121, causing severe losses on hedge funds who were short the Japanese currency. The market action seemed to punish leverage everywhere. On the same day, Chairman of the Fed, Alan Greenspan remarked: "I've never seen anything like this. This is really quite an unusual phenomenon. (...) In reading economic reports, one gets the impression that the economy has collapsed and we might as well all go home and go fishing or something, but the truth is that we are still seeing fairly continued significant momentum (in the U.S. economy)."[16] A week later, on October 15, the Fed came to the rescue once more and unexpectedly cut Fed funds 25 bp to 5.00%.

On November 13, 1998, the IMF-led package to Brazil was officially announced: USD 41.5 billion. For that, Brazil committed to cut the fiscal deficit, reform social security, and maintain the BRL crawling peg. There was also an important target for the Net Domestic Assets in the Central Bank (NDA),[17] which in practice limited the Central Bank's ability to use the IMF dollars to defend the BRL. The announcement of the financial package calmed down the market, local

---

[16] Breakfast at the National Association for Business Economics, October 7, 1998.

[17] Net Domestic Assets in the CB is defined as the difference between the monetary base and the net international reserves in the CB valued in BRL. If the Central Bank sells dollars to prop up the local currency, international reserves fall. When reserves reach a floor implied by the NDA target, the Central Bank can no longer sell dollars, and the only option left is to raise the interest rate to curb USD outflows.

rates dropped, but they stabilized at 25% p.a., clearly an unsustainable level given an inflation forecast of 2% for 1999.

After signing the IMF agreement, the Brazilian authorities set for a road show to explain the Brazilian program to foreign investors. One of the meetings took place on November 17 at the Waldorf Astoria Hotel. It was closed to the press. Among the participants were Minister of Finance Pedro Malan, Head of the Central Bank Gustavo Franco, other government authorities, and the chief econo-mists of the main New York financial institutions. I was lucky to attend it, in lieu of my bank's chief economist who was not in town that date.

Around 25 people were in the Waldorf meeting room. When the door closed, Minister Malan addressed the skeptical group of analysts and investors and said: "since you are well aware of the situation, we will not make a presenta-tion of the Brazilian economy. We are open to questions now." After a few sec-onds of disconcerting silence, he smiled and added: "… unless you want me to talk about the Brazilian economy."

Gradually, the audience overcame the timidity, and engaged in a frank conversation with the authorities. Minister Malan made clear that the structural reforms that Brazil committed to were not easy, but they would do them even without the IMF package because the country had no other alternative. Professor Franco pointed out his concerns about the USD outflows; he did not expect that the outflows would quickly revert as they did in February 1998, after the Asian crisis. What was at stake was the reopening of international capital markets to Brazil. He was hopeful that local companies would soon be able to borrow abroad again, and that eurobonds issuance would normalize.

The authorities were evasive about the exchange rate policy. Mr. Malan cited Professor Paul Krugman of MIT: "If UK devalues it is OK, if Mexico or Korea devalues, it is bad. People do not take for granted things in developing countries the way they do on G7 countries. (Therefore) we do not believe in a controlled maxi-devaluation, especially in the times we are now."

Then Mr. Malan pointed out three reasons for currency attacks in Brazil. First he recognized the country's vulnerabilities to the fiscal situation and balance payments; second arbitrage opportunities between local interest rates and offshore markets, that stimulated USD outflows.[18] Finally (and then his voice went louder and he was visibly upset), "gossips and rumors that were spread in September." He repudi-ated the following "gossips:" (1) academics calling for maxi-devaluation, (2) capital controls (like in Malaysia), and (3) haircuts of private creditors (such as restructuring the domestic debt). "When the three reasons happen together, it is very bad," he said. The mention of the "gossips and rumors" caused some embarrassed grins, because some of the academics whom Mr.Malan repudiated were present in the room.

Unfortunately for the Brazilian authorities, rumors and gossips, however false, only spread when they have some grasp with reality. And the fears about the "haircuts of private creditors" were based on the explosive path of the government

---

[18] Foreign bonds, such as EIs, have fallen so much that they offered better returns than local Brazilian bonds.

debt. Exhibit 2 shows how a ballooning debt coincided with the period when foreign analysts expressed growing concerns over the Brazilian domestic debt. The big jump in January 1999 shows the impact the devaluation had on the net public debt, of which a substantial share was linked to the U.S. dollar.

In fact, right or wrong, some prominent international authorities manifested similar fears:

> It's difficult for someone like from Hong Kong to pontificate on a big country like Brazil. But I know that we are all living in the same boat, and there are some things we have to pool our resources together and help. A few things that I think we have to bear in mind in attacking this issue. First of all it is a very huge issue where the shortage of liquidity is running into hundreds of millions. We are looking at a problem which might be twice as large as the ones we saw in Korea. And it could have a disastrous result if we do not deal with it properly.[19]

In a subtler reference to the inconsistency between super-tight monetary policy and the explosive path of the government debt, Mr.Greenspan would remark later on:

Exhibit 2: Brazilian Public Debt as a Share of GDP. Central Government, States, and Municipalities.

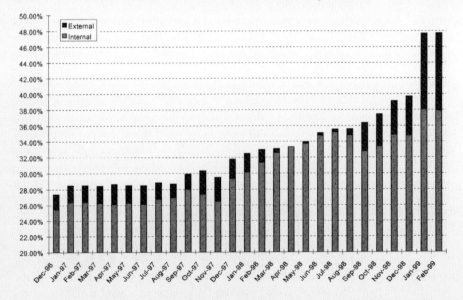

---

[19] Financial Secretary of Hong Kong Donald Tsang on Bloomberg Forum, October 6, 1998.

Brazilian authorities must walk a very narrow, difficult path of restoring confidence and keeping inflation contained with monetary policy, while dealing with serious fiscal imbalances.[20]

The sentiment, after the announcement of the IMF package, was a mix of hope and apprehension. The fiscal targets agreed with the IMF, and required politically sensitive reforms as the target on Net Domestic Assets imposed limits on the dollars available for the Central Bank to sell. The market understood that much depended on the Brazilian government, and if the targets were not achieved, another crisis was likely.

On December 3, the Brazilian Congress rejected two key fiscal measures that raised civil servants' contributions to social security. C bonds fell 3 points on the news, the Bovespa fell 9%. Congress closed for recess in December, and the political deadlock among the government alliance made the calling of a much-needed extraordinary session for January 1999 impossible. Therefore the Congress would only open in late February, leaving the country with a two-month legislative void, amidst strong USD outflows.

The governor of the State of Minas Gerais, Itamar Franco, declared moratorium on January 6, 1999. The state had a eurobond maturing January 15, and Mr. Franco clearly stated that he would not pay it. This would be the straw that broke the camel's back—USD outflows increased sharply.

On January 13, Gustavo Franco, Head of the Central Bank, resigned and Francisco Lopes replaced him. The new Head of the Central Bank announced a widening of the exchange rate band to 1.20–1.32. The top of the band implied a 10% devaluation. The band would slide according to an arcane mathematical formula that Mr. Lopes created. According to his formulator, it was an "endogenous diagonal band." The BRL immediately got to the top of the band. The pressure on the currency intensified even more.

Two days later, on January 15, while currency analysts still fretted to understand what an "endogenous diagonal band" meant, the Central Bank revoked it, and let the BRL float freely. According to government sources, the Central Bank followed an order from President Cardoso, who wanted to devalue while the country still had a comfortable level of international reserves. The failure of Mr. Lopes' attempt at a controlled devaluation discredited him and led President Cardoso to send his Minister of Finance, Pedro Malan, to the Central Bank desk to make sure the BRL would float that day.

Apparently, the flotation was executed unbeknownst to the IMF. The country had undergone one month of utter uncertainty. The IMF agreement had to be totally renegotiated. The Central Bank ended up discredited after Francisco Lopes' failed attempt at a controlled devaluation. He resigned on February 2, and Armínio Fraga Neto, then working for George Soros on the Quantum Fund, was

---

[20] Alan Greenspan, testimony before Banking Committee, U.S. Senate, February 23, 1999.

appointed. Before Mr. Fraga took over, the Senate questioned him on February 26. For three weeks the Central Bank was without any leadership.

At the beginning of March, the country had a new head for the Central Bank, the BRL was around 2.00 (i.e., 30% weaker), and the IMF announced a new agreement with Brazil. Meanwhile, out of fear, the Brazilian Congress approved important fiscal measures, including some that had been rejected in December 1998.

FINAL NOTE

The crises in the three big continents across the world were over by the beginning of 1999. The Hong Kong dollar remained pegged at 7.80 for one dollar, with very low interest rates. The impact of the BRL devaluation on inflation and on growth was surprisingly mild. Foreign direct investment skyrocketed in the following years, accumulating USD 57.7 billion dollars in 1999 and 2000. The side effect of this massive foreign investment was the increase in the country's external liabilities, which were partially responsible for a weakening BRL in the first half of 2001. Another side effect of the Brazilian devaluation was the negative impact on Argentina with its currency board regime. In June 2001, the Argentine economy still suffered from the higher borrowing costs and an over-competitive currency from Brazil.

APPENDIX

Local Interest Rates
Interbank Market

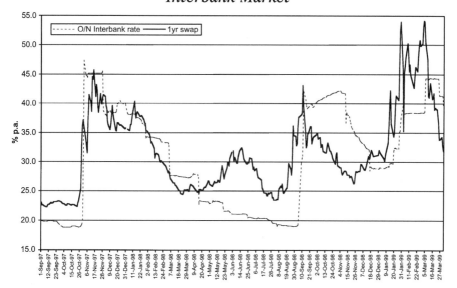

Country Risk

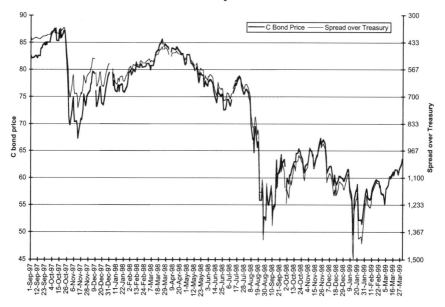

Bovespa
Brazilian Stock Index in Local Currency

Hard Currency Flows to the Local Foreign Exchange Market
Daily Data–Positive Value Means Inflow

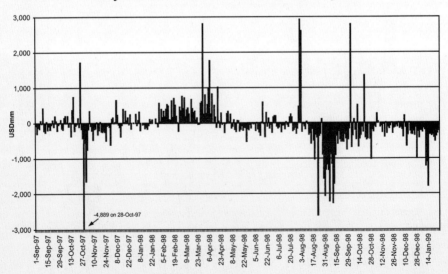

Chapter 11

Local Fixed Income Arbitrage: The Brazilian Case Study

Marcelo Fernandes de Lima Castro
Director
BNP Paribas

T his chapter describes the reasons that countries sometimes present arbitrage opportunities between onshore and offshore rates. The existence of such an arbitrage would in principle contradict the interest parity theorem. However, the first section explains why such a discrepancy may exist. Subsequently, it depicts how to capture such interest rate differentials using Brazil as a case study. The case study is rather complex because it discusses a real-world situation in an environment of local taxes, dual exchange rates, and peculiar fixed income instruments.

Originally, the model presented in this chapter was built in a computer spreadsheet. But since, in the real world, such models usually support real transactions, with real money, one should always understand both the mathematical model as well as building a spreadsheet. The mathematical model represents the closed-form solution of the problem, whereas the computer spreadsheet represents the numerical solution. In the end, the results should obviously match.

WHY LOCAL RATES IN DOLLARS MAY DIFFER FROM LIBOR

The interest parity theorem shows that, assuming no restrictions on capital flows and no arbitrage opportunities, the domestic interest rate in any foreign country should satisfy the following relationship:[1]

$$(\text{LIBOR} + s) \times t = \frac{(1 + i)^t}{(1 + \hat{e}_t)} - 1 \tag{1}$$

---

[1] For t greater than one year, LIBOR is compounded, instead of linear rate. Therefore, equation (1) should be rewritten as:

$$(1 + \text{LIBOR} + s)^t = \frac{(1 + i)^t}{(1 + \hat{e}_t)} \tag{1b}$$

We will use the linear rate version, as depicted in equation (1), because we are dealing with short-term capital flows.

where

> LIBOR = London Interbank Offered Rate
> s = the foreign country risk spread
> i = the domestic interest rate in the foreign country
> t = time
> $\hat{e}_t$ = the expected devaluation of the local currency versus the international currency, in period t

The right-hand side of equation (1) represents the interest rate earned in U.S. dollars[2] by investing in the local market and hedging the currency risk. The left-hand side represents the cost of funding in dollars, taking into account the country risk. Therefore, any inequality in equation (1) would represent a perfect arbitrage situation: if the domestic interest rate in dollars is greater than LIBOR, plus the country risk spread, money would flow indefinitely into the country to capture the interest rate differential. Alternatively, if the local interest rate in dollars is lower than the international benchmark plus the country risk spread, foreign investors and local participants will realize that they are not being properly compensated for running the risk of investing in the local market and will exit the country until its international reserves are exhausted.

Equation (1) is restrictive for policy-makers who may want to independently conduct monetary and exchange rate policy. The most frequent situation is when the Central Bank wants to maintain a high interest rate in an economy with a currency peg or band system on foreign exchange. This can result in a spread over LIBOR higher than what the market attributes as the country risk. As a consequence, foreign capital starts flowing into the country to take advantage of the high spread.

In the short run, the increase of foreign capital inflows can cause an appreciation of the currency and a drop in the local interest rate. To prevent this, the Central Bank may purchase the excess dollars and print money, which is then sterilized by selling local currency denominated bonds. Sterilization operations, however, cannot be performed repeatedly without inconveniently increasing the amount of domestic public debt.

Another solution is to impose some form of capital controls. Such restrictions can reduce the dollar inflows and, at least for some time, enable the Central Bank to control both the currency and interest rates. Therefore, equation (1) may not hold in markets with capital controls, thus creating opportunities for local fixed income arbitrage.

Capital controls usually have been imposed in the following forms: (1) taxes on earnings, (2) upfront fees, and (3) minimum tenor requirements.

Taxes on Earnings

Taxes on earnings are withholding taxes imposed on earnings to reduce the flows of foreign capital into the local market. To include the effect of withholding tax on earnings, equation (1) should be rewritten as follows:

---

[2] It is assumed henceforth that the foreign investor is funded in U.S. dollars.

$$(\text{LIBOR} + s) \times t = \frac{[(1 + i)^t - 1] \times (1 - \text{tax}) + 1}{(1 + \hat{e}_t)} - 1 \qquad (2)$$

where tax = tax rate on earnings.

The difference between equation (1) and equation (2) is the term

$$[(1 + i)^t - 1] \times (1 - \text{tax})$$

which represents the after tax earnings in the local market.

Upfront Fees

Upfront costs are an initial cost that foreign investors have to pay to enter the local fixed income market. The fees are usually payable on the foreign exchange, as the investor sells dollars to buy the local currency. Brazil adopted such a system in 1993. The Brazilian authorities established several types of investments, each one with its own upfront fees (these are called *Imposto sobre Operações Financeiras*—IOF). The Brazilian IOF has varied according to the levels of local interest rates and foreign capitals. Under such a system, it is important to determine the break-even period of time required to recover the initial investment, including upfront fees.

As an example, let's assume that the upfront fee is 5% and that the investor obtains funding at LIBOR + 100 bps. An initial investment of $100 will result in $5 of upfront fee. Therefore, the total initial investment is $105. Let's assume that the local bonds yield 12% per annum in dollars, after taxes. Assuming that the investor's horizon is one year, the initial $100 will be worth $112. Dividing $112 by the initial investment of $105, we obtain an annual return of 6.67%. Assuming LIBOR at 5.5% per annum (p.a.), the 1-year dollar return in the local market is only 12 basis points higher than the investor's funding cost of 6.5% p.a.

Was it a bad investment decision? It depends on the investor's time frame. Notice that, for the second year, the position can be rolled-over without any additional upfront fee. Once the upfront fee has been amortized, the investor has a free option to roll over the position. The option value depends on the forward local interest rate in dollars for the second year, as well as the volatility of such a rate.

In practice, experience has shown that the trade described above is not regarded as attractive. Yet, sometimes a favorable combination of both high local interest rate in dollars and low upfront fees may lead to a break-even period of less than six months.

For the case of capital controls with both upfront fees and withholding taxes on earnings, equation (1) should be revised as follows:

$$(\text{LIBOR} + s) \times t = \frac{[(1 + i)^t - 1] \times (1 - \text{tax}) + 1}{(1 + \hat{e}_t) \times (1 + \theta)} - 1 \qquad (3)$$

where

θ = upfront fee
t = investment time frame

Minimum Tenor Requirements

Some countries impose a minimum period during which remittances are either prohibited or heavily taxed. Sometimes, even within the minimum tenor, the investor is able to capture high rates, although the longer-than-desired minimum tenor may limit the amount of risk the investor is willing to take. There are other situations where the investor likes the country risk, but, since the return is not so attractive, a shorter maturity would be preferable. Here, assessing the future level of local rates is key: once the minimum tenor is reached, the position attains daily liquidity. If, in that moment, high rates still prevail, the initial investment in the country would have paid off.

Another consideration to be made regarding markets with minimum tenor requirements is whether or not an investment in local fixed income securities grants access to other local instruments that would otherwise be barred to foreign investors. A franchise in local swaps, options, and equities can represent an important competitive advantage and may justify an investment in local securities at not really attractive returns.

HOW LOCAL USD INTEREST RATES CHANGE

In the previous section, it was demonstrated that the local interest rate in dollars may differ from the risk-free international rate plus a risk spread, due to taxation and maturity constraints. Defining the local interest rate in dollars as $i_{US\$}$, so that

$$i_{US\$} = \left[\frac{(1+i)^t}{(1+\hat{e}_t)} - 1 \right] \times \frac{1}{t} \tag{4}$$

It is interesting to observe how $i_{US\$}$ behaves. In the previous section, it was shown how capital restrictions cause substantial divergences between the $i_{US\$}$ and Libor. Generally, when the currency risk is low, $\hat{e}_t$ follows the expectation of the inflation differential, and the $i_{US\$}$ will be as high as the real interest rate is expected to be. As the currency risk increases, $\hat{e}_t$ will start trading at a spread over inflation; in other words, those who demand a currency hedge have to pay a premium to convince speculators to go long the local currency. In this situation, other things being equal, $i_{US\$}$ tends to decrease—the more expensive hedge reduces the foreign investor's gains. However, local interest rates can be so high that, despite the more expensive hedge, the $i_{US\$}$ remains high. Finally, when the currency risk is deemed extremely high, the $i_{US\$}$ tends to be always low, regardless of the level of local interest rates; a negative $i_{US\$}$ is rare, but has been observed for short periods of time.

The relationship just described assumes that there is no credit risk involved in hedge instruments nor in dollar-linked bonds issued by the local governments. In times of extreme distrust regarding the government's capacity to pay, the credit risk may play an overwhelming role and cause a very high $i_{US\$}$ in the government dollar-linked bonds.[3] On the other hand, the effect of an increase of the credit risk on the $i_{US\$}$ traded in derivatives markets (e.g., currency swaps) is less clear; usually market players become very selective with their counterparties, and, as result, liquidity disappears.

Exhibit 1 shows the $i_{US\$}$ in Brazil. The market was extremely volatile during the Russian crisis that triggered the devaluation of the Real (July 1998 to January 1999). Concerns about the capacity to pay the super-high real interest rates in local bonds led to a sharp increase in the $i_{US\$}$. Meanwhile, the Brazilian domestic interest rate jumped almost 20% p.a.[4] After January 1999, the IMF confirmed the financial aid to the Brazilian government and perceived the crisis as petering out. As a consequence, the expected devaluation of the local currency—ê of Equation (1)—dropped faster than the Brazilian interest rate. To reinforce the change in expectations, the Brazilian Central Bank aggressively sold U.S. dollar-linked bonds (NBCE) at record-high yields, seeking to strengthen the currency (see Exhibit 2). The better creditworthiness coupled with the abundant supply of currency hedge (i.e., NBCE bonds) led the $i_{US\$}$ to reach 30% p.a. For the remainder of 1999, and also 2000, the downtrend in local real interest rates was the main determinant in driving the $i_{US\$}$ down. In November 2000, as well as in February and April 2001, the uncertainty regarding the Argentine economy caused some volatility on local usd-indexed rates.

Exhibit 1: Brazil – 1-Year $i_{US\$}$
Brazil - 360 days USD-hedged return (spot-adjusted, before taxes) (Swaps USD rate/CDI)

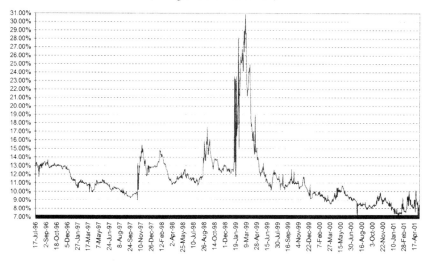

Source: Brazilian Mercantile Exchange

[3] In the Mexican crisis of December 1994–March 1995, *Tesobonos* yielded as much as 40% in dollars due to the lack of international reserves to pay redemptions.

[4] See Chapter 10 for a detailed description of the events that preceded the devaluation.

Exhibit 2: The Central Bank Auctions NBCE to Raise Local USD-Indexed Yields and Attract Short-Term Capital

Primary auctions of Central Bank dollar-indexed bonds (NBCE)

Auction date	Maturity	Amount (R$ mm)	Tenor (months)	Maximum YTM
3-Jul-98	3-Nov-99	500	16	12.50%
10-Jul-98	10-Dec-99	500	17	12.42%
17-Jul-98	17-Dec-99	500	17	12.04%
24-Jul-98	24-Jan-00	500	18	12.57%
31-Jul-98	31-Jan-00	500	18	11.85%
7-Aug-98	7-Feb-00	500	18	12.48%
14-Aug-98	14-Feb-99	500	6	10.08%
21-Aug-98	21-Mar-99	500	7	10.50%
24-Aug-98	29-Dec-99	1,000	16	18.50%
25-Aug-98	12-Jun-99	500	10	14.89%
26-Aug-98	12-Jun-99	500	10	13.80%
27-Aug-98	4-Sep-99	500	12	14.94%
28-Aug-98	28-Aug-99	500	12	15.48%
31-Aug-98	5-Nov-99	500	14	16.38%
1-Sep-98	17-Apr-99	500	7	14.89%
2-Sep-98	4-Sep-99	500	12	14.09%
3-Sep-98	12-Dec-98	1,000	3	11.79%
4-Sep-98	4-Dec-99	500	15	15.47%
8-Sep-98	12-Mar-99	1,000	6	14.94%
9-Sep-98	21-Feb-99	1,000	5	18.97%
11-Sep-98	11-Sep-99	500	12	22.99%
2-Oct-98	2-Jul-00	500	21	16.99%
16-Oct-98	16-Aug-00	500	22	16.79%
23-Oct-98	23-Sep-00	500	23	16.37%
30-Oct-98	30-Oct-00	500	24	16.27%
5-Nov-98	17-Jan-99	600	2	12.99%
6-Nov-98	6-Nov-00	500	24	15.44%
13-Nov-98	13-Dec-00	500	25	14.98%
20-Nov-98	20-Feb-01	300	27	14.94%
27-Nov-98	20-Feb-01	300	27	15.18%
1-Dec-98	11-Mar-99	500	3	12.77%
4-Dec-98	20-Feb-01	300	27	15.48%
8-Dec-98	11-Mar-99	500	3	12.64%
11-Dec-98	20-Feb-01	300	26	15.18%
15-Dec-98	28-Nov-99	500	11	13.77%
18-Dec-98	20-Feb-01	300	26	15.17%
23-Dec-98	20-Feb-01	300	26	14.97%
30-Dec-98	20-Feb-01	300	26	15.13%
7-Jan-99	20-Feb-01	300	25	15.38%
12-Feb-99	20-Feb-01	300	24	15.38%
19-Feb-99	20-Feb-01	300	24	18.99%

Exhibit 2 (Continued)

Auction date	Maturity	Amount (R$ mm)	Tenor (months)	Maximum YTM
4-Mar-99	17-Apr-99	30	1	42.00%
12-Mar-99	2-May-99	500	2	24.50%
12-Mar-99	8-Jun-99	22	3	26.00%
15-Mar-99	8-Jun-99	n.a.	3	32.00%
16-Mar-99	8-Jun-99	600	3	37.90%
18-Mar-99	4-Jun-99	400	3	32.00%
19-Mar-99	12-Jun-99	400	3	31.99%
22-Mar-99	8-Jul-99	600	4	31.98%
23-Mar-99	4-Jul-99	300	3	31.44%
24-Mar-99	8-Jul-99	400	3	31.50%
5-Apr-99	30-Aug-99	400	5	20.99%
7-Apr-99	4-Sep-99	300	5	18.50%
9-Apr-99	4-Jul-99	400	3	15.80%
12-Apr-99	4-Aug-99	400	4	17.09%
19-Apr-99	12-Sep-99	400	5	14.74%
22-Apr-99	4-Oct-99	400	5	14.97%
23-Apr-99	4-Oct-99	310	5	15.47%
3-May-99	13-Oct-99	1,000	5	12.94%
4-May-99	20-Oct-99	300	6	13.00%
28-May-99	24-Nov-99	1,000	6	12.98%
1-Jun-99	24-Nov-99	500	6	13.49%
4-Jun-99	24-Nov-99	500	6	12.95%
10-Jun-99	22-May-00	500	11	12.77%

Notice the Auctions in March and April 1999.

CAPTURING THE INTEREST RATE DIFFERENTIAL

The definition of arbitrage is a risk-free trade with a positive payoff in all scenarios. Opportunities of such arbitrage in local markets are either rare or costly. Trading in local markets involves the following risks:

- convertibility risk
- custody risk
- currency risk
- local interest rate risk
- changes in taxation
- changes in regulations
- credit risk
- execution risk

The main ingredient of the recipe of local fixed income trading is to determine which risks have to be hedged, and which not. As a method that greatly simplifies the reasoning, we shall adopt the following steps for the case study described in this chapter:

Step 1. Formalize the payoffs of each instrument, as well the payoff of the whole basket of instruments. We will call the latter the "payoff function." Amounts and quantities need not be specified at this time.

Step 2. Find quantities and amounts that make the "payoff function" insensitive to changes in the currency and interest rate.

Step 3. Substitute these quantities into the "payoff function," and find the "payoff of hedged position."

Step 4. Formalize the initial investment.

Step 5. Find the yield of the trade, dividing the "payoff of hedged position" by the initial investment.

Step 6. Judge the trade idea, understanding how the parameters change and how they affect the final yield.

CASE STUDY: BRAZILIAN TOURIST EXCHANGE RATE

After July 1994, the Brazilian stabilization plan led to very high domestic interest rates. To avoid a massive inflow of short-term capital, the Brazilian government imposed several restrictions on foreign investments in local fixed income. Yet, all restrictions were aimed at the commercial exchange rate, whereas the tourist exchange market remained free. By mid-1995, foreign investors realized that the Brazilian Central Bank was targeting the Brazilian Real (R$) in the tourist market as well. The perception of currency stability, along with very high domestic rates, triggered an investment boom in the Brazilian tourist rate market. On August 11th 1995, the Central Bank increased the restrictions on local fixed income, and, among other measures, established a 7% upfront fee (called "IOF"[5]) on new investments in the tourist market.

However, the legislation still allowed transfers of money between accounts in the tourist market—the so-called non-resident accounts (CC5 accounts). Moreover, the legislation allowed Brazilians to pay external liabilities, such as imports and dividends, by depositing the equivalent R$ amount in foreign investors' CC5 accounts. Soon a market developed to buy and sell cash held in CC5 accounts. As a consequence, instead of paying the 7% upfront fee determined by the Central Bank, foreign investors could acquire the right to exchange dollars for R$ by paying a fee determined by the market, which ranged from R$0.0020 to R$0.0050. This transaction was locally referred as "purchase of space in the CC5 account."

This situation lasted until December 1995, when the Central Bank called the main dealers and told them to stop doing such transactions because they were causing substantial dollar inflows that had to be sterilized, thus disrupting monetary policy.

In the meantime, this situation offered an opportunity of what was perhaps the closest to a perfect arbitrage. Foreign investors were able to "purchase

---

[5] *Imposto sobre Operações Financeiras.*

space in the CC5 account," exchange dollars for Brazilian currency (R$), and buy short-term local bonds, such as BBCs and LTNs. Most of the investors hedged the local bonds for the currency risk, some also hedged for the slippage risk, and very few bought convertibility protection. After incurring all taxes, costs of purchasing "CC5 space," and hedging, the investor could still earn spreads over LIBOR as high as 600 bps in a 6-month time frame. Tenors shorter than that did not yield a similar return because the foreign capital had to stay for some time invested in local bonds to amortize the upfront costs, such as the "purchase of space in the CC5 account."

The case described below involves hedging three major risks: (1) currency risk, (2) change in the premium between the tourist rate and the commercial rate ("slippage risk"), and (3) convertibility risk. The methodology is the same as in the first case study.

Step 1: Assessing Payoffs

Before we go through all the steps, the definitions about the Brazilian market are worth noting:

a. Money market funds are remunerated on a business days basis. For instance, from Friday to Monday, government securities pay only one-day interest. The interest rate benchmark is "*cdi*," which is the overnight rate for interbank deposits. The *cdi* bears a very close relationship to the *Selic*, which is the Brazilian equivalent of the fed funds rate. Both *Selic* and *cdi* overnight rates are quoted on a 30-day rate basis. As an example, a *cdi* of 4.50% is equivalent to an actual overnight rate of 0.15%.

b. Everyday the Central Bank publishes the closing quote for both the commercial and the tourist exchange rates through the electronic system of the Central Bank at the code "Ptax800 – offer rate." These are the exchange rates governing currency swaps, as we shall see below.

c. The R$ spot rate settles in two days if the investor is buying government bonds. For corporate bonds and derivatives, the settlement is in one day. Consequently, if a foreign exchange transaction is executed to settle government bonds on the following day, the spot rate should be deflated by one overnight rate. Analogously, if a foreign exchange transaction is executed to settle government bonds on the same day, the spot rate should be deflated by two overnight rates. This concept will be evident in equations (6) and (19), below.

d. Virtually all currency swaps refer to the Ptax800 exchange rate with one day lag. Therefore, to avoid currency risk, the investor has to buy dollars and sell R$ one day prior to the swap maturity.

Since this case involves a great deal of variables and parameters, the notation used is summarized in Exhibit 3.

Exhibit 3: Main Market Variables and Parameters

e_{t}	=	ptax800 – offer rate for the commercial rate at day t
e_{t}^{f}	=	ptax800 – offer rate for the tourist rate at day t*
$\bar{e}_{0}^{f}$	=	actual tourist rate that the investor sells dollars and purchases R\$, at the beginning of the trade
cdi_{t}	=	cdi overnight rate at day t. To simplify the equations, the cdi will already be divided by "30"
$\overline{cdi}$	=	Average cdi overnight rate in the period of the trade**
α	=	the average percentage of the benchmark cdi that a government security yields***
CC5	=	the market fee for foreign investors to exchange dollars for R\$ at the tourist rate
ϕ_{t}	=	$\dfrac{e_{t}^{f}}{e_{t}} - 1$ (i.e., the premium between the tourist and commercial rate)****
ϕ^{e}	=	the expected premium on date $n-1$, which can be locked in through currency swaps
$i_{US\$}$	=	the USD domestic interest rate in currency swaps (commercial rate vs. accrued cdi) to hedge the currency risk
$i'_{US\$}$	=	the USD domestic interest rate in currency swaps (commercial rate vs. accrued cdi) to hedge the slippage risk
$i_{US\$}^{f}$	=	the USD domestic interest rate in currency swaps (tourist rate vs. accrued cdi) to hedge the slippage risk
n	=	tenor of the trade, expressed in calendar days
w	=	tenor of the trade, expressed in working days
ψ	=	Annualized cost of convertibility hedge
A	=	the initial R\$ amount of local bonds
A'	=	the initial R\$ amount of the swap to hedge the currency risk
A''	=	the initial R\$ amount of the swap to hedge the slippage risk
P	=	the final proceeds, after taxes, converted into dollars.
P^{hedged}	=	the payoff of the hedged position.
tax	=	15% withholding tax on bond earnings.

* The Tourist rate is also called Floating rate, therefore the choice of the superscript f.

** By definition, $\overline{cdi} = \left[\displaystyle\prod_{j=0}^{n-1}(1 + cdi_{j}) \right]^{1/w} - 1$

*** Government securities should yield 100% of cdi, but due to transaction costs and scarcity factors, the investor usually earns a percentage of the cdi close to 99.50%.

**** Notice that ϕ_{t} is the premium that the tourist rate trades relative to the commercial rate; ϕ_{t} is usually positive (i.e., the tourist exchange rate trades weaker than the commercial rate), but, during the period we focus this case study, ϕ_{t} was indeed negative due to the substantial supply of dollars at the tourist market.

Hedging Currency Risk

This case study assumes that the investor is able to close the foreign exchange transaction at the Ptax800 rate. Therefore, the model disregards execution risk in the foreign exchange market at maturity. To avoid mismatch with the currency swaps, the purchase of dollars must be executed the day before maturity ($n-1$). The Ptax800 tourist rate is then represented as e_{n-1}^{f}. Applying the definition of premium between the tourist rate and the commercial rate we have that:

$$e^f_{n-1} = (1 + \phi_{n-1}) \times e_{n-1} \tag{5}$$

The investor will purchase local bonds that yield a percentage (α) of the local benchmark cdi. As the bonds mature, the investor pays the withholding tax and rolls over the position until the final maturity of the trade. The tenor of the bonds should be short enough to avoid divergences between the yield of the bonds and the benchmark cdi, which is caused by changes in the local interest rate.[6] To simplify, we will assume that the investor purchases bonds equivalent to a $R\$$ amount A, which yields the average daily rate $\alpha \times \overline{\text{cdi}}$, compounded over w business days.[7] Further, the total withholding tax is due at the end of the trade, as opposed to at the maturity of each bond.[8] The bond payoff is then converted into dollars using the tourist rate of the previous day deflated by one overnight rate, as explained in (c) above.

Local Bond payoff
$$= A \times \{[(1 + \alpha \times \overline{\text{cdi}})^w - 1] \times (1 - \text{tax}) + 1\} \div \frac{e^f_{n-1}}{(1 + \text{cdi}_{n-1})} \tag{6}$$

Substituting (5) into (6):

Local Bond payoff
$$= \frac{A \times \{[(1 + \alpha \times \overline{\text{cdi}})^w - 1] \times (1 - \text{tax}) + 1\} \times (1 + \text{cdi}_{n-1})}{(1 + \phi_{n-1}) \times e_{n-1}} \tag{7}$$

The commercial rate versus cdi swap (US/DI swap), traded at the Brazilian Futures Exchange (BM&F), pays the difference between the return of a USD-linked investment at the rate $i_{US\$}$, and an investment at the daily cdi rate. The payoff is converted into dollars using the exchange rate e^f_{n-1}, as defined in equation (5):

$$\text{US/DI swap payoff} = \frac{A' \times \left[\left(1 + i_{US\$} \times \frac{n}{360}\right) \times \frac{e_{n-1}}{e_{-1}} - \prod_{j=0}^{n-1}(1 + \text{cdi}_j)\right]}{(1 + \phi_{n-1}) \times e_{n-1}} \tag{8}$$

Analogously, the tourist rate versus cdi swap (USf/DI swap) pays the difference between the return of a tourist USD-linked investment at the rate $i^f_{US\$}$ and an investment at the daily cdi rate:

$$\text{USf/DI swap payoff} = \frac{A'' \times \left[\left(1 + i^f_{US\$} \times \frac{n}{360}\right) \times \frac{e^f_{n-1}}{e^f_{-1}} - \prod_{j=0}^{n-1}(1 + \text{cdi}_j)\right]}{(1 + \phi_{n-1}) \times e_{n-1}} \tag{9}$$

---

[6] There are ways to hedge this interest risk via interest rate futures. Yet, the strategy of buying short-term bonds simplifies the example without harm for its conclusions.

[7] This simplication is consistent with the definitions and remarks of Exhibit 3.

[8] This could make a significant difference in terms of tax deferral should the trade have a long tenor (n). For the purposes of the current example, however, such a difference is negligible.

Equations (7) and (8) show that the bonds and the US/DI swap follow the cdi overnight rate. Therefore, a proper amount A' of US/DI swaps can hedge the currency risk of local bonds.

Hedging Slippage Risk

The second risk to be hedged is the slippage, therefore, the change in premium between the tourist and commercial rate (ϕ_t). It is possible to set a forward on the premium (ϕ^e) through opposite positions of US/DI swaps and USf/DI swaps, both with the same amount A''. From equations (8) and (9), such a payoff ("premium payoff") can be formalized as follows:[9]

$$\text{Premium payoff} = \frac{A'' \times \left[\left(1 + i^f_{US\$} \times \frac{n}{360}\right) \times \frac{e^f_{n-1}}{e^f_{-1}} - \prod_{j=0}^{n-1}(1 + cdi_j)\right]}{(1 + \phi_{n-1}) \times e_{n-1}}$$

$$- \frac{A'' \times \left[\left(1 + i'_{US\$} \times \frac{n}{360}\right) \times \frac{e_{n-1}}{e_{-1}} - \prod_{j=0}^{n-1}(1 + cdi_j)\right]}{(1 + \phi_{n-1}) \times e_{n-1}} \tag{10}$$

with some arrangements we arrive at

$$\text{Premium payoff} = \frac{A''}{e^f_{-1}} \times \left(1 + i^f_{US\$} \times \frac{n}{360}\right) \times \left(1 - \frac{1 + \phi^e}{1 + \phi_{n-1}}\right) \tag{11}$$

where

$$1 + \phi^e = (1 + \phi_{-1}) \times \frac{\left(1 + i'_{US\$} \times \frac{n}{360}\right)}{\left(1 + i^f_{US\$} \times \frac{n}{360}\right)} \tag{12}$$

Hedging Convertibility Risk

The last risk to be hedged is the convertibility. The convertibility hedge is an insurance policy. If an event of non-convertibility occurs, the investor receives a predetermined USD amount. In this case study, the USD amount should be equal to P, defined as the sum of all payoffs: local bonds plus swaps.

$$\text{convertibility premium} = \psi \times \frac{n}{360} \times P \tag{13}$$

Finally, from equations (7), (8), and (11), we can build the payoff function P:

$$P = \text{Local bond payoff} + \text{US/DI swap payoff} + \text{Premium payoff} \tag{14}$$

---

[9] The reason to distinguish i_{US} and i'_{US} is that the currency and slippage hedges may be closed with different counterparties, and i_{US} may change from one trade to another.

Step 2: Determining Hedge Ratios

Equation (14) shows the payoff of a portfolio comprising local bonds and currency swaps. The next step is to find the right amounts of swaps A' and A'' that make the portfolio P insensitive to changes in the currency e_{n-1} and the slippage ϕ_{n-1}.

In order to determine the right amounts of A' and A'', we should differentiate the payoff function P with respect to the exchange rate at maturity (e_{n-1}) and the premium at maturity (ϕ_{n-1}):

$$\frac{\partial P}{\partial e_{n-1}} = 0$$

$$\Rightarrow A' = A \times \frac{\{[(1 + \alpha \times \overline{\mathrm{cdi}})^w - 1] \times (1 - \mathrm{tax}) + 1\} \times (1 + \mathrm{cdi}_{n-1})}{(1 + \mathrm{cdi})^w} \tag{15}$$

and

$$\frac{\partial P}{\partial \phi_{n-1}} = 0 \text{ and } \frac{\partial P}{\partial e_{n-1}} = 0 \Rightarrow A'' = A' \times \frac{\left(1 + i_{\mathrm{US\$}} \times \dfrac{n}{360}\right)}{\left(1 + i'_{\mathrm{US\$}} \times \dfrac{n}{360}\right)} \tag{16}$$

Step 3: Finding the Payoff of the Hedged Position

Equations (15) and (16) represent the relationship between the swap amounts A' and A'', and the amount of local bonds (A), that hedge the portfolio for changes in the exchange rate and the premium. Substituting these into equation (14), we find the payoff of the hedged position (P^{hedged}):

$$P^{\mathrm{hedged}} = \frac{A}{e_{-1}} \times \frac{\{[(1 + \alpha \times \overline{\mathrm{cdi}})^w - 1] \times (1 - \mathrm{tax}) + 1\} \times (1 + \mathrm{cdi}_{n-1})}{(1 + \mathrm{cdi})^w}$$

$$\times \frac{\left(1 + i_{\mathrm{US\$}} \times \dfrac{n}{360}\right)}{1 + \phi^e} \tag{17}$$

Step 4: Determining the Initial Investment

At the beginning of the trade, the investor sells dollars at the current market rate ($\tilde{e}_0^f$), minus a market fee (cc5), to have the R\$ amount A credited in a CC5 account. Since the purchase of bonds is to be executed on the same day, the exchange rate must discounted by two overnight rates (cdi_0). Therefore, the actual exchange rate will be:

$$(\tilde{e}_0^f - \mathrm{cc5})/(1 + \mathrm{cdi}_0)^2$$

In addition to the purchase of the local bonds, the investor has to pay for the convertibility insurance. As per equation (13), the insurance cost ψ is applied over the amount to be hedged—in this case, the payoff of the hedged position (P^{hedged}).

$$\text{Initial investment} = A \div \frac{(\bar{e}_0^f - cc5)}{(1 + cdi_0)^2} + \psi \times \frac{n}{360} \times P^{\text{hedged}} \tag{18}$$

Step 5: Calculating the Return of the Trade

The return in the period is given by

$$\frac{P^{\text{hedged}}}{\text{Initial investment}} - 1 \tag{19}$$

From equations (17) and (18), with some rearrangement, we arrive at

$$\text{Return} = \left[\Omega \times \frac{e_{-1}^f \times (1 + cdi_0)}{(\bar{e}_0^f - cc5)} \times \frac{(1 + cdi_0)}{(1 + cdi_{n-1})} \times \frac{(1 + \phi^e)}{(1 + \phi_{-1})} \times \frac{1}{\left(1 + i_{\text{US\$}} \times \frac{n}{360}\right)} + \psi \times \frac{n}{360} \right]^{-1} \tag{20}$$

where

$$\Omega = \frac{(1 + \overline{cdi})^w}{\{[(1 + \alpha \times \overline{cdi})^w - 1] \times (1 - tax) + 1\}}$$

Step 6: Judging the Trade Idea

Two risks were left out of the analysis above—credit risk on the Brazilian Futures Exchange (BM&F) and execution risk on the foreign exchange at maturity. All other determinants of the trade are represented in equation (20). It is worth discussing the meaning of each term.

Ω is the ratio of the gross return over the net return of Brazilian money market funds. In practice, the net return is always lower, due to transaction costs (α) and taxes ("tax"). Notice that the higher Ω is, the lower the return of the trade. Furthermore, the minimum value Ω can attain is 1, in the case of no transaction costs ($\alpha = 1$) and no taxes (tax = 0).

The second term of equation (20) is

$$e_{-1}^f \times (1 + cdi_0)/(\bar{e}_0^f - cc5)$$

It represents the ratio of the theoretical initial exchange rate e_{-1}^f over the exchange rate the investor actually gets,

$$(\bar{e}_0^f - cc5)/(1 + cdi_0)$$

Usually, the latter is less favorable than the theoretical exchange rate, causing this term to be higher than 1, thus acting against the investor. Occasionally, in days when the $R\$$ weakens, this term may work at the investor's benefit.

As mentioned in (c) above, purchases of government bonds entail a loss of one overnight rate, which should be recovered at maturity. This is expressed by the third term of equation (20),

$$(1 + cdi_0)/(1 + cdi_{n-1})$$

Notice that the initial overnight rate cdi_0 can be either greater or less than the final overnight rate cdi_{n-1}. Shortly we will see that this effect is negligible in a low-inflation environment when local overnight rates show low volatility.

The fourth term of equation (20) is

$$(1 + \phi^e)/(1 + \phi_{-1}),$$

expressing the difference between the initial premium of the floating rate over the commercial rate (ϕ_{-1}) and the forward premium set via currency swaps (ϕ^e). Therefore, the cost of hedging the slippage risk increases as the forward premium ϕ^e diverges from the initial premium ϕ_{-1}.

The fifth term of equation (20),

$$1/\left(1 + i_{US\$} \times \frac{n}{360}\right),$$

represents the domestic USD interest rate.

Finally,

$$\psi \times \frac{n}{360}$$

is the premium to hedge for the convertibility risk.

Two terms in equation (20), namely the final overnight rate cdi_{n-1} and Ω, should be treated as variables, since they are unknown when the trade is executed. The cdi_{n-1} hardly presents a problem because, in a turbulent scenario, the overnight rate should go up, which would then increase the return of the trade.

Factor Ω is more problematic, as a rise in the overnight rate causes an increase in taxation and, as a result, reduces the net return of Brazilian money market funds. Furthermore, the factor Ω also depends on factor α—the percentage of the benchmark cdi earned by the investor. The percentage of the cdi may vary at each rollover of local bonds, adding uncertainty about the return of the local bonds. One way to lock in such a return is to buy bonds that coincide with the maturity of the trade. However, this is not always possible. To illustrate this point, in the numerical example below, the trade has a 180 days tenor, whereas the bonds liquidity at that time was concentrated around 50 days. Therefore, the investor could not avoid running rollover risk.

Exhibit 4: Exchange Rates, Premium Between Rates, and Overnight Rate (10/2/95 – 10/31/95)

Date t	$R\$$ Commercial e_t	$R\$$ Tourist e_t^f	Premium ϕ_t	Overnight Rate cdi_t
Oct-02-95	0.9555	0.9505	−0.52%	0.14467%
Oct-03-95	0.9585	0.9535	−0.52%	0.14433%
Oct-04-95	0.9585	0.9535	−0.52%	0.14433%
Oct-05-95	0.9585	0.9535	−0.52%	0.14367%
Oct-06-95	0.9590	0.9542	−0.50%	0.14233%
Oct-09-95	0.9585	0.9545	−0.42%	0.14167%
Oct-10-95	0.9585	0.9540	−0.47%	0.14233%
Oct-11-95	0.9585	0.9535	−0.52%	0.14233%
Oct-13-95	0.9585	0.9535	−0.52%	0.14233%
Oct-16-95	0.9585	0.9540	−0.47%	0.14233%
Oct-17-95	0.9585	0.9565	−0.21%	0.14333%
Oct-18-95	0.9590	0.9568	−0.23%	0.14533%
Oct-19-95	0.9593	0.9585	−0.08%	0.14533%
Oct-20-95	0.9613	0.9605	−0.08%	0.14567%
Oct-23-95	0.9615	0.9595	−0.21%	0.14567%
Oct-24-95	0.9617	0.9600	−0.18%	0.14467%
Oct-25-95	0.9617	0.9596	−0.22%	0.14433%
Oct-26-95	0.9625	0.9610	−0.16%	0.14400%
Oct-27-95	0.9622	0.9613	−0.09%	0.14267%
Oct-30-95	0.9617	0.9608	−0.09%	0.14200%
Oct-31-95	0.9619	0.9595	−0.25%	0.14033%

A Numeric Example

Exhibit 4 shows market figures in October 1995, a period that was especially favorable for this trade. Our hypothetical trade took place on October 9, 1995, to mature on April 8, 1996. The market parameters on that date were:

Ptax800 floating rate (e_{-1}^f)	=	$R\$0.9542$
Ptax800 commercial rate (e_{-1})	=	$R\$0.9590$
Therefore, the Ptax800 premium (ϕ_{-1})	=	-0.50%
182-day forward premium (ϕ^e)	=	1.00%
Floating exchange rate (e_0^f)	=	$R\$0.9542$
Overnight rate (cdi_0)	=	0.14167% p.d.
Upfront fee to purchase $R\$$ at the floating rate ($cc5$)	=	$R\$0.002$
Premium of convertibility insurance (ψ)	=	2.00% p.a.
Tenor of the trade (n)	=	182 days
USD interest rate in the first US/DI swap ($i_{US\$}$)	=	21.75% p.a.
USD interest rate in the second US/DI swap ($i'_{US\$}$)	=	21.70% p.a.
number of Brazilian business days comprised in the trade (w)	=	121
withholding tax (tax)	=	10.00%

Three variables still have to be defined: (1) the average overnight rate for the 121 business days of the trade ($\overline{cdi}$), (2) the percentage of the benchmark *CDI* that the investor earns (α), and (3) the final overnight rate (cdi_{n-1}). As a simplification, we conservatively assumed that the final overnight rate is equal to the average overnight rate ($\overline{cdi} = cdi_{n-1}$). Factor α usually ranges from 98.5% to 100% of CDI. Since the actual factor α was unknown at the onset of the trade, a conservative assumption should again be made, which for the purposes of this example was 98.0% of CDI. Therefore, the return of the trade depended on one single variable: the average overnight rate, $\overline{cdi}$. A sensitivity analysis may show how a rise of the $\overline{cdi}$ increases the amount of taxes, with negative impact on the return. Before that, however, it is worth going through the execution of the trade.

On October 9th, 1995, the actual exchange rate would have been R\$0.9542 minus R\$0.002, adjusted for two overnight rates of 0.14167% (because the investor had to purchase local government bonds on the same day). As a result, the actual exchange rate was R\$0.949508. Assuming a USD 10 million investment, the investor should have bought Brazilian bonds worth R\$9,495,080.00.

The investor would then close a swap to hedge the currency risk, receiving 21.75% p.a. plus currency depreciation and paying CDI. Assumptions of α, $\overline{cdi}$, and cdi_{n-1} are necessary to determine the amount of the swap; α has already been determined above. Let's assume 0.1500% for the $\overline{cdi}$ as well as cdi_{n-1} and later see how errors in this forecast might affect the return of the trade. Substituting these values in equation (15), the amount A' of the swap is R\$9,320,628.33.

Additionally, the investor would buy a forward on the premium between the tourist and commercial rate (ϕ^e) at 1.00%. As pointed out in equations (11) and (12), this is done through a combination of two currency swaps, one paying foreign exchange (fx) devaluation at the commercial rate plus a spread and receiving CDI, another one receiving fx devaluation at the floating rate plus a spread and paying CDI. Let's assume that the investor purchased the forward on the premium with another counterparty, and that the spread on the commercial rate swap $i'_{US\$}$ had changed to 21.70%. Therefore, according to equation (12), the spread in the floating rate $i'_{US\$}$ should equal 18.439%, resulting in a forward premium ϕ of 1.00%. Finally, equation (16) sets the amount of the combination of swaps A'' at R\$9,322,751.46. At that point, the investor had already converted the USD 10 million into local currency, purchased local bonds, and closed swaps to hedge both the currency and slippage risk.

The last risk to be hedged is the convertibility risk. In this example, it costs 2% per annum over the insured amount, which should be what the investor expects to receive at maturity, namely, the payoff of the hedged position (P^{hedged}). Substituting our assumptions, including the ones for $\overline{cdi}$ and cdi_{n-1}, into equation (17) we find USD 10,680,999.27. Therefore, the investor should pay 2% p.a. on 182 days over that amount, which equals USD 107,996.77.

Finally, the investor should assess the return of the trade. If the assumptions of $\overline{cdi}$ and cdi_{n-1} turned out to be correct, the trade would yield 5.669% in dollars, or 11.21% annualized. However, the assumptions of $\overline{cdi}$ and cdi_{n-1} could be wrong. In this case, the return would vary in several ways.

It has already been pointed out that the return of the trade is negatively affected as the overnight rate increases. The reason is the increase in taxation. Yet, underestimations of $\overline{cdi}$ also provoke less intuitive relationships: the higher taxation reduces the final proceeds, and, as a consequence, the investor ends up over-hedged for currency and slippage risk. In other words, the hedge amounts were calculated for a given impact of taxation on the final proceeds. As the nominal return of the bonds increases, the tax impact is magnified. As a consequence, the investor should have closed a smaller amount of currency swaps. Indeed, equations (15) and (16) point out that, as the average overnight rate $\overline{cdi}$ increases, the amount of swaps A' and A'' should decrease.

The "over-hedge effect," due to errors in the assumptions of $\overline{cdi}$, causes the investor to become short the local currency. In a stress-case scenario, this is a desirable effect because an upsurge on inflation followed by a rise of local interest rates should increase the probability that the currency devalues faster than inflation. To sum up, the "over-hedge effect" increases the uncertainty over the return of the trade but also mitigates the investor's loss in a stress-case scenario.

Exhibit 5 illustrates this point. The curve "theory" shows the annualized return of the trade assuming no errors for the $\overline{cdi}$ and cdi_{n-1} forecasts. The curve "numeric simulation" shows the return of the trade when $\overline{cdi}$ and cdi_{n-1} were initially assumed 0.15%, and the actual overnight rate ranges from 0.05% to 1.00%. Additionally, the real effective exchange rate devalued 10%.[10] Exhibit 5 shows that, as the scenario deteriorates and the overnight rate increases, the "numeric simulation" performs better than the theory. Nevertheless, the local currency can also act against the investor's overhedged situation. In fact, the gap between the two curves shows how critical the exchange rate becomes once the forecast of the average overnight rate $\overline{cdi}$ turns out to be wrong.

Some considerations should be given to the cost of hedging. The question of whether the investor should really hedge a position for currency, slippage, and convertibility risk are beyond the scope of this chapter. Yet, pure arbitrage situations are extremely rare in the real world. The present case study, for example, is not a perfect arbitrage, since it implies exposure to the domestic interest rate. An intuitive way to assess the cost of hedging is to recalculate the return of the trade, suppressing each of its components one at a time, such as withholding tax, future premium, etc. Following this methodology, Exhibit 6 shows how much upside the investor gives away with each one of the components of the trade, as specified in equation (20). Notice that the currency hedge was excluded from this analysis because the discussion about currency risk is not the subject of this chapter.

We can see that the heaviest cost is the withholding tax that reduces the return by 3.42%. The hedges for slippage and convertibility risk add up to 5.38%. The investor has to decide whether or not these hedges are expensive, based on his or her view of the local market. After thorough research, the investor might

---

[10] The inflation was assumed equal to the annualized overnight rate less a 22% spread, to account for the real interest rate.

eventually decide not to do the hedges, thus enhancing the return of the trade. Then, it should be clear that the trade departs from the initial arbitrage concept, as it acquires more speculative characteristics.

Exhibit 5: Comparison of Numeric Solution and Theory under Various Scenarios of CDI Rates

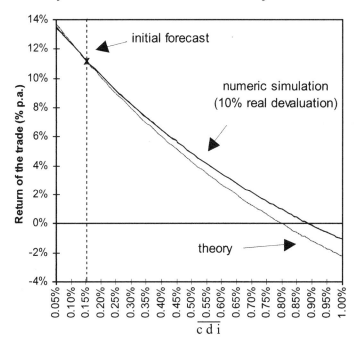

Exhibit 6: Scenario Analysis Under Various Assumptions for the Parameters (swap rate = 21.75%).

Determinants of the trade	% (annualized)	Assumptions
Withholding tax	3.42%	$tax = 0$
Slippage hedge	3.12%	$\phi_{-1} = \phi^e$
Convertibility hedge	2.26%	$\psi = 0$
Bonds transaction cost	0.69%	$\alpha = 100\%$
CC5 market fee	0.43%	$cc5 = 0$
Ptax 800 effect	0.29%	$e^f_0 = e^f_{-1} \times (1 + cdi_0)$
Overnight rate mismatch	−0.02%	$cdi_{n-1} = cdi_0$
Cross residual effect	0.35%	
Total costs	10.54%	
Net return of the trade	11.21%	

Chapter 12

Valuing Options on Fixed Exchange Rates: A Case Study of the Argentine Peso

James C. Kennan
Vice President
BNP Paribas

V aluing options on a fixed exchange rate—or on any asset whose price is set by official decree—is an interesting and potentially troublesome exercise. To the casual observer, options on currencies with fixed pegs may seem illogical, since the cash rate[1] does not move. Yet active options markets have existed on currency pairs despite the presence of explicitly pegged exchange rate regimes. Shortly before the introduction of the Euro, for example, banks continued dealing options among the EMU currencies, such as Deutsche mark versus French franc. Exchange rate crises in which currency pegs were removed, such as Mexico (1994), Russia (1998), and Brazil (1999), have clearly demonstrated that options with strikes "outside the band" are not worthless.[2] By analyzing option prices on pegged currencies, the observer can extract valuable information about the probability that a peg will not hold over a given period.

As with any other asset, prices for such options are determined by supply and demand. But this does not help a trader or analyst who needs to know the relative value of one option versus another, or who has a limited price history and needs to price an option. In this chapter, I provide some simple estimation techniques to help fill in the gaps for relative valuation purposes and to provide a basis for pricing and evaluating such options using practical methods.

---

[1] Generally, the rate for delivery within two business days.

[2] In addition to simple fixed rates, many countries have employed more complicated systems in which the exchange rate fluctuates within a specified band, which may be stationary or "crawling." A crawling band is typically used to reflect inflation differentials between the pegged currency and its anchor. Rather than being pegged to a single currency, many countries have also employed pegs comprised of a basket of currencies. This analysis may be applied to such systems equally well, with allowances for the peculiarities of each regime.

BLACK-SCHOLES AND FIXED PRICES

Brownian motion is a reasonable approximation for the price behavior of a broad range of financial assets. Consequently, the Black-Scholes application of brownian motion to options pricing has become a widely used pricing yardstick, allowing traders to express prices in terms of implied volatility rather than premium, and providing a benchmark for institutions to value non-tradable assets with embedded optionality.

But not all asset prices move in a random walk: the governments of many countries fix the external value of their currencies. As of mid-2001, Argentine law guaranteed "convertibility," obliging the country's central bank to sell one U.S. dollar for every Argentine peso received from a local bank; the Saudi Arabian Monetary Agency promised the delivery of one U.S. dollar for every 3.75 Saudi riyals received; the Hong Kong Monetary Authority likewise promised one U.S. dollar for every 7.8 Hong Kong dollars. Governments have historically employed such policies with the aim of promoting trade or reducing inflation[3].

Despite its apparent irrelevance for pricing options on these fixed rates, the Black-Scholes methodology cannot be so readily dismissed. Although the spot rates on these currencies do not exhibit brownian motion (being essentially stationary), their forward rates typically do. The forward is the rate at which a currency trades for delivery in the future, with legal contracts specifying the dates, rates and places of delivery. Its price reflects the link between the spot foreign exchange market and the two currencies' interest rate markets, a concept known as "covered interest arbitrage." This states that an equal amount of money (calculated at the spot rate) invested in the local currency money markets of two countries must be worth the same at maturity (neglecting taxation, margin, collateralization, etc.). The rate that makes them equal is the forward rate. If they are not equal, one can profit by (1) borrowing one currency, (2) selling it in the spot market, (3) lending the proceeds in the money market of the other currency, and (4) trading the forward against it. The difference between the forward rate and the spot rate thus reflects the interest rate differential between the two currencies.

Exhibit 1 below shows that, although Argentina's spot rate is fixed, its forward rates largely exhibit the same brownian motion of floating currency spot rates. This reflects the fact that with free movement of capital across borders, it is possible to fix a country's exchange rate or its interest rate, but not both.

It is the volatility of this forward rate on which the Black-Scholes equation is based. The σ of the equation represents the volatility of changes in the forward rate that corresponds to the (constant) maturity of the option.

Example. If the spot date today is June 1, the implied volatility of a 1-month at-the-money-forward (ATMF) option is the expected volatility of changes in the forward rate for delivery July 1 over the 1-month period of the option. Observed

---

[3] Bretton Woods and the EEC are examples of trade-related pegs, while various IMF programs have used fixed exchange rates as price-stabilizing anchors.

volatility is calculated as follows. On spot date June 1, we record the forward rate for July 1; on June 2, we again record the rate for delivery July 1 and calculate the daily change as:[4]

$$\ln\left(\frac{\text{fwd}_{\text{June 2}}}{\text{fwd}_{\text{June 1}}}\right) \tag{1}$$

On June 3, we again record the rate for July 1 and compute the daily change from June 2, continuing in this fashion until the last day, when July 1 is the spot rate. We then find σ by calculating the annualized standard deviation of the series of daily changes, by taking the sample standard deviation and multiplying by the square root of the number of work days per year.[5] The rate upon which we base the volatility calculation is thus the "decaying" forward (i.e., a constant maturity, akin to a futures contract). The volatility of this rate can be roughly approximated by the volatility of the rolling forward that is half the maturity being estimated, which is shown in Exhibit 2.

Exhibit 1: History of 1-Year Outright Forwards

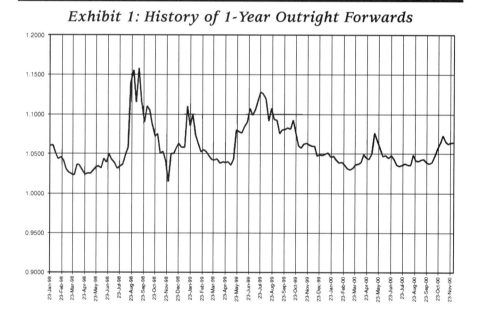

---

[4] We use the natural logarithm in equation (1) to generate a continuously compounded rate.

[5] Calculating standard deviations using daily data is most common, but there is nothing special about this. We could just as easily use hourly data and annualize it with the corresponding factor. Likewise, using the sample standard deviation is most common, but it is arguably more accurate to calculate the standard deviation based on the expected daily change, as

$$\sigma = \sqrt{\sum_{i=1}^{n} \frac{[x_i - E(x)]^2}{n}}$$

where $E(x)$ is the 1-day forward points divided by spot, rather than based on the sample mean, $\bar{x}$.

Exhibit 2: 1-Year Constant Maturity Volatility

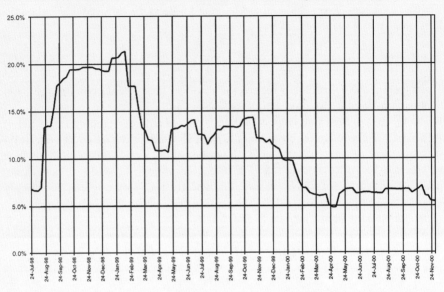

If we graph the daily changes as a cumulative frequency distribution, we can directly compare the observed distribution with a normal distribution. The normal distribution is the primary assumption of brownian motion: changes in the asset price are assumed to be normally distributed. The forward price itself is assumed to be lognormal—a variable has a lognormal distribution if the natural logarithm of the variable (or the return) is normally distributed. The cumulative distribution shows the cumulative percentage of observations at each level of daily change. Exhibit 3 shows the cumulative distribution of returns on the 1-year forward price using the sample period of Exhibit 1, graphed against a normal distribution.

As shown in the exhibit, prices which appear historically stationary may in fact be relatively normal, at least historically speaking. Unlike currencies that are freely floating, however, the historical volatility of the futures rate for pegged currencies rarely approximates the implied volatility used for options pricing; implied volatility is typically much higher.

The large divergence between historical and implied volatilities occurs because the market estimates that the *underlying* distribution of returns is not normal, unlike the *observed* distribution of returns, which is roughly normal. The underlying distribution is the distribution of all possible events, as opposed to the observed distribution, which represents only the events that actually occurred over the period of observation.

Exhibit 3: Actual versus Normal Distribution (Cumulative)

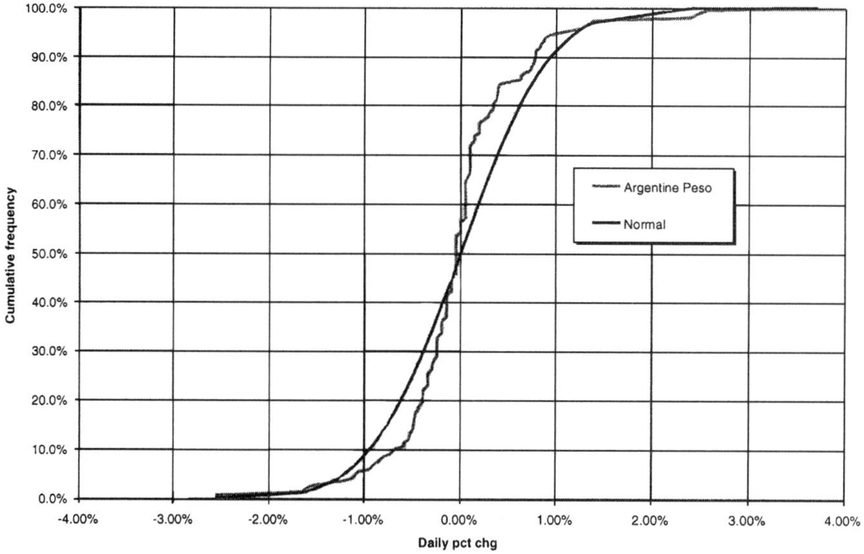

THE UNDERLYING DISTRIBUTION

In the case of a fixed price like the Argentine peso exchange rate, it is easier to visualize this difference between the observed and underlying distributions by referring to the distribution of the future spot rate, rather than the distribution of returns. As noted earlier, if the spot rate exhibits brownian motion, it should be lognormally distributed.[6] The underlying distribution for the Argentine peso can be approximated as bi-modal. Exhibit 4 depicts a comparison of a lognormal and bi-modal frequency distribution of the spot rate at maturity.[7]

The intuition for the bi-modal character of the distribution is as follows. As long as the currency regime holds (i.e., convertibility), the spot rate remains at parity—hence the large spike located at the spot rate. If the rate ever varies significantly from parity, the act of abandoning the peg itself would imply a loss of confidence, reviving fears of a return to Argentina's hyperinflationary past. As of mid-2001, the currency was thought to be overvalued some 20%-30% on a purchasing power parity basis, further shifting the balance of risk toward devaluation rather than revaluation. Because a devaluation would be so potentially destruc-

---

[6] Unlike the normal distribution, the lognormal distribution is truncated at zero. This is because the spot rate itself cannot go below zero (a currency cannot be worth less than nothing), whereas returns on the currency can be positive or negative.

[7] A bi-modal distribution has two distinct modes. Exhibit 4 is a stylized depiction; in reality, the area under the left-hand mode is typically greater than under the right-hand mode, such that the spike located at the spot rate would be very, very high.

tive, particularly considering that much of the country's debt (both domestic and foreign) is denominated in U.S. dollars, the authorities are likely to strongly resist a devaluation. This implies that if a devaluation does occur, it is likely to be very sudden and very large, with no prices observed between the two modes. Note that the forward rate depicted here is the expected (or average) value for the future spot rate for both distributions (lognormal and bi-modal).

One might consider pricing options on a bi-modally distributed asset using a model incorporating two distributions, each with its own standard deviation, or via a Merton-type jump-diffusion model.[8] But the guesswork of estimating parameters for the right-tail distribution make such models impractical. A more intuitive and useful method is to express the ratio of the right-tail relative to the whole distribution via a single probability, allowing one to price options with strikes between the two major modes. This provides a simple linear estimate for a large region where the option price behaves linearly.

The option price reflects information about the currency's underlying probability distribution. Assuming the bi-modal distribution applies, one may infer both the probability and expected magnitude of a devaluation by comparing option prices to the corresponding forward rates.

Exhibit 4: Lognormal versus Bi-Modal Frequency Distribution

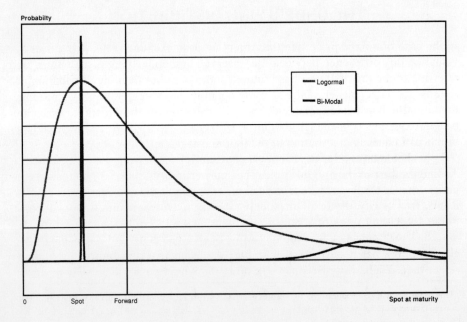

[8] See R. C. Merton, "Option Pricing When Underlying Stock Returns are Discontinuous," *Journal of Financial Economics* (March 1976), pp. 125-44.

The probability of a devaluation can be derived from the price of the at-the-money-forward (ATMF) call on the currency. The buyer of the naked ATMF call should earn a profit if there is no change in the peg, since the option holder runs a much greater risk of devaluation than revaluation. By comparing the amount of expected profit with the cost of the premium, the devaluation probability can be directly computed.

Example. With a spot rate of 1.00 Argentine peso (ARS) per U.S. dollar (USD), a USD deposit rate of 6.0% and a forward rate of 1.05, we can imply an ARS deposit rate of 11.2% based on a maturity of one year.[9] Suppose the ATMF call on ARS (put on USD) trades at a premium of 4.16% of USD (equal to an implied volatility of 11.0%). If there is no change in the peg (i.e., spot equals 1.00 at maturity), the option buyer has an expected profit of:

$$\left(\frac{\text{forward}}{\text{spot}} - 1\right) \times \left(\frac{1}{1 + \text{deposit rate}}\right) \Rightarrow \left(\frac{1.0500}{1.0000} - 1\right) \times \left(\frac{1}{1 + 0.06}\right) \Rightarrow 4.71\% \quad (2)$$

In present value terms, the call option buyer risks 4.16% to make 4.71%, implying a no-devaluation probability of (4.16/4.71) = 88.3%. The devaluation probability is therefore (100.0% − 88.3%) = 11.7%. This can be illustrated using a simple binomial tree.

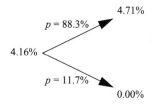

The expected magnitude of a devaluation can be derived from the price of the ATMF put on the currency (which by put-call parity must be the same price as the call on the currency, since the strike is equal to the forward). The buyer of the put should have an expected profit corresponding to the devaluation probability and the cost of the option.

Example. The put buyer risks 4.16% to make an uncertain profit. Using the same parameters as above, we already know the probability of devaluation is equal to 11.7%. The present value of the buyer's expected profit in percent of USD must be:

$$\frac{\text{premium}}{\text{devaluation probability}} \Rightarrow \frac{4.16\%}{11.7\%} \Rightarrow 35.6\% \quad (3)$$

This can also be represented by a simple binomial tree:

---

[9] This can be implied from the forward formula,

$$F = S \times \frac{1 + i_{\text{ARS}}}{1 + i_{\text{USD}}}$$

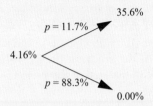

In present value terms, the put option buyer risks 4.16% to make 35.6%, corresponding to an 11.7% devaluation probability. A 35.6% devaluation corresponds to a spot rate of:[10]

$$\frac{\text{strike}}{1 - \text{devaluation magnitude}} \Rightarrow \frac{1.0500}{1 - 35.6\%} \Rightarrow 1.6304 \tag{4}$$

THE PRICING MODEL

As noted above, the main observation motivating the pricing of Argentine peso options is that a short position in the naked ATMF call on ARS[11] makes a profit (equal to the premium) if the peso devalues beyond the forward prior to expiration. The present value of the forward points multiplied by the probability of no devaluation is a first approximation for the price of the ARS call.

This assumes that the probability of revaluation is zero. In practice, the ARS call with a strike of 1.00 does not trade for zero premium, since there are still potential scenarios in which the currency could be revalued (and since no one ever knowingly sells options for free!).[12] Thus there is a small left-tail in the distribution, implying some probability of revaluation. This effectively makes the distribution tri-modal. Prior to 2001, the price of the 1-year 1.00 ARS call typically ranged from 0.15% to 0.30% of USD. This option is frequently quoted in the market and its price is easily observed.

We can incorporate this probability into a pricing formula by simply specifying a price for the 1.00 ARS call. We can also generalize the formula for all strikes above 1.00 and below the region of the right-tail:

$$\frac{P_{\text{strike}} - P_{1.00}}{PV_{(\text{strike} - 1.00)}} = 1 - Pr_{\text{deval}} \tag{5}$$

---

[10] The expected magnitude of devaluation corresponds to the mean of the right-tail distribution as shown in Exhibit 4.

[11] Equivalently, a short position in the ATMF put on ARS that is fully hedged (100% net forward delta).

[12] There is at least one case in recent memory of a government revaluing a pegged currency: in 1986, Saudi Arabia moved its peg of Saudi riyals to U.S. dollars from 3.75 to 3.65 in an effort to squeeze speculative short riyal positions. The operation was successful, and, a month later, the authorities moved the rate back to the old peg of 3.75.

where:

$$P_{strike} \qquad = \text{price of the call on ARS for the desired strike}$$
$$P_{1.00} \qquad = \text{price of the call on ARS with a strike of 1.00}$$
$$PV_{(strike-1.00)} = \text{present value of the (strike} - 1.00\text{) ARS call spread}$$
$$Pr_{deval} \qquad = \text{probability of devaluation}$$

This simply expresses the idea that the difference in price between the ARS call for a given strike (P_{strike}) and the ARS call with a strike of one, relative to the value of the spread, should be equal to the probability of no devaluation over the period of the option. We can then solve for the price of the ARS call for the desired strike:

$$P_{strike} = P_{1.00} + (1 - Pr_{deval}) \times PV_{(strike-1.00)} \qquad (6)$$

Example. If the 1-year 1.00 ARS call is 0.20%, the annual probability of devaluation is 25%, the 1-year forward is 1.0800, and the 1-year USD deposit rate is 5%, then the price of the ATMF call on ARS is equal to

$$P_{strike} = 0.20\% + (1 - 25\%) \times \left(\frac{1.08}{1.00} - 1\right) \times \left(\frac{1}{1 + 5\%}\right) = 5.91\%$$

This price can also be quoted in terms of Black-Scholes implied volatility.[13] In this case, it is equal to 15.6%.

Example. We now wish to price a 1-year USD call ARS put with a strike of 1.1500. We use the same devaluation probability and first calculate the value of the ARS call:

$$P_{strike} = 0.20\% + (1 - 25\%) \times \left(\frac{1.15}{1.00} - 1\right) \times \left(\frac{1}{1 + 5\%}\right) = 10.91\%$$

This implies a volatility of 19.0%. By put-call parity, the USD call (ARS put) must be worth:

$$C = P - e^{-rt}(X - F) = 10.91\% - \left(\frac{1.15}{1.08} - 1\right) \times \left(\frac{1}{1 + 5\%}\right) = 4.74\% \qquad (7)$$

Example. Finally, we price a 1.2500 strike ARS put with the same maturity.

$$P_{strike} = 0.20\% + (1 - 25\%) \times \left(\frac{1.25}{1.00} - 1\right) \times \left(\frac{1}{1 + 5\%}\right) = 18.06\%$$

$$C = 18.06\% - \left(\frac{1.25}{1.08} - 1\right) \times \left(\frac{1}{1 + 5\%}\right) = 3.07\%$$

This implies a volatility of 21.0%.

---

[13] This can be calculated from the premium using Newton's method.

The implied volatilities of these three examples (15.6%, 19.0%, 21.0%) show that the technique inherently implies a volatility smile, which in practice is very much in line with observed market prices. In this particular set of examples, the method provides meaningful prices for strikes up to approximately 1.3500, which begins to encroach on the region of the right-tail distribution. Using equations (3) and (4), the mean of the right-tail distribution is implied by the option price and the probability of devaluation:

$$\text{devaluation magnitude} \Rightarrow \frac{\text{premium}}{\text{devaluation probability}} \Rightarrow \frac{5.91\%}{25\%} \Rightarrow 23.64\%$$

$$\text{mean of right tail} \Rightarrow \frac{\text{strike}}{1 - \text{devaluation magnitude}} \Rightarrow \frac{1.0800}{1 - 23.64\%} \Rightarrow 1.4144$$

Beyond this level, the technique will begin implying negative (and meaningless) option prices. As described, this method cannot be used to price strikes within the region of the right-tail distribution, since it assumes no knowledge of the shape of this mode of the distribution. However, observed market interest in such high strikes relative to the level of forwards has been infrequent.

The probability of devaluation exhibits a term structure similar to that of interest rates and implied volatilities. The annualized probability of devaluation is not uniform through time (though it is identical for different strikes with the same expiration, as in the examples above). For example, if the forward is 1.0200, the ATMF premium is 1.90%, the 1.00 ARS call is 0.03%, and the USD interest rate is 5%, this implies a 1-month devaluation probability of:

$$Pr_{deval} = 1 - \frac{P_{strike} - P_{1.00}}{PV_{(strike - 1.00)}} = 1 - \frac{1.90\% - 0.03\%}{\dfrac{1.02 - 1}{1 + 5\%/12}} = 6.11\% \qquad (8)$$

Annualized, this is equal to:

$$1 - (Pr_{no\ deval})^{12} = 1 - (1 - 6.11\%)^{12} = 53.1\%$$

If the 3-month annualized devaluation probability is, for example, 45%, this is not inconsistent with the 1-month probability of 53.1%. The only arbitrage condition that applies is that the value of the 1-month option cannot be equal to or greater than the 3-month option. There is a very high correlation between the forwards and the probability of devaluation; the higher the forwards, the higher are the implied probabilities of devaluation. The ratio of devaluation probability to forward level cannot be precisely predicted; however, empirical studies of this relationship show a strong linear relationship. There is also a strong empirical relationship between the shape of the forward curve and the shape of the devaluation probability curve.

A NEW COMPLICATION

An interesting twist was added to the Argentine option equation in early 2001, when the minister of the Argentine economy, Domingo Cavallo, proposed that the exchange rate peg be changed from one peso per U.S. dollar to one peso per basket of 0.5 U.S. dollars and 0.5 Euros. Were this change to occur, it would have the effect of superimposing half of the Euro/USD implied volatility on the USD/Argentine peso distribution. Cavallo indicated that he would propose making this change when the EUR/USD spot rate reached 1.00 (it was 0.85 as of June 2001). If and when the EUR/USD rate does reach 1.00, the 1.00 ARS calls are likely to be worth approximately half the value of the EUR/USD at-the-money-spot (ATMS) EUR call USD put options.

The present value of this embedded option can be evaluated by calculating the value of a EUR/USD barrier option.[14] These options are quite liquid and easily priced. For a 1-year tenor, with both the spot rate and forward rate at 0.8500, the USD deposit rate at 5% and the implied volatility at 12%, the EUR call / USD put knock-in option with a strike of 1.00 and a barrier at 1.00 is worth 0.54%[15] of USD notional, making the 1.00 ARS call worth approximately 0.27%. In practice, these options traded above this implied value shortly after the announcement, reflecting uncertainty regarding additional potential policy changes.

CONCLUSION

A careful analysis of a fixed asset's *underlying* distribution, taking into account all possible information—including relevant macroeconomic and policy-related drivers—can assist the trader or analyst in pricing derivatives on such assets. As described above, option pricing on the Argentine peso exchange rate can be expressed in terms of two intuitive factors: annualized probabilities of devaluation and values of at-the-money-spot peso calls. The Black-Scholes formula is not a deterministic pricing model used by traders to predict option values; instead, it allows them to transform their discussion of prices into terms of implied volatility. Likewise, the simple model suggested here is not intended to predict option prices—though it does aim to provide a basis for relative valuation. Instead, it provides a practical benchmark that, like implied volatility, can be more intuitively discussed to formulate option prices.

---

[14] A barrier option is an option that is activated (or de-activated) when an underlying reference rate, e.g. the spot rate, reaches a specified level. These are also referred to as "knock-in" and "knock-out" options, to indicate whether the option will be activated ("knocked in") or de-activated ("knocked out") if the barrier level is reached.

[15] This is the (skewed) market price, using a 25-delta risk reversal of 0.4 for the EUR puts and a 25-delta butterfly of 0.3; theoretical value (under the Black-Scholes assumption of a flat volatility surface) is approximately 0.43% of EUR.

Section III

Credit Issues

Chapter 13

Challenges in the Credit Analysis of Emerging Market Corporate Bonds

Christopher Taylor
Director
Emerging Market Telecom/Media
Global High Yield Research
ING Barings

E merging market corporate bonds can be an attractive asset class. That is, they have the potential to provide investors with attractive risk-adjusted returns. However, the asset class also raises unique challenges that require a disciplined approach to manage.

APPROACHES TO INVESTING IN EMERGING MARKET CORPORATES

There traditionally have been two approaches to investing in emerging market corporate bonds: top-down and bottom-up. Neither approach is necessarily contradictory or mutually exclusive. However, in practice they are often treated as such. The top-down approach essentially treats investing in corporates as "sovereign-plus." The bottom-up approach can treat emerging market corporate bonds as "U.S. credits-plus." Investors have become more sophisticated in recent years—to a large extent due to the recurrent crises in Mexico, Asia, Russia, and Brazil, and to the consequent massive sell-offs throughout Emerging Markets. But there are still many inefficiencies. We believe that investing in emerging market corporate bonds can be most profitably done utilizing techniques practiced for high-yield bonds, but the macro-environment and micro-factors unique to individual countries must be taken into account. In other words, a matrix approach is needed.

Prior to the Mexican crisis in 1995, little attention was paid to corporate fundamentals. Most investment was "name lending"—the local blue chips would get loans at rates slightly above sovereign bonds. Hence the treatment of emerging market corporates as "sovereign-plus." Often this was justified, since many of these blue-chips had credit ratios and characteristics that, in the United States, would have earned them investment-grade ranking. However, several times these investment decisions were made based on name and reputation rather than sound credit decisions, and investors got stuck with low-quality bonds.

Conversely, many investors bought these names based on their strong credit ratios and attractive yields relative to U.S. names with similar ratios. However, comparing ratios across borders obscures as much as it reveals. Investors should pay close attention to ratios and other credit statistics. Investors should also adjust for the fact that (1) emerging markets are inherently more volatile (thus ratios should be stronger), (2) inflation accounting distorts results (especially when inflation is increasing), (3) accounting standards are less rigid in many emerging markets, (4) the legal system is less developed and reliable in many of these countries, (5) recessions tend to be more severe, and (6) governments tend to intervene (and support their companies) more.

These factors should not deter investors from acquiring these bonds. We believe that investors are usually adequately compensated for these risks, considering the high yield on most emerging market corporates. However, it does mean that investors should be aware of these risks and, more to the point, of how to manage them.

Each subsequent crisis (Asia in 1997, Russia and Brazil a year thereafter) has brought more discipline to emerging market corporate bonds. As investors gain more experience, they have adjusted their approach to the asset class. Underwriting standards have improved significantly.[1]

EMERGING MARKET CREDITS VERSUS U.S. CREDITS WITH SAME RATING

In theory, a BB rated emerging market bond should have the same default risk as a BB U.S. bond. In other words, the BB corporate rating should already incorporate sovereign risk. Many of the emerging market corporates that we look at have solid investment grade ratios for U.S. standards. But, of course, these issuers are not based in the United States; they are located in a region where the economic and political environments are more volatile. This is why these issuers are rated BB rather than investment grade. However, to argue that a BB company should carry a premium relative to U.S. BB credits is discounting twice, since the BB rating already incorporates a penalty for sovereign risk! The solid investment-grade ratios are what enabled these companies to survive even a drastic downturn, such as occurred in Mexico and Argentina in 1995, or in Brazil and Argentina during 1999.

Asian corporates are different, since prior to the Thailand collapse they were by-and-large not constrained by the sovereign ceiling. They also had more

---

[1] See, for example, Christopher Taylor, "Suggested Guidelines for New Issuance," *Global High Yield Research*, ING Barings, 2000.

access to local and commercial bank credit than Latin corporates traditionally had. Consequently, Asian corporates as a general rule had higher leverage, higher levels of short-term debt (i.e., more potential for liquidity problems), and less transparent accounting. Thus, despite their higher ratings, they encountered more problems when their economies collapsed.

Most companies in Latin America have proven that they can survive even drastic macro-economic turbulence. With an economic decline and liquidity squeeze equivalent to what the U.S. experienced during the 1930s, a large majority of these companies managed to survive. We doubt that many U.S. single-B or even double-B companies would have been able to survive a downturn and liquidity squeeze so severe. To be sure, there were defaults in Latin America in the past several years. But, considering the extent of the regions economic volatility, the percentage is relatively low.

Of course, credit risk is not the only factor influencing bond pricing. Trading risk (e.g., volatility and liquidity) is another significant variable. Latin bonds are inherently more volatile and less liquid than U.S. high-yield bonds. Ironically, the latest market crisis comes out of the United States, not emerging markets. Since the 2000 NASDAQ crash, emerging market corporate bonds have taken a significant hit, along with U.S. high-yield bonds. Investors in emerging market corporate bonds should be aware that their asset class suffers whenever any other asset class sneezes. This is true even when their own fundamentals—corporate or sovereign—are relatively strong.

Investors should ensure that they are adequately compensated for this extra trading and liquidity risk, even when they believe default risk is already priced into the assets. A good approach might be to compare yields on a basket of similarly rated U.S. and emerging market corporates. Whenever spreads for the latter come too close to the former (say within 100 to 200 basis points), one might wish to reduce exposure. This does not always guarantee good results. For example, during 2000, single-B U.S. corporates underperformed similar Latin corporates, since the former had more speculative, venture capital-like characteristics. However, by and large, Latin corporates outperform their U.S. counterparts in bull markets and underperform in bear markets. But, we emphasize that this is because of trading and liquidity risk, not default risk.

TIERING THE CREDIT

Often, trading in emerging market bonds—especially those whose ownership is concentrated with locally based investors—is based on a company's local reputation, as opposed to credit fundamentals. But a blue chip reputation and credit strength may or may not be related. Instead, we recommend that investors rank credits in three categories based on standard credit risk measures (e.g., cash flow ratios, risk and volatility of industry, size of company, competence of management, etc.). Of course, many of the perceived blue chips will still be top-tier credits if ranked by such a methodology—but not always. Short-term, companies that are perceived locally to be blue chips will probably trade better than those that have top-tier characteristics according to U.S.-style methodologies.

But, in the end, credit fundamentals are usually the determining factor in whether a bond is repaid. Especially now that many emerging markets are opening up to competition and slaying the inflation dragon, perception will sooner or later catch up with reality. In the past, many blue chips became big or remained big not because of strong management. Instead, it was because of their political connections or high import barriers, and/or their ability to export thanks to high inflation and weak currencies, and/or because competitors could not emerge due to limited access to capital or lack of political connections. However, in a more stable environment with a healthier currency and better access to capital and lower import barriers and privatization, new competitors are emerging and management competence becomes the key variable.

In countries where reform has been underway for some time now, many of the blue chips whose managements were incapable of dealing with the new environment have already been eliminated. In other countries, there is still a significant divergence between companies which are locally viewed as blue chips and those that are top-tier credits based on more relevant credit guidelines. We caution that short-term U.S. investors could get frustrated since a significant part of emerging market trading is still dominated by "name trading." However, most market participants have become more sophisticated and are more likely to do thorough credit analysis. Over time, we continue to believe that the divergence between perception and credit reality will continue to close, and thus investors who today do their credit homework should outperform those who buy based on name trading.

Tier one credits are those that are constrained by the sovereign ceiling, meaning those that would be solid investment grade if they were located in a more stable environment. Tier two credits are not necessarily constrained by the sovereign ceiling. If they were located in a typical OECD country they would probably be BB or possibly borderline investment grade. Tier two credits tend to have some significant credit issues which bear watching, but not significant enough to cause a serious risk of default. Tier three credits, in contrast, have significant default and/or rescheduling risk. These credits should have a sizable risk premium, since in emerging markets creditors usually have little recourse under local law in the event of default, and local courts are somewhat inefficient.

JUDGING COMPANIES BY INFORMATION PROVIDED

Many investors are turned off from investing in emerging market corporate bonds by the historically pathetic levels of disclosure these companies provided. There are still some companies which treat investors shabbily. (Often, not coincidentally, these companies are perceived blue chips whose credit fundamentals do not measure up to market perception.) However, we believe that, in general, the level of disclosure continues to improve significantly. Many emerging market companies—especially the better managed ones—have learned to treat investors as a key constituency rather than a nuisance to be tolerated. On the other hand, there are still quite a few poorly managed companies that do not provide their investors with even minimum acceptable information flow.

We believe that investors should demand a healthy premium for the bonds of companies which do not service their investors' legitimate information requirements properly. Lack of information flow and poor credit risk and weak management often go hand in hand. These companies are usually riskier, since foreign investors are usually the last to learn of any bad news. Also, the lack of information and bad news are usually correlated, since most companies would be more than happy to spread any good news. An unwillingness to open up to investors is often an indication of a traditional-type management that is incapable of changing with the times. And even if these uninformative issuers were good credits, we have learned that the bonds of companies that do provide good information to investors usually hold up better in a bear market and rebound faster in any recovery.

We have developed several rules of thumb. First, avoid private companies (i.e., ones that don't report to a stock exchange) unless their bonds are registered with the SEC and they have a New York–based investor relations firm. With private companies, it becomes very difficult to get hold of financial results once they take a turn for the worse. Private company bonds virtually always lag otherwise equivalent-risk bonds. Also, secondary trading tends to be very illiquid, especially in bear markets.

Second, demand a premium for issuers that do not have a New York–based investor relations agency. Usually those companies that are not prepared to incur the expenses of an investor relations agency also have an unconstructive view towards investors. Often there is a close correlation between managements that treat investors as an important constituency (and thus usually have better performing bonds), and those that have the skill set needed to compete in a liberalized and rapidly changing economic environment. We should emphasize that there are several emerging market issuers that have excellent investor-relations programs without having a New York-based agency supporting them, but they are the exceptions.

Third, demand a premium for companies that do not file U.S. generally accepted accounting principles (GAAP), or at the least an annual U.S. GAAP reconciliation. In other words, demand a premium for 144A bonds over SEC-registered bonds. We are not necessarily saying that other GAAP's are less conservative. Indeed, we can point to examples where U.S. GAAP is too liberal (e.g., depreciation allowances) or too cumbersome (e.g., deferred taxes). However, at least U.S. GAAP is the devil the greatest number of investors know. Also, it seems to be the most comprehensive and the most thorough in disclosure.

We can think of several instances where a good cash flow company turned into a marginal one when statements were converted into U.S. GAAP—maybe because a "small" subsidiary or some parent company operations had to be consolidated or because a new policy on accounts receivable or inventory obsolescence or revenues accrual had to be recognized. Essentially, what we're saying is that it is easier to have a higher degree of confidence in the companies that report under U.S. GAAP. Full U.S. GAAP numbers would be ideal, but an annual reconciliation is acceptable. Often companies, once they have to show a reconciliation, will change their local-GAAP policies so as to avoid too large a discrepancy between the two standards.

Nonetheless, we believe that investors should always check the reconciliation, just to understand the differences in what is reported quarterly (local GAAP) and what is filed at year-end with the SEC (U.S. GAAP). If the differences are only tax related or (non-cash) depreciation and amortization, one can have a high degree of confidence in quarterly numbers. If the differences are more substantial, investors should question management more thoroughly and take quarterly results with a grain of salt.

Also, for a new issue, the standards of due diligence and disclosure in the prospectus are higher in an SEC-registered issue than in a 144A. We find that, in most instances, disclosure in 144A prospectuses is relatively limited. On the other hand, SEC-registered deals require a legal opinion regarding adequate disclosure, which forces the underwriter (and issuer) to do a more thorough job in due diligence and disclosure. Therefore, we think investors should demand an adequate premium for 144A issues compared to SEC-registered deals. Of course, this premium should vary according to credit risk. If the issuer has high-quality credit ratios, it should be very small. On the other hand, for high-risk credits, this premium should be substantial.

In Asia, disclosure and transparency have improved since their crisis a few years ago. Nonetheless, by and large, accounting standards remain significantly below par and much worse than Latin practices. Ironically, the more blue-chip-like a company is perceived to be, the worse its transparency is likely to be. We recommend that investors think twice before investing in non–U.S. GAAP Asian companies. If one decides to do so, pay close attention to discover whether any accounting tricks are being played. For example, many issuers are notorious for not consolidating heavily indebted subsidiaries or for disclosing significant guarantees or other contingent exposure to liability.

DEBT STRUCTURE MATTERS: COVENANTS

Historically, many Eurobonds were poorly structured, although admittedly this has improved in recent years. In the past, if there were covenants at all, they were usually a maintenance ratio such as debt/capital. These ratios are not very meaningful even in the United States (after all, debt is repaid with cash, not with a capital ratio), but especially not in emerging markets where underdeveloped legal rules and/or inefficient local court systems make enforcement and/or recourse if these covenants are violated rather difficult. We can think of several instances where emerging market companies violated their debt/capital covenants and went right on paying dividends or making acquisitions. The whole idea of covenants is to give investors leverage if things don't go as planned. Also, capital-based maintenance covenants give companies an incentive to incur off-balance-sheet debt or inflate their asset values. Since such debt is often secured and/or effectively has first claim on cash flows, these covenants effectively work against the interests of bondholders rather than protecting them.

These issues do not matter so much for blue chips with strong financial ratios (but not perceived blue chips with poor credit ratios). For top-tier credits, good bond-structuring is relatively unimportant (assuming the credit does not deteriorate while the bonds are outstanding!). However, for companies with weak ratios, emerging market investors should, in our opinion, pay more attention to structure, since this can have a significant impact in how a credit develops. Usually if an investor buys a second tier bond, it is with the hope that the story will improve, or, if the yield is sufficiently attractive, that the story will stabilize. A well-structured bond should give investors comfort that management won't take actions to worsen the credit, and it gives investors leverage to prevent management from doing so. Instead, we have seen perceived blue chips with negative cash flow and an acquisition track record issue bonds without any covenants at all. Investors have only themselves to blame if these deals blow up.

The key credit variables revolve around cash-flow ratios. There is plenty of room for disagreement as to which particular ratio is best, but, conceptually, most analysts agree that some form of ratios that measure cash flow earnings relative to fixed cash payments (e.g., EBITDA/Interest or debt/EBITDA) provide the best measurement of credit risk. (In contrast, a capital-based ratio solely measures on-balance-sheet debt relative to historical investments—in other words, it is a backwards-looking ratio). Thus, it follows that if one wants to create a covenant that best protects creditors, it should be a cash-flow-based ratio. Also, although one can never create a forward-looking ratio, at least one can ensure that a ratio is as current as possible by requiring calculations on a pro forma basis. Most importantly, we believe that investors should require covenants that measure all fixed calls on cash flow, including off-balance-sheet debt and mandatory preferred. Finally, any covenants should be self-enforcing, which is crucial in a region where legal recourse is difficult.

The high-yield market has, over the years, developed effective covenants. It has learned how to tie management's hands if it doesn't meet its projections, without this adversely affecting bondholders or requiring major legal expenses by creditors. This is done by means of comprehensive "incurrence" tests. Some form of cash-flow-based ratio is chosen to measure management's projections of cash-flow relative to future fixed obligations, with some margin for error. Essentially, management can do whatever it wishes, but if it wants to borrow or pay dividends or buy back stock or upstream money to its parent, it must meet this ratio (on a pro forma basis).

For example, a debt/EBITDA incurrence test in an issuer's covenant package is 4 times. On a historical basis, the company has 3 times debt relative to EBITDA, but if management wanted to borrow more (e.g., to pay dividends) it would have to calculate the ratio based on the new debt level. It could incur as much debt as it wanted, so long as the ratio remained below 4 times (usually known as "the ability to incur $1 of additional debt under the incurrence test"). This offers investors effective assurance that management's actions won't cause credit ratios to deteriorate beyond a certain point. If properly drawn, this clause makes it very difficult for management to borrow extra money for acquisitions or to pay dividends, etc.

Of course, general business risks could cause a credit deterioration, but no covenant can protect against such developments. Indeed, a maintenance covenant can worsen the situation by forcing management to focus on playing games (e.g., accounting tricks or off-balance-sheet liabilities) to avoid violating the covenant at the very time when they should be focusing on improving the business fundamentals.

Just as important for emerging market investors where the legal system is not necessarily a reliable ally, incurrence covenants are to some extent self enforcing. No bank will lend money or no board will declare dividends if that very act is a violation of the covenants. Under maintenance covenants, no such self-policing mechanism exists. The company is already in violation, so why shouldn't the board go ahead with other plans (e.g., pay dividends or pursue acquisitions), even if those cause further deterioration?

DEBT STRUCTURE MATTERS: CRITICAL ROLE OF MATURITY PROFILE

One lesson we should have learned from the recurring crises in emerging markets is that short-term debt is bad. Especially commercial paper proved itself to be a rather fickle source of finance for companies, whereas commercial bank debt could only be rolled over with difficulty—not to mention with significantly higher interest rates. We are encouraged that many emerging market firms have improved their debt profile and retired shorter-term debt, even if it cost them a few hundred basis points extra. Even in the United States, commercial paper is usually not considered an appropriate and reliable source of capital for non-investment-grade companies. Certainly in emerging markets, where capital availability is even more volatile, commercial paper must definitely be an inappropriate form of financing. It usually disappears just when it is needed most (i.e., during a major crisis).

We believe that those issuers that still use high-risk short-term debt (in particular, commercial paper) should probably be avoided, even if other credit fundamentals appear sound. A willingness to tolerate a risky level of short-term debt says something about management, and, in emerging markets, we prefer to invest in well-managed companies. Most emerging markets have underdeveloped lending systems with only short-tenor debt available. This debt usually automatically rolls over, becoming effectively long-term debt ("evergreen"). Thus, we can understand how traditional management was comfortable with high levels of short-term debt. However, this automatic "evergreen" does not apply to foreign debt, where refinancing risk is significant. Companies that rely on significant amounts of short-term debt should be avoided.

Companies with bad ratios but no immediate refinancing requirements can usually muddle through for a while. In contrast, during crises, companies with stronger financial ratios but steep refinancing requirements can be pushed under. After all, a default is not caused by unfavorable financial ratios (unless maintenance covenants trip them up) but rather by an inability to pay debt obligations. Thus, if there are no obligations coming due for a long time, the risk of default is reduced significantly, no matter how bad the ratios are in the interim. Debt structure (i.e., upcoming debt maturities) is the most important credit variable in emerging markets, even more so than cash flow ratios.

A closely related issue is debt arbitrage. Many emerging market companies borrow in U.S. dollars to avoid steep local interest rates. The flip side of these high local rates is good returns on cash deposits. Thus, many companies over-borrow hard currency and invest it in local instruments. During the good times this is a profitable strategy, but, when a crisis hits, the chickens can come home to roost. We simply do not like companies that engage in such arbitrage. Not only is it risky when there are devaluations, it also sends some negative signals about management. It says that management likes to gamble and also, to some extent, that management does not see many profitable investment opportunities in its core business. If management's core businesses were strong, it wouldn't be wasting its energy on non-core activities, such as financial arbitrage, trying to boost short-term profitability.

BREACHING THE SOVEREIGN CEILING

As a general rule, we believe that virtually all emerging market corporates should trade at a premium to their sovereign bonds. However, there can be a few exceptions. In Argentina, several of the top-tier credits trade tighter than Argentine sovereign bonds. This might be partly due to the strong fundamentals of Argentine corporates and, in several instances, their ownership by strong foreign parents. But, these conditions can also apply to other countries. The main reason we are comfortable with Argentine corporates trading through the sovereign is due to

Argentina's currency board. The currency board makes exchange controls and/or restrictions less likely; therefore the theory behind the sovereign ceiling argument becomes less relevant.

The sovereign ceiling argument is essentially one of structural subordination. Simplistically, it says that if the sovereign needs foreign exchange, it will have first call on hard currency, to the detriment of other creditors with hard-currency debt, such as corporates. Therefore, corporates should always carry a risk premium relative to sovereigns. (This is another reason why we do not like corporates with significant amounts of hard-currency short-term debt or commercial paper: the sovereign is more likely to restrict access to foreign currencies for short-term obligations than it is for repayment of long-term debt, especially bonds.) In most countries, the structural subordination argument is valid. With a currency board, however, the government essentially removes its first call on hard currency, and therefore corporates are no longer structurally subordinated. The central bank is not "lender of last resort" to the government, and therefore the government no longer has a superior status structurally.

Of course, one should always be cautious about government risk. Currency boards were created by politicians and thus can be abolished by them. Therefore, one should focus carefully on the longevity of the currency board and its popular support. If one contracts with an insurance company in Bermuda or buys a mutual fund in the Bahamas—both of which have currency boards—sovereign risk is hardly an issue. This analyst does not even know what the economic or political risk in either country is, but that proves our point. If one is confident that a currency board will remain in place, local political and economic risks become almost irrelevant to the credit story.

Of course, one is less secure in Argentina because the currency board has been in place for only a few years, whereas in Bermuda and the Bahamas there has been at least half a century of confidence building. Nineteenth century Latin America has plenty of examples of currency boards being abolished and/or manipulated once the going got tough. Therefore, one should always be more skeptical about Argentina than one would be in small Caribbean islands with a different legal and political tradition. However, we believe that the 1995 and 1999 crises proved that the currency board has solid across-the-board popular support in Argentina. Because of this, we remain reasonably confident that for the foreseeable future—or at least until most of the corporate Eurobonds that we cover have been safely retired—the currency board will remain in place. Thus, for very strong local blue chips there is justification for their trading through the sovereign ceiling. We note that S&P also accepted this argument and rates several companies' credit ratings higher than that of the sovereign. Having said that, even in Argentina sovereign risk remains a factor to be considered.

As a general rule, any time a corporate trades tight to a sovereign bond, the risk-reward equation goes against the corporate. At best, the corporate will slightly outperform the sovereign, assuming market sentiment remains bullish. At worst, if market sentiment sours, the corporate will significantly widen against the sovereign.

Thus, a good rule of thumb remains to sell if spreads become too tight to the sovereign. Even for those selected corporates where investors are comfortable that trading very tight to—or even inside—the sovereign is justified (e.g., in Argentina or in those with strongly committed multinational parents), we recommend that investors pay close attention to historical spread levels. Only if they are rich relative to historical levels are they likely to offer attractive risk-adjusted returns.

STABILITY OF A COUNTRY'S CURRENCY

All other things being equal, we look for countries with historically stable currencies. We usually disregard whether the currency is short-term overvalued or undervalued, since, in the long run, purchasing power parity usually holds. According to this theory, inflation usually catches up with a devaluation, thus, in the longer term, arbitrage risk (borrowing in hard currency, revenues in local currency) is relatively modest. However, countries with volatile currencies usually have more risk of dysfunctional macro-economic policies. In the short term, these policies may actually benefit certain corporates (e.g., economic stimulation benefits companies that sell to the domestic market, whereas weak currencies benefit exporters and producers—usually commodities—whose prices are dollarised). However, in the long term, these policies increase cash flow volatility and cost of capital (or even reduce access to capital) and thus credit risk. Since, by their very nature, corporate bonds are long-term instruments, this is what matters.

For example, in Mexico, inflation has already largely eroded the (alleged) short-term advantage of the December 1994 devaluation. In the interim, however, the government was forced to incur sharply higher interest rates and thus a severe recession in order to stem the resultant capital flight and inflation (which almost always follow devaluations). Thus, over a 2-year timeframe, the currency arbitrage risk was minimal (inflation and thus unit prices caught up with the devaluation), but, in the interim, sales volumes collapsed and cost of capital skyrocketed. For some time, this severely impacted some of the issuers' creditworthiness, even the exporters that were the alleged beneficiaries of the devaluation. Worse, capital markets were shut to new issuance, thus sharply increasing refinancing risk.

Our point is that for long-term bonds the currency mismatch (between local currency revenues and hard-currency borrowing) is not a major concern *per se*, since purchasing-power parity usually holds (barring extreme exchange and price controls). However, countries with unstable currencies tend to have unstable macro-economic performances as well, and these are a major negative from a corporate credit perspective. One reason we are quite comfortable with Mexico at present is because, since the devaluation debacle, the government has learned its lesson and places a heavy emphasis on currency stability and avoids imbalances in the underlying macro-economic fundamentals. In other words, the central bank has the upper hand over the economic growth advocates, and therefore economic growth—albeit slower at first—has become more stable and sustainable. Since stability and sustainability of cash flows (as opposed to short-term growth) are key credit variables for corporate bonds, conservative monetary policies are a significant positive.

We believe that one reason Argentine corporate bonds traditionally trade tight relative to sovereign bonds is because, with the currency board, currency instability has been all but eliminated. Thus, the strength or weakness of the local currency is no longer a factor in corporate earnings, which makes them more predictable. Argentina has gone one step further and abolished inflation accounting (low inflation is fundamentally associated with a stable currency). This, of course, enhances the quality and reliability of earnings, which should further reduce the risk premium required.

INFLATION ACCOUNTING

Inflation accounting makes it more difficult to truly understand what is going on in a company. Given that we all have time pressures, we prefer to invest in companies where we can easily and quickly understand what is going on. Also, given the complexities of inflation accounting, one is never quite certain whether one correctly understood what the numbers said. When we present an investment idea to investors, we prefer to be confident that we understand it ourselves; inflation accounting makes us somewhat less likely to stick out our necks. One rule of thumb we have developed is to disbelieve any numbers where inflation is above 50%, unless they have been translated into hard currency at the time of the transaction.

In some Eastern European and Middle Eastern countries, the income and cash flow statements are not restated, only the balance sheet. We find this methodology preferable to using comprehensive restatements as used in some Latin American countries. In our opinion, the income statement is reasonably reliable so long inflation is modest; however, even with around 20% inflation, the cash flow statement is distorted so as to make it almost meaningless.

In Argentina, inflation accounting was abolished in 1995. In our opinion, this justifies a lower premium for their corporate bonds since we can more easily and better understand the numbers and thus are less likely to get caught by surprise. In Brazil, inflation accounting was abolished in 1996, but unfortunately most companies continue to use it. Worse, most companies do not separately disclose the inflation and devaluation component of their interest expense, making it virtually impossible to calculate true interest expense. Since interest expense is a key variable in determining a company's credit risk, this is a negative for which investors should demand a significant premium.

In Mexico, inflation accounting still reigns with full force. Fortunately, however, inflation has come down significantly since the 1995 devaluation debacle. A big positive for Mexican corporates is their stock exchange's electronic database for reporting earnings. This database requires all Mexican companies to report relatively quickly (5 weeks after each quarter end, and 9 weeks after year end) and in relatively good detail. We believe this good level of disclosure helped many investors get comfortable with Mexican credits and helped in the relatively rapid rebound after the devaluation debacle. If Mexican reporting had been as slow as in Argentina or as uninformative and difficult to collect as in Brazil, we doubt many investors would have been willing to reenter the Mexican corporate sector after the devaluation—certainly not as rapidly as they did in other countries.

For many emerging market credits, a key earnings variable is the strength of the local currency. Now that inflation in most countries is coming under control, the many companies that were able to compete based on their weak currency will have to start competing based on their core competencies. Many will not be able to not compete in this environment, and we believe investors should avoid these names altogether since their margins will only deteriorate. A good rule of thumb we have learned is to avoid companies that complain about the strength of the currency and loudly call for a devaluation rather than proactively investing or restructuring so that they can compete regardless of the strength of their currency. Proactive companies will survive in the longer term (even if, in the shorter term, they have to borrow to finance these investments).

Also, with inflation coming down rapidly (which is directly related to a stable currency), cost control becomes a more important issue (e.g., as salaries rise to catch up with inflation), and operating margins no longer benefit from the inventory effect (i.e., inventory bought at lower prices results in lower cost of goods sold and better margins after the finished unit is sold at higher prices). This affects everyone's margins. Thus, investors should bet on companies that are focused on operating margins and results, not just top-line (sales) growth. We can think of several examples of companies that tried to grow (or acquire) their way out of uncompetitive cost structures. They almost always fail.

EXPORTERS VERSUS DOMESTICS

For most countries, the corporate sector (and the economies, for that matter) can essentially be broken into two sectors: the dollarized sector and the non-tradeable sector. Roughly, in most Latin countries, a third to a half of the companies (and of the economy) is dollarized. In export-oriented countries, the percentage may be higher. In essence, producers in this sector base their prices on U.S. prices and/or international commodities. Thus, even though they may sell domestically and invoice in local currencies, they are reasonably hedged if they borrow in hard currencies. Products whose prices are dollarized include virtually all commodities, such as mining products, chemicals, and paper, as well as internationally traded products, such as autoparts, glass, electrical equipment, and transportation services (e.g., shipping, airlines).

Note that this definition of "dollarized" includes a broader sector than just exports. The key is whether a producer has the option to export. For example, a paper or packaging producer may sell virtually all of its output domestically. However, if domestic prices were too low relative to international prices, it could always shift sales abroad. Thus it has pricing power domestically and therefore can tie its prices to international rates. Unless the government imposes major price controls (always a risk after devaluations), these companies are relatively hedged against devaluations.

The dollarized sector is usually the biggest beneficiary from devaluations or weak currencies in general. In dollar terms, there would not be much change in their revenues, but their local currency-based costs decline. (Of course, what they gain in better margins they usually lose in higher cost of capital and lower domestic volumes, but that's another story.) With stable currencies, as a general rule, one can expect dollarized producers to see tighter margins. In countries that have had a stable currency for a longer time, most vulnerable producers have already been eliminated.

In other countries, however, this weeding out process has only just begun. Once a currency strengthens, even the strongest producers will see a tightening of margins. Of course, on the positive side, the better-run companies will be able to lower their cost of capital and extend their debt maturities. In countries with high inflation and volatile currencies, companies find it unusually difficult to get financing beyond one year, and even then at high rates. To a large extent, the lower cost of and easier access to financing offsets the margin pressure.

However, the uncompetitive firms (and their unions) usually put heavy political pressure on the government to devalue (or adopt economic policies that in the end will cause a devaluation). Also, one harsh side effect of this necessary restructuring is unemployment, which puts political pressure on the government to reflate the economy (which almost inevitably causes devaluation). All these pressures increase the risks for all of the country's issuers, even the strong ones, until the transition process is several years old and these uncompetitive firms have been restructured or eliminated.

Assuming unchanged international commodity prices, revenues in dollar terms for these dollarized companies should be stable despite local currency instability. However, until inflation and interest rates decline to international levels, inflation and high real-interest rates will continue to increase local currency-based borrowing costs. Thus, until the currency and inflation are totally stable, the strength (or weakness) of the currency and trends in inflation will remain key variables in companies' quarterly earnings and debt-coverage ratios. Since this adds an extra element of instability and uncertainty—and thus risk—to companies' earnings, investors should ask for a risk premium for issuers in inflationary countries or in those with volatile currencies.

Negative trends on margins due to strong currencies can, to some extent, be offset if these companies can sell more value-added products domestically.

Companies tend to export very commoditized products, but locally sell more customized products. As a general rule, domestic sales tend to have more value added and thus better margins. For instance, a paper producer might export standardized paper rolls, but for domestic customers it may cut and/or coat the paper, thus increasing proceeds per ton by several hundred dollars. With more stable currencies and lower inflation often come more confidence and higher disposable income and thus a stronger domestic economy and more sales opportunities.

In addition, exports have higher transportation costs and generally command a somewhat lower price in the international market than locally due to the absence of tariff protection. (Although tariffs in the third world are declining, they are often still sizable.) As a very general rule, however, we do not believe that the higher-margin domestic sales fully offset the negative impact of the stronger currencies on margins for dollarized companies, although there are exceptions to prove our rule. The key is to do one's credit homework to thoroughly understand how each company is impacted by stronger currency and declining inflation on the one hand, yet benefits from stronger domestic spending and better access to capital markets on the other. Focus on long-term trends, not quarter-to-quarter changes.

REGULATORY RISK

A final word of caution when investing in bonds of companies dependent on the domestic sector, especially utilities: regulatory risk. Of course, this risk that concerns us is present in the United States and European utilities and telecommunication companies, too. Instead, it is the process. In the United States, no matter how antiquated and cumbersome utility regulations may be, at least there is a clearly defined process that enables all to know how to participate and ensures some level of fairness. In contrast, it seems at times that the process in several emerging market countries is somewhat opaque and may be arbitrary. Sometimes, local companies' political clout can be a key variable in this process.

For example, a permitted price increase is "waived by consent" in order to help the government's inflation-control program. Fortunately, most utilities with bonds outstanding in emerging markets have strong coverage ratios, so these events only have a modest credit impact. However, for the few marginal utilities investors should certainly demand a premium to offset this risk. Unless a utility has strong support from an investment-grade parent (or is sovereign owned), investors should always demand a reasonable risk premium compared to sovereign bonds to offset regulatory risk. This is a risk factor investors should get comfortable with, for it is entirely possible that all of the sudden a significantly different regulatory regime will be imposed with little or no warning. To be fair, many emerging markets seem to have learned that this scares off investors and are trying to amend their ways.

SUMMARY

We believe that investors who use the skills gained in analyzing U.S. credits (bottom-up) can make significant risk-adjusted returns in emerging markets since they understand how to analyze cash flows. This has not traditionally been a common skill in emerging markets, where top-down analysis has been the traditional approach. However, we have raised the above issues in this chapter since there are also many factors unique to emerging markets, which we sometimes see U.S. investors not taking into account. Our point is that one should use high-yield style credit skills, but one should also be prepared for the unexpected. Do not assume that a Brazilian utility is just like a U.S. utility, but understand the differences as well. When all is said and done, however, use high-yield style disciplines. If you cannot get good information from management or cannot get a good grip on cash flow, stay away from the bond altogether. On the other hand, if management is modern and informative and helps you get comfortable with (which in our mind is usually synonymous with understanding) the risk, you can increase the probability of higher risk-adjusted returns.

Chapter 14

Debt Covenants: Applications in Emerging Markets

Allen Vine
First Vice President
Merrill Lynch & Co.

David Sohnen, CFA
Vice President
Merrill Lynch & Co.

T he intense turmoil in global financial markets in the fall of 1998 forced a review of many long-standing investment concepts, changed the trading practices of many investment houses, and commenced a search by the financial community for less-volatile ways to make money. In hindsight, the events of 1998 are increasingly viewed as inevitable, given the unknown risks of new sovereign and corporate issuers, the sharp increase in the speed of capital flows, and the profound changes in the investor base. At the same time, little in terms of new analytical tools has emerged to deal with the new challenges.

It is not clear whether new analytic techniques can be developed that could encompass the complexity of the modern financial markets. Sovereign risk, technical flows, and other key market drivers appear as inscrutable today as ever. Yet, the pressure to outperform has remained. The question now is what mechanisms can investors use to protect their capital while pursuing high-yield opportunities?

One effective mechanism, standard in the U.S. high-yield market but largely neglected in emerging markets, is the application of debt covenants. This chapter highlights how wider use of this tool can substantially enhance the safety of corporate investing, especially in the emerging markets, by forcing higher degrees of discipline on underwriters and transparency on issuers.

THE PURPOSE OF COVENANTS

Covenants are designed to protect creditors' access to cash flow and the underlying income-producing assets to service their loans by subjecting the issuer to certain restrictions. In the event of default, covenants delineate the seniority of asset claims. Covenants pertaining to a bond issue are generally included in the indenture—a formal contractual agreement between an issuer and bondholders (typically represented by a designated trustee)—where certain considerations, including protective provisions, redemption rights and call privileges, among others, are established.

By subjecting issuers to restrictive covenants, investors can achieve a higher degree of protection for their investment on the basis of the credit quality of issuers. Preventive measures, as opposed to reactive measures, can be particularly effective in markets where legal mechanisms make it difficult for creditors to enforce their rights. The issue of enforceability of claims is particularly relevant in emerging markets since, to date, there has been little precedent for bondholders being able to protect their rights through bankruptcy proceedings and liquidations.

Generally, covenants rely on tests to ensure that an issuer maintains a certain level of credit quality. Incurrence covenants protect the interests of existing lenders by preventing a company from issuing additional debt if such issuance would violate certain predetermined covenants. For example, if a covenant allows maximum leverage of 5.0× and a new issuance of debt would cause leverage to rise above 5.0×, the issuer would not be allowed to sell additional debt.

Maintenance covenants require companies to remain within certain prescribed credit ratios. For example, if covenants require a minimum coverage ratio of 2.0× and coverage slips to 1.8×, the company would typically be in default. If the debt were then accelerated, a bankruptcy court could assume control, provided that creditors do not accept consent offers by the company or a prepackaged bankruptcy-restructuring plan. In this manner, bondholders can demand repayment while the issuer is still generating positive cash flow, rather than wait for mounting operating losses to reduce the firm's value.

To be effective, covenants need to capture the essence of risks faced by debtholders. The risks include, but are not limited to, the following:

- Insufficient cash flow to cover interest.
- Insufficient liquidity to meet amortization requirements.
- Acquisition, merger, consolidation, and asset transfer activities that adversely affect a company's cash generating ability.
- Adverse changes in the ownership structure.

Covenants need to warn creditors when these conditions may be arising and help protect investors when these conditions do occur. Some of the specific functions that covenants need to accomplish include the following:

- Deter aggressive use of leverage to the detriment of existing lenders.
- Trigger alarms while a company is still in a solid financial and/or operating position and allow bondholders greater recovery.
- Install further protection in the issues of weaker companies by securing sinking funds or prefunded interest payments.

Due to their relative safety, investment grade bonds generally include three basic covenants: (1) restrictions on debt, (2) restrictions on sale-leaseback transactions, and (3) consolidation, merger, and sales of assets.

High-yield indentures usually include a majority of the main covenants and, occasionally, other firm-specific covenants. This has been especially the case since the high-yield market turmoil in the 1989-1991 period.

In emerging markets, corporate debt has been largely issued with limited sets of covenants, despite the repeated bouts of sharp market volatility and bond-holder difficulties in enforcing claims. On a positive side, investors have made significant gains in securing greater transparency from emerging market issuers since 1995. The application of covenants can substantially enhance the usefulness of this hard-won transparency.

DEBT INDENTURES

The debt indenture is a legal document that imposes a number of restrictions, key among which involve an issuer's ability to raise additional debt and make distributions to shareholders. The indenture also details the execution, registration and delivery of the bonds, and the characteristics of the bond issue, such as coupon rate, maturity, numbering, and method of payment, among others.

Definitions of Covenants

Debt Incurrence and Limitation on Indebtedness

A debt incurrence and limitations on indebtedness provision limits a company's ability to incur additional debt unless there is sufficient cash flow to service all debt. Here, the interests of current bondholders are placed ahead of those of other potential creditors. As with other covenants, the limitation on indebtedness establishes an incurrence ratio. Usually, the covenant will specify a minimum coverage ratio, leverage and/or debt to total capitalization ratio (pro forma for the issuance of the new debt) before the company can incur additional indebtedness. In this instance, investors are concerned about coverage tests and the amount of cushion at the outset of the deal, the amount of subsidiary debt and preferred stock and subsidiary debt alternatives.

Limitations on Restricted Payments

A limitations on restricted payments covenant prevents the parent company and subsidiaries from distributing assets to junior creditors and equity holders before senior creditors. Senior creditors have the first claim on a firm's assets in the event of a bankruptcy. Notably, senior creditors often try to avoid such proceedings, wherein their interests are renegotiated to reflect the interests of junior creditors and equity holders. As a result, the provision's principal purpose is to restrict stock repurchases, dividends, subordinated debt repurchases, or early repayments, investments or guarantees of affiliate debt. The potential for default is monitored and limitations are established to mitigate the chance of such an event. If all the requirements are observed, the company will usually be able to make "restricted payments" of up to 50% of consolidated net income.

Restricted and Unrestricted Subsidiaries

By keeping subsidiaries "unrestricted," an issuer can grow its business outside the reach of covenants. In addition, a company can leverage such a subsidiary but avoid consolidating its debt into debt totals used for incurrence or maintenance tests. Therefore, covenants restrict or limit payments to unrestricted subsidiaries. This covenant is often used to address joint ventures or foreign investments.

Limitations on Dividends and Other Payments

A limitations on dividends and other payments covenant prohibits or limits unannounced or unexpected dividends at both the parent and the subsidiary levels. Without this protection, an issuer could decide to liquidate the company and divert cash flow to equity holders by paying out the entire proceeds as a special dividend to its stockholders. Also, the covenant may prevent the availability of subsidiary cash flow to pay parent company debt.

Net Worth Maintenance

A net worth maintenance provision requires the issuer to maintain a minimum level of net assets, or equity, as a cushion in the event of credit quality deterioration. Without a sufficient cushion, the company may be in default and will usually be required to repurchase outstanding debt at par plus accrued interest or at the applicable redemption price plus accrued interest. This maintenance covenant is generally tested at the end of each quarter on a rolling 6-month basis.

Limitations on Transactions with Affiliates

A limitations on transactions with affiliates indenture prevents self-dealing and restricts the issuer from dealing with affiliates on a less than fair basis when it comes to the sale of assets, the terms of loans or the provision of products and services. The gauge is the "arm's length" measure that proposes a relatively equal bargaining position between contracting parties. The provision also restricts the issuer from engaging in business on a less than fair market value basis with stockholders who own more than 5% of the company's stock, unless the terms are approved by a majority of the "disinterested" members of the board of directors.

Limitations on Sale of Assets

A limitations on sale of assets provision prevents an issuer from selling assets, especially securitized assets, that would take away the security of current bondholders. In addition, the issuer promises not to sell assets outside the bondholders' claims for less than fair market value (the proceeds must be within 70% and

100% of fair market value) or for a certain percentage in cash (typically 75%). The key concern in this instance is that stripping of assets could leave the company as a shell, thereby leaving little, if any, value for creditors in a liquidation scenario.

Without this covenant, the issuer could sell the asset to an officer of the company or a newly created subsidiary that is not under the bondholders' jurisdiction, leaving subordinated bondholders with no security. Occasionally, a covenant on a senior-debt issue will require that the company use a certain portion of proceeds from asset sales to retire senior debt, usually within one year.

Limitations on Sale-Leaseback Transactions

The company is limited in sale-leaseback transactions to leases with (1) a finite period, (2) renewable rights and (3) unrestricted companies. A sale-leaseback to any wholly owned subsidiary is allowed as the assets of a subsidiary can be used to pay bondholders in the case of liquidation. If the subsidiary is wholly owned, bondholders need not share the proceeds with any other parties.

Limitations on Mergers, Consolidation or Transfer of Assets

A provision that restricts mergers, consolidations and sales of all of an issuer's assets protects the bondholder against the impairment of the issuer's credit profile. Typically, mergers are forbidden unless (1) the company is the surviving entity, or the surviving entity is a U.S. or Canadian company that assumes the bond indenture; (2) the merger does not result in default; (3) the surviving entity's net worth is equal to or greater than the company's prior net worth; and (4) the company's pro forma interest coverage conforms to the covenant's minimum ratio.

Limitation on Liens

A limitation on liens covenant protects the relative seniority of income-producing assets. As a result, the company is forbidden to incur any liens (with specified exceptions) unless the notes are equally secured. This covenant typically applies to subordinated debt but can apply to other types as well.

Negative Pledge

In a negative pledge, the company promises not to pledge assets to secure a bond issue that have already been used to secure a currently outstanding issue.

Change of Control

A change of control provision protects creditors from a change in control (subject to a variety of definitions) by requiring the company to repurchase the bonds within 30 days from the change in control, usually at 101% of par plus accrued interest. The change in control is typically triggered following the purchase of control of the voting stock. If the company is unable to repurchase the entire bond issue within 30 days of a change in control, it would be in default.

Events of Default

Event of default provisions define the conditions under which the company would be in default. These include, among others: (1) delays of more than 30 days in paying interest on outstanding debt, (2) inability of the company to meet minimum ratios for more than 60 days and (3) any legal action against the company that would disable it from repaying loans. If any one of these is violated, the trustee may declare the company in default and could accelerate the maturity of all notes to be paid immediately so that all bondholders can receive equal payments.

Cross Default

A cross default clause states that if the company has defaulted on any material debt (usually defined as a dollar threshold level), all debt would be in default. In the event of a cross default, the trustee can accelerate the maturity of outstanding debt.

Other Issues Covered in Indentures

In addition to containing covenants, the indenture reviews the basic characteristics of the bond issue, including the items discussed below.

Optional Redemption

Optional redemption covenants related to optional redemption usually discuss the following:

- Length of the option's exercise period, usually four to five years.
- Call premium, often half the coupon (for instance 105 for a 10% coupon bond), declining to the first call at par.
- An irrevocable notice period, typically 30 days.

Puts Puts enable investors to demand repayment, usually three to five years after issuance. Brazilian issuers, for example, have widely sold putable bonds, as there are tax advantages in Brazil for bonds with maturities of at least eight years. Given limited investor demand for long-dated Brazilian corporate bonds, many investors were enticed with put options, which can shorten effective duration.

Equity Clawbacks Some indentures, particularly for technology or telecommunications issues, may offer equity clawbacks, usually at an issuer's discretion. This enables a company to purchase part of the outstanding debt issue with proceeds of an equity offering. Key issues include the type of equity financing (initial public offering versus primary add-on or public versus private), the length of exercise period, the amount of principal that may be redeemed, and the call premium.

The theory behind this provision is that it enables the issuer to take advantage of equity proceeds to deleverage the credit, while at the same time benefiting bondholders by improving the capital structure of the issuer and presumably the trading levels of the outstanding bonds. Recently, provisions have become more standardized, with the length of exercise period typically around three years and the percentage to be retired in the 30% to 35% range. This provision is less common among deals smaller than $100 million as that level is often the minimum that assures secondary liquidity.

Sinking Fund, Excess Cash Flow Sweep In the 1980s, sinking funds were standard, although they have become less common lately since bullet maturities afford issuers greater flexibility to direct cash flow to capital expenditures and working capital. An alternative to a sinking fund is an excess cash flow sweep, which is generally structured as an "offer to repurchase" and is used to reduce the average life to maturity. Excess cash flow sweeps and other mandatory redemptions enable investors to revisit their investment decisions.

BANKRUPTCY

In the event of default, bondholders typically attempt to quickly restructure the company's debt, even if it entails canceling large portions of existing debt, since full liquidation can take several years and involves substantial legal costs. Bondholders are usually forced to hold the bonds unless specifically prevented from doing so by investment charters, as secondary market demand at reasonable prices often disappears. If a company's business is viable and going-concern value exceeds estimated liquidation value, investors can typically expect to receive a mix of new equity and new debt in a restructuring.

Forced Reorganization and Liquidation

If a company is in violation of covenants and shows unwillingness to address such violations, bondholders can take advantage of the remedies provided in their bond documentation. Most Eurobonds require between 25% and 51% of bondholders to act in concert to accelerate the maturity of the bonds.

When an out-of-court or prepackaged bankruptcy is not possible, the last alternative is to reorganize under local bankruptcy law. If a company defaults as a result of operations becoming permanently impaired, as opposed to short-term liquidity problems, creditors can usually seek liquidation of the company. In emerging markets, bondholders can benefit by quickly approaching U.S. courts to limit issuers from giving local creditors priority treatment.

The seniority of claims can resemble the following:

- Unpaid wages to workers up to one year.
- Payment of back taxes to the government.
- Real estate mortgages, unless claims are unsecured.
- Senior secured creditors, usually banks.
- Senior bondholders.

- Junior bondholders.
- Equity holders (often receive nothing, as net worth is typically negative at this point).

Bankruptcy Plays

Generally, investing in bankruptcies can offer substantial returns, given the high levels of risk. Occasionally, an issuer can emerge from bankruptcy in a stronger position, or it can be acquired by a better-capitalized competitor. Sometimes, heavy selling can send bond prices below liquidation value or below the cash flow–generating power of the company as a going concern, creating opportunities for bolder investors.

A company will generally be liquidated if the value of assets exceeds the cash flow they can generate. However, creditors seldom force companies into liquidation as bankruptcy costs are high and since the book value of assets is often overstated and proceeds of liquidations often fall short of total debt. Of the 1,096 bankruptcies in the U.S. between 1970 and 1990 that Professor Edward E. Altman studied,[1]

- 248 companies (22.6%) emerged as public companies.
- 199 companies (18.2%) emerged as private companies.
- 164 companies (15.0%) were liquidated.
- 72 companies (6.6%) were merged or acquired.
- 412 companies (37.6%) were in bankruptcy, but still in reorganization at the time of the study.

Even if all 412 companies that were still under reorganization were liquidated, 47.4% of the sample continued either on their own or as part of another corporation. However, applying the breakdown of the 683 companies that completed the bankruptcy process to those companies that were still in reorganization, 85% would have continued as public or private companies or were merged/acquired.

Complications in Emerging Markets

The degree of a country's integration in the world economy and local markets are among the key factors determining the extent to which creditors can recoup their money in case of the issuer's distress in emerging markets. Importantly, the defaults and reorganizations that followed the Mexican Peso crisis in 1995, suggest that companies with assets in the U.S. and/or strong foreign owners have generated higher recovery values for investors compared to companies that had no such attributes.

Liquidation is seldom a feasible choice in emerging markets, where government and corporate contracts are often not fully enforceable and where local banks and creditors tend to get priority treatment. In addition, the difficulty in estimating recovery values and the risk that liquidation will be processed legally

---

[1] Edward I. Altman, *Corporate Financial Distress and Bankruptcy: Second Edition* (New York, NY: John Wiley & Sons, 1993), pp. 66-67.

and fairly make bondholders lean towards reorganization and equitization of existing debt versus liquidation.

Also, a significant percentage of restructurings in emerging markets has followed sovereign crises, which have generally involved sharp currency devaluations and deep recessions. The flight of capital from the affected regions and the sharp increases in interest rates have often made the purchase of assets, even at distressed prices, tougher to make attractive or possible.

IMPORTANT COVENANTS

Prevention is generally the best defense, in our view, especially in markets where legal defense may be limited. For that reason, we believe that a certain set of covenants should be almost mandatory for all corporate debt issues from companies that are clearly not investment grade.

Limitation of Indebtedness

One of the key covenants that can preventively protect bondholders is *limitation of indebtedness*, which would limit a company from issuing additional debt except in small aggregate amounts. The less debt outstanding, the easier debt service should be and the fewer claimants who could seek liquidation proceeds in the worst case scenario.

Negative Pledge

A *negative pledge* extends a limitation on indebtedness by restricting a company from using the same asset to secure more than one loan. The provision should also prohibit large amounts of new off–balance sheet debt.

Restricted Payments

The *restricted payments* provision is important because it prevents a company from transferring value to major stockholders, subsidiaries or other parties that could detract from the firm's value.

Change of Control

A *change of control* provision and limitations on mergers and acquisitions give bondholders the assurance that a merger would enhance firm value, or creditors can demand repayment. These provisions take on a special value in emerging markets for issuers with strong foreign ownership. The loss of this ownership can result in a significant deterioration of an issuer's overall credit attractiveness.

Maintenance Ratios

Maintenance ratios, such as minimum coverage and maximum leverage (including off-balance sheet debt), ensure that there is sufficient cash flow to cover debt service, even if profitability declines. However, minimum debt to capitalization or net-worth ratios are subject to ambiguity under certain accounting regimes and in highly inflationary environments. Thus, they generally can only be effective if done under U.S. GAAP standards and in a low inflation environment.

Cross Default

The *cross default* provision should protect creditors from a "selective" default by a company. The provision enables bondholders to demand 101% of par plus accrued interest if the issuer defaults on any other obligation, often above $10 million. If an issuer defaults on any material obligation, the company is likely experiencing limited liquidity and will have difficulty servicing remaining debt.

Prefunding and Performance Goals

For start-ups and companies without substantial short-term cash flow prospects but with attractive long-term fundamentals, prefunded interest payments can be attractive. Escrowed interest payments can make investors feel more secure and enable start-ups to focus on building their businesses. Covenants can require issuers to reach certain goals during the prefunded interest period in lieu of maintenance ratios.

Limitations

It is important to recognize that even with these covenants, many limitations are likely to remain, including credit events caused by sovereign developments, privatization of quasi-sovereigns, dollar-constrained clauses, break-ups of conglomerates, complex holding structures, special purpose vehicles, start-up companies, and the loss of sovereign support for banks.

CASE STUDIES

Following are five case studies of Latin American companies that issued bonds in the early to mid-1990s, a period when covenant packages were very limited and did not include essential protective mechanisms for debtholders. In many cases, existence of simple incurrence tests could have prevented companies from over-leveraging. This, in turn, may have prevented some issuers from defaulting or at least preserved more value for creditors.

Buenos Aires Embotelladora (BAESA)

Buenos Aires Embotelladora (BAESA) was the largest bottler of Pepsi products outside the U.S. in the mid-1990s, with operations in Argentina, Brazil, Chile, and Uruguay. The company also distributes a proprietary brand of water, Budweiser beer and other beverages. In 1994, BAESA invested approximately $400 million in the construction of soft drink production and distribution facilities in its franchise areas in southern Brazil, and, in 1995, the company announced plans to spend an additional $400 million in its Brazilian business.

Starting in 1995, weakening sales volumes in Argentina and Brazil led to a restructuring of operations, with layoffs in Argentina and a separation of Brazilian manufacturing and distribution operations. The company's operating performance was further negatively affected by start-up costs for expansion in Minas Gerais and Mato Grosso do Sul in March 1996.

In February 1996, BAESA sold $200 million in Eurobonds, mostly to refinance short-term debt. The issue was rated BB- by Standard & Poor's, which cited lower sales volumes and increased competition from Coca-Cola products, offset by high profit margins and the company's importance to Pepsi.

Restructuring Process

By July 1996, Pepsi took management control of BAESA. Despite cost cutting, operating performance in the first nine months of 1998 deteriorated further, and BAESA was in violation of debt covenants that rendered $200 million in debt immediately due, in addition to $545 million in other short-term debt. Several months later, BAESA stopped making interest and principal payments altogether.

In October 1996, shareholders filed a class action lawsuit in the U.S., claiming that management misrepresented the financial condition of BAESA and artificially inflated the value of the company's debt and equity. Shortly thereafter, BAESA avoided liquidation by agreeing with the bondholders to defer interest and principal payments for six months. The company also received a $40 million commitment from Pepsi.

In April 1997, after the October standstill agreement expired, BAESA announced a restructuring plan whereby it would eliminate existing stock and give creditors a combination of cash, new equity, and additional debt. Following the plan's announcement, BAESA's bonds rose from a price of 65 to the low 70s. A month later, in May 1997, after a weak earnings report, BAESA's shares were delisted from the New York and Buenos Aires Stock Exchanges as net worth fell into negative territory following the company's fifth money-losing quarter.

In an effort to raise cash, BAESA sold its Costa Rican unit for an undisclosed sum and the company's Brazilian unit as well as bottling plants to Companhia Cervejaria Brahma for $110 million in cash and the assumption of $45 million in debt. In addition, Brazilian creditors forgave $85 million in debt, leaving around $25 million in debt in Brazil.

In January 1998, creditors and shareholders accepted BAESA's July 1997 plan enabling the matter to be settled out of court. Under the new agreement, BAESA agreed to exchange $113 million in new debt and 98% of the equity for $700 million in already existing debt and accrued interest.

Post-Restructuring Performance

Total revenues fell 1% to $99.5 million in the first quarter of fiscal 1999 and EBITDA decreased 19% to $9.2 million as Argentine volumes rose 8%, offset by a 7.8% drop in the average sales price per case. Sales of third party products, such as beer, wine and other products, fell 50% to $2.3 million on lower prices.

Uruguay sales decreased 14.9% to $8.4 million in the quarter on a 13% decline in case sales volume and lower market share. BAESA's joint venture with CCU in Chile reported a profit in the first fiscal quarter of 1999 as a 5.8% decline in sales was offset by a 7.6% devaluation of the Chilean Peso.

In late 1998, BAESA's restructuring plan was updated, whereby the company would exchange $113 million in new debt and 98% of the company's equity for $727 million in existing debt. Pro forma for the restructuring, BAESA had shareholder equity of $80.6 million. In January 1999, the company's stock was delisted from the New York Stock Exchange, but it may continue to trade on the Argentine Bolsa.

Summary
Since BAESA's Eurobond issue did not contain covenants restricting large investments or minimum maintenance ratios, the company amassed over $700 million in debt while credit statistics deteriorated to the point where BAESA was unable to service debt. BAESA's restructuring plan resulted in a large loss for bondholders, as the company exchanged $113 million in new debt and 98% of BAESA's $80 million in equity for $700 million in existing debt, which resulted in a return of approximately 27 cents on the dollar.

Grupo Sidek

Through its subsidiary Grupo Situr, Grupo Sidek was engaged in the real estate and time-share market and was a leading Mexican hotel owner and operator. Grupo Simec, Sidek's steel subsidiary, was a leading mini-mill steel producer and manufacturer of a broad range of non-flat structural steel products.

Restructuring Process
In February 1995, Sidek became the first Mexican company to default in the wake of the peso crisis, choosing to not repay a $19.5 million corporate note despite the company's $60 million cash position. Sidek virtually stopped communicating with investors, and subsidiary Situr's bonds dropped to a price of 50 on the news, as most of the company's bonds would be in default due to a cross-default provision. The company later reversed its decision and made the payment.

In September 1995, creditors granted Sidek a 3-month extension to repay $170 million of the company's $1.5 billion in total debt. The company planned to sell golf courses and hotels in order to repay the $170 million credit line.

In February 1996, Sidek and subsidiaries agreed with creditors to defer principal payments during the restructuring process. However, the company announced that Simec was not a part of the restructuring and would continue to operate as an ongoing business. In the meantime, Sidek agreed to monetize between $700 million and $1 billion worth of assets and restructure its debt into four categories:

- Debt incurred in the 1995 bailout package would become 4-year floating-rate secured notes.

- Debt secured by assets that were generating significant cash flow would be exchanged for 10-year secured 10% notes that became floating-rate notes after one year. Principal repayments are scheduled to begin in 2001.
- Debt secured by collateral and unsecured debt of subsidiaries with real estate properties worth more than their debts would become new 2.5-year convertible notes, which receive the cash flow generated by the previously secured assets, which could be forcibly converted into shares at expiration.
- Unsecured bondholders would receive 2.5-year convertible notes that could be forcibly converted at maturity.

Sidek completed the restructuring by March 31, 1998.

Post-Restructuring Performance

Grupo Sidek's sales fell 3.8% to $340 million in the first nine months of 1998, and operating income turned positive to $20.8 million. Grupo Situr's third quarter revenues rose 29%, including Simec's operations. In 1997, Sidek transferred its stake in Sidek to Situr, which increased Sidek's ownership of Situr from 60% to 92%. Real estate sales jumped 78%, though hotel and timeshare revenues fell 11% due to lower average occupancy rates.

Grupo Simec's sales in the first nine months of 1998 fell 1% to $175 million as a 1.0% rise in sales volumes to 478,411 metric tons was offset by a real 3% drop in average prices. A 7% cut in operating expenses resulted in a 23% rise in operating income to $25.5 million. Following the company's debt restructuring, most of Simec's $323 million of debt matures between 2007 and 2009, with some principal amortizations beginning in the year 2000.

Summary

Restrictions on payments and asset sales as well as maintenance ratio requirements could have limited Sidek's use of debt to finance real estate and hotel development. In order to finance the aggressive acquisition and development of hotels and resorts, Sidek borrowed heavily and monetized accounts receivables. Moreover, the company used the same accounts receivables to secure multiple borrowings, which would not be allowed under the "negative pledge" covenant.

Grupo Mexicano de Desarrollo

Grupo Mexicano de Desarollo (GMD) was engaged in the construction of a broad range of infrastructure projects throughout Mexico, including highways and toll roads, bridges, tunnels, water works, dams, airports, and port facilities in the early to mid 1990s. The company also participated in industrial, housing, and commercial construction projects, as well as real estate development. GMD conducted most of its construction operations through four subsidiaries, which were guarantors for the Eurobonds. The company was controlled by the Ballesteros family, which has been involved in the construction business for over 50 years.

Since 1990, GMD had played a major role in the Mexican government's program to develop a modern highway network, with the construction revenues of concessioned toll roads contributing about 76% of revenues during the five years that ended on December 31, 1995. In an attempt to accelerate the building process, the government had asked private contractors such as GMD to construct highways and collect tolls to recoup their investments. However, the companies encountered trouble when highway traffic fell below projections. Revenue generation was also negatively affected by the devaluation of the peso in 1994 and the slowdown in the Mexican economy.

GMD's credit profile deteriorated rapidly with the collapse of the toll-road concession market. The credit crunch was further toughened as a large percentage of the company's toll-road concession revenues were non-cash, in contrast to its costs and liabilities. (The company had $250 million of 8¼% notes and $120 million of floating debt outstanding.) GMD defaulted on its $250 million Eurobond interest payment in August 1997, soon after the Mexican government seized the construction and toll highway concessions.

Restructuring Process

In August 1997, GMD delayed a $10 million interest payment on its $250 million Eurobond issue as it waited for the results of the Mexican government's toll-road restructuring plan. The government announced that it would repurchase GMD's concessioned toll roads for $309 million in cash, or roughly one-third of GMD's investments in those roads. GMD recognized a $653 million write-down on those investments and defaulted on the Eurobond interest payment.

GMD's largest "asset"—a $309 million cash payment from the Mexican government under a toll road rescue plan—would be the majority of the payout to creditors. The company also had sold 49.9% of its water works unit to Enron for $12.5 million in cash and the assumption of $25 million in debt.

U.S. bondholders feared that GMD would use most of the cash payment to repay local creditors. However, in April 1998, a U.S. federal court ruled that GMD would have to pay $82.4 million to international bondholders following its default. In May 1998, a lower federal court in the U.S. ordered the company to set aside assets to pay off the bondholders and barred GMD from pledging limited assets to other creditors. The ruling could set a precedent that may lead other courts to rule in favor of international creditors in foreign-based company bankruptcies.

In June 1999, the U.S. Supreme Court upheld a lower court's ruling that GMD must treat all creditors equally. GMD had sued to overturn the lower court's injunction against disbursing funds received from the Mexican government to Mexican creditors, which would have left the company little or no remaining funds to settle with U.S. creditors. GMD established an exchange offer whereby the $250 million 8¼% Guaranteed Notes due 2001 were swapped with newly issued certificates of the GMD Bondholder Trust estate established March 2000 in Bermuda. A Mexican master trust encompasses both the GMD Bondholder Trust and Mexican bank creditors. On May 15, 2000, GMD made its required deposit of $197.5 million into the Mexican master trust for the benefit of Mexican bank creditors and tendering note holders. The GMD Bondholder Trust estate makes up 48.44% of the Mexican master trust. The master trust is expected to distribute 51.56% of its assets to Mexican banks in cash in exchange for the release of its debt, and 48.44% to the GMD Bondholder Trust in exchange for the release of its debt. This breaks down to around 38.3% of par. For the benefit of its creditors, GMD has been permitted to continue operations, but on a much smaller scale.

Summary

GMD's covenants required it to maintain a net worth equal to 130% of the $250 million of Eurobonds outstanding, or $325 million. However, since the company wrote-up the value of its investments by 70% versus 10.5% inflation, it was forced to write-off $653.2 million following the announcement of the toll-road restructuring plan from existing equity of approximately $471.2 million, which resulted in negative net worth.

Had the company accounted for toll-road investments at more realistic values, GMD would likely have reached the minimum net worth of $325 million well before the announcement of the government's plan and could have been forced to restructure operations accordingly, in an effort to prevent future losses.

Covenants based on equity or capital are often ineffective, as these figures can be overstated, especially in countries with high rates of inflation. Moreover, GMD's covenants did not include effective incurrence or maintenance ratios, such as minimum coverage or maximum leverage. GMD's coverage and leverage were rendered meaningless well before the default as the company generated negative EBITDA. More restrictive covenants could have led to an earlier restructuring, at which time the company had greater means to satisfy creditors.

Alpargatas

Alpargatas is an Argentine footwear and textile company that manufactures Nike, Converse and Fila brand sneakers under license.

Cheap imports in the early 1990s and the 1995 recession in Argentina, which forced Alpargatas to abandon plans to spin off its shoemaking unit, hurt the company. In late 1997, the company was forced to suspend the sale of $175 million in debt after the Asian market turmoil caused a worldwide market decline. The company reported losses of $77 million in fiscal year 1997 compared to a loss of $16 million in 1996.

Restructuring Process

Alpargatas defaulted on $70 million of 9% convertible notes after delays in securing new financing left the company without adequate cash. Alpargatas tried to restructure debt through a $90 million stock sale, a $225 million new bond issuance, and a $200 million syndicated loan.

The stock sale needed approval of the shareholders, who saw the stock drop 61% in the nine months that ended in March 1998 after a previous debt restructuring was scuttled. Since the shares were trading at $0.23, less than the $1 minimum level at which the company could issue shares, Alpargatas received shareholder approval for a five-to-one reverse stock split to boost the share price. Newbridge Latin America, a buyout fund partly owned by the Texas Pacific Group, pledged to buy any unsold shares and had purchased $80 million of convertible bonds in 1997.

The funds from the stock sale and debt issuance were going to be used to refinance the $450 million of outstanding bonds and other debt as of March 1998; $265 million of the debt matured in 1999. The company had also planned to sell $50 million of non-core assets. In April 1998, the company asked creditors to wait for up to six months for repayment of debt while it worked out the details of the restructuring.

In July 1998, the Asian crisis dampened demand for risky emerging market debt and Alpargatas cancelled plans for the $225 million bond issuance. The company then offered to swap existing debt for a mix of shares and new debt and to also sell new shares as planned.

In October 1998, a Brazilian unit of Alpargatas filed for court protection from creditors. The company then held talks in New York with creditors to restructure debt through the issuance of new 15-year bonds at a 6% coupon. The company's stock price more than doubled at the end of the month to $0.17 from prior weeks' levels on expectations that talks with bondholders would enable Alpargatas to restructure more than $500 million in debt, install new management, and return to profitability.

In November 1998, Banco de la Provincia de Buenos Aires, one of the company's major creditors, said that it would analyze the restructuring proposal but could reject it outright instead of making a counteroffer. The shares jumped 47% from October 10 to November 10. Alpargatas called a 35-day work stoppage from January 1, 1999 at its textile plant in Tucuman due to financial problems brought on by the import of foreign products under conditions detrimental to the local industry.

A review of Alpargatas' credit statistics from 1993 through 1999 clearly shows how covenants would have protected bondholders. After generating 2.0× interest coverage and 6.0× leverage in 1993 and 1994, credit statistics deteriorated to nearly distressed levels in 1995 through 1997 and worsened in 1998 and 1999. Meanwhile, the company added a total of $300 million of debt in 1998 and 1999. Maintenance ratios would have sounded alarms in 1995, when coverage halved to 1.0×, and incurrence tests would have prevented the company from adding so much debt while operating performance was declining. The company was unable to support the added debt, most of which was short-term bank debt, and bondholders ended up holding 7% of the equity of the company, which value fell precipitously when the company's shares were delisted.

Grupo Synkro

Grupo Synkro currently designs, manufactures, distributes, and sells apparel, cosmetics and insecticides. The company makes socks, stockings, synthetics, sneakers, and cosmetics and had approximately a 50% share of the Mexican hosiery market.

In 1994, the company acquired Kayser-Roth, a U.S. hosiery company, for $170 million, funded with short-term debt. Following the Mexican peso crisis, the company's large short-term debt doubled in peso terms while operations slumped due to slowing economies in Argentina and Mexico. In addition, rocketing interest rates on the company's short-term floating-rate debt forced a restructuring and recapitalizing of the company.

Restructuring Process
In July 1996, Synkro completed the restructuring of $60 million of Kayser Roth's debt to GE Capital.

In August 1997, Synkro completed the restructuring of $494 million in debt. Holders of Synkro's $50 million Eurobond turned one-third of the bonds into equity, one-third into 5-year 12% bonds, and wrote off the rest. Holders of Synkro's remaining bonds swapped their debt into new equity. Synkro also repurchased $80 million of the new shares with a buyback fund that the company established before the crisis.

In 1998, Synkro sold the Camino Real hotel chain and its sneaker unit, Calzado Puma, among other subsidiaries. In late 1998, Synkro sold Kayser-Roth, which the company purchased three years prior for $170 million, to Americal for $62 million.

Post-Restructuring Performance
Despite a 5.5% decline in revenue in the first nine months of 1998, Synkro posted a slight increase in operating profit to $6.8 million. As of September 30, 1998, Synkro had approximately $110 million in short-term debt and approximately $24 million in long-term debt.

Summary
Covenants restricting payments for acquisitions, such as the company's $170 million purchase of Kayser-Roth (funded with short-term debt), could have helped Grupo Synkro avoid bankruptcy and the subsequent restructuring. Had bondholders blocked the acquisition, the company would have had much less short-term debt, which is what largely caused the default.

Chapter 15

New Standards for Sovereign Credit Analysis and Risk Management: The Lessons of the Asia Crisis

Paul A. Pannkuk
Executive Director
Head of Sovereign Risk Management
Morgan Stanley

S overeign risk analysis has evolved, and become far more sophisticated, over the last 20 years. Significantly, a great evolution in the discipline occurred in the aftermath of the Asia crisis of 1997.

This chapter was written to facilitate a better understanding of the origins of Asia's economic and financial crisis, and, on a practical level, was designed to enhance the rigor of Morgan Stanley's internal analysis. It encourages an interdisciplinary approach to sovereign analysis that enables a more comprehensive country view, while making judgments on the appropriateness of alternative policy options.

The chapter explores the incentives prompting the movement of capital into and out of emerging markets since 1992, and briefly examines the varied causes of instability in the countries most seriously affected by the subsequent loss of investor confidence. It gives particular emphasis to sources of instability in these markets that are not easily detected by traditional sovereign credit analysis. The chapter also discusses the appeal of capital controls as a barrier to capital market instability and argues that they are no alternatives to good macro-policies. It considers the benefit of fixed or pegged exchange rates and highlights the importance of additional vigilance for countries that adopt these currency regimes. And it discusses the implications of these economic developments for credit research and recommends steps that could improve our ability to detect

With acknowledgement to the members of Morgan Stanley's Sovereign Credit Group—Scott Turner, John Seel, Alexis De Mones, and Supriya Menon—for their support and insight in covering the economic and political developments that define the parameters of risk in emerging market finance at our firm.

such system-threatening problems in the future, thereby reducing the dramatic swings in capital flows that occurred in 1997 and 1998.

The Russia case study incorporates some of these improved analytical techniques and insights into the sovereign analysis. And it serves as an illustration of effective risk management, in that its conclusions prompted a reduction in Morgan Stanley exposures over the ensuing five months such that the Firm experienced no losses in the aftermath of that country's subsequent devaluation and default.

LESSONS FROM THE ASIA CRISIS: A NEW STANDARD OF CREDIT ANALYSIS

The developing economies of Asia, absent China, experienced near unprecedented economic downturns in 1997 and 1998. At the same time Japan, further weakened by the crisis in neighboring countries, immobilized by its own hapless public policy record, and crippled by a hopelessly weak banking sector, posed an enormous risk to international financial stability. Russia, driven to the brink of insolvency by inept fiscal management, devalued its ruble and suspended payments on domestic and (some foreign) currency bonds and bank debt in the summer of 1998, leaving investors with losses in excess of $100 billion. Brazil's unsustainably large foreign and domestic currency public and private sector borrowing requirements produced exchange rate pressures, in the fall of 1998, which nearly halved foreign currency reserve levels by end-December of that year and led to coordinated multilateral financial assistance that still failed to prevent an abandonment of the government's pegged currency band in mid-January 1999. Turkey's economy faced similar pressures for the same reasons.

These events unfolded in such rapid succession, and with such initial surprise, that they left emerging-market investors reeling and in rapid retreat. The flight of capital from emerging markets between the summer of 1997 and the spring of 1999 was far greater than could have been anticipated prior to Thailand's devaluation—almost certainly greater than was justified—and is most commonly explained by the herd mentality that produces contagion. Further confusing investors was the fact that each country's problems were unique and demanded unique prescriptions (see Appendix I). Nevertheless, the collapse of investor sentiment triggered by inappropriate economic policies and inadequate regulatory frameworks (1) produced dramatic economic downturns in scores of countries around the world; (2) prompted devaluations which overshot reasonable targets; (3) depleted countries' foreign currency reserve levels; (4) decapitalized public and private commercial banks and corporates; (5) diminished world asset values by hundreds of billions of dollars; and (6) reduced world economic growth in 1998 to its lowest level in more than a decade.

The shattered confidence of emerging-market investors prompted concern about the free flow of capital to sovereign borrowers and financial institutions and renewed debate over the usefulness and effectiveness of capital controls in developing country economies.

International Capital Markets, Pre-1997: The Pursuit of High Yield

By 1992, emerging-market country debt stocks had generally fallen to manageable levels with the help of very successful Brady debt reduction policies. Debt service ratios improved accordingly, aided as well by stronger domestic economic and export growth rates. Lulled by the reality of an improving macro-economic and policy environment in nearly every major emerging-market economy in the world, international debt and equity markets directed vast amounts of new money to developing country borrowers in the pursuit of yield. This trend only accelerated after the Mexican devaluation induced the market turbulence of 1994. Yet, as the credit quality of most public sector, and many private sector issuers improved, risk premiums fell in tandem with growing international liquidity and declining U.S. and European interest rates. By mid-1997, the price differential between AA rated issuers and BB rated issuers had fallen to less than 300 basis points.

The improving macro-economic policy environment across the range of developing country borrowers (albeit from a comparatively poor policy history) even encouraged investors to take longer maturities at reduced rates. The ease of raising capital, and the trend among sovereigns with large financing needs to diversify the range of borrowing entities empowered to act on their behalf, significantly reduced the pressure on governments over this period to continue their rigorous pursuit of micro-economic policy adjustment, having largely achieved macro-economic stability. Yet, despite the growing laxity of (especially financial sector) reform in many borrowing countries, market access remained intact as international liquidity continued to expand.

The turnaround of this trend had its roots in the massive expansion of export production in Asia in the mid-1990s, and particularly in China's emergence as a major competitive force. The unification of China's exchange rate system in late 1993 and the subsequent stabilization of its overheated economy set the stage for a tremendous flow of direct foreign investment into the PRC. Much of the resulting output was aimed at export markets. China's new ability to leverage its vast force of cheap labor created pressure on the labor-intensive industries that had driven the growth of other Asian economies. This eroded the competitiveness of Southeast Asian exports and worsened their external imbalances, increasing concerns about the valuation of their dollar-pegged currencies. These concerns were heightened as evidence grew of systemic flaws in regional banking sectors, encouraging holders of local currency (or of foreign currency) emerging market debt to switch to higher rated U.S. dollar instruments. The July 1997 devaluation of the Thai baht caused a renewed flight to dollars across the region and accelerated the downward spiral in Indonesia, Korea, and Malaysia.

Currency Turmoil: Themes and Differences

While each of the currency crises had its own root causes, there were a number of overriding themes and developments that encouraged investors to retreat from these economies.

- The most obvious was the existence of under-regulated and highly protected banking sectors, all of which had access to international capital markets, and all of which (save Hong Kong) developed huge exposures to their domestic economies while accommodating interest rate, foreign currency, and maturity mismatches. Each country had experienced very fast growth in bank lending, which left banks overextended—to the property sector in particular. This caused rapid asset quality deterioration as property values fell and as devaluation hit economic growth.

- Most of the crisis economies of Asia had put in place managed exchange rate pegs that demanded responsible fiscal and monetary policies. The massive liquidity support provided for banking sectors in Thailand, Indonesia, and Korea, along with the external imbalances caused in part by the failure of these economies to keep ahead of the competitive pressure from China, suddenly rendered their currency regimes unsustainable.

- Central government involvement in the expansion decisions of industrial sector producers/borrowers resulted in higher corporate leverage ratios and encouraged considerable overcapacity in manufacturing (especially in Korea), which further reduced (export) prices in an environment of diminished demand and complicated already strained private sector debt servicing capabilities.

Each country affected has experienced the wrath of fleeing investors, largely in proportion to its dependence on foreign (and domestic) borrowings. In addition, each government's response to problems in its banking sector affected the severity of the pressure on its currency and the magnitude of its economic downturn. Capital's flight to quality largely, if temporarily, eschewed emerging markets.

The Value and Effectiveness of Capital Controls

As a result of, and in reaction to, the events of 1997 and 1998, many investors and a number of prominent economists called for a re-examination of capital controls as a means of imposing constraints on the highs and lows of market sentiment. Proponents of this initiative suggest that the absence of controls encouraged the unrestrained free flow of short-term portfolio investment and bank loans that proved unstable and unpredictable as a source of external financing for emerging market borrowers.

The capital structures of Chile and China are often cited as examples of the beneficial effects of well targeted restrictions on financial flows into countries whose evolving economic policies (1) attract substantial, if not excessive, capital inflows, yet (2) are still insufficiently developed to ensure sustained investor confidence over the long term. (See Appendix II for details of these two countries' experience with capital controls.)

Based on an examination of these two countries' experience, and the experience of other sovereigns with incentive systems designed to limit swings in financial flows, empirical evidence would suggest that capital controls, however comprehensive or benign, have historically proven only partially effective in controlling the movement of funds into and out of emerging market economies. Targeted *restrictions* and *disincentives* to the free flow of capital may help safeguard economic and financial stability by limiting short-term, and therefore tenuous, portfolio investments and bank loans to transition economies. Countries that typically develop excessively large short-term liabilities, however, are nearly always found to have encouraged these capital inflows in an attempt to finance excessively large current account deficits.

Ultimately, sound macro-economic and financial policies, together with prudential bank regulations, have consistently proven a more effective regulator of investment patterns, however large. Certainly, appropriate policies are a more *efficient* allocator of funding in a global economy than are government-imposed controls designed to limit cross-border capital movements.

Sovereign Analysis: The Assumed Safety Net

It remains the widespread impression of investors that the economic and financial demise of nearly all of Asia, of Russia, and perhaps of Brazil and Turkey completely eluded the sovereign radar screen. Traditional sovereign risk analysis would appear to have overlooked the ominous developments that were unfolding before the eyes of the world.

Some would argue that sovereign and high-yield credit analysis were blindsided over a period of years by the consistent availability of rapidly expanding international liquidity in pursuit of lucrative and comparatively attractive investment opportunities. Others would suggest that no analytical judgment could have predicted the overreaction of investor sentiment to policy shortcomings that merited more modest market corrections.

A critical shortcoming of traditional sovereign analysis before the Asian crisis was the underemphasis on bank and corporate credit quality. Despite the deficient disclosure of bank data, it is clear that asset quality in the financial systems of nearly all of the affected Asian countries was deteriorating well before the crisis began. In addition, there had been a significant increase in corporate leverage in much of the region before the crisis, which increased the risk to the banking sector. This information did not show up in traditional sovereign creditworthiness ratios, though most of the bad assets of these financial sectors have ultimately become obligations of the sovereign.

In Asia, absent the inclusion of deteriorating banking sector liabilities, ratios of fiscal balance/GDP, government debt/GDP, and government interest payments/budget revenue were stronger in mid-1997 than those associated with most

"AAA" and "AA" rated OECD countries. International reserve levels in all of these countries exceeded the standard three months of import coverage test until Asian central banks began to spend these savings to prop up overvalued currencies and protect inappropriate fixed-exchange-rate regimes and illiquid banking sectors. Very high current account/GDP deficits of Thailand, Malaysia, Indonesia, and Korea were considered sustainable, as long as market liquidity remained intact, because they were financing foreign-currency-earning industrial capacity in a low-international-interest-rate environment, a factor that eased debt service.

Traditional measures of sovereign creditworthiness are still valuable advance indicators in many economies. For example, fiscal and local currency debt ratios grew seriously deficient in Russia in 1997, though that country's current account balance/GDP and gross external debt/current account receipts ratios remained comparatively strong until mid-1998. Continued fiscal deterioration only began to adversely affect foreign (in addition to domestic) currency debt ratios beginning in late 1997 and continuing into the first half of 1998, even as commodity export prices declined precipitously in 1998 and spreads on emerging market debt tripled.

At least two conclusions can be drawn from this analysis:

1. *A sovereign issuer's rating will change, sometimes dramatically, when a precipitous decline in liquidity is perceived to threaten the sovereign's ability to service its debt.* In other words, instead of looking at static credit measures, there is a need to stress-test some of these ratios.

2. *Traditional sovereign analysis has not yet proven to be a consistent leading indicator of credit risk.* This may be due, in part, to the historic absence of a coordinated sovereign, bank, and corporate analytical approach to the measurement of country leverage and sovereign exposure.

The Role of Credit Analysis

If these and previous conclusions are valid, it follows that improved risk analysis, aided by greater fiscal, financial, and corporate sector transparency, must be considered the ultimate approach in regulating and apportioning capital flows to emerging market borrowers. There are four main areas in which special attention is needed in determining ratings. These recommendations are based on the experiences and the lessons acquired from the Asian crisis and are related to financial sector regulation, fiscal transparency, currency regimes, and coordinated analysis.

Financial Sector Regulation

The existence of weak regulatory regimes and the lack of transparency in the operation of financial systems encouraged the buildup of maturity and interest rate mismatches and large, unhedged, foreign currency exposures in each of the crisis economies of Asia (save Hong Kong), and in Russia. Overinvestment and slowing economic growth also eventually contributed to the deterioration in asset quality that was often inadequately recognized and provisioned for.

Notwithstanding the reform programs currently being implemented in these areas, emerging market countries will require time to develop the strong supervisory and risk management systems already in place in more advanced economies. Beginning in 1998, the Basle Committee started the process of developing a more rigorous "Core Principles for Effective Banking Supervision," which are intended to serve as a basic reference and minimum standard for supervisory and other public authorities. Consistent with these principles, in 1998 the IMF developed a framework for financial sector surveillance, "Toward a Framework for Financial Stability," to guide the analysis of banking systems by identifying key areas of vulnerability. In late 1998 the World Bank met with representatives of the "big five" international accounting firms to suggest they not sign (nor allow their foreign country affiliates to sign) unconditional audits of banks in emerging market economies if they failed to comply with (enhanced) international accounting standards.

Recommendation These standards and guidelines must be considered increasingly appropriate to the analysis of emerging market banking sectors, just as they are now an accepted standard of financial sector analysis throughout most of the OECD area. In some cases, the application of these standards will replace assumptions of implicit sovereign support, especially for quasi-publicly held emerging market banks which have limited public policy roles, and for which little financial information is available. In the face of inadequate disclosure, worst-case assumptions should prevail, absent explicit government support, and these conclusions should be reflected in internal ratings. To the extent that implicit, and perhaps even explicit, government support is discounted and ratings fall, decisions to take exposure additional to that associated with the rating assigned should be made within the context of realistic risk parameters.

Fiscal Transparency
The IMF in the 1990s completed work on a Code of Good Practices on Fiscal Transparency to guide member countries in enhancing the accountability and credibility of fiscal policy as a key component of good governance. In this regard, governments which run fiscal surpluses while encouraging directed state bank lending to priority government projects (sometimes in place of direct fiscal expenditure) should be required (at least partially) to adjust budget surpluses to accommodate the contingent liability created by these unprovisioned loans (many of which must be considered nonperforming by any international commercial standard). Greater fiscal transparency must be required to enable appropriate adjustments.

Recommendation Pressures related to fiscal laxity account for a disproportionate number of internal country downgrades and have often interrupted sovereign access to international and (even) domestic capital markets. Internal ratings should continue to reflect this weak link where it exists, with increased attention to the actual or estimated contingent liability created by state bank policy loans. Within the context of fiscal laxity, attention should also be accorded the implications of "fiscal crowding out" as it affects interest rate policy, long-term private sector growth prospects, and liquidity, all factors which influence domestic and foreign currency debt and debt service ratios. These concerns might be considered especially acute in fixed-exchange-rate regimes.

Floating Exchange Rates, Currency Pegs and Currency Boards

Floating exchange rates should be viewed within the context of market pricing, just as long-term interest rates are considered a reflection of future inflation expectations and the price of long-term financing within an economy. In this regard, the market value of a country's exchange rate is a reflection of its perceived present and future economic performance. It reflects a view of the appropriateness of fiscal and monetary policy, and a judgment of a country's trade and balance of payments position.

Mature economies need not, and should not, rely on currency boards to engage the confidence of international investors. Nor should governments with mature political systems use currency boards or fixed exchange rates to enforce policy discipline that can be adopted, even with some appropriate flexibility, under floating exchange rate regimes. In these countries, currency depreciation can, and often does, trigger appropriate policy adjustments, which in turn stabilize exchange rates.

Currency boards are appropriate to, and have worked in, countries recovering from prolonged periods of economic mismanagement and hyperinflation. They often introduce a degree of discipline to economic policy, in part by putting monetary policy in a straight-jacket, requiring capital inflows to enable economic (and money supply) growth. They can increase confidence in future currency values, encourage capital flows, and allow lower interest rates on average. They also often block political pressures on governments attempting to implement sound but difficult economic policies. Exit strategies from these rigid currency regimes often prove useful after stability has been institutionalized.

The Asian crisis proved that pegged currency regimes, however structured, are unsustainable without appropriate fiscal and monetary discipline. Once central banks in these countries abandoned that discipline, pressure on their currencies grew to levels that could not be sustained even with destructively high interest rates. At that point, currency depreciation was abrupt and dramatic. Stable currency regimes also require adequate bank supervision and oversight to ensure that private sector borrowers are not building up dangerous levels of unhedged, especially short-term, foreign currency debt.

Recommendation There should be a heightened awareness of economic policy within the framework of currency boards or currency pegs (in other words, in economic frameworks which do not allow exchange rate adjustments to compensate for lax fiscal or monetary policies). Deteriorating fiscal and/or monetary policy discipline should be viewed as a red flag for potential currency pressures. Such breakdowns in economic policy are likely to require very high real interest rates to maintain currency regimes (Brazil, Thailand, Indonesia, Korea, Malaysia), which historically have been destructive of growth and bank asset quality. Substantial current account imbalances and the need for high levels of potentially volatile, short-term debt and non-debt foreign currency financing in these economies should also be serious warning signals. Internal ratings must take these considerations into account when assessing credit risk and determining potential exposure levels.

Coordinated Analysis
Historically, little coordination has existed between sovereign, bank, and corporate analysis. Sovereign analysts failed to account for the overexposure of the Thai and Malaysian banking sectors, and for the overreach of the Korean corporate sector:

Recommendation To enhance coordination and the increased flow of information between analytical groups, sovereign analysts should be required to participate in all committees where banks or corporates from countries included in their coverage area are reviewed. Likewise, bank and corporate analysts must be required to participate in sovereign committees when country ratings provide a sovereign ceiling for the banks and/or corporates they review.

A Global Framework for the Restoration of Private Sector Capital Flows to Emerging Market Economies
The most obvious and appropriate way in which the architecture of the international monetary system can be improved is through the development and implementation of international standards designed to strengthen the operation of financial markets. These principles must work to (1) foster effective financial market supervision and regulation; (2) improve the institutional infrastructure of both borrowers and lenders; and (3) enhance surveillance and market discipline.

Standard credit analysis will benefit from these initiatives, and from the greater transparency they will encourage. The broad fundamental lessons outlined above may also enable lenders and investors to better avoid macro-economic and financial risk, and thereby preclude the repetition of past mistakes.

Internal risk analysis, to the extent that it benefits from these initiatives, can serve as a partial and appropriate brake on the unrestrained flow of funds into vulnerable economic and financial environments. Improved analysis also offers the best protection against losses, ultimately and most appropriately protecting the Firm's capital.

Broad investor acceptance of, and demand for compliance with, international standards of sovereign and corporate transparency would prove an even more effective insurance against the excesses that provoke international crises. These standards, preferably devised by a group of international public and private sector players who may also act as economic and/or financial advisors (the World Bank, the International Monetary Fund, the Bank for International Settlements, and interested investment and commercial banking institutions), would set forth a framework for evaluating key credit issues including data disclosure, financial oversight, and the legal protection available to creditors. Compliance with these standards would be voluntary and would not require a bureaucratic overseer. However, by highlighting gaps in regulation and disclosure, the standards would promote lenders' awareness of the potential credit risks they face. Since compliance with the standards would presumably lead to a lower cost of capital, there would be a market incentive for borrowers to come into compliance. The objective is the prevention of credit losses and the protection of public and private institutional capital. Enhanced international economic and financial stability would be a vital side benefit.

The Country Review Process

With the criteria and methodology in place, country analysts should review sovereign counterparts on a regular basis. Highly rated industrialized countries should be reviewed less often than lower rated emerging-market sovereigns. Countries whose political and/or economic circumstances are precarious or evolving, and with whom business appetite is strong or growing, should be reviewed more frequently.

Written reviews and detailed spreadsheets with economic performance data and ratios should be presented to Sovereign Committees annually. Core members of these committees should include the head of Worldwide Credit, the head of Counterparty Credit, the entire team of sovereign analysts within the Credit Department, and other interested department members, including bank and industrial analysts who cover counterparties in the country under review. The head of the Sovereign Group should chair the Sovereign Committee.

After an often detailed discussion and question-and-answer session, the Sovereign Committee should agree on an internal rating for the country under review. Internal rating scales might logically mirror the rating agencies' rating scales, though individual country ratings may not necessarily match the ratings assigned by the rating agencies. Like the rating agencies, a BBB rating should represent the cutoff for investment grade credit quality. Countries rated in the BBB, BB, and B rating categories should be assigned country limits.

Setting Country Limits

Sovereign limits are assigned to countries in the mid- to lower range of the rating scale in an attempt to contain the aggregate potential exposure of all public and private sector counterparts domiciled in those economies where business appetite might exceed the Credit Department's risk appetite. Very little, if any, term exposure is incurred with CCC rated counterparts, although fully collateralized, or strategic, transactions are occasionally approved on a case-by-case basis in these troubled sovereigns.

Country limits are determined with a view to containing losses at prudent levels relative to capital. Yet, individual country limits are maintained at a very small percentage of the Firm's total capital base. Realistically, a more meaningful consideration might entail a judgment about containing country losses such that these unforeseen events, should they occur, would be small enough to preclude market reactions that might adversely impact the value of the Firm's equity.

Loss limits are defined in terms of potential exposure. This calculation, derived from an increasingly sophisticated risk model, estimates the replacement value of a portfolio of counterparty trades in the event of that counterparty defaulting at some point within the maturity structure of the portfolio.

A Potential Exposure Model

Estimating the replacement value of a trading portfolio at some future date, be it three months and 30 years, is complicated by the fact that interest and exchange rates on any future default date are unknown. The model's value, therefore, is based on a comprehensive set of assumptions, simulating thousands of "plausible" or "theoretically realistic" alternative economic scenarios stretching 30 years into the future.

The starting point in each country-specific scenario is the point at which the economy finds itself in its current business cycle. Future business cycles are then projected on the basis of historical averages of the country's economic expansions and contractions. Monetary policy is assumed to reflect these business cycles, and alternative interest rate scenarios are projected on the basis of the monetary policy assumptions. Future exchange rates are projected with the help of these economic assumptions as well. The model assumes the maintenance of purchasing power parity in industrial countries, but not in emerging-market economies, which more often maintain currency boards, exchange rate regimes that are pegged to a basket of currencies, or managed floats. Assumptions may include future entry into the European Monetary Union, or economic event risks including coordinated regional liquidity crises.

In the end, the potential exposure of a proposed trade is determined by the worst case scenario, as derived from the model, with a confidence ratio of 99%.

Alerting Business Units

The Credit Department, on a case-by-case basis, approves large trades, especially involving products that are highly sensitive to exchange rate and/or interest rate movements. These transactions are always model-tested to determine the potential exposure they create. Trades are approved if they fit within the established limit structure, often after netting against a portfolio of existing transactions with the same counterpart.

Trading Limits

Business units are notified when current and potential exposure levels reach 75% of a country or counterpart limit. Business unit heads are also alerted after each

Sovereign Committee meeting when country ratings and limits are changed. When ratings fall and limits are reduced, business units are usually encouraged to reduce current and potential exposure levels in an orderly way. Trades are sometimes unwound if they are booked in violation of established limit structures. Unwinds are also considered after internal country ratings downgrades, when existing exposures suddenly exceed new limit structures. This is especially relevant when exposures are considered vulnerable to the economic and financial constraints prompting the downgrade. In most downgrade situations, existing exposures that exceed new limits are allowed to fall off over a period of weeks or even months.

Potential Problems

Occasionally, a perceived or anticipated deterioration in the economic and financial outlook of a country is dramatic enough to prompt a reconsideration of all exposures to that sovereign. When this happens, meetings are arranged by the head of Credit with Firm managers and business unit heads to communicate a revised view of (1) the deteriorating environment; (2) the assumptions underpinning the forecast; and (3) the potential loss entailed in maintaining existing—or even reduced—exposures.

CASE STUDY: RUSSIA

Illustrative of the value of the new standards for credit analysis is the case of Russia as perceived in January 1998, after a review of Russia's deteriorating political and economic fundamentals resulted in a downgrade of the sovereign in credit committee. In the aftermath of these meetings, a decision was made to reduce proprietary positions and avoid bridge loans. When Russia devalued the ruble and defaulted on local currency obligations the following August, losses to Morgan Stanley were minimal to nonexistent. The text of the actual review follows.

Russia: A Mid-Year Update of Deteriorating Credit Fundamentals (February 1998)

Russia's economic fundamentals have materially deteriorated since our review of July 1997, largely in response to the government's inability to enact comprehensive tax reform which would (1) set the stage for a structural reduction in the country's chronic and unsustainably large fiscal imbalances, and (2) slow the rapid accumulation of foreign and local currency debt. Significantly, public sector foreign currency debt grew to $142 billion last year, from $123 billion at end-1996, as the government tapped foreign as well as local currency funding sources to finance fiscal deficits and continued rapid capital flight (presumably attributable to tax avoidance). Russia's foreign currency debt/current account receipts ratio rose to a comparatively high 189% at end-1997, from 158% a year earlier. Russia is no longer an under-leveraged country.

On the local currency funding side, declining inflation has exacerbated the situation, as the cumulative value of these fiscal deficits, the nominal accumulation of public sector local-currency debt, and the ratio of local currency debt/GDP are no longer being eroded by rising prices. Domestic currency fiscal debt as a percent of GDP rose in 1997 to an estimated 52%, having fallen from 270% at end-1992 to 48% at year-end 1996, when annual inflation exceeded the rise in nominal public sector borrowings by as much as sixfold.

These deteriorating fundamentals have resulted in downward pressure on the ruble in recent months, prompting the Central Bank to (1) spend FX reserves in the currency's defense, prompting a decline from US $20.4 billion in June 1997 to $13 billion in early February 1998, and (2) raise the discount rate, from 26% in October 1997 to 42% in January 1998, despite falling single-digit inflation.

Spreads on much-needed foreign currency borrowings have also risen dramatically since October, another factor which will make deficit reduction and deficit financing more difficult and could raise liquidity concerns about the timely replacement of Russia's $30 billion of foreign currency short-term debt. High foreign and domestic interest rates will almost certainly push (recorded) GDP growth back to negative in 1998.

Russia's problems have been highlighted and perhaps exacerbated by the erosion of investor sentiment resulting from Asia's financial crisis, and by the increased scrutiny of investors to economic fundamentals in emerging-market economies.

Political Developments

Of significance on the political front, President Yeltsin's sporadic attention to reform has failed to extract from a resistant Duma a credible tax reform bill which would put in place a tax code that would, over time, reduce tax avoidance and facilitate the development of a viable public sector. Future Russian governments will be required to (1) respond to the legitimate social needs of a population which has undergone considerable hardship as the economy has transformed itself to private ownership and market pricing; (2) invest in much-needed physical infrastructure which could also encourage private investment in plant and infrastructure; and (3) budget reasonable expenditure priorities without incurring unsustainably large fiscal imbalances and the accumulation of public sector debt.

Yeltsin's verbiage is often appropriate, but his government has thus far failed to implement programs that would lend credibility to his stated policy objectives of creating a reliable revenue base, reducing fiscal imbalances, and encouraging an environment for sustainable growth. Complicating matters, he continues to exhibit a tendency to lend support to competing groups of reformers and/or to powerful economic elites for no more than a few months at a time, then switching allegiance if only temporarily. Thanks to Yeltsin's divide and rule philosophy of governance, the Russian cabinet is a collection of "rival warriors" rather than a united administration. This clearly reduces the momentum of consistent and coherent policy making.

Policy Developments

There is little consistency on the policy front; on the whole, sound monetary policies are undermined by lax fiscal policies.

Fiscal Policy

Movement toward comprehensive tax reform has stagnated in the Duma, saddled with more than 3,200 amendments which, if enacted, would undermine the intent of this fiscal initiative. The government's objective is to simplify the tax code, remove duplicative tax levies, lower tax rates to encourage broad-based compliance, and raise the revenue/GDP ratio from its present 12% to a level of around 35% over a 5-year horizon (the European Union average revenue/GDP ratio is 42%). In the absence of comprehensive tax reform, it is our view that (1) fiscal deficits will not *structurally* decline; (2) social and infrastructure investment expenditure will not rise to appropriate levels; and (3) Russia's chronic capital flight (tax avoidance) will not be curtailed. Deficit spending in a declining inflation environment will exacerbate the government's fiscal debt/GDP ratio and raise the interest component of fiscal expenditure that will further crowd out discretionary spending.

Economic indicators have already suffered dramatic deterioration resulting from the postponement of tax reform. Foreign as well as domestic currency debt ratios have risen because the government has chosen to finance its overall public sector deficit (including the deteriorating fiscal balances of the regional governments) in local as well as international markets to lower its overall interest burden. Russia's foreign currency debt/current account receipts ratio has climbed from 144% at end-1995 to 189% at end-1997. Local currency debt as a percent of GDP has begun rising again, to an estimated 52%, following a dramatic decline from 270% at end-1992 to 48% at year-end 1996, a result of the corrosive effect of inflation during those years.

Access to international markets is likely to be somewhat more restricted in 1998, while the cost of foreign currency debt has risen dramatically in recent months, raising liquidity concerns for the government as it endeavors to finance unrestrained deficits. If the Yeltsin Administration is forced to rely for deficit financing solely on domestic markets, where interest rates have risen faster than international spreads, the interest component of this budget will almost certainly force the administration to fall out of compliance with IMF conditionality, further restricting the access of all Russian borrowers to foreign capital. Budgetary assumptions (with average interest rates of 25%) are already unrealistic. No formal initiatives have been taken or interim budgets introduced to correct these assumptions. In his address to the nation on February 17th, Yeltsin called for proposals (by May) to cut expenditure and restore the budget's original deficit targets. The problem with this approach (other than its May timetable) is that deficit reduction over these past five years has consistently relied on expenditure cuts (or under-spending budget targets), leaving a bare bones budget with little room to pare back (except, perhaps, in areas which are supported by strong special interests). There is no reason at the moment to believe that comprehensive and sustainable structural adjustments that will reverse the deterioration in Russia's economic fundamentals are likely to be implemented in the near term.

Monetary and Exchange Rate Policy

Monetary and exchange rate management is the one bright spot in this policy environment. An independent Central Bank, led by the very capable Sergei Dubinin, has limited money supply growth, and adjusted domestic interest rates and the reserve requirements of the banking sector to secure an impressive reduction in inflation and a stable ruble (the currency has, in fact, appreciated in real terms over the past two years, while inflation is expected to average a modest 8.5% this year, down from 14.3% in 1997). Dobinin has reaffirmed his intention to raise interest rates to whatever level necessary to maintain low inflation and a stable real exchange rate. Regrettably, the lack of fiscal discipline will require very high real interest rates over the coming two years if the Central Bank is to achieve these goals. This scenario will slow growth in the recorded economy and could require the further draw down of the country's shrinking foreign currency reserves, should currency pressures intensify.

Privatization

Further privatization of the natural resource sector, and the revenues these initiatives will earn, will reduce the size of a projected fiscal imbalance being pushed higher by rising interest rates. These revenues as currently estimated, however, are unlikely to exceed or even match the additional interest expense incurred by rising domestic rates and international spreads. Each percentage point increase in the rate or spread charged costs the government around $300 million in additional interest expense. Nevertheless, if deficit financing from abroad is more limited than in 1997 and revenues continue weak, accelerated privatization would be the only way for authorities to fulfill spending commitments under the 1998 budget and avoid stalemate with the Duma over the revised budget. Significantly increasing privatization revenues could be difficult, however, as it would require a shift to more competitive cash auctions open to foreign investors. Domestic financial groups seeking to gain control over the remaining lucrative state assets at low prices will almost certainly oppose such a course.

Legal/Legislative

Although property rights legislation, bankruptcy laws, contractual laws, and land reform and ownership decrees nominally exist, they have not been enforced sufficiently widely or consistently to be considered operational in practice. Weak implementation has been paralleled by judicial conflicts that have resulted in outright confusion as to which laws have precedence, especially as far as taxation and property rights are concerned.

Inadequate regulation and the absence of a functioning legal system limit direct foreign and domestic investment and commercial bank lending, and significantly inhibit the growth potential of the Russian economy.

Enterprise Reform, Competition, and Other Related Structural Issues

Sluggish enterprise restructuring because of weak political resolve to intensify competition and strengthen market forces remains a major impediment, along with renewed high real interest rates, to an early return to significant output growth. Weak financial discipline prevented further restructuring among partly and/or fully privatized firms. Reforms needed to better target social transfers and housing subsidies remain on the drawing board, preventing both government and enterprises from reducing wasteful spending. Gross enterprise arrears rose by the equivalent of 11% of GDP between January and August 1997, to 43% of GDP. Most enterprises shifted from nonpayment of wages and suppliers last year to tax arrears, complicating the fiscal dilemma. Bitter controversy among powerful financial groups seeking valuable assets the government has tried to privatize more competitively has helped weaken political support for government efforts to advance reforms.

Banking Sector and Banking Supervision

Further moves to strengthen bank supervision have helped to prevent systemic problems during the financial turmoil that began in October, but many banks have been adversely affected by reduced profitability because of lower Treasury bill yields through September and large losses on government securities and equity holdings thereafter. Nonperforming loans have risen at most banks, although 90% of them are said to be covered by some form of collateral and/or provisions. Efforts to improve the regulatory framework focused on loan classification and provisioning, as Russian accounting standards have moved closer to an international standard.

Economic Performance

Recorded real GDP rose by an estimated 0.4% in 1997. Limited enterprise restructuring constrained output despite strong growth in bank lending to nongovernment borrowers. Weak incentives, poor financial discipline, and confiscatory taxes hampered enterprise restructuring again last year. Higher interest rates and the cessation of new bank lending to nongovernment borrowers will likely cause the economy to contract by 2% or more in 1998.

External Accounts

Stronger growth in import volumes and stagnant exports (with export receipt values actually falling, a result of declining commodity prices) have combined with higher net interest payments to narrow Russia's current account surplus in 1997 to an estimated $500 million, down from a record $9.1 billion surplus in 1996. Lower oil and natural gas prices will again inhibit export growth in 1998, while higher foreign currency interest payments associated with rising debt levels and interest spreads will boost service payments. While import demand is likely to slow with a return to negative GDP growth, a current account deficit of at least $5 billion is projected, a factor which will add to the country's foreign currency borrowing requirement.

Complicating matters, non-debt foreign investment is expected to fall in 1998, from the $6.4 billion level achieved in 1997, as the ongoing stock market correction, less favorable investment sentiment, and deteriorating economic fundamentals reduce foreign currency capital inflows.

Debt

Russia's foreign currency debt grew by nearly $20 billion in 1997, and is projected to increase by as much as $30 billion in 1998 as the government endeavors to fund in international capital markets or with international bank debt (1) an anticipated current account deficit; (2) a portion of the overall public sector deficit (including the deficits of regional governments); and (3) continued capital flight, which has helped deplete foreign exchange reserves. Total foreign currency indebtedness stood at $142 billion at year-end 1997, equal to 189% of current account receipts. This ratio will likely grow to 231% if an additional $30 billion is added to the debt stock in 1998. Russia is no longer an under-indebted country and could be a very highly indebted country by year-end.

Of significance, short-term debt increased by more than $10 billion in 1997, to $29.5 billion. Nearly $1 billion was secured in December to facilitate year-end debt service payments and shore-up declining foreign currency reserve levels, which increased from $12.5 billion at end-December to $13.5 at end-January, equal to just over three months of import coverage. Short-term debt approximates 21% of total foreign currency obligations, a moderately high ratio. But in absolute terms, $30 billion in short-term debt obligations presently equals more than 200% of foreign currency reserve levels, up from 90% in June 1997.

Combined with the more than $3 billion of debt repayments falling due on long-term obligations this year, and an estimated $13.7 billion of interest on total foreign currency debt anticipated in 1998, Russia's debt service schedule could look significantly more onerous than the 22% (debt service/current account receipts) ratio calculated on long-term amortization plus interest on total debt calculated on the assumption of short-term debt rollovers.

Absent a significant loss of confidence in Russia's creditworthiness, Russia's short-term debt could grow by an estimated $10 billion in 1998, as borrowers are forced to shorter maturities. This trend would make Russia even more vulnerable to a liquidity squeeze should a sudden loss of confidence occur.

CONCLUSION

The lessons derived from the country crises of 1997-1999, and the analytical benefits and data and accounting standards they have produced, have immeasurably enhanced the discipline of sovereign risk analysis and helped minimize the risks to capital of banks and investment firms that underwrite and trade emerging-market paper. This development has emerged as financial products have developed in complexity and global capital markets have become more diverse. It is increasingly clear that those financial institutions that best identify, assess, monitor, and manage credit, market, funding, and operational risk will also most effectively ensure their financial stability and profitability.

APPENDIX I

COUNTRY SUMMARIES

Thailand

Thailand's decade-long commitment to prudent fiscal and monetary policy was ultimately overshadowed by the government's acquiescence in a massive flow of short-term capital through an under-regulated financial sector, and by its attempts to prop up that financial system when it came under pressure. Although much of the capital inflow was used to expand productive capacity, the maturity mismatch between short-term funding and long-term investment became a major source of risk for the industrial sector. In addition, the inflow also funded a real estate boom and a current account deficit that grew to nearly 8% of GDP by 1997. The strain that this imbalance placed on the pegged currency regime was magnified when the Chavalit government provided massive liquidity support for the country's 91 finance companies, nearly all of which were suffering from asset quality deterioration as the property market slowed. The pressure on the Baht intensified through early 1997. The government's use of high interest rates to defend the currency undermined economic growth but failed to offset growing market fears about the state of the financial sector. Demand for dollars grew substantially after the decision to devalue on July 2, 1997, as corporations and banks tried to cover their foreign exchange exposures. This led to a massive overshooting of the Baht/dollar exchange rate, which fell from a slightly overvalued 25.3 in early 1997 to a vastly undervalued 54 in January 1998.

Indonesia

Indonesia's equally prudent fiscal and monetary policies and its long-successful managed float of the rupiah gave investors confidence to finance a vast array of expensive public sector infrastructure projects. Meanwhile the corporate sector enjoyed access to international capital markets, its creditworthiness seemingly enhanced by the unlimited availability of cheap labor and by the government's policy of managing competition through the distribution of ownership rights. Within this policy context, the banking sector was chronically weak, and the lack of prudential regulation encouraged massive reliance on unhedged foreign debt in the corporate sector. These flaws became critical after Thailand's devaluation, which proved to be the demise of rupiah stability. Bank Indonesia's decision to abandon the currency band led to a rush for dollars as the corporate sector tried to cover its short-term debt. As in Thailand, the central bank also provided a massive liquidity injection to the banking sector, which added to the devaluation of the rupiah. And the Suharto Administration's reluctance to adhere to IMF conditionality refocused the world's attention on the government's willingness to sacrifice sound micro-economic policy for economic nepotism.

Korea

Korea's short-term debt overhang originated with a government mandate to the country's large corporate sector to vigorously expand capacity and aggressively gain world market share. The chaebol pursued this goal with the help of foreign and domestic currency borrowings, mainly from the country's under-regulated banking sector, which enjoyed access to international capital markets and maintained significant maturity mismatches. Overexpansion ultimately resulted in a series of corporate bankruptcies and/or debt servicing problems, which prompted foreign capital flight, forced a devaluation of the won, and focused investor attention on the need for chaebol restructuring and enhanced banking sector regulation. All of these factors eventually overwhelmed the government's history of sound fiscal and monetary policy management.

Malaysia

Malaysia's better-regulated banking sector was, nevertheless, hugely exposed to the economy; total loans equaled 170% of GDP at year-end 1997. The country was similarly dependent on foreign capital to finance its current account imbalance. Large *non-debt* inflows were maintained with the help of sound and investor-friendly policies and a managed currency float, sustained with the help of high real interest rates and a balanced fiscal account. While domestic banks were relatively over-exposed to the real estate boom, Malaysia's banking sector problems, its foreign and domestic currency debt service, and pressures on the currency were manageable. However, Malaysia's external orientation exposed it to a severe competitive impact as regional currencies and trade volumes fell. This external impact added to a softening property market and the high leverage of its corporate sector, creating rising asset quality problems in the banking sector. The government's unwillingness to address these structural problems compounded concerns about its economic management. This intensified when the government discussed, and then imposed, controls on currency convertibility and other investor options—including the repatriation of foreign capital within one year—that limited the flow of foreign funds into and out of the financial sector. The result was an accelerated economic downturn, driven by the need to produce and sustain an adjustment in the current account.

Hong Kong

Hong Kong's 1998 distress can be attributed largely to its external orientation, which allowed a direct spillover from the regional crisis on its tourism, financial services, and trade sectors, and to a severe correction in its inflated property market. Real estate prices were peaking when Thailand devalued, and the regional crisis worsened a price correction that would have been significant in its own right. With declines of 60% in residential property prices in just over a year, private consumption was hit by a huge negative wealth effect. These problems were complicated by Hong Kong's continued adherence to a currency board, which limited the government's ability to compensate for external shocks. The currency board was the target of periodic speculative attacks, fueled by concerns about the stability of the renminbi, about the outlook for Hong Kong banks, and about the government's commitment to free-market policies. These pressures, which created short-term interest rate spikes, recurred throughout the year despite the Special Administrative Region's maintenance of huge foreign currency reserve levels and an accumulated fiscal and land fund reserve equal to an additional 27% of GDP. Hong Kong's comparatively well-regulated banking sector boasted strong capitalization and aggregate nonperforming assets equal to less than 2% of total loans outstanding in 1998. However, the severity of the recession encouraged market sensitivity as investors looked for signs of a weakening in Hong Kong's economic policy resolve.

Japan

Japan has mystified the world with its inability to reform its ailing and poorly regulated banking sector, the single most important precondition to the restoration of domestic demand and GDP growth in that country. Deregulation of the comparatively closed economy is also urgently needed. This should be undertaken in tandem with recent fiscal stimulus measures and, of necessity, before the government tackles its deteriorating fiscal position and the mountain of debt that these budget policies have created. (Gross fiscal debt is offset, for the time being, by a surplus in the social security reserve fund.) Japan's large and sustainable current account surplus and huge foreign currency reserve levels should insulate the economy from any dependence on international capital and may cushion the yen in the face of declining international confidence. Bankruptcies and the cost of a financial sector bailout, however protracted, will limit growth prospects over the medium term.

Russia

Russia's economy collapsed under a burden of fiscal debt denominated in both foreign and domestic currencies. The economy's most serious problem was an absence of fiscal discipline since 1991, as the government failed to reform an inadequate tax regime. Without the resources to carry out its basic commitments, the government largely squandered its privatization proceeds, trading undervalued shares in natural resource-rich companies for loans from a handful of individuals/banks to cover its fiscal ineptitude. The skewed distribution of wealth and political power that resulted continued to inhibit the pursuit of appropriate policy remedies. The collapse of Russia's unregulated and unregulatable (given its ownership structure) private commercial banking sector vastly expanded the economy's problems. In sum, Russia again found itself a highly indebted country with few immediately available resources at its disposal to rectify the situation. A foreign currency debt restructuring became inevitable.

Brazil

Brazil's persistent and unsustainably large fiscal imbalances—the deficit equaled 7½% of GDP in 1998, a development that is especially problematic in a low-inflation environment—increasingly extracted a heavy price from the central bank, which kept interest rates high in real terms to support the country's managed currency peg and, since January 15, 1999, to support a floating exchange rate. November's $42 billion IMF support package was accepted by the government in an attempt to buy more time to legislate and implement fiscal and constitutional initiatives designed to close the budget gap. However, these initiatives faced political opposition and the fiscal deficit grew, largely because of persistently high real domestic interest rates. Following the dramatic depreciation of the real, Brazil was faced with the task of reducing its foreign and domestic currency borrowing and refinancing requirement, which as recently as year-end 1998 was estimated in excess of $90 billion. Success in this initiative required a massive reduction in both fiscal and current account imbalances, the achievement of which inevitably produced a contraction of GDP growth. Devaluation exacerbated foreign currency debt service and raised fears of debt restructuring or rescheduling.

APPENDIX II

CAPITAL CONTROLS: EXAMPLES

The Experience of Chile

In the early 1990s, Chile experienced a surge in capital inflows that created a conflict between the local authorities' desire to maintain tight monetary policies and the country's need for foreign non-debt funding to facilitate the expansion of a competitive export sector. In 1991, the central bank attempted to resolve this dilemma by imposing a 1-year unremunerated reserve requirement (URR) on foreign loans. This policy was primarily designed to discourage short-term borrowing without affecting long-term foreign investments. The fixed holding period of the reserve requirement implied that the financial burden diminished with the maturity of the investment. Between 1991 and 1997, the rate of the URR was increased and its coverage extended in several steps to cover most forms of foreign financing except foreign direct investment. In other words, all loans, fixed income securities, and most equity investments were subject to the URR, with only foreign direct investment and primary issuers of ADRs exempted from the reserve requirement.

Evidence regarding the effectiveness of the Chilean controls in reducing short-term external debt is somewhat ambiguous. National data suggest that the introduction of capital controls significantly affected the maturity composition of net capital inflows after 1995 when these controls were strengthened and the reserve requirement increased. Data from international sources, however, describe a somewhat different picture. The IMF reports that BIS figures for short-term external borrowings substantially exceed those reported in Chilean sources and suggest the existence of a large amount of foreign currency loans issued by Chilean affiliates of foreign banks, outstanding import credits, and a significant mis-reporting by borrowers of external credit. The maturity structure of foreign bank borrowing appears quite different from that implied by the national data as well. At the end of 1997, loans with maturities of up to one year represented 49% of total foreign currency loans, whereas the Chilean data for the equivalent component of the total external debt is 11%. BIS data would suggest a significant number of avenues around such controls, rendering them essentially ineffective.

The Chilean government has abandoned the URR, apparently having decided it must encourage all foreign capital inflows in a suddenly illiquid marketplace.

The Experience of China

China's closed capital account (the current account has largely been freed) is popularly cited as an appropriate exchange control for a partially reformed economy. Analysts argue that these controls protect an economy with (1) a comparatively undeveloped domestic bond market; (2) a banking sector dominated by four large state-owned banks, which in aggregate house 80% of the country's foreign and domestic currency deposits and which continue to act at the behest of the government in support of state enterprise liquidity, irrespective of asset quality considerations; and (3) little effective banking sector regulation.

All medium- and long-term foreign commercial borrowing in China requires the prior approval of the State Administration of Foreign Exchange (SAFE). Borrowing quotas continue to be allocated under the annual plan. Joint-venture enterprises and wholly foreign-owned companies are required to balance their foreign exchange receipts and payments, and foreign borrowing must be reported to the SAFE. Transfers of foreign currency out of the country must also be reported and approved.

Significantly, these controls have not been wholly successful in keeping money from leaking out of the country. Most of these funds have found their way to Hong Kong in search of higher yields than could be achieved in the PRC. These leakages are traditionally recorded in the errors and omissions column of the capital account. In 1998, errors and omissions amounted to an estimated $20 billion. When fears of devaluation grow, capital flight increases. Data for the first ten months of 1998 suggest a trade surplus of $38 billion and actual foreign direct investment inflows of $31 billion through the end of September. After accounting for invisibles and other flows (including errors and omissions), the capital account should have been in surplus by an estimated $40 billion. Yet official foreign currency reserves grew only marginally during this period—to about $144 billion at end-October from $140 billion at end-December 1997—suggesting a dramatic acceleration in the flow of capital over the border, this time in pursuit of protection from currency instability.

Chapter 16

Default and Recovery Rates in Emerging Markets

Tsvetan N. Beloreshki
Senior Consultant
National Economic Research Associates, Inc.

INTRODUCTION

Fixed income markets have achieved a remarkable progress in understanding credit risk. A number of sophisticated analytical models and quantitative techniques have been developed to analyze the behavior of fixed income instruments. This greater theoretical understanding has enhanced the ability of issuers, intermediaries, and investors alike to identify and take advantage of available investment opportunities. As evidenced by the multiple emerging market crises and liquidity droughts that occurred in the 1980s and 1990s, however, the insights gleaned from theoretical models alone are hardly sufficient.

By its nature, emerging markets is one area of financial markets that requires that investors possess a combination of multidisciplinary knowledge and experience, as well as a rich arsenal of quantitative and qualitative tools, in order to succeed in this extremely treacherous but potentially rewarding field. As a result, it is sure to punish investors for overreliance on any single methodology as a means of understanding the nature of credit products.

The purpose of this chapter is to discuss the role two omnipresent yet rarely discussed phenomena—default probabilities and recovery rates—play in the valuation of debt securities, as well as their relation to more traditional measures of credit risk, such as credit spreads. In doing so we will provide a historical perspective, economic analysis, and an analytical framework that will allow for the incorporation of default probabilities and recovery rates into an investor's decision-making process.

FIXED INCOME SECURITIES THROUGH THE PRISM OF DEFAULT PROBABILITIES AND RECOVERY RATES

The credit risk implicit in holding a bond depends on (1) the probability that the issuer may default, (2) the expected recovery contingent upon an event of default, and (3) the term structure of default and recovery rates. All other things being

311

equal, the value of fixed income instruments is related inversely to the probability of default on the part of the underlying issuer, and positively to the expected recovery rate (see Exhibit 1).

The term structure of default and recovery rates can be quite complicated and can affect the value of the underlying fixed income instruments in a variety of ways. In general however, the higher the correlation between default and recovery rates, the higher the value of a fixed income security. While it might be reasonable to expect that states of the world characterized by a high expected probability of default would tend to be associated with low post-default recoveries, the empirical evidence on this relationship is inconclusive.[1]

From that point of view, investment decisions as to whether or not to hold a fixed income instrument reflect investors' expectations of future default probabilities and recovery rates and how these relate to the ones implied by the marketplace. All other factors constant, a rational investor will invest in (a class of) credit instruments that maximizes his net yield advantage, defined as the differential between the spread S (between the securities' yield and the risk-free rate), and the expected default loss rate $p \times (1 - R)$, where p and R are the probability of default and the recovery rate, respectively. As a result, the decisions of all economic agents lead to a market equilibrium in which the market default and recovery expectations are reflected into debt instruments' credit spreads and their corresponding valuations.

Exhibit 1: Bond Value as a Function of Expected Default and Recovery Rates

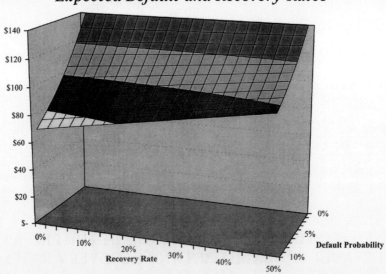

[1] Martin S. Fridson, M. Christopher Garman, and Kathryn Okashima, "Recovery Rates: The Search for Meaning," Merrill Lynch & Co., Global Securities Research & Economics Group, High Yield Strategy (March 13, 2000).

Default Probabilities, Recovery Rates, and Credit Spreads

There is a direct link between the compensation for credit risk and the probability of default. In a risk-neutral one-period framework, an investor will be indifferent between receiving e^{r_f} dollars with certainty, or $e^{r_f + S}$ dollars with probability $1 - p$, where r_f is the risk-free rate, S is the credit spread over the risk-free rate, and p is the periodic probability of default. Then, in the absence of liquidity and other technical factors, the spread is a compensation for the risk of default:

$$e^{r_f} = (1 - p) \times e^{r_f + S} \Rightarrow e^{-S} = (1 - p) \Rightarrow 1 - S \approx 1 - p \Rightarrow p = S \qquad (1)$$

The approximation $e^{-S} = 1 - S$ is derived from the Taylor expansion of an exponential function about zero, and assumes that the credit spread S is close to zero.[2]

More generally, assuming a recovery rate R, the risk-free payoff is equal to the sum of the expected payoffs weighted by their respective probabilities of occurrence. Thus the relation between default probability and recovery rate becomes:

$$e^{r_f} = [p \times R + (1 - p)] \times e^{r_f + S} \Rightarrow e^{-S} = p \times R + 1 - p \Rightarrow p = \frac{S}{1 - R} \qquad (2)$$

Equation (2) implies that for a given credit spread level, higher recovery rates imply higher default probabilities. In addition, expected recovery rates have a more pronounced effect on the valuations of securities of weaker credits. This fact goes a long way towards explaining the wide dispersion of the credit spreads of lower-rated debt instruments. To the extent that similar credit ratings on rated debt instruments reflect similar expected probabilities of default, the variance of credit spreads would be largely attributable to differences in the market recovery rate expectations.

The above analysis can be extended in a straightforward fashion to incorporate (1) multiperiod settings and (2) deterministic or random periodic probability of default. One major feature of this relationship, however, remains constant. The joint contribution of default probability and recovery rate to the above relationship makes it impossible to obtain separate estimates for each of them from credit spreads alone. In other words, having observed market valuations and credit spread levels, one can estimate default probability only after incorporating recovery rate assumptions, and vice versa. Thus, we see the need for more precise default probability and recovery rate estimates.

DEFAULT

An event of default is generally defined as the failure to meet a principal or interest payment on the due date (or within the specified grace period), contained in

---

[2] This assumption may not be applicable to lower-quality credit instruments, such as emerging markets debt. In such cases, higher-order approximations may be appropriate.

the original terms of the debt issue. The default frequency or probability can then be defined as the likelihood that a debt instrument of a particular obligor will default within a given time frame.

In the context of sovereign obligations, the above definition of default is usually extended to include forced exchange offers of new debt, which impair the value of the original debt and/or contain terms that are less favorable than those of the original issues. Among the different ways through which such a dilution of original terms can be achieved are (1) extinguishing obligations at a discount from their original face value (e.g., Brazil in 1986–1987, 1990); (2) rescheduling principal and/or interest in ways that impair investors' interests (for example, extending principal and/or reducing interest payments, e.g., Russia and Ukraine 1999); and (3) conversion into new currency of less than equivalent face value (e.g., Ghana 1979). As a result, transactions involving forced exchange offers (similar to those linked to the issuance of Brady bonds), debt/equity swaps related to government privatization programs, and/or buybacks for cash are generally considered events of default by the major credit agencies (Standard & Poor's, Moody's, and Fitch).

Importance of a Robust Definition of Default

Arriving at a robust and uniform definition of default has long been a goal for industry participants. Despite the relative importance of the problem and the multiyear efforts of the major credit rating agencies and global trade associations, the industry entered the 21st century with a plethora of unresolved issues and few prospects for their prompt and successful resolution.[3]

Documentation Risk

In particular, the International Swaps and Derivatives Association's (ISDA) definitions of credit events (e.g., restructuring, bankruptcy, obligation acceleration, and obligation default) are broader than the definition of "default" as applied by the major credit rating agencies, as well as much of the market. As a result, the risk of a synthetic investment, by way of a credit derivative, may not be equivalent to and may in fact exceed the risk of a cash investment in the same credit. For example, if not structured properly, a credit default swap may pass along the risk of triggering a loss following events that are not actually defaults (e.g., mere credit deterioration) instead of the risk of loss following an actual default.

The failure to address this issue in a systematic and consistent way threatens to undermine origination and secondary market activities in certain segments of the marketplace. This is particularly true for the structured products and synthetic instruments markets, which rely explicitly on credit event definitions. As a result of their particularly high exposure to such "documentation risk" issues, counterparties in credit derivative contracts face the challenge of providing a definition of a default trigger event that is clear, precise, and sufficiently broad in scope.

[3] For a more detailed discussion see Jeffrey S. Tolk, "Understanding the Risks in Credit Default Swaps," *Moody's Investors Service* (March 16, 2001).

Litigation Risk

As has been discussed above, events of sovereign default are contemplated in emerging markets transactions and are reflected in the overall price of a given instrument. Nonetheless, litigation activity related to emerging market instruments tends to increase following sovereign and corporate defaults. Practical problems such as the expense of lawsuits, sovereign immunity, and/or the difficulty of dealing with foreign entities in court, as well as the lack of resources of the entity itself, effectively bar litigation against sovereign and/or corporate issuers by most investors. As a result, the risk of litigation in emerging markets transactions stems mostly from the interactions between the transaction counterparties (e.g., brokers and customers), not between the investor and the original issuer.

In every transaction, each investor essentially has the right, but not the obligation, to commence legal action against other market participants. A rational investor would only exercise this right contingent upon sustaining significant investment losses.[4] As a result, investors in general hold a litigation option, which they can exercise against broker/dealers, security underwriters, etc.

The emerging markets arena is one that is almost custom-tailored in terms of accommodating investor claims challenging investment suitability and valuation. A number of factors characteristic of the sector tend to enhance the value of investors' option to litigate, and they result ultimately in higher litigation costs for a number of market participants. These costs include (1) high volatility of underlying instrument(s) and significant expected losses contingent upon the occurrence of credit events; (2) transaction complexity (e.g., use of leverage, structured products such as collateralized debt obligations,[5] embedded options, lack of transparency, and relative illiquidity); (3) informational and financial sophistication asymmetry between transaction counterparties (e.g., between broker/dealers and retail customers); and (4) direct and/or indirect litigation costs differential between the counterparties in a transaction.

As a result, emerging markets investors would be more likely to exercise their option to initiate broker/dealer disputes and legal actions, and any failure on the part of a broker/dealer to provide a full, unambiguous, and robust definition of all terms of the transaction (regardless of how trivial they may seem in the eyes of an experienced finance professional) could potentially precipitate unwelcome legal action. Typical claims in emerging markets litigation and arbitration cases include disputes as to appropriate default references, credit (and default) trigger events (in particular, credit event triggers used for the unwinding of structured products and credit-linked notes), and the appropriateness of default and recovery rate assumptions.

---

[4] This barrier-like feature is due to the fact that a rational investor would initiate a lawsuit only if the expected benefits from litigation outweigh potential costs (e.g., in terms of both time and resources spent in litigation as well as potential reputation loss suffered by an investor plaintiff).

[5] A collateralized debt obligation (CDO) is an asset-backed securitization. CDOs encompass collateralized loan obligations (CLOs), in which the collateral being securitized is primarily loans, and collateralized bond obligations (CBOs), in which the collateral is primarily bonds.

Cross-Default

One potential pitfall for both buyers and sellers of credit protection on sovereign risk is the uncertainty of whether default on one class of debt (e.g., sovereign's domestic obligations) triggers a payout on derivatives pegged to another class of debt (e.g., foreign currency borrowings).

A number of fixed income instruments contain provisions that trigger default in one security in the case of an event of default on another. Technically, a cross-default provision is a covenant by the issuer such that should there be a default in a payment under its other borrowings, such nonpayment is considered an event of default in respect to the issue to which the cross-default covenant applies. In the case of corporate issuers, such a covenant generally extends to the borrower's subsidiaries and/or guarantors.

In general, cross-default provisions enhance investor confidence and, under certain circumstances, can have a significant effect on the valuation of securities. This is true both in the case when the cross-default provisions involve the issues of a single issuer, and in circumstances when multiple issuers are involved. In the former case, the potential adverse consequences related to a default on an issuer's total debt may impose significant enough costs to preclude (partial) default, and as a result, may tend to improve perceived credit quality. For example, the threat of future lack of access to the capital markets and significant reputation loss may be sufficient to offset an issuer's temptation to miss a coupon (or principal) payment on one of its issues in the face of a temporary liquidity problem. In the latter case, the extension of a weak credit's cross-default provisions onto a stronger credit can provide a significant support for the weak credit and its market value. To the extent that the market views and values the two credits jointly, the explicit guarantee provided by the stronger credit represents a form of credit enhancement.

It should be noted that an implicit guarantee by a stronger credit can sometimes prove just as valuable. In one of the most publicized examples of inter-governmental tension, in 1999 the governor of the State of Minas Gerais in Brazil placed a moratorium on the repayment of all debt and threatened to delay the payment on the state's Eurobond due on February 10, 1999. Given the fragility of investor confidence in Brazil at the time, the republic was reluctant to allow a sub-sovereign entity to default and fully covered the state's payment shortfalls.

Finally, cross-default provisions need not be reciprocal. The fact that default of security A triggers a cross-default of security B does not necessarily imply that default of security B triggers a cross-default of security A. For example, Russia's 1998 decision to effectively default on its unrated Soviet-era foreign obligations (PRIN and IAN loans) did not trigger default on Russian Eurobond debt issues. However, a Russian default on its Eurobond obligations would have triggered default on all Soviet-era debt. This lack of reciprocity in cross-default provisions had significant repercussions for investors, led to severe losses, and in some cases even precipitated legal actions. Imagine the position of a credit derivatives trader who believed he was flat by virtue of "hedging" his long Russian protection position referenced on the Russian Eurobonds with an offsetting short Russian protection position referenced on the Russian PRIN loans. While the value of the former would have increased due to general widening of Russian credit spreads, the loss on the latter would have been far greater, leading to a substantial net loss.

RECOVERY RATES AND DEFAULT SEVERITY

Default or loss severity is generally defined as the expected loss following default, after accounting for any recovery proceeds on the defaulted asset. It is generally represented as the difference between par (or purchase price) and recovery rate.

Recovery rates on defaulted debt are most often expressed as the percentage of par (or cents on the dollar) value that can be recovered by the creditor (securityholder). One minus the recovery rate represents the loss rate to the investor. For example, if an investor receives $25 for a $100 bond in default (either through an open-market transaction or through receiving proceeds as a result of bankruptcy reorganization or settlement), then the recovery rate equals 25%, and the corresponding loss rate becomes 75%.

Alternatively, for securities issued and/or trading at significant discount, recovery rates can be represented as the percentage of pre-default market value that is expected to be recovered in the event of a default.

Should a given security be actively quoted and traded in the marketplace, a recovery value estimate can be obtained by examining post-default market valuations of distressed debt. The main assumption underlying this approach—that the markets are sufficiently efficient to correctly anticipate the financial outcome of the restructuring process—may be objectionable given the relative illiquidity and thinness of the marketplace where such securities are traded. This problem could be particularly acute as related to emerging markets, and could potentially result in the introduction of significant noises into the estimation of recovery rates.

An alternative method for estimating default severity, often favored by distressed debt investors, holds that recoveries should be based on the valuation of distressed debt after the ultimate resolution of the default (or reorganization) process. While this methodology has certain advantages and avoids the problems presented by the former, it can present additional challenges. Most importantly, its application necessitates the valuation of recovery packages that often include complex financial structures comprising debt, equity, and other assets that may be difficult to value.

Additionally, any comparisons between the two methods would necessarily depend on the appropriate choice of discounting procedure.

DEFAULT AND RECOVERY RATES IN EMERGING MARKETS

Throughout modern history, defaults on foreign currency debt instruments have taken place repeatedly, and on a substantial scale. Past defaults reflected a variety of factors including wars, revolutions, lax fiscal and monetary policies, and external economic shocks. At the outset of the 21st century, as cross-border capital flows and bond issuance have flourished, fiscal discipline, debt management, and the contingent liabilities arising from weak banking systems, in particular, represent significant policy challenges for many sovereign and corporate issuers.

It is imperative for investors to understand the many factors that affect the issuer's analysis, and to adjust their beliefs as to the likely distribution of future default probabilities and recovery rates accordingly. Some of the factors that could lead to a potential default are exogenous (e.g., strength of the world financial system, likelihood of liquidity crisis and contagion, commodity prices). Others are endogenous or issuer-specific. These include indicators that reflect the economic strength and political stability of the issuer's country, its debt structure and payments schedule.

While an emerging markets obligor may have been led to consider default because of deteriorating underlying economic conditions, an ultimate decision to default is typically based on both economic and noneconomic factors. Such an analysis would typically weigh the benefits of debt reduction and/or forgiveness against the potential costs associated with reputation loss, political fallout, temporary loss of market access, and reentry barriers. For example, because of the creditors' limited legal redress, emerging market governments can default selectively on their obligations even when they possess the financial capacity for timely debt service. As a result, an issuer's willingness to pay is an issue distinguishing sovereigns from most types of issuers and is reflected in the different default rates observed on various classes of rated and unrated sovereign debt.

Another important characteristic of default and recovery rates specific to emerging markets is the difficulty in performing accurate credit assessments. This problem is caused by, among other things, lack of information, different financial reporting standards, and lack of transparency in many developing countries. Additionally, in the case of corporate credits, frequent central government intervention may render analysis of the stand-alone credit strength of a given company difficult to achieve.

Empirical Evidence on Emerging Market Defaults

Much of the historical experience related to emerging markets and sovereign defaults is reflected in the ongoing research of a number of financial institutions and trade associations. Particularly exhaustive and complete in this area is the work done by Moody's and Standard & Poor's. Therefore, I will refrain from repeating their analyses, and will rather focus on a number of key issues characteristic of emerging markets.

High Historical Probability of Default

Emerging markets debt has a well-deserved reputation for being one of the riskiest classes of investment securities. In addition to high volatility (the annualized volatility of the JP Morgan EMBI+ Composite Index exceeded 17.8% over the period between 1993 and 2000), it has historically been subject to significant risks of default.

Standard & Poor's has tracked the history of sovereign emerging markets defaults back to the early 19th century.[6] One need not look that far to assess the severity of that risk. At least 78 issuers, or 38.8% of all sovereigns, have been documented to default on their foreign currency debt obligations between 1975 and 1999. Sovereign defaults occurred nearly every year (in 22 out of the 25 years in the period), and a significant portion of defaulted sovereigns remained in default for extended periods of time.

Recurring Nature of Defaults in Emerging Markets

In the sovereign sector, successful debt restructurings do not necessarily signal lower future default rates and lasting improvements in creditworthiness. Most of the 78 sovereign issuers that defaulted on their foreign currency bond and bank debt in the last quarter of the 20th century did so more than once during the period. For example, Russia and Ecuador defaulted in 1999, a mere few years after completing Brady-style deals on their bank debt in 1995 and 1997, respectively. Similarly, Argentina, Brazil, and Venezuela have defaulted at least twice on their local currency debt obligations.

Local Currency versus Foreign Currency Sovereign Debt

Sovereigns have a significant ability to compartmentalize different classes of debt. For example, they can unilaterally subordinate certain types of outstanding obligations to others (e.g., Russia 1998). Investors' legal redress against such actions is limited, and this fact should be reflected in their investing decisions. The above factors can lead to different default and recovery characteristics of different classes of emerging markets debt.

A substantial majority of sovereigns has historically continued servicing local currency debt[7] without interruption after defaulting on foreign currency debt. As a result, the default frequency of local currency sovereign debt tends to be significantly lower than that of foreign currency obligations.

At the same time, the recovery rates on local currency debt are adversely affected by the powers of sovereign issuers to impose unilateral default resolutions. In addition, the foreign currency devaluations that frequently accompany such periods of crises (e.g., Russia 1998) tend to exacerbate investors' losses even further,[8] and translate ultimately into higher loss severity for holders of local debt as compared to foreign currency obligations investors.

---

[6] "Sovereign Defaults: Hiatus in 2000?" Standard & Poor's (December 15, 1999).

[7] Local currency debt is debt denominated in the legal tender of an issuer's country of domicile.

[8] Attempts to hedge such exposures through nondeliverable forward foreign currency contracts with local counterparties have systematically failed, due to the high correlation between counterparty and sovereign default risk.

These empirical facts are consistent with the idea that, through their taxation powers and control over the domestic financial system, sovereign governments generally have a stronger capacity (e.g., through their ability to inflate away their debt obligations) and willingness to service local rather than foreign currency debt. Credit ratings issued by the major agencies for local currency debt reflect primarily the risks of regime switch (e.g., civil wars) that could lead to repudiation of debts, the predictability and strength of the legal system, and other macroeconomic variables (e.g., depth and liquidity of the payment system, danger of hyperinflation). As a result, in many instances, local currencies sovereign credit ratings may exceed those for foreign currency debt.

Sovereign versus Corporate Debt

The lowest-risk issuer in any country is generally the government of that country. Sovereigns command vast foreign currency holdings (e.g., foreign reserves, hard-currency revenues from the export of state-owned commodities). Through the imposition of transfer restrictions, they can appropriate foreign exchange from other sectors of the economy in order to discharge their own obligations. Finally, a government can rely on its central bank's regulatory powers, its own legislative authority, and its monopoly on coercive force. For example, sovereign entities may take actions to (1) restrict convertibility of the local currencies into hard currencies; (2) direct borrowers to default on all or some of their cross-border obligations; or (3) require that all hard currencies held be converted into local currency. Such actions would effectively restrict the corporate entities' ability to make repayment of their foreign currency debt obligations. In effect, the credit quality of any corporate issuer is bounded by the credit of the creditworthiness of the sovereign.

RECOVERY RATES: ECONOMICS AND EMPIRICAL EVIDENCE

While default occurrences have been relatively well documented and researched, this is not the case with recovery rates. This problem is quite pronounced even for well-developed and relatively liquid marketplaces such as those for bank loans[9] and U.S. corporate bond issues. It is even more acute as it pertains to emerging market corporate and sovereign defaults. As a result, one of the main issues associated with the evaluation of the empirical evidence on default severity is the lack of a long and consistent historical data series.

Recovery rates on secured and unsecured exposures seem to contain a large random factor, and are highly variable across counterparties. This fact, however, is to be expected given the uniquely different circumstances that apply in almost every business and sovereign failure. Furthermore, it is not clear to what extent estimates obtained using data from one fixed income market segment can

---

[9] Greg M. Gupton, Daniel Gates, and Lea V. Carty, "Bank Loan Loss Given Default," Moody's Investors Service (November 2000).

be applicable to another. For example, the recovery rates assumptions applied to corporate bonds or loan agreements which are governed by U.S. law may not be appropriate for non-U.S. jurisdictions with different insolvency provisions and historical experience. Finally, as discussed above, recovery rates and default probabilities together are an intrinsic part of almost all debt securities valuation, and their separation could prove quite challenging.

While the above issues are significant, a certain degree of insight into the nature of default severity can be gleaned from at least four sources, namely (1) economic and financial theory; (2) empirical evidence; (3) historical industry experience; and (4) statistical estimation from market information.

Economic Determinants of Recovery Rates

Economic theory points to a number of factors that could explain some of the variability in recovery rates across different fixed income instruments. The following are among the most frequently cited ones: (1) seniority; (2) post-default management; (3) instrument type; (4) industry; and (5) other technical factors.

Debt Seniority

The importance of debt seniority in determining recoveries is widely recognized in the finance industry. All else equal, post-default recoveries are predicted to increase with seniority in the capital structure. For a given seniority class, however, recovery rates may vary greatly over time.

Debt issue covenants provide for contractual subordination of certain obligations to other more senior obligations. As a result, senior debt receives priority treatment in the event of default. Subordinated debt becomes a residual claimholder, and its interests are satisfied only if and to the extent that all senior obligations have been completely discharged.

A 1996 study by Altman and Kishore[10] documented default severity and recovery rates for a large sample of U.S. corporate issuers, and found strong evidence supporting the hypothesis that seniority plays an important role in determining default recoveries (see Exhibit 2). Subsequent studies[11,12] using different issue samples confirmed the above evidence of the expected recovery gradation: senior secured debt was followed by senior unsecured, subordinated, and junior subordinated instruments.

Post-Default Management

Effective post-default management and a disciplined workout tend to be associated with higher recovery rates. Among the more important issues involved

[10] Edward I. Altman and Vellore M. Kishore, "Almost Everything You Wanted to Know about Recoveries on Defaulted Bonds," *Financial Analysts Journal* (November/December 1996), pp. 57–64.
[11] Edward I. Altman, Vellore Kishore, and M. Christian Saxman, "Recoveries on Defaulted Bonds Tied to Seniority Rankings," Standard & Poor's (July 22, 1998).
[12] "Default and Recovery Rates of Corporate Bond Issuers: 2000," Moody's Investors Service (February 2001).

include the nature of the (expected) debt renegotiation process (e.g., structure of creditors' interests, deviations from absolute priority rules, etc.), as well as the ability to take full advantage of available additional guarantees and credit enhancements. Finally, given the difficulties associated with emerging markets foreign debt default negotiations, one cannot overemphasize the importance of the legal framework within which a debt renegotiation takes place.

The timing of default disposition is also important. Generally, the longer the time between default and valuation, the higher the valuation will be. If, because of a security indenture or some other pressure, a defaulted asset has to be sold within a shorter time frame immediately following default, the recovery rate may have to be discounted accordingly to reflect an accelerated sale. Aside from the "fire sale" element of immediate asset disposition, the relative lack of information and the increased uncertainty during this period would generally lead to higher volatility in pricing and, therefore, still lower valuations.

Instrument Type

The type of debt instrument—loans or bonds—affects recovery rates as well. Loan recovery rates tend to exceed those for bonds. The main reason is the nature of the relationship between lender and borrower. Bank loans benefit from tighter covenant restrictions, closer scrutiny, and superior monitoring (e.g., such as periodic compliance reviews) by the lenders. In addition, both sides generally have strong incentives to view the default as a continuing process of renegotiation and to maintain an ongoing dialogue.

Exhibit 2: Recovery Rates by Industry and Seniority: Defaulted Bonds, 1971-1995

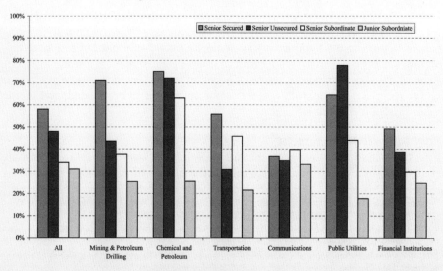

Industry

In the case of corporate bond issues, one would expect recovery rates differentials to be affected by certain industry-specific factors. It has also been documented that there is high variability of recoveries across different industry groups relative to the mean recovery price.[13] This indicates that knowledge of industry- and issuer-specific characteristics is of paramount importance. While higher recoveries in certain industries[14] could be at least partially explained by a greater preponderance of senior bonds in the higher-recovery sectors, the authors of the studies concluded that the nature and liquidity of the firms' assets and the industry's competitive structure (determining future earnings certainty/predictability among others), as well as other industry-related variables, help explain differential recovery rates.

This idea can be extended to sovereign credits as well. For example, one would expect that sovereigns with a more diversified industrial and export base are in a better position to take advantage of opportunities to achieve post-default efficiency gains (e.g., through privatization of state-owned assets). As a result, they can achieve faster economic recovery, return to a path of sustained economic growth, and ultimately offer investors better terms for the restructuring of their debt obligations.

Other Technical Factors

Finally, in the continuing search to pinpoint those variables affecting default severity, one might reasonably look to any number of technical factors, including (1) original credit rating of a bond issue; (2) time between the origination and default date; and (3) issue size. However, the empirical evidence suggests that, at least in the U.S. corporate market, the above factors have no material effect on recovery rates.[15]

Empirical Evidence on Recovery Rates from U.S. Corporate Markets

The U.S. corporate market is relatively liquid and transparent. Its default and recovery experience has been documented over a long period of time, and reliable data are readily available. Therefore, the empirical evidence and estimates of recovery rates can be viewed both as a useful reference point and as an upper bound for what one can reasonably expect to observe in emerging markets debt instruments.

Long-run average recovery rates for U.S. corporate issues appear to be fairly stable at about 40.2%. At the same time, recovery rates have exhibited high variability over shorter time horizons—post-default recoveries have been as high

---

[13] See Fridson, Garman, and Okashima, "Recovery Rates: The Search for Meaning."

[14] The highest average recoveries were documented in the public utilities (70.47%), and in the chemical, petroleum, and related products (62.73%) industries.

[15] See Fridson, Garman, and Okashima, "Recovery Rates: The Search for Meaning."

as 72.0% in 1981, and as low as 21.7% and 24.7% in 1980 and 1990, respectively. Most recently, in 1999 the average recovery rates for U.S. corporate issuers declined significantly to 28.7%,[16] which is still within one standard deviation of the historical average.

The 1958 pioneering study by Hickman,[17] which focused on corporate default history over the 1900-1943 period, documented recovery rates in large issues of between 35% and 43% depending on whether the obligations were rated investment or non-investment grade five years prior to default. A subsequent study[18] focused on 533 Standard & Poor's-rated straight-debt corporate issues that defaulted after January 1, 1981.[19] The authors estimated that investors who liquidate a position in defaulted securities shortly after default can expect to recover on average, 43.77 cents on the dollar. The standard deviation of this estimate (25.81) indicates a substantial degree of variation.

Another study[20] used data on 954 debt instruments issued by companies which emerged from bankruptcy in the between 1987 and 1996. Its findings, a median recovery rate of 44.94 cents on the dollar with a standard deviation of 37.38, are largely consistent with Altman's study.

Empirical Evidence on Recovery Rates from Emerging Markets

Accurate and detailed historical data on post-default recoveries on loans and bonds for issuers in emerging market regions generally are sparse or nonexistent. In general, however, recovery rates for defaulted emerging markets assets are lower than those for U.S. obligors. This fact reflects both a historical track record of lower realized recoveries and lower secondary market liquidity for emerging market instruments, particularly in periods of systemic problems in the international financial markets. Finally, any analysis of recoveries must adjust for relevant country-, industry- and/or issuer-specific factors.

In the context of emerging markets, expected recovery rates depend on a number of key variables. Among those, one needs to consider (1) the likelihood of debt restructuring as opposed to outright repudiation of debt obligations; (2) the terms of the restructured securities (e.g., principal debt forgiveness, extension of debt repayment schedule, submarket coupon schedule); (3) the credit spread at which the defaulted instrument will trade after completion of the restructuring

---

[16] Edward I. Altman (with Naeem Hukkawala and Vellore Kishore), "Defaults & Returns on High Yield Bonds: Analysis through 1999 and Default Outlook for 2000–2002," New York University Salomon Center (January 2000).

[17] W. Braddock Hickman, *Corporate Bond Quality and Investor Experience* (Princeton: Princeton University Press, 1958).

[18] See Gupton, Gates, and Carty, "Bank Loan Loss Given Default."

[19] The study excludes identically rated subsidiaries of rated companies, as well as companies whose debt is guaranteed by another entity or entities.

[20] "Suddenly Structure Mattered: Insights into Recoveries of Defaulted Debt," Standard & Poor's (May 24, 2000).

process; and (4) the length of time it takes to conclude the restructuring. Based on the expected distribution of the above factors, one can assess the upside–downside risk profile and profit potential of a given credit over the medium-to-long-term.

Because of the importance issuers assign to securing and maintaining access to capital markets, outright debt repudiation is generally a highly unlikely event, and should be assigned a correspondingly low probability. An appropriate illustration is Russia's 1998 decision not to repudiate the debt owed by the former Soviet Union, and instead seek a speedier return to the international capital markets.

Mexico was the beneficiary of the original restructuring under the aegis of the Brady Plan in 1989. That debt renegotiation allowed the country to write off approximately 30% of its outstanding loans, and set a precedent for subsequent debt restructurings. Between 1989 and 2000, over 30 countries completed debt and debt service reduction negotiations, with the typical restructuring deal resulting in about 30%–35% forgiveness of a sovereign's debt. For example, in 2000 Russia achieved a 36.5% write-off from the London Club[21] on its $32 billion debt.

In certain cases, however, debt write-offs were significantly higher (e.g., Poland 50% in 1991 and 1994; Bulgaria 48% in 1994). This is particularly true for certain low-income countries, which have had high debt burdens and, in all likelihood, will continue to have them to an even greater extent. Among the worst restructuring terms for investors were those associated with the 1997 restructuring of Côte d'Ivoire's debt, which provided for the reduction of $6.5 billion of debt owed to commercial banks by $4.1 billion in nominal terms, or close to 63% of the total amount restructured.

Past debt restructurings provide an indicator as to the spreads at which newly issued restructured assets tend to trade. Data from restructurings completed in the 1980s and 1990s show that over 40% of the assets issued as a result of restructuring negotiations had issue spreads of between 500 and 1,000 basis points. Approximately half of those securities had issue spreads over 1,000 basis points. Perhaps even more importantly, the empirical observation that no securities traded at issue spreads exceeding 3,000 basis points could prove useful for investors interested in identifying undervalued distressed securities.

As discussed above, the debt restructuring process involving emerging market obligors could be quite protracted and thus adversely affect expected recovery rates. The complexity and duration of the process generally depend on the magnitude of the issuer's financial problems—or in the case of a sovereign, on the status of its banking system as well as internal political uncertainties. In addi-

---

[21] The *London Club* is a group of commercial banks that meets in London to negotiate rescheduling of outstanding commercial debt of countries in a condition of imminent default. After agreement on the multilateral rescheduling, each creditor bank may enter a bilateral agreement with the principal obligator bank in the debtor country. The *Paris Club* is an *ad hoc* group of creditor nations that meets in Paris with debtor countries that are in a condition of default or imminent default to negotiate rescheduling of outstanding debt and that have approved programs with the International Monetary Fund. The Paris Club Advisory Committee makes recommendations for a multilateral policy on bilateral debt settlements. Debt relief is formally provided by bilateral agreements between each creditor and debtor country.

tion, the structure of creditors' interest and their ability to present a unified nego-tiating position would greatly enhance the chances of a speedy and successful outcome.

Not surprisingly, emerging market restructurings take longer than the 2–2½ years typical for U.S. corporate bankruptcies.[22] The length of the default reso-lution period varies significantly across sovereign issuers. While some defaults have been resolved in a relatively short time frame, a number of sovereign obliga-tions have been in defaults over extended periods of time—for example, Zimba-bwe (1965–1980), Bolivia (1989–1997), and Panama (1987–1994). As of the end of 2000, three countries—the Solomon Islands, Angola, and the Dominican Republic—have yet to reach a resolution on their local currency obligations, even after being in default for 5, 8, and 19 years, respectively. Still, the general trend has been towards shortening the negotiations duration, with the average restruc-turing taking about 2–4 years as compared to over 5 years in the mid-1980s.

The tangible effects of the above factors are evident in the results of the 1998 Citibank study of Latin American loan losses,[23] which is probably the most extensive piece of research in this area. The authors used a sample of 1,149 Latin American defaulted loans that were resolved between 1970 and 1996 to estimate the loss in the event of default (LIED). *LIED* can be defined as "the present value of all costs of credit incurred on a loan through the full workout process, expressed as a percentage of the initial default amount."[24] In other words, LIED measures the amount of write-offs, interest drag, and expenses incurred in the process of default resolution.

The study estimates the average LIED at 31.8%, which corresponds to an average recovery rate of 68.2%. The write-offs (21.6%) and the interest drag (14.6%) are the two dominant determinants of LIED. The distribution of LIED is unimodal, with a standard deviation of 28.8% and a strong right skewness. The skew results from the high concentration (over one third of all issues) of observa-tions with losses between 0% and 15%, and the small number of loans with losses approaching (or even exceeding) 100%.

Finally, yet another indication of applicable recovery rates estimates comes from the assumptions used by the major market participants, such as investment bro-ker/dealers and credit rating agencies, in assessing credit risks. As shown in Exhibit 3, the general consensus in the industry seems to be centered around the 20%–25% range for sovereign credits and in the 10%–15% range for corporate issuers.

To the extent that these estimates are often used in the issuance of struc-tured products (e.g., CBOs and CDOs), it is reasonable to view them as somewhat conservative. This is so because the threat of litigation and/or reputation loss

---

[22] Altman, Kishore, and Saxman, "Recoveries on Defaulted Bonds Tied to Seniority Rankings."

[23] Lew Hurt and Akos Felsovalyi, "Measuring Loss on Latin American Defaulted Bank Loans: A 27-Year Study of 27 Countries," Citibank (1998).

[24] Hurt and Felsovalyi, "Measuring Loss on Latin American Defaulted Bank Loans: A 27-Year Study of 27 Countries."

would cause the financial institutions involved to tend to err on the side of caution. That said, historical experience indicates that under certain circumstances, actual realized recovery rates can be significantly lower.

MARKET-IMPLIED DEFAULT PROBABILITIES

While factors predicted by economic theory combined with empirical and industry experience data provide valuable benchmarks to help gauge recovery rates, from a practitioner's point of view the most useful and relevant source of information on expected recovery rates and default severity is the marketplace for fixed income cash and structured product instruments.

Estimation of Recovery Rate Bounds from Market Information

Given the difficulties associated with the precise estimation of loss severity and recovery rates, significant value can be added by estimating the bounds within which one would expect future recovery rates to be realized. One estimate for the upper bound of recovery rates can be derived from equation (2) by noting that

$$e^{r_f} = [p \times R + (1-p)] \times e^{r_f + S}$$

$$\Rightarrow e^{-S} = p \times R + (1-p) = p \times (R-1) + 1 \geq R \Rightarrow R \leq e^{-S} \quad (3)$$

In other words, the recovery rate R is bounded from above by the value e^{-S}.

Exhibit 3: Industry Recovery Rate Assumptions

Security Class	Lehman Brothers[1]	S&P[2]	Moody's[3]	Fitch IBCA[4]	
	n/a	12-month lag	Immediate	Immediate	24-month lag
Senior Secured Bonds	n/a	60%	n/a	n/a	n/a
Senior Secured Bank Loans	50%	50%	n/a	60%	80%
Senior Unsecured Debt	n/a	25%	n/a	40%	65%
Subordinated Debt	n/a	15%	n/a	20%	25%
Non-Emerging Market Bonds	30%	n/a	n/a	n/a	n/a
Emerging Market Sovereign Debt	Min(25%, 30% MV)	25%	n/a	20%	20%
Emerging Market Corporate Debt	Min(10%, 15% MV)	15%	n/a	15%	15%

Sources:
[1] Lehman Brothers, Alliance Investments, Limited Offering Memorandum
[2] *Global CDO/CLO Criteria*, Standard & Poor's, p. 106; *Collateralized Debt Obligations*, Banc of America securities, June 1999, Figure 52
[3] Commonly Asked CDO Questions: Moody's Responds, Moody's Investors Service, February 23, 2001
[4] Rating Criteria for Cash Flow Collateralized Debt Obligations, Fitch IBCA, Duff & Phelps (November 4, 1999), p. 6

Should the recovery rate on a given security exceed the above bound, one can arbitrage the differential by forming a costless portfolio of a long risky and a short risk-free asset, and locking in a positive profit π equal to

$$\pi = [p \times R + (1 - p)] \times e^{r_f + S} - e^{r_f}$$

$$= e^{r_f + S} \times (p \times R + 1 - p - e^{-S}) > e^{r_f + S} \times (1 - p) \times (1 - R) \geq 0$$

(4)

An alternative approach would be to apply statistical methods to estimate recovery rates from the available historical market data. Bayesian techniques, in particular, could arguably be the most appropriate choice given (1) the small sample sizes involved, (2) the need to supplement quantitative methodologies with one's subjective beliefs, and (3) the opportunity for updating and learning as new information becomes available. The implementation of Bayesian techniques depends on the choice of a prior distribution, which in turn depends on each particular investor's market view and experience.

One technique that does not depend on one's subjective views uses some well-known properties of uniform distributions and ordered statistics. Uniform distribution may be a good starting point in such an estimation since it can be viewed as a noninformative prior distribution.

Let $X_1, X_2, \ldots, X_N$ denote N recovery rate observations for a given class of credit instruments. Given the nature of recovery rates, a reasonable assumption for their distribution would be that the observations X_i are identically and independently distributed from a uniform distribution $X_i \sim U(\vartheta, 1)$ i.i.d.[25] Then $[(N + 1) \times X_{\text{Min}} - 1]/N$ is an unbiased estimator of ϑ.[26] Under an alternative, less restrictive assumption $X_i \sim U(\vartheta_1, \vartheta_2)$ i.i.d., it can be shown that the $[N \times X_{\text{Min}} - X_{\text{Max}}]/N - 1$ and $[N \times X_{\text{Max}} - X_{\text{Min}}]/N - 1$ are unbiased estimators for ϑ_1 and ϑ_2, the lower and upper bound of the uniform distribution, respectively.

Inferring Default Probabilities from Market Information

It should be noted that the necessary market information may be derived both directly, via prices and spreads of traded securities, and indirectly via the structured product markets (e.g., default swaps premiums, asset swap spreads, credit-linked note levels). As discussed above, default probabilities can be inferred from readily observable market information combined with appropriate recovery rate assumptions. A number of methodologies could be utilized for that purpose.

One basic and easy-to-implement model calculates risk-neutral default probabilities by equating the expected cash flows of a fixed income security with its observed market prices. Its assumptions—term structure of the recovery rate R_t and the periodic probability of default p_t conditional on non-default in the prior periods—could easily be relaxed, given additional information.

---

[25] Note that the parameter ϑ is not necessarily bound by zero from below.
[26] See the appendix to this chapter for the complete derivation.

At each coupon payment, we can form expected cash flows by assuming a binomial default distribution. That is, the default process at each payment date is analogous to flipping a "tail" after N successes (payments). Because of independence, the probability of surviving to time t becomes $(1-p)^{t-1}$ for a constant periodic probability of default p_t. Then the probabilities of default and non-default at time t are $p \times (1-p)^{t-1}$ and $(1-p)^t$, respectively. As a result, at each payment date the expected cash flow is $E(\text{CashFlow}_t) = p \times (1-p)^{t-1} \times R_t + (1-p)^t \times CF_t$, where CF_t is the scheduled payment at time t. In a risk-neutral world the market price should then equal the sum of the asset's expected cash flows discounted at the risk-free rate, i.e.,

Market Value $= \Sigma_t PV(E(\text{CashFlow}_t))$

$$= \Sigma_t \frac{p \times (1-p)^{t-1} \times R_t + (1-p)^t \times CF_t}{(1+r_t^f)^t} \tag{5}$$

Since equation (5) represents the market value of a credit instrument solely as a function of R_t and the periodic probability of default p_t, one can derive the latter from known instrument value and R_t.

Inferring Default Probabilities from Issuer-Specific Credit Curves

Emerging market practitioners utilize a number of methodologies to derive yield curves that reflect the credit characteristics of a given issuer. This technique can be extremely valuable, since it allows for the incorporation of all available market information regarding a given issuer including maturity, type, and currency denomination. The spreads implied by these credit curves can then be used to derive the cumulative and conditional issuer-specific forward probabilities of default over any time period.

Given the enormous amount of data problems and noise characteristic of the emerging markets, the simplicity and ease of implementing the bootstrapping technique make it a reasonable choice. The bootstrap method for calculating market-implied default probabilities uses as its inputs the market values of all securities (e.g., bonds, default swaps) based on the same credit. To the extent that there is an equation of the form (5) corresponding to each available maturity date T_1, $T_2, \ldots, T_M$, one can calculate the market implied forward probabilities of default by discretizing over $T_1, T_2, \ldots, T_M$. In this way, given an appropriate set of assumptions as to the distribution of the forward probabilities of default over any period $[T_i, T_{i+1}]$, one can solve sequentially a system of M equations similar to equation (5) above. [27]

---

[27] For a more rigorous treatment of techniques for extracting implied forward default probabilities, see Richard Martin, Kevin Thompson, and Christopher Browne, "Price and Probability," *Risk* (November 2000).

Exhibit 4: Implied Cumulative Default Probabilities – August 1998

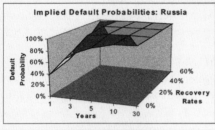

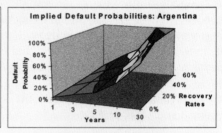

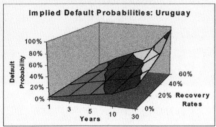

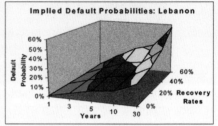

Exhibit 5: Implied Conditional Default Probabilities – August 1998

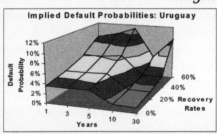

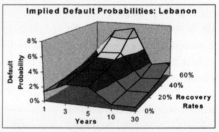

Exhibits 4 and 5 illustrate the market-implied cumulative and conditional probabilities of default for a number of sovereign credits. As expected, market valuations in the summer of 1998 indicated an extremely high probability of default for Russia even as compared to other emerging market sovereigns. It is fair to make the observation that the 1998 Russian sovereign default came as a surprise only to those market participants who failed to credit the wisdom of the marketplace.

Separating Recovery Rates and Default Probabilities Using Structured Products

One of the great advantages of the structured products marketplace is that it offers investors financial securities custom-tailored to suit their particular investment needs and views. For example, financial instruments can be structured in ways to offer, among others, alternative maturities, payoff structures, cash flow profiles, credit exposures, and currency denominations. The fundamental benefits from these structured products arise from their role in completing the markets for the securities of the credit(s) to which they are linked. As a result, market prices of structured products are frequently used to infer parameters such as probabilities of defaults and recovery rates.

The recovery rates expectations associated with a certain credit can be inferred from the valuations of instruments traded in the credit derivatives marketplace, an ever-expanding area of emerging markets. For example, default put options are derivative instruments that provide protection against adverse credit events and default of the referenced credit. In general, the buyer of protection pays an upfront premium (or in the case of default swaps, a set of periodic payments), and receives a predetermined default-contingent payoff.

The default-contingent payoff associated with a default put written on a bond is generally defined as $\text{Max}(K - R, 0)$, where K is the put strike and R is the recovery rate. In a standard default put $K = 1$. In other words, upon default the default put would pay the protection buyer the difference between par and recovery value. The premium (value) of a standard default put DP_{Standard} providing default protection over a period T equals to the discounted expected loss, and can be expressed as:

$$DP_{\text{Standard}} = e^{-r_f \times T} \times p(T) \times \text{Max}(1 - R, 0) = e^{-r_f \times T} \times S \times T \qquad (6)$$

where S and $p(T)$ are the credit spread and the probability of default, respectively.

Note from equation (6) that the standard default put is not sensitive to recovery rate assumptions. This is not the case for default puts with any other default payoff structure, including the so-called binary default puts. The default-contingent payoff associated with a binary default put written on a bond is generally defined as some predetermined constant C. In other words, upon default the binary default put pays a fixed amount C. The premium (value) of the binary default put DP_{Binary} equals the discounted expected loss, and can be expressed as:

$$DP_{\text{Binary}} = e^{-r_f \times T} \times p(T) \times C \qquad (7)$$

Using equations (6) and (7) one can derive the following result:

$$R = 1 - \frac{DP_{\text{Standard}} \times C}{DP_{\text{Binary}}} \qquad (8)$$

Therefore, using both standard and binary default puts market valuation data one can estimate the expected recovery rates associated with the credit they are written on. For example, if a standard and a binary ($C = 0.8$) default put on the same credit are quoted at 200 and 500 basis points respectively, then the implied recovery rate would be 32%.

CONCLUSION

Achieving better understanding of the nature of default is of paramount importance to all credit markets participants, but the importance is even heightened for investors in emerging markets fixed income instruments. The nature of the issue and the scarcity of data present a formidable problem of constructing good predictive models with which to forecast the behavior of defaults and the loss severities associated with them. Until such models become available, investors and all other market participants will benefit from using a wide array of quantitative and qualitative techniques to help guide their investment decisions.

APPENDIX

Since $T(X) = X$ is a sufficient statistic[28] for uniform random variables distributed $U(0, \vartheta)$ i.i.d., and $E(X_{\text{Max}}) = N/(N + 1)$, then $[(N + 1)/N] \times X_{\text{Max}}$ is an unbiased estimator of ϑ.[29]

Let $X_1, X_2, \ldots, X_N$ denote N recovery rate observations for a given class of credit instruments from a uniform distribution $X_i \sim U(\vartheta, 1)$ i.i.d. The marginal and cumulative density functions describing the above uniform distribution are $f(X) = 1/(1 - \vartheta)$ and $F(X) = (X - \vartheta)/(1 - \vartheta)$, respectively. Then $Y(X) = X_{\text{Min}}$ is a sufficient statistic, and from the properties of ordered statistic we obtain its density function

$$f(X_{\text{Min}}) = N \times \left(\frac{1 - X}{1 - \vartheta}\right)^N$$

Since $E(1 - X_{\text{Min}}) = [N/(N + 1)] \times (1 - \vartheta)$, it follows that $[(N + 1) \times X_{\text{Min}} - 1]/N$ is an unbiased estimator of ϑ.

Alternatively, let $X_i \sim U(\vartheta_1, \vartheta_2)$ i.i.d. The marginal and cumulative density functions describing the above uniform distribution are $f(X) = 1/(\vartheta_2 - \vartheta_1)$ and $F(X) = X - \vartheta_1/(\vartheta_2 - \vartheta_1)$, respectively. Then $T(X) = (X_{\text{Min}}, X_{\text{Max}})$ is a sufficient statistic,[30] and from the properties of ordered statistic we obtain the following density functions:

$$f(X_{\text{Min}}) = N \times \frac{(X - \vartheta_1)^{N-1}}{(\vartheta_2 - \vartheta_1)^N}$$

---

[28] See George Casella and Roger L. Berger, *Statistical Inference* (Belmont, CA: Duxbury Press, 1990), Example 6.1.3.

[29] This fact was used during World War II by American and British intelligence to estimate the total number of German tanks. British and U.S. statisticians based their estimates on a small, but reliable, sample of manufacturing serial numbers of captured equipment (specifically the tire molds and tank gearboxes). These resulting estimates proved to be superior to other means the Allied intelligence gathered for these figures, and more accurate than Germany's own estimates.

[30] See Casella and Berger, *Statistical Inference*, Example 6.1.7.

and

$$f(X_{\text{Max}}) = N \times \frac{(\vartheta_1 - X)^{N-1}}{(\vartheta_2 - \vartheta_1)^N}$$

Since

$$E(\vartheta_2 - X_{\text{Min}}) = \frac{N}{N+1} \times (\vartheta_2 - \vartheta_1)$$

and

$$E(X_{\text{Max}} - \vartheta_1) = \frac{N}{N+1} \times (\vartheta_2 - \vartheta_1)$$

it follows that

$$\frac{N \times X_{\text{Min}} - X_{\text{Max}}}{N-1}$$

and

$$\frac{N \times X_{\text{Max}} - X_{\text{Min}}}{N-1}$$

are unbiased estimators for ϑ_1 and ϑ_2, respectively.

Chapter 17

Tevecap

Bruce Stanforth, CFA
Emerging Markets Fixed Income Analyst
BNP Paribas

The analysis of emerging market corporate credits has evolved over the years, and has moved toward a more U.S.-based, high-yield approach. However, analysis that might apply for a credit based in Kansas does not necessarily translate to an emerging market credit. In addition to a rigorous, high-yield style credit review, there are a number of factors that need to be especially considered with respect to emerging market credits. If these factors are analyzed properly, investments in emerging markets should lead to above average—and often extraordinary—investment returns. If ignored, however, a security with a high probability of default may be purchased

These factors are examined in the case of Tevecap, a Brazilian pay TV company. Tevecap was in a relatively non-competitive industry that was expected to experience explosive growth over the ensuing decade. However, Tevecap eventually defaulted on its bond obligations. This default had little to do with the long-term growth prospects for the industry, prospects that are still considered to be strong. Rather, Tevecap's history underscores the importance of properly accounting for factors unique to emerging markets.

SPECIAL CONSIDERATION IN EMERGING MARKET FIXED-INCOME ANALYSIS

In many respects, emerging market fixed-income analysis has improved substantially in recent years. Initially, corporate credit investigation analysis, such that it was, consisted largely of name recognition and perhaps a brief sovereign view. Corporates (and financial institutions in particular, which dominated the early days of emerging market issuances) were largely family-owned and managed. If investors were familiar with the reputation of the family and it was favorable, the credit was considered money good. The next step in the analysis was to add a macroeconomic view. For example, if Mexico was poised for growth and Mexican government securities were deemed to be good investments, then the strategy would be to buy an assortment of Mexican corporate securities with well-recognized ownership.

Although this approach was obviously incomplete, it was not quite as flawed as would appear at first glance. Even today, much of the price of an emerging market corporate is determined by sovereign risk factors. In addition, many of the investors were retail based, and the first non-government issuances were short-term bonds from financial institutions. Given the lax state of financial institution regulatory oversight in the majority of emerging market countries, financial statement analysis for banks was of limited use, a condition that unfortunately applies to this day.

As the market evolved, institutional investors became more active, and the variety and complexity of corporate bonds increased. Analysis moved closer in line with a traditional high-yield style. Under a high-yield approach, heavy emphasis was placed on an overall sector outlook, cash flow fundamentals, and high-yield covenant protection. So-called high-yield "crossover investors" would apply this type of analysis, usually combined, once again, with a rough macroeconomic outlook on the respective country or region.

While the high-yield style of analysis was certainly a major upgrade over the name recognition-based system of the past, if used in isolation it carries its own set of drawbacks. These drawbacks stem from the fact that a U.S. style high-yield approach can overlook a number of factors critical to emerging market investing. We will review the resulting pitfalls, and show how they can result in an incomplete analysis of emerging market credits. While some of the elements below also apply to a straight high-yield type of analysis, they take on added importance when analyzing emerging market credits. These pitfalls are the following:

1. Undertaking incomplete economic and sovereign analysis
2. Assuming that financing will be available
3. Underestimating the importance of sponsorship
4. Utilizing inappropriate types of financing
5. Overestimating minority investor's rights.

BACKGROUND FOR TEVECAP

The above roadblocks are illustrated in the case of the Brazilian pay TV operator and programmer, Tevecap. Tevecap operated pay television programming and distribution systems in Brazil, and had participation agreements with HBO Partners, ESPN Brazil, and MTV Brazil. Tevecap owned three systems: TVA Sistema, TVA Sul, and Galaxy Brazil. The company also controlled Abril Video Amazonia, the country's largest home video distribution company. In addition, the company held minority interests in companies involved in the production of programming, and the distribution of pay TV services using MMDS technology. Tevecap and its operating ventures distributed programming through five different technologies: MMDS, cable, Ku-Band, C-Band, and UHF. Tevecap also focused on being a content provider in Brazil.

Tevecap was divided into three separate operating divisions: TVA Distri-buidora which included cable, MMDS, and C-Band operations; TVA Programa-dora which incorporated the company's programming assets; and TVA Satellite which consisted of the company's satellite collaboration in conjunction with DirecTV of the United States.

Tevecap was majority-owned by the Abril Group of Brazil. Abril's own-ership stake was originally 54%, and subsequently increased to 62.2%. The Abril Group was one of the two largest Brazilian media groups, with a particularly strong emphasis on publishing. The company published eight out of the top ten magazines in Brazil, and its flagship publication, the magazine "Veja," reportedly had the fourth-highest magazine circulation in the world. The other shareholders in the group were strategic investors ABC/Hearst (17.4%), Falcon International (12.3%), and the Chase Private Equity Fund (8.1%).

Investors were attracted to some enticing aspects of the Tevecap story. Brazil and most of the rest of Latin America were experiencing both an economic and financial rebirth. After years of stagnation, Latin American economies were undergoing a transformation back to an investor-friendly formula of privatization and an overall opening of the economy, away from the state-controlled model of doing business. After a brief respite following the Mexican Tequila crisis in late 1994, foreign investment flooded back into the region. Latin American Brady bonds, for instance, returned over 30% in 1995 and 1996.

Brazil, in particular, was seen as an investor favorite. The Cardoso gov-ernment implemented the anti-inflation Real Plan in late 1994. Its success in bringing down inflation was spectacular, it fell from an annualized rate of 91.6% in 1994 to 22% in 1995, and to less than 10% in 1996.

Not only was the sovereign outlook positive, but Tevecap had some very attractive features going for it. The company was well positioned to take advan-tage of expected explosive growth in pay TV services in Brazil. Due to a number of factors, pay TV services had previously not been widely offered in Brazil. Pay TV penetration in Brazil (measured as the percentage of households that have pay TV services) was only slightly above 5% in 1996. This rate was not only signifi-cantly less than the United States, which had penetration levels above 60%, but also well below the 50% rate of Argentina, Brazil's neighbor to the south.

As a result, forecasts of pay TV growth in Brazil were generally at least around 20%–30% per year. According to the consulting company Kagan, the num-ber of pay TV subscribers was expected to rise from 2.5 million in 1997 to 12.4 million in 2007 (see Exhibit 1). This was one of the more conservative estimates. In early 1998, Tevecap President Raul Rosenthal, citing large pent-up demand ,stated that Tevecap was expecting the total Brazilian cable market to reach 10 million sub-scribers by the end of 2000, from the 2.5 million figure at the end of 1997. In addi-tion, the economics of the pay TV business are characterized by high start-up fixed costs, but low variable costs. As a result, EBITDA margins were expected to settle in the 50%+ range, a figure in line with cable companies in the United States.

Exhibit 1: Brazil Pay TV Penetration Rates

(MM)	1997	2007
Total pay TV subscribers	2.5	12.4
Monthly Revenue/Sub	$43.9	$56.25
Annual Revenue/Sub	$527.0	$675.00
Penetration of TV Households	6.9%	29.2%
Penetration of Total Households	6.3%	26.4%

Source: Kagan's Latin American Cable/Pay TV 1998. Reprinted with permission.

ANALYSIS OF TEVECAP

On the face of it, the fundamentals appeared favorable for a long-term investment in Tevecap. Investor enthusiasm for Tevecap enabled the company to issue US$250 million in Senior Notes under 144A registration. The bonds were issued in the fourth quarter of 1996 with a 2004 maturity and a coupon of 12 5/8. However, as explained below, Tevecap's subsequent difficulties underscore the importance of the potential pitfalls that are unique to emerging market credits.

Incomplete Sovereign and Economic Analysis

Cross-over, high-yield investors normally have a country view, but often this view is limited to a simple economic outlook such as basic GDP growth assumptions. In fact, the performance of companies varies considerably under different economic scenarios. In addition, it is often overlooked that even if the long-term economic outlook is positive in an emerging market country, there is likely to be immense economic volatility in the short term. Business plans will perform differently under this volatility. Moreover, political and regulatory matters can often outweigh economic factors, and require their own separate analysis.

The optimistic projections regarding Tevecap's business growth quickly ran into difficulties. First, the awarding of new pay TV licenses by the Brazilian regulatory authorities was supposed to be granted quickly. Instead, many court challenges tied up the process of awarding these licenses indefinitely. Although these court challenges may have had limited validity, the Brazilian regulatory and court systems were unable to resolve the matter quickly. As a result, Tevecap was unable to expand its business as it originally intended. Since repayment of the vast amount of the debt under the business plan was premised on the assumption of explosive growth, this was a serious setback.

Another setback came in the summer of 1997 when Thailand devalued its currency. This devaluation set off a chain of events that resulted in substantial harm to investor confidence in emerging markets. While these events barely registered a ripple in developed economies like the United States, it was quite harmful to Tevecap's business. The problem was twofold. First, investor confidence was such that access to funding for all but the strong blue chip companies began to shut down. Second, this lack of investor confidence also applied to Brazil as a whole and, as a result, money stopped flowing freely into the country. In addition, pressure was put on Brazil's local currency exchange regime. International reserves began to flow out of the country, and real interest rates, already high, rose considerably. This, in turn, resulted in recessionary pressures in the Brazilian economy.

Nor was the effect on the Brazilian economy purely financial. Worldwide commodity prices—long the life blood of many Latin American economies—began to fall following the problems in Asia, and this fall in prices resulted in lower economic growth in the region. These concerns became exacerbated following the default in Russia, and the ensuing global liquidity squeeze. Brazilian GDP growth, which had averaged 3.6% between 1995 and 1997, collapsed to –0.1% in 1998.

The effect of the economic downturn on Tevecap was severe. The pay TV business has a high correlation with the underlying economy, and the fall in Brazilian GDP negatively affected Tevecap's growth. The financial results of Tevecap are provided in Exhibit 2. Revenues, which increased by 55% in 1997, grew by only 7% in the year following the onset of the economic troubles in Asia. Moreover, the company's customer churn rate and bad debt rate increased. Churn (i.e., turnover) rates on the satellite pay TV business for instance, increased to 24% per year in the second quarter of 1998, up from only 5% in the first quarter, as the recession affected the willingness and ability of customers to pay. The churn rate was exacerbated by the company's recent, previous targeting of the lower income segments (by offering a "super basic package" at around US$20—compared to some US$35 for the regular package). Tevecap was able to increase its penetration levels under this strategy, but suffered a disproportionate amount of delinquent accounts when the economy fell into a recession. As a result, EBITDA, which had jumped five times in 1997, slowed to 13% growth in the four quarters following the onset of the problems in Asia. This fall in EBITDA was such that the company was never able to generate enough operating cash to pay off even the interest on its debt obligations.

No one foresaw the effects that a devaluation in Thailand would have on emerging markets worldwide. However, the fact that some "shock" would affect Brazilian GDP was entirely predictable. Furthermore, a thorough analysis might have anticipated the weaknesses of the Brazilian judicial system, and Tevecap's vulnerability to a fall in domestic GDP growth.

The Assumption of Available Financing

While pricing can vary widely in U.S. high-yield markets, it is rare that solid, creditworthy corporates are not able to access fixed-income markets. This is decidedly not the case in emerging markets, in which "liquidity squeezes" are common occurrences, and foreign and domestic sources of financing can shut even the strongest companies off from financing altogether. As such, companies with solid business plans and strong growth prospects could be forced to close operations, due to an inability to continue funding their operations. This underscores the importance of investing in companies that will be either fully funded, or have access to additional sources of financing.

Exhibit 2: Tevecap Financial Results (US Dollars in Millions)

	30 Sep 96	31 Dec 96	31 Mar 97	30 Jun 97	30 Sep 97	31 Dec 97	31 Mar 98	30 Jun 98	30 Sep 98	1996	1997	LTM 9/97	LTM 9/98
Number of Months	3	3	3	3	3	3	3	3	3	12	12	12	12
Income Statement Items:													
Net Sales	60.2	69.4	67.2	82.7	92.4	86.0	82.1	81.0	85.8	211.9	328.3	311.7	334.8
Cost of Sales	33.0	60.7	46.8	55.8	26.2	45.2	49.6	48.1	50.6	148.0	174.1	189.6	193.5
Gross Profit	27.2	8.7	20.4	26.9	66.1	40.8	32.5	32.9	35.2	63.9	154.2	122.1	141.4
Gross Margin %	45.2%	12.5%	30.3%	32.5%	71.6%	47.4%	39.6%	40.6%	41.1%	30.2%	47.0%	39.2%	42.2%
S,G & A	29.9	16.8	25.9	31.5	70.5	53.7	44.9	45.0	49.8	89.4	181.6	144.7	193.4
S,G & A %	49.7%	24.2%	38.5%	38.1%	76.4%	62.4%	54.7%	55.5%	58.1%	42.2%	55.3%	46.4%	57.7%
EBIT	-2.8	-8.2	-5.5	-4.6	-4.4	-12.9	-12.4	-12.1	-14.6	-25.5	-27.4	-22.7	-52.0
EBIT %	-4.6%	-11.8%	-8.2%	-5.6%	-4.8%	-15.0%	-15.1%	-14.9%	-17.0%	-12.1%	-8.3%	-7.3%	-15.5%
Depreciation & Amortization	8.3	10.1	10.4	12.5	15.3	18.1	19.1	21.3	22.5	30.2	56.3	48.3	81.0
Other Cash Income	0.0	3.8	5.0	1.4	-6.4	9.9	0.0	0.0	0.0	6.4	9.9	3.8	9.9
EBITDA	5.5	2.0	4.9	7.9	10.9	5.2	6.7	9.2	7.9	4.6	28.9	25.6	29.0
EBITDA %	9.1%	2.8%	7.3%	9.6%	11.8%	6.1%	8.2%	11.4%	9.2%	2.2%	8.8%	8.2%	8.7%
Interest Expense	6.5	7.9	11.3	13.6	15.0	16.5	17.0	17.8	16.4	18.9	56.5	47.9	67.7
Other Financing Cost (Inc.)	0.2	-5.0	-3.9	-4.2	8.0	0.0	0.0	0.0	0.0	-15.3	0.0	-5.0	0.0
Adjusted EBITDA	5.5	11.1	15.4	6.7	30.6	-20.5	12.4	9.2	32.8	11.0	38.8	63.7	33.9
EBITDA / Interest	0.8	0.2	0.4	0.6	0.7	0.3	0.4	0.5	0.5	0.2	0.5	0.5	0.4
(EBITDA—Cap. Exp.) / Int.	-8.5	-4.9	-3.0	-4.5	-4.1	-3.3	-1.4	-1.8	-1.9	-8.3	-3.7	-4.1	-2.1
Adj. EBITDA / Interest	0.8	1.4	1.4	0.5	2.0	-1.2	0.7	0.5	2.0	0.6	0.7	1.3	0.5

Exhibit 2 (Continued)

	30 Sep 96	31 Dec 96	31 Mar 97	30 Jun 97	30 Sep 97	31 Dec 97	31 Mar 98	30 Jun 98	30 Sep 98	1996	1997	LTM 9/97	LTM 9/98
Number of Months	3	3	3	3	3	3	3	3	3	12	12	12	12
Growth Rate Analysis:													
Revenues	33.9%	15.3%	−3.1%	23.0%	11.6%	−6.9%	0.0%	−1.4%	5.9%		55.0%		7.4%
Cost of Sales	28.3%	84.0%	−22.9%	19.2%	−53.0%	72.3%	9.7%	−3.0%	5.1%		17.7%		2.0%
Operating Expenses	21.5%	−43.9%	54.0%	21.7%	123.7%	−23.9%	0.0%	0.1%	10.8%		103.0%		33.6%
EBITDA	805.1%	−64.3%	149.8%	61.3%	37.4%	−52.0%	0.0%	37.5%	−14.5%		522.5%		13.1%
Liquidity:													
Current Ratio	0.5	1.5	1.0	0.8	0.7	0.6	0.6	0.5	0.4	1.5	0.6	0.7	0.4
Quick Ratio	0.3	1.4	0.9	0.7	0.5	0.4	0.4	0.4	0.3	1.4	0.4	0.5	0.3
Days in A.R.	35.0	44.8	48.1	52.0	56.5	49.2	62.8	67.7	49.1	58.7	51.5	56.5	49.1
Profitability:													
Gross Margin	45.2%	12.5%	30.3%	32.5%	71.6%	47.4%	39.6%	40.6%	41.1%	30.2%	55.3%	39.2%	42.2%
Net Margin	−23.1%	−14.4%	−24.7%	−21.9%	−21.9%	−42.3%	−38.1%	−40.6%	−30.5%	−24.3%	−24.8%	−20.7%	−27.7%
Return on Avg. Assets	−8.8%	−2.5%	−3.5%	−3.6%	−3.7%	−6.2%	−4.9%	−5.1%	−4.0%	−12.8%	−13.9%	−3.3%	−4.2%
Return on Avg. Equity	−26.6%	−10.2%	−20.7%	−30.6%	−59.2%	−274.6%	−41.6%	−56.4%	−113.5%	−52.8%	−798.0%	−30.2%	−96.3%
Credit Scoring Ratios													
EBITDA/Gross Interest	0.8	0.2	0.4	0.6	0.7	0.3	0.4	0.5	0.5	0.2	0.5	0.5	0.4
Adj. EBITDA / Gross Interest	0.8	1.4	1.4	0.5	2.0	−1.2	0.7	0.5	2.0	0.6	0.7	1.3	0.2
Debt Service Coverage	0.8	0.2	0.3	0.4	0.4	0.2	0.3	0.2	0.3	0.2	0.3	0.4	0.3
Current Ratio	0.5	1.5	1.0	0.8	0.7	0.6	0.6	0.5	0.4	1.5	0.6	0.7	0.4
EBITDA Margin	9.1%	2.8%	7.3%	9.6%	11.8%	6.1%	8.2%	11.4%	9.2%	2.2%	8.8%	8.2%	8.7%
Debt / 12 Mos. EBITDA	5.0	37.1	14.6	11.6	9.5	22.1	17.0	17.8	16.4	62.8	16.0	16.1	16.6
Debt / Total Cap.	51.4%	76.2%	80.5%	88.3%	95.4%	98.6%	84.8%	91.6%	99.1%	76.2%	99.6%	95.4%	99.1%
HC Rev as % of Total Rev.	0.0%	0.0%	0.0%	0.0%	0.0%	0.0%	0.0%	0.0%	0.0%	0.0%	0.0%	0.0%	0.0%
Cap Exp as % of Avg. Capital	113.0%	42.6%	43.6%	66.3%	66.8%	51.3%	25.1%	33.4%	31.5%	42.3%	51.8%	51.0%	35.1%

Sources: BNP Paribas estimates, company filings.

Tevecap's problems were exacerbated by its original development strategy. The company's business plan was to compete in all three of the major technological areas (cable, wireless, and DTH). In many respects, this was a sound strategy. At the time, each of these three technologies had its own theoretical advantage (cable—cities, MMDS—towns, and DTH—rural areas and upscale market). In addition, it was still not clear whether one of these technologies would ultimately prove to be competitively dominant over the others. By developing all three technologies, Tevecap was covering its bases.

However, by developing all three technologies, Tevecap would have to fund all three of them. In the first quarter of 1998, Tevecap said it planned to boost spending on equipment and infrastructure to meet an expected increase in demand from the domestic market. After outlaying some US$240 million in capital expenditures in 1997, the company planned to invest US$140 million in 1998, and around US$100 million a year, per year for the four following years. Tevecap was very proud of these planned expenditures. The Chief Financial Officer Douglas Duran claimed that their planned expenditures were "more than some automakers are doing."

Assuming continued, strong growth prospects and ready access to domestic and international capital markets, this might have been a viable strategy. However, under this strategy, free cash flow was an estimated negative US$270 million in 1997, and another US$130 million in the first nine months of 1998. (See Exhibit 3.) As access to capital dried up following the Asian crisis, these needed expenditures quickly turned into an albatross.

Discounting the Importance of Sponsorship

While sponsorship is obviously important with all credits, with emerging market credits, it is almost always the most crucial factor in analyzing the long-term creditworthiness of an investment. This importance can be illustrated by the fact that all of the defaulted Latin American Eurobonds over the last decade share one thing in common: none of them had an investment-grade controlling owner or sponsor.

As previously mentioned, macroeconomic environment can be extremely volatile in developing countries. GDP growth in Indonesia, for instance, grew at a rate of 8% in the three years leading up to the devaluation in Thailand in 1997, but the next six quarters from the fourth quarter in 1997 GDP growth averaged −9.7%. While this might be an extreme example of volatility, substantial volatility in GDP growth in emerging markets is normal. With such wide growth swings, a committed, deep-pocketed, long-term shareholder is necessary to be able to ride through the inevitable liquidity squeezes and be available to act as a lender of last resort.

Exhibit 3: Cash Flow

Cash Flows:	30 Sep 96	31 Dec 96	31 Mar 97	30 Jun 97	30 Sep 97	31 Dec 97	31 Mar 98	30 Jun 98	30 Sep 98	1996	1997	LTM 9/97	LTM 9/98
Number of Months	3	3	3	3	3	3	3	3	3	12	12	12	12
EBIT	-2.8	-8.2	-5.5	-4.6	-4.4	-12.9	-12.4	-12.1	-14.6	-22.7	-27.4	-41.8	-52.0
+D&A	8.3	10.1	10.4	12.5	15.3	18.1	19.1	21.3	22.5	48.3	56.3	73.8	81.0
EBITDA	5.5	2.0	4.9	7.9	10.9	5.2	6.7	9.2	7.9	25.6	28.9	32.0	29.0
−Interest Expense	6.5	7.9	11.3	13.6	15.0	16.5	17.0	17.8	16.4	47.9	56.5	66.3	67.7
+ Chg in Working Capital	—	5.3	5.5	-2.6	26.1	-35.6	4.1	-15.4	24.9	34.3	-6.6	-20.8	-22.0
− Capital Expenditures	60.6	40.7	38.8	69.0	72.2	60.0	31.1	41.4	38.3	220.7	240.0	204.7	170.8
= Free Cash Flow	-61.6	-41.4	-39.8	-77.3	-50.3	-106.9	-37.3	-65.4	-21.9	-208.7	-274.2	-259.8	-231.5

Sources: BNP Paribas estimates, company filings.

In times when access to capital markets is not available, companies will likely try to tap their bank lines where available. It is doubtful that new funds will be obtainable, but banks already tied into these companies can be obligated to roll over existing funds. In addition, the local development bank can often act as a lender of last resort. If debt or equity financing is not available, the options are limited. Companies will be forced to either rely on existing sponsors, find new equity partners, sell off assets, or restructure/default on debt. Besides providing access to relatively inexpensive financing, a strong sponsor can be crucial in other respects. Often foreign or large shareholders are needed to expand the pool of buyers, lower costs from suppliers, and enhance economies of scale.

For Tevecap, lack of access to financing quickly became a serious concern. Although the capital markets window opened up slightly in the spring of 1998, this opening was selective. While Tevecap's parent, Abril, might have been deemed "strong" enough to issue in this market, it is unlikely that Tevecap would have been able to obtain financing. At any rate, the refinancing window was quickly shut with the worldwide liquidity crisis in the summer of 1998, which culminated in the default on Russia securities.

As Tevecap was unable to obtain financing from the capital markets or financial institutions at either the international or domestic level, its only recourse to financing came from its shareholders. Abril, the majority owner, provided financing in terms of shareholder loans and capital injections. Notably, in early 1998, Abril did put additional capital into the venture, and increased its ownership stake to 62.2%. However, minority shareholders, ABC/Hearst, Falcon, and the Chase Private Equity Fund, declined to inject additional capital. Although, to some extent, this lack of additional funds came amidst different objectives and outlooks for the company, it also reflected a lack of confidence in the business plan. This should have been an obvious warning sign for investors. Abril also continued to lend Tevecap money and, at one point, related company loans reached US$115 million in 1998. However, with the extended liquidity squeeze, Abril was facing its own funding difficulties. Although it was finally able to pay off its own US$100 million Eurobond that was putable in 1998, its willingness and ability to indefinitely support Tevecap—and its substantial cash burn—was no longer assured.

Type of Financing

As discussed earlier, access to additional sources of financing cannot always be taken for granted in emerging markets. As such, companies that finance long-term ventures with short-term financing have a high probability of developing liquidity problems. In the absence of committed lines with banks, or very strong sponsorship to see them through the inevitable liquidity crunches, this will almost inevitably lead to a liquidity crunch, and a forced selling of assets.

Tevecap's liquidity and method of financing came back to haunt it. Unlike some other start-up ventures, it chose not to issue either a zero or prefunded coupon that would have alleviated it from the burden of expending cash on its interest expense during the start-up phase of its operations. The interest expense added to the company's short-term payments burden, and exacerbated the company's liquidity problems. The company was carrying up to US$70 million in short-term debt, and had interest expense of another US$15–US$20 million for an operation that was substantially free cash flow negative.

A further difficulty faced by emerging market companies is that to access long-term funding, emerging market companies usually have no other option than to receive funding in "hard" currencies (i.e., US$, euro, yen, etc.). Local market and local currency financing are available only for short tenors, and rarely for over two years. As such, companies with predominantly local currency revenues often have little choice but to lock themselves into a mismatched revenue-liability position. Their revenues will be in local currencies, and yet their liabilities payable in dollars, euros or other hard currencies.

This subjects these companies to the risk of devaluation, an event that can have a debilitating effect on the balance sheet, and, yet is an event over which the company itself has no control. This devaluation risk does not mean that local currency revenue generating companies should not fund themselves through hard currencies, but it does underscore the importance of sponsorship and access to financing. On the other hand, emerging market companies with exports or hard currency revenue generating products, a high degree of local costs, and a relatively small amount of hard currency liabilities should experience improved financials with a local currency devaluation.

In early 1999, under pressure from the ongoing international liquidity squeeze, the Brazilian government finally abandoned its currency control system, and let its currency float freely. In a matter of months, the Brazilian Real depreciated from 1.21 BRL/US$ to as low as 2.15 BRL/US$ in March of 1999, before eventually settling in around 1.75 BRL/US$. The detrimental effects of the devaluation on Tevecap were immediate. The vast majority of Tevecap's debt was in dollars, as was a high percentage of its costs. However, virtually all of its revenues were in the local currency. As a result, upon the devaluation, the company experienced an overnight deterioration in its credit ratios. The last quarter's numbers, before the devaluation, showed that, on a pro-forma basis, the devaluation resulted in a deterioration of debt to EBITDA from an already high 13.7 times to 27 times, with the currency depreciating to 1.75 to the dollar instead of 1.21. Interest coverage dropped from an already low 0.5 times to 0.3 times. Exhibit 4 shows Tevecap's financial ratios under various exchange rates.

Overestimating Minority Investors' Rights

Equity holder investor rights in Latin America are often an oxymoron, and while the situation is improved for debt holders, it still is less than ideal. The lack of investor rights comes in several forms. Financial disclosure has improved dramatically over the years, but still can suffer from lateness, hidden liabilities, arbitrary income statement recognition, and misleading local accounting practices.

Exhibit 4: Tevecap's Financial Ratios under Various Exchange Rates

BRL/ US$	Last Qtr. Annual.	Total Debt	S-T Debt	L-T Debt	For. Cur. Debt	Loc. Cur. Debt	Loc. Cur. Capital	EBITDA/ Interest	Debt/ EBITDA	Debt/ Capital
1.21	33.2	455.5	73.5	382.0	390.0	65.5	0	0.5	13.7	100%
1.75	23.0	621.1	—	—	575.8	45.3	0	0.3	27.1	100%
2.00	20.1	615.4	—	—	575.8	39.6	0	0.3	30.6	100%
2.25	17.9	611.0	—	—	575.8	35.2	0	0.3	34.2	100%

Sources: BNP Paribas estimates, company filings.

Another disclosure problem is inflation accounting, which is in practice in several emerging market countries. Although inflation accounting has its theoretical justification, it results in accounting figures that are largely meaningless – at least in terms of representing a company's operations. Net income under Mexican inflation accounting, for example, is often largely attributable to the gain/loss from the company's net liability position in the local currency or dollars. Although the currency composition of a company's debt is not unimportant, net income figures under inflation accounting reflect more about the country's currency over that period than the company's operations.

Another difficulty facing minority investors is inadequate and poorly enforced bankruptcy laws. Investors involved in distressed debt are well aware that even if their interests are properly represented, bankruptcy proceedings often go on for years in many emerging market countries. This can arm emerging market debtors with a large ace-in-the-hole when it comes to negotiating with creditors. This ace comes in the form of threatening to seek bankruptcy protection, as creditors have only one guarantee if their claims are placed in bankruptcy proceedings—that of a long delay before they receive any cash flows. While creditors worldwide bemoan the delays, inefficiencies, and unequal access in bankruptcy proceedings, these problems are often exacerbated in emerging markets. Although conditions are improving, perhaps the only remedy to these weak laws is for analysts to take into consideration the owner's reputation and past history with the investment community.

Not all of these difficulties with being a minority investor applied to Tevecap. Despite Tevecap's difficulties, the company's management received generally favorable marks in the investment community. Many of the company's difficulties were clearly out of its control, and, by prevailing Brazilian standards, the company had a strong track record on disclosure and openness to investor inquiries. Unfortunately, the same level of disclosure did not apply to the controlling shareholder, Abril. Tevecap's parent company had no public equity outstanding (Brazilian media companies are prohibited by law from issuing equity), and it was difficult for investors to get a full and timely disclosure on the parent's financial situation.

Following the devaluation in Brazil, it was becoming increasingly clear that Tevecap would not be able to survive in its present form for much longer.

With access to external financing shut off, and the parents unable or unwilling to provide further support, the company turned to the prospect of selling off assets in order to raise cash. Tevecap had been in negotiations to sell off its pay TV satellite division to Hughes for quite some time, but consummation of the sale was delayed. In the fourth quarter of 1998, the company divested its satellite operations, and, in the summer of 1999, an agreement was finally reached. Abril/Tevecap agreed to sell its satellite TV operations to Hughes Electronics Corp. and Venezuela's Cisneros Group to raise cash to pay down debt. Abril/Tevecap also sold its 10% stake in Galaxy Latin America and its 100% stake in Galaxy Brazil.

Concurrently, Abril/Tevecap put out a tender offer to Tevecap bondholders. The tender offer was to pay US$500 per US$1,000 principal amount of the notes, plus an additional US$150 per US$1,000 principal amount of the notes for the consent fee (i.e., the waiving of protective covenants on the bonds).   The net cash proceeds of the sale to Hughes for a reported US$140 million would be used to fund a tender offer for the US$250 million face value of the notes.

This sale to Hughes was contingent upon receiving consent from the bondholders that the tender offer would be accepted, and that all restrictive covenants would be eliminated, as well as a provision that permitted the completion of the proposed sale. While bondholders did receive a premium over the prevailing market price (which was priced in the low 50s), the transaction still represented a 35% discount to par. Unfortunately, bondholders who tendered were faced with little choice. Tevecap's management had reiterated that, if the proposed sale was not consummated (which was contingent upon the acceptance of the tender offer), it expected that the company would continue to suffer recurring operating losses. This, in turn, would bring into question the company's viability as a going concern, and force the company to restructure/default on its debt. Bondholders that chose not to tender the notes would also be left without covenant protection or liquidity in the bonds. Investors were essentially forced to accept the Tevecap offer, and the vast majority tendered their bonds. Standard & Poor's considered the "forced' tender offer as an equivalent to a default.

A few months after the Tevecap tender transaction, Abril sold a 12.5% stake in Universo Online's (UOL) to a group of private investors for US$100 million. This transaction valued Abril's total stake at US$400 million. Hypothetically, a complete selling of Abril's UOL business would have provided more than enough cash to completely fulfill Tevecap's debt obligations, with no detrimental effects on the company's underlying cash flows. This led to renewed speculation in some quarters that Abril had not treated minority investors properly.

CONCLUSION

As we have seen, both emerging markets and its investors have changed considerably over the past decade. Investors have become more systematic and rigorous in their analysis. At times, however, they have discounted the importance of factors unique to emerging market corporate debt, such as the importance of sponsorship, and the availability of financing during volatile market conditions. Emerging markets remain very volatile, but those investors who can successfully analyze the potential pitfalls can enjoy very attractive investment returns.

Chapter 18

Dao Heng Bank

Andrew M. Aran, C.F.A.
Senior Vice President, Corporate/Credit Research Director
Alliance Capital Management Corporation

D uring the fall of 1997, Asian credits were depressed by the South East Asian currency debacles of 1997 (Indonesia, Thailand, and Korea all received IMF assistance to stabilize their currencies), creating significant uncertainty about the region's growth prospects. Volatility continued into 1998, and escalated following the Russian sovereign default and the collapse of Long Term Capital Management, a large arbitrage hedge fund, resulting in numerous market and credit dislocations as excessive leverage was unwound. In the process, market liquidity dried up, and investors bore the brunt of significantly lower prices for anything outside the largest and best known credits. Fundamental credit analysis during this period was paramount. One example of a company whose bonds were caught in both the no-bid zone and challenged by the region's worsening operating environment was Hong Kong based Dao Heng Bank (DHB). In this chapter, I summarize the analysis undertaken in reviewing the risks, strengths, and weaknesses inherent in that credit. Solid, dedicated, credit research allowed managers to take advantage of the investment opportunity.

Sections:

Company fundamentals—DHB's scope and business description.

1. Analytical efforts—discovery and rediscovery process—historical financials and due diligence
2. Risk factors—challenges facing DHB
3. Mitigants—strengths supporting the credit
4. Interim results
5. Conclusion
6. Postcript

SITUATION

The merits of investing in the DHB's bonds would have first been considered in January 1997, as the new issue was marketed in New York. After a road show presentation, a one-on-one meeting was held with a senior manager of the bank to further investigate the bank's operational philosophy and financial profile.

Historically, the bank maintained high liquidity, a diversified and well secured loan portfolio, and strong capital adequacy. Operating in Hong Kong, it also had a natural exposure to real estate, interest rates, and foreign exchange fluctuations.

Following the crisis in Thailand, numerous speculative attacks were directed against the Hong Kong dollar (pegged versus the U.S. dollar) resulting in higher interest rates, slower economic growth, and heightened uncertainty. Analysts' expectations for banks were rapidly being reduced, and investors were concerned that higher interest rates would lead to a recession, a squeeze on lending margins, an increase in problem assets, and a reduction or elimination of earnings. These uncertainties, together with substantive markdowns in other Asian debt issues, led to illiquid Asian debt markets and a substantive decline in Dao Heng's debt prices. In the fall of 1998, Dao Heng Bank's US$350 million, 7¾% subordinated notes due January 24, 2007 (rated Baa1, BBB by Moody's and Standard & Poor's, respectively, and underwritten by Merrill Lynch in January 1997) dropped from $80 to $69, offering a yield to maturity of 14%. The stock was also depressed during this time trading to a low of HK$6.8 on September 3, 1998, down from HK$24.40 on April 23, 1998.

THE COMPANY

Dao Heng Bank, is Hong Kong's fourth largest bank, with HK$131.8 billion in assets (USD 17 billion), providing commercial and retail lending, deposit taking, and trustee related services. The bank is 70% owned by Guoco Group, 30% owned by Malaysia's Hong Leong Group. Over 90% of assets, revenues, and earnings are derived in Hong Kong with other operations in the China, Philippines, and Taipei.

The bulk of the Company's services are delivered through its Personal Banking, Direct Banking, Commercial Banking, and Chinese divisions.

As of mid 1998 (the Bank has a June 30th fiscal year), Personal Banking operated over 80 branches and 10 remote access ATMs in Hong Kong. The Company enjoyed a solid reputation, evidenced by Dao Heng being one of five banks tapped by the Hong Kong Mortgage Corporation (HKMC) to sell mortgages to HKMC (The Hong Kong Mortgage Corporation) in support of the Government's long-term housing plans. Residential mortgage lending, always an important business for the bank, represented over 25% of loans. Credit card operations grew rapidly in the 1996-1998 fiscal years, exceeding 500,000 cardholders, and HK$3.3 billion in receivables as of June 1998. The bank's direct and indirect real estate exposure was over 53% as of mid 1997 as shown in Exhibit 1.

ANALYSIS

In analyzing the merits of investing in the subordinate debt issue in January 1997, the basic considerations were made. Comfort was drawn from the bank's solid reputation, conservative balance sheet, low overhead, high liquidity, and ample capital adequacy. Although consumer lending almost doubled between fiscal year 1994 and 1996, as it gained market share in credit cards and personal loans, underwriting standards appeared conservative. Management meetings revealed a solid, service oriented strategy, conservative underwriting policies, and a bias for high liquidity and a strong capital base. As shown in Exhibit 2, liquidity was high as 45% of assets were short-term and high-quality, capital was high with a 14% tier one regulatory capital ratio, and profitability good, with a 1.9% return on assets. Follow up discussions were held with management in January and March 1998.

RISK FACTORS

The risk factors are summarized below.

Exhibit 1: Loan Portfolio; June 1997

Property investment	20.8%
Trade finance	9.7%
Manufacturing	10.0%
Property development	5.4%
Property investment	4.8%
Transport & equipment	0.9%
Other commercial	6.4%
Residential mortgages	27.2%
Credit cards	4.2%
Other consumer	4.8%

Source: Company statements

Exhibit 2: Dao Heng Bank Financial Highlights

(FY ended 6/30; HK$ bln)	6/1997	6/1996
Total assets	125.5	103.5
Total loans	64.5	52.4
Equity	10.6	9.2
Tier one capital	14%	15%
Liquidity ratio	44.5%	45%
% Delinquent loans	1.29%	0.4%
% General loan loss reserves/loans	1.0%	1.0%
Return on average assets	1.9%	1.6%
Net interest margins	2.8%	2.9%

Note: Semi-annual financial reports are published by the bank.

Market

Bank earnings are predominantly a function of the spread between rates earned on assets and funding costs, other fees and operational costs, and asset quality. These elements are heightened in an environment like Hong Kong's, where the margin between borrowed funds (at HIBOR – Hong Kong Interbank Lending Rate) and earning assets (priced at the Prime rate) is influenced by volatile interest rates and capital flows, reflecting an inflexible currency peg that quickly impacts money flows. Partly reflecting these fundamental uncertainties, the Hong Kong banking market is characterized by short-term funding (three months or less), with lending typically secured in a culture favoring timely repayment of obligations.

Economy

Interest rate volatility and an inflexible foreign exchange system renders marginal economic growth hostage to business, investor, and consumer confidence. Higher interest rates would, at minimum, slow growth. Slower growth was likely to lower operating margins. Delinquencies, prompting lower earning asset yields and increased reserves for possible loan losses, would also lower earnings.

Asset Quality

Loans to Hong Kong borrowers were likely to be adversely impacted by higher interest rates and lower economic demand. Loans to borrowers in the Asian region, particularly China, were also likely to come under pressure. Dao Heng's assets and loans grew a rapid 21% and 23%, respectively, in its fiscal year ending June 30, 1997, prior to the Asian financial turmoil. Growth had been even higher in 1995 and 1996. Would aggressive growth leading up to 1997 result in rising delinquencies?

Ownership

Its primary shareholder was Malaysian. Would it withdraw capital from Dao Heng to support its weakening real estate operations in Singapore, Hong Kong, and the Philippines?

MITIGANTS

Following are mitigating factors.

Market Risk

High capital adequacy and liquidity maintained at Hong Kong banks is one mitigant to market risks. Economic risk is addressed by diversification, collateral, and underwriting standards. Earnings were pressured as the spread between the two turned negative in November 1997, and did not revert to positive until February 1998.

Exhibit 3: Dao Heng Bank Financial Highlights

(FY ended 6/30; HK$ bln)	6/1998	6/1997
Total assets	122.6	125.5
Total loans	64.7	64.5
Equity	11.1	10.6
Tier one capital	15.6%	14%
Liquidity ratio	52.7%	44.5%
% Delinquent loans	1.25%	1.29%
% General loan loss reserves/loans	1.35%	1.0%
Return on average assets	1.0%	1.9%
Net interest margins	2.3%	2.8%

Note: Semiannual financial reports are published by the bank.

Asset Quality

Diversification, collateral, and strong underwriting all contribute to controlling lending risk. As stated previously, over 53% of the bank's lending exposure was real estate related. Importantly, half of that exposure was residential mortgage lending in a market where residential real estate is a scarce commodity, well secured, and where home ownership is culturally an important milestone. About 95% of loans were local (Hong Kong), with only 1% of assets in the Philippines (a subsidiary established in 1995), and another 0.2% of assets in loans to other Asian country borrowers.

Ownership

Dao Heng represents Hong Leong Group's crown jewel, and recognizes the need to preserve its valuation. It has never required extraordinary dividends, as is more likely to sell shares in the bank to a strategic or financial investor than to diminish its value. Hong Kong banking regulators have strict rules limiting intercompany lending to affiliates.

INTERIM RESULTS

As shown in Exhibit 3, by mid 1998, growth in loans and assets had slowed, reserves for possible loan losses were up, and net interest margins and profitability were down. The anticipated increase in delinquencies had yet to be evidenced, but was still expected.

The six months ended December 1998, showed substantive degradation in asset quality, no loan growth, stable margins, but higher loan loss reserves, decreasing profitability (see Exhibit 4). Capital adequacy was strengthened from already solid levels offsetting lower, but still comfortable liquidity. Operating earnings were weaker than reported, as a one time gain from the early redemption of US$81 million face value in the 7¾% subordinated notes due 2007. Problem loans increased in trade finance, corporate lending, taxi financings, PRC domiciled borrowers, and credit card borrowers. Rescheduled loans were allowed representing 0.95% of total loans. On December 31, 1998, residential mortgage delinquencies represented a manageable 0.89% of assets.

CONCLUSION

Dao Heng's management's focus quickly turned defensive in fiscal year 1998, as delinquent loans were already increasing in 1997, and Hong Kong interest rates rose to support its U.S. dollar peg. Fortunately, management entered this period of challenging operating conditions with good underwriting standards, high liquidity, and strong capital. Management confidence was expressed by the open market purchase of subordinated debt in the fall of 1998. Initial due diligence, followed by periodic management discussions, assisted analysts and portfolio managers in holding securities that had poor liquidity and were distressed until the bank's performance stabilized, and market liquidity improved.

POSTSCRIPT

For the year ending June 2000, Dao Heng's return on assets rose to 1.26%, reflecting higher net interest margins and lower delinquencies, as shown in Exhibit 5. On November 9, 2000, Standard & Poor's changed the outlook on Dao Heng Bank's debt ratings to positive from stable, reflecting improved profitability, stronger capital, and asset quality that allowed it to "weather the Asian economic crisis better than many of its domestic peers".[1] Moody's had listed Dao Heng's A3 senior debt and Baa1 subordinated debt ratings for possible downgrade in September 1998, affirmed ratings in December 1998, and upgraded its outlook on ratings to stable from negative. The subordinated notes were trading at $95 as of September 30, 2000, yielding 8.816%, 300 basis points over comparable U.S. Treasuries. The stock reached HK$42.40 on November 6, 2000.

Exhibit 4: Dao Heng Bank Financial Highlights

(FY ended 6/30; HK$ bln)	12/1998	6/1998
Total assets	124.5	122.6
Total loans	63.8	64.7
Equity	11.4	11.1
Tier one capital	16.50%	15.60%
Liquidity ratio	51.00%	52.70%
% Delinquent loans	3.62%	1.25%
% General loan loss reserves/loans	1.23%	1.35%
Return on average assets	0.82%	1.00%
Net interest margins	2.26%	2.30%

Note: Semiannual financial reports are published by the bank.

[1] Standard and Poor's press release 11/9/2000.

Exhibit 5: Dao Heng Bank Financial Highlights

(FY ended 6/30; HK$ bln)	6/2000	6/1999	12/1998
Total assets	142.0	131.9	124.5
Total loans	65.3	64.9	63.8
Equity	12.5	11.7	11.4
Tier one capital	17.80%	17.00%	16.50%
Liquidity ratio	48.00%	49.00%	51.00%
% Delinquent loans	3.60%	3.80%	3.60%
% General loan loss reserves/loans	1.23%	1.23%	1.35%
Return on average assets	1.26%	0.94%	0.82%
Net interest margins	2.61%	2.43%	2.26%

Note: Semiannual financial reports are published by the bank.

Index